Youth Culture, Language Endangerment and Linguistic Survivance

BILINGUAL EDUCATION & BILINGUALISM

Series Editors: Nancy H. Hornberger, *University of Pennsylvania, USA* and Colin Baker, *Bangor University, Wales, UK*

Bilingual Education and Bilingualism is an international, multidisciplinary series publishing research on the philosophy, politics, policy, provision and practice of language planning, global English, indigenous and minority language education, multilingualism, multiculturalism, biliteracy, bilingualism and bilingual education. The series aims to mirror current debates and discussions.

Full details of all the books in this series and of all our other publications can be found on http://www.multilingual-matters.com, or by writing to Multilingual Matters, St Nicholas House, 31–34 High Street, Bristol BS1 2AW, UK.

Youth Culture, Language Endangerment and Linguistic Survivance

Leisy Thornton Wyman

MULTILINGUAL MATTERS
Bristol • Buffalo • Toronto

Library of Congress Cataloging in Publication Data
Wyman, Leisy Thornton.
Youth Culture, Language Endangerment and Linguistic Survivance/Leisy Thornton Wyman.
Bilingual Education & Bilingualism: 85
Includes bibliographical references and index.
1. Education, Bilingual--Alaska. 2. Yupik children--Languages. 3. Yupik children--Education. 4. English language--Study and teaching--Alaska--Foreign speakers. 5. English language--Study and teaching--Yupik speakers. 6. Linguistic change--Alaska. 7. Alaska--Languages. I. Title.
LC3733.A5W96 2012
370.11709798--dc23 2012009133

British Library Cataloguing in Publication Data
A catalogue entry for this book is available from the British Library.

ISBN-13: 978-1-84769-740-0 (hbk)
ISBN-13: 978-1-84769-739-4 (pbk)

Multilingual Matters
UK: St Nicholas House, 31–34 High Street, Bristol BS1 2AW, UK.
USA: UTP, 2250 Military Road, Tonawanda, NY 14150, USA.
Canada: UTP, 5201 Dufferin Street, North York, Ontario M3H 5T8, Canada.

The policy of Multilingual Matters/Channel View Publications is to use papers that are natural, renewable and recyclable products, made from wood grown in sustainable forests. In the manufacturing process of our books, and to further support our policy, preference is given to printers that have FSC and PEFC Chain of Custody certification. The FSC and/or PEFC logos will appear on those books where full certification has been granted to the printer concerned.

Typeset by Techset Composition Ltd., Salisbury, UK.
Printed and bound in Great Britain by Short Run Press Ltd.

Contents

Acknowledgments

First and foremost, *quyanaqvaa* to the people in the pseudonymous village Piniq for the privilege of working on this study and book. Many, many people in Piniq have supported me and my family, and generously shared their lives, stories and concerns. Every day in my teaching and research I have used wide-ranging lessons learned from my former students in the Real Speaker group, even if I have only offered a selective version of my experiences with them here. The families, community leaders, and the Get By youth within deserve my deep thanks, as well, for allowing me to research their language use and everyday lives. I am grateful to the principals, teachers, associate teachers and teacher aides in Piniq for sharing observations, granting access to classrooms and providing feedback along the way.

In this book, I share information collected for the narrow, yet important, purpose of helping educators and scholars understand young people's language learning and language use. All my experiences with community members in Piniq, however, helped me make sense of this work. Over the past 20 years I have been profoundly moved by the warm reception I have received upon each return visit to Piniq. It would have been easier to write a book solely about community members' strength, wisdom, generosity and humor than a book that also focuses on the challenging situation of rapid language shift and endangerment, as I have done here. I pray that I have lived up to the responsibility that comes with so many accumulated acts of friendship and trust, and with my choice to write this book, in particular.

Many additional Alaskan colleagues deserve my thanks. Alice Fredson graciously and patiently provided translation assistance with good humor and attention to detail. Paul Ongtooguk shared valuable advice about how to work as an outsider in Alaska Native communities, and helped me place the Piniq case in historical perspective. I am especially grateful to have deepened my understanding of Yup'ik language education through work with Patrick

Marlow, Fannie Andrew, Abby Augustine, Elena Dock, Grant Kashatok, Mary Jane Mann, Veronica Michael, Gayle Miller, Rachel Nicholai, Paul Paul, Nita Rearden and Tim Samson. I am also thankful for the feedback and insights of Walkie Charles, Oscar and Sophie Alexie, Ray Barnhardt, Phyllis Morrow, Chase Hensel, Bev and Carl Williams, Ann Fienup-Riordan, Michael Krauss, Steve Jacobson and Yup'ik educators in the LKSD bilingual institute and SLATE language planning and assessment classes.

Many scholars at Stanford University provided key support and helped lay the groundwork for this study. Shirley Brice Heath inspired me with her studies of the ethnography of communication and youth language, and mentored me as I designed and carried out my original ethnographic research. Guadalupe Valdés profoundly influenced my understanding of bilingualism and the Piniq study through her research and teaching, and many helpful discussions. My thanks go to Penny Eckert for her critical insights and enthusiasm, and her work on language, gender, youth and language shift. I thank Joshua Fishman, in addition, for his many relevant contributions to sociolinguistics and for feedback on research design and preliminary findings. For early feedback, I also thank Ray McDermott, Mica Pollock, Lissa Soep, Jane Collier, Miyako Inoue, Kenji Hakuta, Melissa Brown, Les Field, Jacqueline Shea Murphy and Jason Raley.

While working on this book, I was very fortunate to collaborate with a talented group of researchers on a series of comparative conference panels, volumes, chapters and articles on Indigenous youth language. For their collegiality and scholarly contributions, I thank Teresa McCarty, Sheilah Nicholas, Tiffany Lee, Pila Wilson, Kauanoe Kamana, Jacqueline Messing, Shelley Tulloch, Deborah Augsberger, Mary Eunice Romero, Barbra Meek and Ofelia Zepeda. Over the past six years at the University of Arizona, I have also had the pleasure of working with an outstanding group of colleagues and students. I thank the LRC community for support and many enlightening discussions. For feedback on this book, I especially thank Perry Gilmore, Norma González, Iliana Reyes, Brendan O'Connor, and students in my classes on Language and Youth Culture, Educational Linguistics, and Indigenous Languages, Cultures and Schooling. I also thank fellow faculty members and students of the American Indian Language Development Institute (AILDI) for helping me learn about Indigenous language educators in 'the Lower 48'.

The research within was made possible by funding from a Spencer Foundation Dissertation Fellowship, National Science Foundation Linguistics Doctoral Dissertation Improvement Grant #BCS-0001914, and the College of Education at the University of Arizona. Sections of Chapters 6 and 7 have been adapted and expanded from a previous article with permission from the

Journal of Language, Identity and Education (Wyman, 2009). For permission to conduct the formal study within and help during the sharing of research findings, I thank the 'Piniq' Traditional Council and local school board, and the Lower Kuskokwim School District. I also greatly appreciate the team at Multilingual Matters, including Nancy Hornberger and Colin Baker, Tommi Grover and the anonymous reviewer, for their feedback and patience.

Heartfelt thanks go to friends in San Francisco, Vancouver and Tucson for supporting my young family during my many research trips away from home. I am indebted to my parents John and Julia Thornton for decades of consistent interest and encouragement, and my in-laws Bob and Sue Wyman for help with childcare. Last but not least, I thank my unusual husband Michael for supporting me in too many ways to name, and my children Jules and Evy for bringing me tremendous joy and perspective throughout their lives.

Mistakes within are solely the fault of the author.

Introduction

Young people play pivotal roles in shaping the most dramatic sociolinguistic phenomena of our times, including the global consumption and employment of new technologies (Sefton-Green, 2009), the negotiation of language practices in immigration (Dorner et al., 2008; Mendoza-Denton, 2008) and the spread of new cultural forms such as Hip Hop (Alim et al., 2009). In this book, we will consider young people's roles in yet another key worldwide sociolinguistic phenomenon: the increasing endangerment of the large bulk of the world's languages. Scholars predict that 50–90% of the world's languages will no longer be spoken by the end of this century (UNESCO, 2003) and recent decades have seen an upsurge of scholarly concern and discussion over what to make of the phenomenon. Many books and articles discuss the loss of global linguistic diversity and the trend toward language shift and endangerment in specific communities. Researchers are also describing efforts to document, teach and reclaim languages on the brink of disappearing (for recent examples, see Harrison, 2007; Hornberger, 2008). College-level courses, international conferences and websites devoted to related topics, such as the documentation of Indigenous ecological knowledge, have multiplied in recent years. In the burgeoning field, academics have now begun to analyze the very discourses of language endangerment and accompanying arguments for linguistic rights (see, for instance, Duchêne & Heller, 2007; Hill, 2002; May, 2005).

Few studies to date, however, have investigated how youth broker language maintenance, shift, endangerment and/or language revitalization. Unless young people learn heritage languages and grow up to raise new speakers, language shift can progress rapidly within the course of a generation (Fishman, 1991, 2001). Scholars note that young people's individual and collective language decisions can 'ripple through societies to create a tidal wave' of sociolinguistic change (Harrison, 2007: 9), and are beginning to attend to the ways in which youth act as 'everyday language

1

policymakers', in endangered language communities (McCarty *et al.*, 2009). Still, we have much to learn about how such 'tidal waves' happen, and how young people navigate and transform the sociolinguistic worlds around them.

Once youth under a certain age have uniformly stopped speaking their heritage language, collective changes in patterns of language use may appear to evidence a concise 'choice' on the part of a particular generation to abandon a heritage language. If we see youth speaking mostly English, for instance, we may assume that their parents chose not to pass on a heritage language at home. On the other hand, if we see young people wearing clothes or singing lyrics related to global media flows, we may also – based on the most superficial observations – assume that youth themselves have been lured away from marginalized communities and linguistic practices by the promise or imagination of a flashier, more privileged life elsewhere. Yet these assumptions are problematic. Adding a second language to a community does not mean that a community or even a subgroup of a community will inevitably stop speaking their heritage language. A growing body of research further demonstrates that many Indigenous youth in rapidly shifting communities are not simply abandoning their heritage languages by 'choice', but rather express powerful yearnings to become confident heritage language speakers (discussed in McCarty & Wyman, 2009). As we will see in this book, youth may value and actively attempt to maintain heritage languages with one another, even as their own changing peer practices drive processes of language shift and endangerment. Further, as this book demonstrates, vicious cycles of reduced *resources for* and *increasing doubts* about bilingualism can emerge quickly and become the force behind the 'tidal wave' of change described above *in spite of* young people's, as well as adults', efforts to maintain heritage languages.

To understand how youth, families and communities move along trajectories of language endangerment in such settings, we must examine how language learning and beliefs about languages change over time within complex *linguistic ecologies* – social networks of language use that root within, and extend beyond specific communities and geographical places (Hornberger, 2002; Kramsch, 2002). We must additionally consider how educators and community members look to youth to gauge the prospects for the future of heritage languages, and consciously and subconsciously tailor their practices over time accordingly. Importantly, we must further recognize how youth themselves negotiate challenging positions vis-à-vis their heritage languages, demonstrating what I will call *linguistic survivance* – the use of languaging and/or translanguaging to creatively express, adapt and maintain identities under difficult or hostile circumstances – as they (1) grow up in rapidly changing sociolinguistic environments and (2) are educated in schools under pressure.

Overview of the Study

Central Alaskan Yup'ik Eskimo, commonly referred to as Yup'ik, was one of only two out of 20 Alaska Native languages still spoken by children in 1980 (Krauss, 1980). Between 1980 and 1995, the number of Yup'ik speakers dropped from 13,000 to 10,000, indicating that Yup'ik was rapidly disappearing. In 1995, children spoke Yup'ik comfortably in only 14 out of 64 Yup'ik villages (Iutzi-Mitchell, 1992; Krauss, 1997). By 2007, veteran Yup'ik educators reported that increasing numbers of children in some of these villages, as well, were beginning to speak mostly English (Wyman *et al.*, 2010a, 2010b).

This book examines a decade in the life of Piniq (pseudonym), a remote Yup'ik village with less than 700 residents located roughly 500 miles off the road system in southwestern Alaska near the Bering Sea. Portrayed within is a community in a rapidly evolving, yet early and uneven stage of language shift. Told here is also the story of two cohorts of youth in Piniq. Youth in the older group spoke mostly Yup'ik with one another in the mid-1990s, and were later described by local Yup'ik teachers as 'the last real speakers' of Yup'ik. The majority of youth in the younger group, in contrast, spoke mostly English with peers *only five years later* in 2000 and 2001, even as they used bilingualism to 'get by', as community members put it, with adults and one another.

Over the course of the book, we will follow individuals and groups in Piniq, witnessing how young people used language as they participated in schooling, moved in and out of village and urban spaces, interacted with teachers, peers and family members, attended church, consumed global forms of media, interpreted village political struggles, took their first jobs and learned gendered subsistence practices. Additionally, we will consider how youth in Piniq responded to strong local messages about the importance of speaking Yup'ik as their own heritage language skills diverged and eroded in a context of ongoing language shift. Examining the changing contours and internal complexities of bilingual peer culture over the course of a decade, we will explore the ways Piniq youth navigated the interstices of global, State, school, community, family and peer practices, brokering both linguistic continuities and language endangerment. Importantly, we will also see how adults and youth used language to mediate broader societal changes, as local youth culture emerged as a driving force of language shift.

A Context of Dramatic Change

The historical backdrop of this book is one of dramatic social, spiritual, economic, political and technological change. In the 1930s, when the grandparents of the youth in this study were children, people in Piniq lived a largely self-reliant subsistence lifestyle in one of the last areas of Alaska to experience the incursion of the outside world. Yet, even at that time, Piniq was undergoing rapid social transformation as villagers wrestled with the aftermath of devastating epidemics introduced by distant prospectors and traders, and additional outside pressures. The 'Great Death' or combined influenza and measles epidemic of 1900 was a calamitous event in the history of the Yup'ik region, decimating entire villages and causing estimated deaths of 25–60% of the Yup'ik people (Fortuine, 1989; Napoleon, 1991). After experiencing widespread sickness, villagers in Piniq adopted Moravianism, a form of Christianity. As elsewhere at the time, men and women in Piniq also began to live together in family units, and abandoned traditional Yup'ik dancing at the urging of missionaries (Napoleon, 1991).

In the 1930s, the village of Piniq itself was new, located as far up a river as a barge could reach with the materials to build a missionary-run school, formed by families moving from two earlier village sites. The first school in Piniq offered English language instruction, punishment for speaking Yup'ik and openly espoused assimilationist goals. At the same time, villagers continued a seminomadic lifestyle, spending winters in Piniq, and springs, summers and falls at tundra camps, following seasonal patterns for bird and seal hunting and fishing. Villagers also continued to speak Yup'ik as their everyday language of communication.

The years between those early changes and the early 1990s were ones of continuous transformation. As elsewhere across the Far North, Piniq saw the introduction of a web of local bureaucracies during the second half of the 20th century (Dorais, 1997; Nadasdy, 2003; Patrick, 2005, 2007; Reder & Wikelund, 1993). With the growing incursion of the United States government, villagers elected a chief and established a traditional council, hoping to maintain village autonomy. The Piniq traditional council later grew to administer programs for the Department of Health and Human Services such as Aid for Families with Dependent Children and a low-income housing program, and ran a state-funded utility company and tribal court. Federal and state government agencies set up a local post office and health clinic. In 1971, the Alaska Native Claims Settlement Act created more layers of bureaucracy and challenged villagers' collective land ownership, as Piniq legally became a village corporation and part of a broader regional corporation.

Over the same period, Piniq steadily increased its connection to the outside world through changing forms of education, transportation and technology. As described in Chapter 3, in the late 1950s and 1960s, youth left Piniq to attend Bureau of Indian Affairs boarding schools in faraway places like Oklahoma and Oregon. In the early 1970s, the creation of a local public high school also increased the presence of outsiders in Piniq, as groups of predominantly white teachers were lured to the village by teacher salaries, the promise of adventure, interest in other cultures and/or their own hopes of finding meaningful work. Around the same time, elementary educational practices radically changed when Piniq developed a local bilingual program, and community members were employed as educators in the local school.

From 1970 to 2000, the frequency of local flights to the regional hub town of Bethel increased from one flight a week to five flights a day, weather permitting. Migration also increased as villagers moved back and forth between urban and rural Alaska in strategic efforts to take advantage of jobs and post-secondary education elsewhere, while maintaining local connections (Fienup-Riordan, 2000; Huskey et al., 2004). With the advent of the first, shared phone in Piniq in the 1970s, villagers stayed in closer contact with relatives elsewhere; by 2000, almost all local households had phones. Between 1990 and 2000, the installation of satellite dishes and internet connections at the local school and traditional council created new, everyday means of accessing the outside world.

Within elders' lifetimes, the village economy also became mixed with a global cash economy. A few villagers opened local stores; starting mid-century, many more villagers began to participate in commercial salmon and herring fishing. In the heyday of the fishing industry in the 1980s, some villagers were able to earn enough money for the year by fishing in places like Dillingham or working in canneries over summers. However, by 2000, fishing had become less profitable in the 'boom-and-bust' cycle of commercial natural resource extraction. The local economy was distressed, and 72% of employed community members worked in one of the new local bureaucracies. The school was the largest local employer; within the school, a quarter of the certified teachers were Yup'ik, and additional villagers found jobs as bilingual associate teachers, aides, maintenance workers and staff. According to 2000 US Census figures, however, less than 40% of the Piniq labor force was employed. Discounting household revenue from annual Alaska Permanent Fund Dividend checks generated from oil extraction on the North Slope ($1963.86 in 2000 for each household member), average households existed only slightly above the state poverty level, and 20% of local families were below the poverty level.

Placing the Piniq Study in Time and Place

By 1992–2001, the approximate decade of the study within, villagers in Piniq took many of the earlier dramatic changes from the elders' childhood, such as the new village location, the adoption of Christianity and related moves toward nuclear families and school attendance, for granted. Villagers also participated actively in national and state politics and educational systems, and consumed global flows of media and technologies. Still, almost every aspect of community life involved negotiation of what villagers called *yuuyaraq* – the way of the Yup'ik people and a unique local knowledge system – with the outside world. As community leaders worked to establish self-determination as an Alaska Native people, villagers often described the tensions between desires for local autonomy and the increasing role of government-dominated bureaucracies and regulatory systems. Local language socialization and young people's everyday language practices sat squarely within these broader struggles.

Indigenous language issues in Piniq were further 'embedded in a political discourse centered on land and the role that land plays in Aboriginal cultures, including their spiritual values and languages' as elsewhere in the Far North (Patrick, 2007: 51), and as the following chapters document. In the latter part of the 20th century, as increasing bureaucratization and movement transformed the Yup'ik region socially, politically and economically, subsistence rights were important grounds on which villagers in Piniq and other Yup'ik community members fought cultural extinction (Morrow & Hensel, 1992: 40). The Yukon-Kuskokwim Delta where Piniq is located is marked by tremendous natural abundance, and subsistence practices played a large role in shaping local life throughout the study. Villagers procured the bulk of their food through extensive year-round activities on the Bering Sea, a connected regional network of rivers, sloughs and lakes, and the flat, wet tundra environment around them. Millions of diverse birds migrated annually to the region. Local residents hunted birds in the fall, and birds, seals and walrus in the spring. In summer, villagers collected eggs, berries and other edible and medicinal plants from the tundra, and fished for tomcods, herring, salmon and halibut as yet another important food source. With the dropping temperatures of late fall and winter, subsistence activities slowed, yet continued as villagers used traps for catching blackfish and hooks for catching smelts under river ice (for descriptions of Yup'ik subsistence, see Frink, 2002; Hensel, 1996).

Villagers additionally depended on commercial harvesting as well as federal and state subsidies to fund modern rural life. When families increased their income, they bought material goods to support and extend subsistence practices (Fienup-Riordan, 2000; Langdon, 1986); in economic downturns, as well, villagers used money to buy boats, motors, snowmobiles, gas, guns, bullets, special clothing, marine radios, global positioning systems, freezers and electricity for gathering and storing food. In the face of economic pressures, some villagers referred to subsistence as the alternative, more stable part of the mixed rural economy, pointing out how they could always get food from the land, unlike poor people living in urban settings. In 2000 and 2001, however, land-use regulation was moving into Piniq in unprecedented ways, creating concerns about the continuity of subsistence, as well as linguistic practices.

Bringing Youth and Bilingualism into the Picture

The focus on young people's practices and perspectives in this book stems from a specific type of research: the ethnographic study of language and youth culture (Bucholtz, 2002). Historically, researchers have analyzed adolescents as inconsequential to adult concerns or as incomplete versions of adults. Recent language and youth culture research, in contrast, focuses on youth as interpreters and shapers of society, with an emphasis on youth agency and production (Bucholtz, 2002; Soep, 2006), and youth stylistic performance (Alim *et al.*, 2009; Eckert, 1989; Mendoza-Denton, 2008).

Ethnographic inquiry into the connections among different aspects of young people's lives can problematize and clarify debates about language, culture, society, development and globalization (Alim *et al.*, 2009; Maira & Soep, 2005; Roth-Gordon & Woronov, 2009). Close analysis of language and youth culture can also highlight the complex ways in which youth language practices and ideologies emerge and play out within rapidly changing sociolinguistic settings (McCarty & Wyman, 2009), as social, economic and political systems produce inequalities in complex worlds (Bucholtz, 2002). To date, most studies of language and youth culture have taken place in diverse urban settings. Yet community members, scholars and educators working in seemingly homogenous, rural settings can also gain important insights into processes of language maintenance, shift and revitalization by recognizing how youth use multiple types of linguistic resources to perform unique identities and make sense of their world.

Even in apparently monolingual peer cultures, youth appropriate dialects and/or affect various accents or registers of language to mark their ongoing constructions of identity (Bucholtz, 1999). Youth pick up language from global media flows, weaving related styles, terms and references into their everyday talk for situated local purposes (Alim *et al.*, 2009; Rampton, 2006). Youth in diverse urban settings also 'cross', appropriating one another's language in face-to-face encounters (Rampton, 1995). Together, these practices demonstrate the intertextuality and creative layering of young people's talk.

Young people in bilingual and multilingual communities similarly draw upon and employ wide-ranging linguistic resources to negotiate varying stances in different ways, at different times, in different places with different people. Recent research demonstrates how Indigenous youth in seemingly remote settings live in linguistic ecologies that are far more complex than the word 'bilingual' or even 'multilingual' implies (McCarty & Wyman, 2009; McCarty *et al.*, 2009). Bilingual youth may not only know two languages but multiple varieties of each of those languages to varying degrees (McCarty *et al.*, 2006; McKay & Wong, 1996; Zentella, 1997). Youth in bilingual communities may also use varying languages, media terms, 'voiced' words of others, and dialects of languages to express stances or to position themselves in interactional moments in classrooms (Jørgensen, 1998, 2005), family homes (Wei, 2002) and out-of-school spaces (Mendoza-Denton, 2008; Roth-Gordon, 2007). Youth may express and perform multiple situated identities using aspects of wide-ranging linguistic repertoires, rather than simply choosing one language as the main language of peer culture (Bucholtz & Hall, 2005; McKay & Wong, 1996; Zentella, 1997).

However, youth may also grow used to positioning themselves as heritage language listeners and 'overhearers', versus speakers, when they have not had enough opportunities to hear, practice and use heritage languages in meaningful conversations in real-life settings (Kulick, 1992; Valdés, 2005). These youth are still bilingual and may activate their heritage languages to productive levels someday in the future should their circumstances change, or should they attend heritage language programs (McCarty & Wyman, 2009; Messing, 2009). Yet it is often difficult to distinguish what heritage language learners can do and what they are willing to do with their linguistic repertoires.

Individual bilingual youth develop varying linguistic skills in relation to life circumstances, language learning experiences and assumptions about language that differ within, as well as between populations, generations, peer groups and families (Kagan, 2005; Valdés, 2005). Like adults, youth also seek to understand inequality and difference, interpret a range of ethnic, gender, social class, regional and generational relationships, and use language accordingly (Rampton, 2006). Heritage language learners in shifting Indigenous communities continuously negotiate the everyday uses of their heritage language against the privileged position of dominant languages, and commonly express feelings of linguistic insecurity (McCarty & Wyman, 2009). If youth have been teased or punished for using a language, they may also internalize societal messages about stigmatized languages or language varieties, and hide their linguistic skills (Lee, 2007; McCarty et al., 2006; Messing, 2009; Pye, 1992). Bilingual youth may additionally 'cloak' and 'uncloak' language competencies as they coconstruct stances toward sociopolitical circumstances and/or educational environments (González & Arnot-Hopffer, 2002; Mendoza-Denton, 2008).

Thus, in any given community at any given time, youth may produce language in ways that complicate general assumptions about language choices and identity. There may also be many reasons why youth appear not to use a heritage language at any given moment. Language shift is a notoriously complex phenomenon to document in progress, since researchers must track how multiple internal and external pressures combine through multilayered processes to produce dramatic changes in community language use over time (Fishman, 1991, 2001; Sommer, 1997). Adopting a youth culture perspective, we gain a more nuanced understanding language shift and endangerment as both locally situated and translocally produced. Careful consideration of young people's communities, relationships, positions, practices and performances can also illuminate remaining possibilities for bilingualism in settings of rapid language shift.

At the same time, scholars must negotiate additional considerations and tensions when studying youth culture in *Indigenous* settings of language shift and endangerment, given global, national and local struggles for Indigenous rights (McCarty & Wyman, 2009). In order to situate youth practices in rapidly changing sociolinguistic contexts, and to work through the theoretical, methodological and ethical challenges of studying Indigenous young people's lives and language use, this book uses three conceptual lenses: language ideologies, language socialization trajectories and linguistic survivance.

Language Ideologies

The 'choice' to abandon a language involves social assessments about the possibilities and purposes of bilingualism, as well as value judgments about the role of the heritage language in maintaining community. While communities may appear as if they are suddenly 'choosing' to abandon a heritage language, often changing *language ideologies* – power-laden, seemingly commonsense

assumptions about languages related to communities' sociohistorical circumstances – lay the groundwork for shift before it becomes apparent (Dorian,
1989; Gal, 1979). Ideologies of language 'envision and enact ties to identity,
to aesthetics, to morality and to epistemology' and 'underpin not only linguistic form and use but also the very notion of the person and the social
group, as well as such fundamental social institutions as religious ritual,
child socialization, gender relations, the nation-state, schooling, and law'
(Woolard, 1998: 3). Since language ideologies exist at least partially out of the
realm of our conscious mind, they are also subject to distortion and illusion,
and often contribute to unpredictable outcomes in language reproduction
(Kulick, 1992; Silverstein, 1981).

To understand the complex ways that language ideologies help produce
inequalities in society, researchers examine wide-ranging, multileveled
phenomena from broad institutional policies to the microlinguistic details
of face-to-face communication, as well as community norms, beliefs and
discourse patterns. 'Community', here, can be defined in multiple ways;
people can also participate in multiple communities with differing language
ideologies, and individuals can hold contradictory views of language. As we
will see in the pages that follow, discourses of pride and shame commonly
produce powerful 'ideological crosscurrents' for youth in endangered
language settings (McCarty *et al.*, 2006; see also Lee, 2007; McCarty &
Wyman, 2009). Language ideologies also proliferate quickly when
community members and/or outsiders try to make sense of language
endangerment, document or maintain an endangered language (Hill, 2006;
Wyman, 2009).

The study of language ideologies is helpful for uncovering assumptions
in educational policies and practices, as well as the many overt and subtle
ways in which educators, families, youth and even young children award
status to certain linguistic practices, while erasing and undermining others.
Scholars have only recently begun to explore, however, how young people
make sense of, enact and reshape language ideologies through interpre-
tive and interactive processes (e.g. see González & Arnot-Hopffer, 2002;
Mendoza-Denton, 2008), and a very small number of studies have looked
closely at the ways young people's language ideologies intersect with processes of language shift and endangerment (Kulick, 1992; Meek, 2007). To
identify how young people's language ideologies come about and shape sociolinguistic transformation in the pages that follow, we will consider young
people's and adults' stated and implicit beliefs about language, analyzing
these beliefs in light of sociohistorical changes and power relationships in
and out of Piniq.

Language Socialization Trajectories

To understand young people's experiences and roles in language shift, we must also understand how changing language resources and learning processes shape the ways in which young people 'learn to speak only one language even though two languages are present in their environment' (Pye, 1992: 75). *Language socialization* – the study of socialization through the use of language, and socialization to use language (Schieffelin & Ochs, 1986) – is a particularly useful lens for integrating analysis of language ideologies and language learning practices in communities experiencing language shift (Garrett & Baquedano-Lopez, 2002; Kulick, 1992; Meek, 2007). Historically, language socialization studies in Indigenous communities have been 'burdened by both ignorance and myth' (Heath, 2008). Recent scholarship, however, has deepened our understanding of how Indigenous youth in many societies have been and in some cases still are socialized to understand their place in the world and their relationships to others through rich language practices ranging from stories, naming rituals, chants, catechism and greeting routines to lectures and interactional routines, as well as activities ranging from intent observation, imitation, practice and the physical learning of skills in apprentice-style learning (Crago, 1992; Lomawaima & McCarty, 2006; Nicholas, 2009; Philips, 1983; Rogoff *et al.*, 2003; Simpson & Wigglesworth, 2008).

Of course, the ways in which community members have passed on local knowledge have also changed over time as Indigenous peoples have experienced the extreme pressures of colonization, and environmental, educational and social changes (Brayboy, 2008; Crago *et al.*, 1993; Garrett & Baquedano-Lopez, 2002; Makihara & Schieffelin, 2007). To illuminate how sociohistorical motivations and linguistic processes spread sociolinguistic change through communities, scholars often examine differences within and between *cornerstone generations* of shift – the last generation to use a heritage language before clear-cut patterns of shift have taken hold, and the first generation to noticeably shift toward predominant use of a nonheritage, dominant language (Gal, 1979; Kulick, 1992; Meek, 2007). Groundbreaking longitudinal studies of urban immigrant communities have documented how young people's experiences, educational opportunities and language ideologies can vary within generations and change over time, shaping learners' linguistic repertoires and language shift (Valdés, 1996; Zentella, 1997). As we will see in this book, Indigenous peoples in seemingly remote, homogenous 'small scale' rural settings, as well, participate in highly dynamic and complex linguistic ecologies, criss-crossed by uneven flows of people, ideas and discourses. To understand young people's positions vis-à-vis Indigenous language endangerment, we will track how historically emergent language socialization processes shaped both similarities and striking differences in the ways two *cornerstone peer groups* learned and used language over a short period of five to 10 years time. We will also track how learners' changing social networks, pressures, opportunities and educational experiences shaped emergent language competencies, choices and ideologies (Luykx, 2003: 40–41, see also Garrett & Baquedano-Lopez, 2002).

Gender, as an inherent concept organizing human activity, is commonly evident in language socialization and language shift patterns (Luykx, 2003). Many language shift studies have sought to explain how changing language ideologies prompt women in a particular society to adopt a dominant language faster than men (or vice versa) (for a review of studies building on Gal's groundbreaking early work in this area, see Pavlenko *et al.*, 2001). Studies have also examined the ideological processes through which whole languages can become associated with stigmatized and gendered identities, with implications for language shift (Kulick, 1992). In many places, Indigenous youth have been and/or still are socialized to take up men's and women's gendered roles, responsibilities and practices (Lomawaima & McCarty, 2006; Kulick, 1992; Nicholas, 2009; Paugh, 2005). The Far North, as a site 'of living social struggle, cultural production, political contest, and environmental scrutiny', also raises significant issues relevant to understanding how both gender and ethnolinguistic identities are tied up with continuities and changes in a global world (Rosner, 2009: 489). At the same time, notions of gender and ethnicity map imperfectly onto young people's multilayered identities and the forces underlying their linguistic behavior (Eckert & McConnell-Ginet, 2003; Mendoza-Denton, 2008; Rampton, 2006). As we will see in this book, young people's language ideologies and linguistic practices must also be carefully analyzed in light of individual and collective language learning opportunities over time.

Currently, scholars are reconceptualizing how language learners integrate heterogeneous sets of linguistic resources and experiences across historical and shorter timescales (Lemke, 2000), and local and translocal spaces (Blommaert, 2005, 2010), with implications for the formation of language practices and identities. Scholars have also begun to document how individualized yet overlapping *language socialization trajectories* account for similarities, differences and dynamism in young peoples' linguistic and cultural repertoires, and social and academic identities (Wortham, 2006). In the chapters that follow, we will compare the language socialization trajectories of individuals, peer groups and families in Piniq in order to see how youth developed and used their linguistic repertoires under varying circumstances, and how, over time, youth took up and enacted positions as nonspeakers versus speakers of Yup'ik, with consequences for community-wide language shift. We will also examine how youth used heterogeneous linguistic competences within varying *communities of practice* – groups who came together, and developed 'activities and ways of engaging in those activities . . . common knowledge and beliefs, ways of relating to each other, (and) ways of talking' in the course of mutual endeavors (Eckert & McConnell-Ginet, 2003: 57; Lave & Wenger, 1991). By analyzing young people's typical and atypical language socialization trajectories in and out of school, within and beyond the physical boundaries of Piniq, we will further situate local processes of Yup'ik language maintenance and shift within a broader Yup'ik linguistic ecology stretching across multiple villages and urban spaces within Alaska.

Overall, the study of language ideologies and socialization trajectories allows us to analyze how young people in Piniq mediated changing *beliefs about* and *resources for* bilingualism, and how their resulting language practices drove Piniq along a path toward language endangerment. Our third analytical lens, *linguistic survivance*, pushes us to consider youth in Piniq as members of a particular Indigenous community engaged in broader historical and contemporary struggles.

Linguistic Survivance

Vizenor, the well-known Anishinaabe poet, novelist and literary scholar uses the term 'survivance' to highlight the complex combinations of survival and resistance that evidence Indigenous people's 'continuing presence over absence, deracination, and oblivion' (Vizenor, 2008: 1, 1994). Scholars in multiple fields have built on Vizenor's discussions of survivance to help account for the diverse ways in which individuals and communities creatively express power, self-determination and specific worldviews, thereby renunciating dominance, 'the unbearable sentiments of tragedy, and the legacy of victimry' (Vizenor, 2008: 1). In Native American studies, the concept of survivance is widely used to highlight how Indigenous peoples appropriate and adapt rhetorical conventions to resist and/or comment on hostile circumstances while expressing connection to unique Indigenous identities (e.g. Stromberg, 2006; Vizenor, 2008).

In educational circles, as well, the term 'survivance' has also recently been used to raise profound questions about the ways in which teaching and learning relate to people's maintenance of collective identities under circumstances threatening their annihilation. Survivance does not solely relate to Indigenous people's experiences, and can be used by varying groups to help understand how 'adaptation and strategic accommodation' help peoples 'survive and develop the processes that contribute to community growth' (Brayboy, 2005: 197). Rural education scholars, for instance, have used the term 'survivance' to refer to non-Indigenous peoples' struggles to maintain unique, historical connections to rural spaces and land-use practices, while raising reflexive questions about Indigenous colonization in those spaces (Corbett, 2009). Indigenous education scholars have also extended the term to compare Native American education efforts to Jewish peoples' efforts to educate their children during the Holocaust (Villegas et al., 2008, discussing Kardos, 2002).

As Brayboy, a leading Indigenous education scholar writes, Vizenor's concept of survivance is particularly useful for articulating American Indian and Alaska Native experiences with persevering in hostile contexts, and for keeping Indigenous claims to personhood in focus, while sidestepping commonplace analytical tropes and binary pitfalls (Brayboy, 2005: 197). Indigenous peoples are often portrayed as either heroic or tragic, as traditional or modern, as maintaining cultural continuity or resisting pressure from outside forces, as noble and original ecologists or as tainted modern peoples with no respect for land. Such binary analyses fail to recognize the complexities and contradictions that arise from histories of domination, adaptation and Indigenous people's ongoing struggles for self-determination (see Brayboy, 2008; Field & Fox, 2007; Lomawaima, 1994; Smith, 1999).

In contrast, the notion of survivance takes the complexity, contingency and diversity of contemporary Indigenous practices as a given. The analysis of what I call *linguistic survivance* similarly sidesteps the pitfall of imposing binary interpretations upon Indigenous people as simply 'speakers' or 'nonspeakers' of endangered languages, illuminating the ways that individuals and communities use specific languages, but also second languages, language varieties and linguistic features, as well as bilingualism and *translanguaging* – the moving across or intermixing of languages and language varieties (García, 2009) – as they shape collective identities, practices and knowledge systems in challenging or hostile circumstances, and through participation in translocal, as well as local, spheres of influence.

As the book documents, forms of linguistic survivance can vary dramatically within communities, and acts of linguistic survivance may or may not stem processes of language shift and endangerment. Undoubtedly, the focus on linguistic survivance also raises new questions: How do we situate linguistic survivance in relation to varying, sometimes contradictory forms of Indigenous adaptation and activism? When are attempts to define Indigenous linguistic and cultural identities empowering and/or disempowering for communities, individuals and youth? How do we reconcile complex views of languages as ever-changing, open systems, and communities as porous and internally diverse, with claims about the potential impact of the loss of a specific language for a specific people?

As the portraits of community members, educators, families and youth within demonstrate, definitive answers to those questions may be beyond our reach. At the same time, the use of linguistic survivance as a heuristic can bring into focus local meanings of language use, bilingualism and biliteracy, and the 'diversities of experience' (Nicholas, 2009; Smith, 1999) and forms of 'complex personhood' (Tuck, 2009) found within Indigenous, as well as non-Indigenous communities. The analysis of linguistic survivance can also highlight how local and translocal forms of power contribute to the ongoing production of everyday linguistic practices. As such, a focus on linguistic survivance serves as a powerful corrective to the types of analyses and rhetorics that render specific community struggles and strengths invisible, providing more nuanced understandings of language maintenance, shift, endangerment and reclamation, local knowledge and human adaptation, in settings of sociolinguistic transformation.

Organization of the Book

Chapters 1–3 provide background information for analyzing local youth culture during language shift. All studies are shaped by researchers' subjectivities, assumptions and choices; in Chapter 1, I discuss commonplace considerations in the study of language shift/endangerment and Indigenous youth, and how my evolving relationships within Piniq and the Yup'ik region influenced the longitudinal documentation and representational choices within.

Chapter 2 overviews local language ideologies at the time of the study, and documents how adult bilingual brokers adapted historically rooted language socialization practices within village institutions in Piniq to creatively negotiate the dramatic societal changes described above. Chapter 3 provides a historical and contemporary view of the local school in Piniq as a particularly important, yet contested arena for language learning, ideological reproduction and linguistic survivance.

Chapters 4–7 move into analyzing young people's language use from 1992 to 2001 in detail. Chapter 4 sets the stage for examining changing dynamics in local youth culture by documenting the language socialization trajectories, language ideologies and discourse norms of the older 'Real Speakers' of Yup'ik, or RS group. Using the concept of linguistic survivance, the chapter further illuminates how members of the RS group used Yup'ik, English and bilingualism/biliteracy to navigate a turbulent high school, and participate in a collaborative effort to connect secondary classrooms to community funds of knowledge (González et al., 2005; Moll, 1992) in the mid-1990s. The chapter also tracks RS group members' language uses and linguistic survivance in their early years after high school.

Chapter 5 traces how families' language socialization dynamics quickly changed between the RS and the younger 'Get By' or GB youth in the study, as parents, youth and children responded to decreasing support for Yup'ik language maintenance in the local school, uneven patterns of migration, and the 'tip' into English in local peer culture. Detailing two families' efforts to maintain Yup'ik at home with young children in 2001, the chapter further highlights the role of young peoples' peer socialization in shaping ongoing language shift and countercurrents of Yup'ik language maintenance and reclamation.

Building on the previous chapters, Chapter 6 overviews how individuals and subgroups of GB youth negotiated language ideologies, decreasing and uneven opportunities for learning Yup'ik, and their challenging positions as icons and inadvertent agents of language endangerment. The chapter also highlights the myriad ways GB youth underscored Yup'ik language allegiance and integrated wide-ranging linguistic resources within local youth culture, even as they spoke mostly English.

Chapter 7 examines how GB youth, in general, and young hunters, in particular, negotiated eroding opportunities for Yup'ik language learning with continuing opportunities for learning gendered subsistence practices. Focusing on boys' everyday storytelling about subsistence, the chapter also highlights how youth mediated connections between land-use and language practices during the rapid transformation of the local linguistic ecology.

The conclusion discusses overarching themes and implications of the Piniq study in light of recent trends within the fields of sociolinguistics, Indigenous education and language planning. In the epilogue, I draw on recent collaborative research efforts (Wyman et al., 2010a, 2010b) to note how changes in educational policy, regional Yup'ik language shift and language activism, and the community of Piniq from 2001 to 2010 underscore findings from the ethnographic study within.

1 Researching Indigenous Youth Language

Most researchers who set out to study language shift in-depth have arrived once language shift has already taken place, or, alternately, once all young people under a certain age no longer use a heritage language productively (for important exceptions, see Luykx, 2003; McCarty *et al.*, 2009; Gal, 1979; Zentella, 1997). This longitudinal study, in contrast, grew out of a teacher-researcher effort to connect youth to local knowledge in a village that happened to be on the cusp of a rapid language shift. My relationship with the community of Piniq started when I took a job as a secondary teacher there in 1992. Like many well-meaning teachers working with students from diverse backgrounds, I had deep questions about how to connect school learning with students' lives. As with many non-Indigenous teachers working in Indigenous contexts, I also had deep questions about how to overcome historical school policies that had erased and oppressed local community practices. I came to Piniq fresh out of the Teach for Alaska teacher education program at the University of Alaska Fairbanks (Noordhoff & Kleinfeld, 1993), where program directors strongly recommended that we 'get to know' our students so that we might counteract longstanding dynamics of distrust between schools and Alaska Native villages (Wyman & Kashatok, 2008). As teachers-in-training, my colleagues and I were also encouraged to join community activities in order to develop relationships with community members, and learn how to connect our classrooms to what others at the time called community funds of knowledge – 'historically accumulated and culturally developed knowledge and bodies of knowledge and skills' (Moll, 1992: 133).

Getting to Know the 'Real Speakers'

As a high school teacher in a small school from 1992 to 1995, I taught a seven-year span of students (*n*. 75), many of whom I had the privilege of teaching for three years in a row. Among these students were the tail end of the group that community members later identified as the 'the last ones who really spoke Yup'ik', the RS group. I also taught a three-year span of younger students who were on the cusp of language shift. As one of three secondary teachers, I generally taught each group of students for two hours a day, and ran study halls after school.

Part of a village teacher's job was also to run after school activities and to travel by plane for extracurricular overnight trips to other villages and the hub town of Bethel. The school district funded extensive student travel at the time, and district policy required a certified teacher to accompany students. As the only new, single, young certified teacher in Piniq, I was by far the most willing to take on chaperoning duties. Perhaps in response to my own enthusiasm for spending extra time with students, or more likely due to the small selection of teachers to choose from, I became the chaperone of choice and accompanied RS youth on almost every overnight sports trip during my first year teaching.

From 1992 to 1995, I continued to chaperone sports trips, and organized a third of the students in the RS group to participate in academic competitions in Bethel. I also spent time with the combined junior/senior class – who later came to be identified as the 'very last group to speak Yup'ik to one another' – as an advisor organizing fundraisers, a trip to the Alaska Federation of Natives meeting in Anchorage, a senior trip around Alaska and a trip for students to study state government in Juneau. When traveling with students, inclement weather often prevented our return to the village for up to five days. As a result, such trips provided extended opportunities for observing students interacting with one another and with students from other villages. Given various extracurricular activities, I spent over one thousand hours with the RS group out of class over the course of three years. I also observed or worked with all but six students in the RS group in at least one extra-curricular activity. In Piniq, I further got to know many of my students' parents, and saw students in situations ranging from relaxing at home, attending local feasts, to traveling by snowmobile to church events in neighboring villages.

Every week from 1992 to 1995, I spent at least two hours writing up my experiences and observations, tracking my progress as I tried to 'get to know' my students and tailor my educational efforts. After joining the Alaska Teacher Researcher Network in 1993, I approached my work as a teacher-researcher. The bulk of my classes were English and English Language Development; since some villagers were already voicing concerns about language shift, many of my notes from this time concerned students' language use, comments about language learning, English, Yup'ik and bilingualism, and the ways local metamessages about language seemed to reflect or contradict local practices and beliefs about socialization. In weekly reflections, I also documented my own struggles as a white teacher to counteract historical and racialized dynamics of distrust between the school and the local community.

My teacher-research centered on finding ways to make connections between my classroom and the community of Piniq. As part of this research, as described briefly in Chapter 4, I worked with students, Yup'ik teachers, traditional council members and other community members on a project in which youth interviewed local elders, transcribed and translated resulting interviews, and used locally gathered information to complete academic work in English, Yup'ik and an Alaska Native history course. Through this collaboration, I was able to foster respectful relationships with students and community members, building on young people's strengths and interests in the classroom, and deepening my understanding of language, culture and education.

The intergenerational work raised deep questions, however, about how local language practices were situated socially, historically and politically, and what this meant for the schooling of youth in a setting of language endangerment. Community concerns and my own questions led me to graduate studies; from 1995 to 2000, I studied education, linguistics and anthropology at Stanford University, returning semiannually to continue collaborative work documenting elders' narratives and once to be a graduation speaker. On these trips, I noted what had happened to my students, caught up with as many youth and families as possible, and visited with community members in Piniq. I also talked with veteran local educators and a rotating cast of nonlocal teachers and administrators about their observations of ongoing educational changes and language shift.

Early in my studies, I noted how commonly language shift studies seemed to portray community members as mere linguistic victims of larger power dynamics. At that time in my scholarly writing I started using the pseudonym 'Piniq', a locally recognizable word made from the Yup'ik cognate *pini-* or 'strength' and the hybrid word ending *-(a)q*, as an everyday reminder not to lose sight of the tremendous cultural, human and linguistic strengths I had seen in the Yup'ik youth and adults I knew.

The Uneven Puzzle of Early Language Shift

In the summer of 2000, I returned to Piniq for 14 months of research on young people's bilingualism. Upon reentering local life, I first confronted a puzzle: while I had lived away from the village for only five years, community members reported that a *language tip*, or rapid language shift (Dorian, 1989), had taken place among the youth. Community members referred to young people as 'those English-speaking kids' and claimed 'kids these days speak only English'. Schoolteachers and a new local administrator noted that young children were coming to school speaking mostly English, and assumed that parents must not be speaking Yup'ik to children at home.

To hear some community members and educators talk, one would get the impression that no young people could speak or were speaking Yup'ik, and that families were simply choosing to use English. Yet, as I walked around and visited families with adolescent and pre-adolescent children, I saw many young people using Yup'ik at home with parents, and subgroups of youth using Yup'ik with one another. In most of the young families I knew, the oldest siblings spoke Yup'ik, yet the youngest siblings spoke English. Within a considerable percentage of families, however, even preschool-aged children spoke Yup'ik comfortably.

As I came back to live in Piniq, in some ways I stepped back into my previous community roles. I volunteered in school, sang in the local church and resumed rounds of visiting and taking steam baths with friends. This time, however, I returned with a husband and a young child. I also lived in village housing without running water, rather than in teacher housing. As a result, I was much more aware of family joys and responsibilities, and immersed in the daily work of life in rural Alaska. I was also much more available to participate in community life and to work on my own Yup'ik skills.

During the 14 months of research, I filled in previous blind spots by paying attention to the lives of parents and children in Piniq, and participated in the yearly cycle of events, including holiday celebrations and women's subsistence activities, ranging from egg hunting to skinning a seal. Helping my husband learn to fit in locally as a man, caregiver and novice hunter, as well as integrating our son into community life, provided additional dimensions to the research, forcing me to consider local gender roles as well as expectations surrounding childrearing. Interviews and many more conversations with elders, parents, educators and school district personnel further helped me consider how bilingualism in Piniq was inherently part of continuing struggles to maintain a Yup'ik way of life, and local responses to wide-ranging historical changes.

Identifying Cornerstone Peer Groups

Identifying the last generation, let alone the last peer group, to actively use a heritage language and the first group to use mostly a nonheritage language is a challenging task when language tip is in progress. At the time of the research, however, Piniq was a small community with multistranded relationships. People in Piniq were related to one another as family members and coparticipants within overlapping networks and communities of practice: as classmates, educators, neighbors, basketball teams, search and rescue teams, as coworkers and coboard members in the school or council and as comembers of church, singing, hunting and fishing groups. According to Yup'ik cosmology, people were also spiritually connected through naming relationships, enacted through gift-giving, comments and special attention to one's relatives in name (e.g. Fienup-Riordan, 2000).

Thus, people in Piniq knew one another and knew about one another. They knew one another's children and about the personal histories of families and individuals. People paid attention to one another when they met neighbors and kin on the boardwalk, at church, out on the tundra or ocean, at the local store, in steam houses, at the health clinic and while visiting Bethel or other villages. People saw one another interact within and across multiple contexts again and again, and had a deep knowledge of one another's life circumstances and language use.

Community members were quick to identify which youth were the last to use primarily Yup'ik with one another. Veteran Yup'ik educators who had worked with students throughout their school years also shared a wealth of information concerning the academic trajectories, language skills and circumstances of individuals and groups of youth. Since local families had up to 10 children, a number of parents had children spanning the decade that marked a language shift in local youth culture. Talking to these and other parents about their childrens' language use further confirmed the observations of educators and community members about the dramatic changes taking place between the RS and GB group.

District Yup'ik Proficiency Test scores based on structured Yup'ik interviews in 1998 showed a remaining basic level of Yup'ik language proficiency in the years immediately following the RS group, but also confirmed community impressions that Piniq was in an early stage of language shift, as we see in Table 1.1. The scores in Table 1.1 also suggested that young people's Yup'ik skills were highly uneven in early language shift, as later research subsequently confirmed.

Last but not least, in order to establish an emic view of the tip to English within local youth culture, I used observations of the youth themselves. Throughout the study, young people in Piniq were confronted regularly with ways they did or did not measure up to adult expectations for language use. Like bilinguals in general, they were at times hard pressed to articulate details of their daily language practices. Nevertheless, youth in Piniq grew

Table 1.1 Language status of Piniq students in 1998, as designated by the Lower Kuskokwim School District

	Grade K–3 (n. 68)	Grade 4–8 (n. 58)	Grade 9–12 (n. 37)
Non-Yup'ik speaker	35%	17%	13%
Limited Yup'ik speaker	26%	21%	11%
Fluent Yup'ik speaker	38%	62%	75%

up with an overall sense of who was and was not 'really speaking Yup'ik' according to community expectations. Community members, Yup'ik educators, parents and youth all identified the RS group, born in the late 1970s, as the last youth to use mostly Yup'ik with one another.

Building the Comparative Study

One of the challenges of language shift research is to tease apart complex, rapidly changing situations to determine the sources of linguistic change. Compared within are the language socialization trajectories and peer dynamics of two consecutive cohorts of youth: (1) the 'Real Speaker', or RS group and (2) the younger liminal group with very uneven Yup'ik skills often described by community members as just able to 'Get By' in Yup'ik, GB hereafter. Comparing the RS and GB groups illuminated how contingencies, societal changes and evolving language ideologies concerning the purpose and possibilities of bilingualism, as well as Yup'ik language ability and learnability, became significant and had increasing impact over time, influencing the tip into English in local youth culture.

On my return, I had the privilege of following up with my former students, hearing the joys and challenges they faced as young adults living in Piniq, flowing between village and urban life, or back and forth to their spouses' villages. In 2000–2001, I observed and interviewed many former students who stayed in Piniq as young adults, and found out what had happened to youth who had left. Interviews with parents and teachers of the RS group further helped me supplement my notes and observations of the RS group during the 1990s, and notes from follow-up visits in the following years.

During 2000–2001, I also conducted 11 taped semistructured interviews and 12 conversational interviews (reconstructed in notes the same day) with RS youth. These interviews focused on RS group members' reflections on their childhoods, experiences as secondary level youth and experiences with language and life after high school. RS interviewees included individuals who reflected the general level of bilingualism in the group, as well as outliers who leaned more heavily toward English or Yup'ik use. The RS interviewees also represented varying life paths after high school, including youth who had left and stayed in Piniq, and those who had flowed among post-secondary programs, training opportunities and jobs in urban hub towns and cities. Importantly, the group also included a number of young parents.

Getting to Know the 'Get By' Group

During fieldwork in 2000–2001, I faced the challenge of 'getting to know' the younger GB group. Many GB youth remembered me vaguely as someone they had seen singing Yup'ik in church or in a short-lived village rock band, and/or someone who taught their older brothers and sisters. To focus on GB peer culture I volunteered daily in the local seventh grade classroom. School assessments showed that the class had particularly mixed Yup'ik skills. The local Yup'ik teacher in charge of the class used Yup'ik extensively in the classroom to focus students on learning tasks, praise and sometimes scold students, and explain topics in Yup'ik or a mixture of Yup'ik and English. Participating regularly in the classroom helped me identify patterns in bilingual talk directed at GB youth, and to observe some of the ways in which youth used language to get by with adult Yup'ik speakers.

Within the undercurrents of classrooms, hallways and school-related activities, students use language to work out identities that might not receive approval from adults, given discourses of schooling, and/or discourses about students' heritages (Blackledge & Creese, 2008; Canagarajah, 1997). Students' peer-directed casual talk, everyday interactions and even seemingly off-task humming and singing in school can highlight young people's linguistic creativity and sophistication, social use of language and multilayered worlds (Moses & Wigglesworth, 2008; Rampton, 2006). Students also use private asides, comments, jokes, stories, word play, teasing and insults to construct stances that are complex, creative and sometimes pedagogically oppositional (Canagarajah, 2004; Gutiérrez et al., 1995).

The seventh grade classroom offered daily opportunities to observe students interacting with their peers. To compare the seventh grade class with other groups, I also shadowed the first, fifth and sixth grade classes for a day each, and observed school events including class parties, a fifth and sixth grade sleepover and sports events such as Native Youth Olympics (described in Chapter 6) and basketball tournaments. To gain an on-the-ground view of students' lives out of school, I followed the sixth and seventh grade class members and other GB students into village life, where I observed as many activities as possible, ranging from community-based after-school programs, Sunday school, egg hunting on the tundra, two cousins learning how to cut up a seal and church rallies in other villages.

Throughout the 14-month period, a rotating group of preadolescent and younger children was eager to visit our house, try our food, play with my son Jules and conduct their own observations of the resident *kass'aqs* (*white people/outsiders*). Small groups of children also came to play with one another using our toys and art supplies. In the spring, summer, and early fall months, especially, we had a steady stream of young visitors to the point that, after one particularly heavy spell, a girl surprised my husband when he opened our door with the question, 'Is this Emily's secret clubhouse?' Often children would come in small groups of friends multiple days in a row, leaving only when asked, or less frequently, staying through dinner. I observed many of the same young children when visiting family homes.

With parental permission and young people's assent, in some cases I taped GB group members and children when they came to my house to play with friends, or, less often, when individuals came to chat. I also let it be widely known and demonstrated how I was teaching my son Jules Yup'ik, and young people's interactions with Jules provided further insight into community discourse norms and young people's language ideologies (Scollon & Scollon, 1981). Periodically young visitors helped me as I took on new kinds of household and subsistence- related work. Often these instances and conversations further highlighted young people's local knowledge.

Throughout the study, many members of a group I call the young *nukalpiat* (*great hunters*) in the RS and GB groups were particularly underserved in school and especially vocal about language endangerment. As a result, I focused closely on this group's learning trajectories and everyday language practices before and during language shift. I initially spent most of my time interviewing GB junior high-aged boys, since I predicted this would be the hardest group to access.

I also supplemented my research with younger members of the GB group with more limited observations and interviews with a five-year span of high school students. As with the younger students, I observed these youth in as many situations as possible, conducting mostly single observations of a church youth group, classes with Yup'ik-speaking teachers, after-school study halls, school sports practices and events, hallways at lunchtime, prom preparations, the prom itself and graduation ceremonies.

Interviews were difficult to complete given the round of human subjects permissions to be collected, and the constraints of finding private spaces within Piniq. The high school group was least represented in the study given my inability to focus on them extensively, and the challenge of scheduling high school student interviews during the school day. I interviewed six high school students overall, and one high school boy multiple times as a primary informant. The GB data includes 24 taped interviews with 13 boys and 6 girls.

I interviewed most GB group members in a school closet just big enough for three chairs. At other times, I interviewed youth at the traditional council, my home or on the floor of a school storage area. I conducted many interviews with small groups of two or three youth in varying combinations; this allowed me to tape young people negotiating their wide-ranging linguistic repertoires with one another as well as with me as a researcher, and to closely consider young people's codeswitching in collaborative storytelling (Nortier, 2008). The youth stories in Chapter 7, for instance, were gathered in taped group interviews, unless otherwise noted.

Documenting Family Language Socialization Trajectories

Community members would often relate a child's general use of English or Yup'ik to family circumstances, especially whether a family had lived somewhere else or included a parent whose dominant language was English. Within many local families with children in the Getting By group who stayed in Piniq, younger siblings also used less Yup'ik than older siblings. School personnel and parents generally noted which families made up a strong subgroup of Yup'ik users, and had young children who spoke Yup'ik comfortably. To systematically examine the impact of various contingencies such as childhood mobility, sibling order, parental language background and childhood friendships on the Yup'ik use of individuals and peer groups, I constructed basic genealogies and general family life circumstances of the 74 families of the 153 children in the GB group.

Chapter 5 is also based on interviews with 11 parents about their experiences socializing RS and/or GB children. In the 1990s and 2000, there were no local proponents of speaking English to children in Piniq. A very small number of individuals initially chose to speak English to their children for reasons discussed in later chapters, yet most families generally used both Yup'ik and English, or more consciously maintained Yup'ik-only policies at home. Parent interviewees included (1) a few individuals who chose to speak English to their children, (2) many parents who initially chose to speak to their children in Yup'ik, yet were finding themselves 'tipping' toward using increasing English at home and (3) a few parents who were particularly vocal proponents of Yup'ik maintenance.

To double-check the ways that various contingencies were affecting students' uses of language, I compared informal assessments and interview data with school test scores and Yup'ik educators' observations. Veteran local educators and district administrators also helped me reconstruct the language program history of the village school. By synthesizing data on migration, school programming and community language use patterns, with data from individuals, peer groups and families, I was able to situate the rapid shift in local peer culture. Over time, I was also able to see how various contingencies were contributing to the language use of individuals and groups, and to predict in many instances what groups of young children would be speaking out and about in the village at any given time.

To consider changing dynamics of family language socialization, I also looked more closely at the language socialization trajectories of two nuclear families. Both families initially had very consciously attempted to maintain Yup'ik with their children, with varying success. Family 1 was a young family in which the parents spoke Yup'ik to each other and Yup'ik and English to the children. Over 14 months, I observed the children in family 1 at least once a week in their home, their grandmother's home, my house, or, in warmer months, out and about on the boardwalk, with the exception of a stint when the children lived in another village. The children from family 1 played regularly with their older GB cousins; with permission I also observed and selectively taped the children as they interacted with cousins, peers and adults. I further shadowed James, the oldest child in family 1, for a day in first grade.

Family 2 was part of a group of families in which younger as well as older siblings spoke Yup'ik. In 2001, the parents of family 2 were also making a very conscious ongoing effort to advocate for Yup'ik use locally, and to maintain Yup'ik as the sole language of home communication. To learn how young children in strong Yup'ik-speaking families were learning to speak Yup'ik comfortably during a community-wide language shift, I initially tried to hire four GB youth to work as youth ethnographers examining their younger siblings' language use. Due to changing family situations and the girls' mobility, as well as perhaps the unusual nature of the job, only one of the four ended up staying with the task. Lillia, a GB youth and an older daughter from family 2, worked with me over a number of months as a coresearcher to create an overall profile of her younger brother Willie's language use. She also taped herself interacting with Willie on three occasions, transcribing the tapes and going over data with me. Excerpts from this data appear in Chapter 5.

Locally, there were as many variations of language socialization practices as there were families (e.g. González, 2001; Zentella, 1997), and Chapter 5 is not meant to represent in detail all village families' experiences with language maintenance and language shift. At the same time, the two family cases provided an important window into commonly described local experiences and parents' varying strategies during the early, rapid yet highly uneven phase of language shift, even if that window is only partially open.

Linguistic Survivance and 'Getting By'

Given the wide-ranging language competences among the GB group in 2000–2001, another major task of the study was to unpack community notions of what constituted speaking and knowing Yup'ik. Accelerated language reduction, syncretization and mixing often cooccur with a language's demise (Dorian, 1989; Hill & Hill, 1986; Jaffe, 2006). Adults and youth in Piniq who spoke Yup'ik comfortably commonly reported difficulty with the 'hard words' of elders. Many middle-aged adults were prone to extensive word borrowing from English. Parents, teachers and some youth themselves also pointed out how young people's Yup'ik speech evidenced rapid lexical and morphosyntactic changes.

The backdrop of language change among Yup'ik language speakers raised many questions in community members' minds about the viability of Yup'ik, yet scholars warn against reading linguistic change as a straightforward sign of language erosion. Youth in at least one setting have developed teenage versions of Indigenous languages (Langlois, 2004). Furthermore, no formal linguistic change serves as an inherent marker of language endangerment. Some linguistic changes and even convergences with a dominant language may evidence the vitality and flexibility of a language, while attempts to maintain 'pure' forms of language and/or nostalgia about a pristine linguistic past can obscure innovation, contradiction and creativity in linguistic processes (Gal, 1989), as well as existing language competences of speakers and learners in shifting communities (Hill & Hill, 1986; Woolard, 1989). Such competences may serve as important resources in language maintenance efforts (McCarty & Wyman, 2009; McCarty et al., 2009). In the study, I noted community members' concerns about particular types of language change; I also carefully considered whether and how specific changes were shaping inter- and intragenerational communication.

When adults assessed young people's Yup'ik competences, they typically commented on a young person's ability to interact with older generations, and, as I describe in Chapter 2, the desire for youth to learn directly from Yup'ik-dominant elders was one of the prime motivating forces for maintaining Yup'ik. However, community members' analysis of how language shift was occurring, and which groups were 'really speaking' hinged on a second key phenomenon: 'the writing on the wall' of the virtual disappearance of Yup'ik as the language of local youth culture over the course of a decade. The more I pieced together how broad pressures on Yup'ik language learning were impacting bilingual peer culture, and how changing language use within peer culture, in turn, was amplifying those pressures via a wide variety of language socialization processes, the more I, too, came to see this shift in general peer language use as an important turning point in community-wide sociolinguistic transformation. Even as young people's Yup'ik use dramatically decreased with the GB group, however, local peer culture was markedly bilingual. There was little evidence that Yup'ik was becoming stigmatized among GB youth; in contrast, a popular group of students used Yup'ik extensively, while others who used Yup'ik at home described insecurities around speaking Yup'ik within local peer culture. Community members and young people often recognized the existing bilingual skills of students who did not 'really speak', by clarifying that 'he/she can get by' in Yup'ik. The third task of the study was thus to consider what constituted 'getting by' in Yup'ik with adults versus peer groups for the growing group of young people who expressed and evidenced insecurities around speaking Yup'ik. Observations, taped events and interview data highlighted the patterned and unusual ways that most young people in Piniq who 'didn't really know Yup'ik' used extensive Yup'ik receptive skills, basic Yup'ik productive skills and knowledge of local discourse norms to negotiate everyday interactions.

Studying Indigenous Youth and Communities

Indigenous peoples around the world are increasingly asserting their rights to determine the types of research that will be useful to their communities (Smith, 1999). Researchers in Indigenous communities must situate their research accordingly, negotiating specific research questions, the theory and practice of research, and community members' needs. *Youth* researchers in endangered Indigenous language settings must further negotiate attempts to gain access to young people's emic experiences and communities of practice with (a) adult language planning and educational efforts and (b) the rights of local Indigenous authorities to determine ethical, appropriate and permissible types of community-based research (McCarty & Wyman, 2009: 281).

From 1992 to the time of this writing in 2010, my varying relationships with Piniq and the Yup'ik region shaped my research trajectory and ongoing choices about methodological approaches, analysis and the representation of the findings within (Brayboy & Deyhle, 2000; Clifford & Marcus, 1986). The most obvious challenges of conducting research in Piniq stemmed from the layers of distance between community members, participating youth and me. I am a white, Yup'ik language-learning woman from a Unitarian Universalist, suburban, midwestern background. In the mid-1990s, I was a teacher-researcher in my mid- to late twenties. In 2000–2001, I was a former teacher and a mother in my mid-thirties. Throughout the period represented within, I was locally known to be sympathetic toward Yup'ik language maintenance efforts; most of those years and since I have been involved with related collaborative research projects. As such, I became an 'outsider-insider' (Brayboy & Deyhle, 2000) over time, yet I remain a guest, versus a community member, in Piniq and the Yup'ik region.

Youth researchers recognize adults as important socializing and authorizing agents in society, yet generally maintain a primary focus on youth as cultural actors, emphasizing the importance of uncovering young people's 'own acts of cultural critique and cultural production' (Bucholtz, 2002: 535). However, my own, and later, my family's presence as guests in Piniq was allowed due to the role model I set as an non-Native adult willing to collaborate with adult village members to guide youth toward community-determined goals. Throughout the research within the small setting, I continuously negotiated my positioning vis-à-vis young people and the village overall, taking into consideration my previous roles and multi-stranded relationships with adult community members, my desire to use research approaches that would be deemed locally respectful and useful, and emerging research goals. I avoided situations that would have been perceived as bizarre behavior for a local adult, such as spending most of my time with youth. While I focused the study on young people's emic views and creative expressions during language shift, I also tried to document and historicize local youth culture in light of intergenerational language maintenance efforts.

Given the ways the school regularly rotated its administrative leadership and secondary teachers, I continuously negotiated my presence in the local school, as well. In order to spend time studying young people's everyday linguistic practices and experiences, in 2000–2001, I turned down an offer to step into the role of full-time math teacher and avoided placing myself in the position of having direct authority over students. At the same time, I volunteered in the seventh grade classroom as a way to give back to the school and community.

Language Use in the Study of Language Shift

As a researcher, I had my own language socialization trajectory; my ability to understand and speak Yup'ik, recognize local 'village English' and codeswitching patterns, and articulate observations in academic terms changed dramatically between 1992 and 2001. Early on as a village teacher, I felt stretched between the obvious demands of my job, and the less obvious but equally important task of becoming part of the community. If I spent 14-hour days teaching six class preps and running after school activities, at times practically living in the school, I ran the risk of falling into the stereotype of the outside teacher who never ventured into the village (Wyman & Kashatok, 2008). On the other hand, if I 'visited around too much', I felt more connected to the village and gained an appreciation for students' lives and language out of school, yet sometimes felt the work of the classroom slide and students' resentment.

From 1992 to 1995, I petitioned for, and then attended a beginning Yup'ik videoconference class for teachers. I also immersed myself in Yup'ik in the local church in Piniq, where I worked on my Yup'ik pronunciation for regular choir, duet and solo performances. Over time, I learned how to understand and use predictable statements in Yup'ik as I interacted with adult friends and participated in a weekly women's steaming group. As a white teacher, I received regular, strong positive feedback on my attempts to speak Yup'ik as a sign of respect for the community, along with some good-natured teasing from friends and students for blunders, yet my Yup'ik remained at the level of niceties.

During my time away as a graduate student in the Bay Area, I studied Yup'ik for a year with a tutor. I then studied on my own, working my way through a Yup'ik grammar book while my son slept in a stroller in a coffee shop. Later, when I returned to live in Piniq, I was immersed in Yup'ik in community activities with adults, and benefited greatly from interacting with a friend who appointed herself my Yup'ik teacher in nightly steams. I never attained Yup'ik fluency, but developed the ability to understand and tell short stories, and to participate in the daily life of Piniq in Yup'ik. In 2000–2001, I consciously positioned myself as a Yup'ik speaker, commonly using Yup'ik with adults and strong Yup'ik speakers in the GB group. Most community members knew that I spoke Yup'ik, and many villagers interacted with me on an everyday level in Yup'ik. The longer I spent in Piniq, the more I also 'got by' using my increasing skills in Yup'ik, local patterns of codeswitching and a localized version of English.

Language is one way the researcher impacts the situation she studies. The data within reflect my changing status as a Yup'ik speaker, my ongoing linguistic negotiations and young people's interactions with me as a researcher, with somewhat contradictory effects. Many, but not all of my strong Yup'ik-speaking previous students from the RS group maintained relationships with me primarily in English. Some members of the GB group, in contrast, used mostly Yup'ik with me.

Although I was interested in comparing young people's and adults' language use, adults were particularly reluctant to be audiotaped in situations in which I heard the most Yup'ik. In nightly steam baths, for example, women friends shared stories of daily events and jokes in the rich Yup'ik patter of local adults (e.g. Woodbury, 1998). After trying unsuccessfully to get permission to tape these sessions, I respected my friends' wishes to keep their primary social activities private. Nevertheless, steam baths provided opportunities to observe how adult women interacted with one another, and how some GB girls who mostly spoke English used Yup'ik with adults. Witnessing community members teach young children and myself situated 'steam bath Yup'ik lessons' helped me consider local uses of Yup'ik, and continuing intergenerational possibilities for bilingual development.

Sociolinguists have long noted that the language of interviews affects outcome, and early on in the study I had to choose whether to hire someone to help me conduct interviews in Yup'ik, or to conduct interviews myself primarily in English, interspersed with my basic Yup'ik. Each choice presented methodological drawbacks and ethical dilemmas. If someone in the community had conducted the interviews with me, I may have had a much better opportunity to document how strong Yup'ik speaking youth interacted with local adults in Yup'ik, and the interviews would have undoubtedly produced different data. Yet, as Chapter 2 describes, talk in Piniq at the time was structured to a certain extent by the expectation that young people would primarily listen to local adults. Some adults interacted regularly and comfortably with youth, though working on the elders project, I had also heard young people express insecurities about the ways their Yup'ik use differed from adults' Yup'ik use, and seen some youth veer away from one another and particular adults based on individual or family relationships. In some cases, it took years for me to learn the underlying cause of specific avoidances and silences.

Working in a setting of ongoing language shift presented another set of difficulties, since I was dealing with mostly 'semi-speakers' (Dorian, 1989). In 2000–2001, growing numbers of youth were meeting local adults' commonplace requests to speak Yup'ik with silence, and many young people did not display clear-cut preferences for speaking in Yup'ik or English, but spoke in a mix of both languages. Positioning my son and myself as Yup'ik learners at times opened doors for youth to articulate their knowledge of Yup'ik, and their experiences 'getting by', in ways that they might not have with fluent Yup'ik-speaking adults. I consciously spoke Yup'ik with young children in the study, and asked children to help me teach my son Yup'ik. A few children readily accepted me as a Yup'ik speaker, though after a few weeks of quiet or minimal responses on the part of James, the oldest child of family 1, I grew to mirror James' use of Yup'ik to English. Out and about in Piniq, I generally interacted with youth in the Get By group in Yup'ik and English.

When space constraints, unpredictable flows of local work and the initial challenges of figuring out how to document the complexity of the situation made it difficult to find and integrate an adult community member as a coresearcher, I chose to conduct interviews with youth myself. I told interviewees that they could speak to me in Yup'ik or English and that if I did not understand something right away, I would go back to the tapes and figure it out. One student spoke mostly Yup'ik in interviews, while many others used mostly English with codeswitching into Yup'ik. Predictably, since adult community members' English was generally stronger than my Yup'ik, interviews with adults usually ended up being conducted in English with intermittent Yup'ik phrases, words, sections and stories. Comparing taped interactions to everyday observations and interviews helped me consider how participants framed their interactions with me and vice versa. Later I hired Alice Fredson, an accomplished Yup'ik translator with experience on wide-ranging projects in the Yup'ik region, as a language consultant on the project. Alice corrected my translations and spelling, and transcribed and translated lengthier sections of taped Yup'ik data.

The types of data collected for the RS and GB groups differ in important ways. I was in a different position vis-à-vis the youth involved when I made observations of each group's bilingual peer culture. As a teacher, I had more authority over the RS youth in the mid-1990s, yet I also had more time to develop relationships and a level of trust with students through collaborative projects and years of follow-up visits. In 2000 and 2001, I was a researcher with much less authority over members of the GB group, yet I worked with them for a shorter amount of time, and played a much more peripheral role in their lives.

The observations of the consecutive groups of youth were different in nature. In the mid-1990s, I was a teacher-researcher documenting weekly events for action research with RS youth on a community funds of knowledge project focused on local adults. In 2000–2001, I was a university-based researcher using the tools of ethnography to more closely document and understand young people's everyday negotiations of language shift. In the same timeframe, I went from being a non-Yup'ik speaker to someone who demonstrated basic proficiency in Yup'ik in my regular interactions with community members.

Taken together, my various choices and positions had obvious implications for the data collected. 'Detailed, dense longitudinal studies of language use and acquisition are rare enough for single individuals over a time course of months,' and quickly become unfeasible when researchers attempt to extend their analyses to whole communities of language users (Beckner *et al.*, 2009: 12). Each group represented within – elders, families and educators, RS and GB groups – could have constituted a full-length study. In maintaining a broad enough focus to understand how ideologies, learning opportunities and language practices shaped one another over time in local life, I was forced to sacrifice some details. Not having the chance to work wholeheartedly with the GB group as a teacher, as I had with my former students, was also one of the most frustrating aspects of my return.

At the same time, by positioning myself to look comparatively across sections of community life, I was able to analyze layers of language ideology and socialization processes that might have been obscured had I focused on a small group of individuals or one subgroup in the small, but very complex setting. Getting to know the younger students as a group well enough to see both recurring patterns and dramatic changes against the backdrop of village life gave me invaluable perspective into the questions that drove my research. The resulting view of community life also allowed me to contextualize local youth politically and historically, to parse and synthesize multilayered patterns, and to place interesting findings that had little to do with language shift in perspective.

My strengths, limitations and subjectivities as a researcher, my relationships with participants and others, my linguistic negotiation of the research process itself and my analytical and representational choices heavily shaped the research within. In the pages that follow, I mark how and when information was gathered, and reflexively note how my positioning may have shaped specific interactions. This complex task I must also partly leave to the reader.

Vetting the Work Locally and Regionally

Between 2001 and 2010, I conducted member checks with research participants and shared research findings with Yup'ik community members to increase the accuracy and validity of the work within. In Piniq, I discussed major findings and the language programming history of the village school with community educators and language maintenance advocates through individual meetings and focus groups. With interpretation and organizational help from traditional council members, I then presented findings in English and Yup'ik to roughly 35 community members in a public meeting. Coordinating my efforts with those of district administrators, I further discussed the study with Piniq school board members as a backdrop for school-based language planning efforts in 2008, and presented the work to local and nonlocal teachers in the K–12 school.

During this period, parents of the families spotlighted in Chapters 4 and 5 reviewed the use of their stories and quotes in context, as did the 30+ adults and RS youth participants quoted within, with the exception of a few white educators who had left the region. Some older GB youth including Ellen, Mary, Lillia, Jack and David reviewed and approved their quotes in context; individual RS and GB youth also confirmed the general accuracy of Chapters 5–7. While member-checking quotes and descriptions, I offered to remove and/or edit any representations that might concern community members, and asked if community members would like me to stress particular or additional points. In response, most research participants approved their quotes and descriptions, while others requested minor edits and/or clarification.

To honor emerging understandings of Indigenous research protocols and to address the challenges of member-checking data from younger GB youth, I also asked village adults for comments on the work within. Two community members and educators who worked with all of the RS and GB youth graciously read the entire study, providing valuable perspective on the work. Two former and current traditional council members and a nonlocal Yup'ik educator generously provided feedback on Chapters 2 and 7. At the request of a community leader, I removed a small amount of data from an earlier draft of this book. Four relatively short-term white educators provided additional feedback on the school dynamics presented in Chapter 3.

Over the same 10-year period, I further developed the book by discussing the work with a broader range of educators and upcoming Yup'ik scholars in the Yup'ik region. Early on, I shared written summaries of the study and presented findings to district school board members and administrators. From 2005 to 2007, I discussed major findings with roughly 60 Yup'ik educators, Yup'ik graduate students and scholars in language planning classes at the Yup'ik Language Institute in Bethel and the University of Alaska Fairbanks. I also gained a broader view of regional Yup'ik language revitalization efforts through visits to Ayaprun Elitnaurvik, a groundbreaking Yup'ik immersion school for children in Bethel (described in Aguilera &

LeCompte, 2007) and another immersion program connecting adult Yup'ik language learners to elders (described in Alexie *et al.*, 2009).

Remaining in conversation with Yup'ik educators about my own research trajectory (Smith, 1999), I also built on the Piniq case, 'putting anthropology to work' (Field & Fox, 2007) alongside Yup'ik educational leaders Yurrliq Nita Rearden, Ciquyaq Fannie Andrew and Cikigaq Rachel Nicholai, as well as Gayle Miller, the head of academic instruction in the Lower Kuskokwim School District (LKSD, hereafter) and my colleague Patrick Marlow of the University of Alaska Fairbanks. Chapter 3 evidences how new educational policies emphasizing high stakes testing were coming into place in 2000–2001, changing the everyday work of schooling in Piniq. In the later project, discussed in the epilogue, my colleagues and I documented the effects of these policies on language programs, and Yup'ik educators' observations of language maintenance, shift, and revitalization across 11 Yup'ik villages (Wyman *et al.*, 2010a, 2010b).

The multilayered vetting process and the follow-up work described above strengthened my understanding of the Piniq study, allowing me to situate my findings in relation to the regional Yup'ik linguistic ecology and the ongoing struggles of community members, educators, language activists and their allies. I alone, however, am responsible for any mistakes within.

Notes on Presentation of Data

All personal and place names within are pseudonyms in order to protect the privacy of research participants. Yup'ik is presented in italics throughout the text. English translations are italicized in parentheses directly following most Yup'ik morphemes, words and phrases. For more extended quotes in Yup'ik, original segments appear without translation first, with English translations following in italics. For extended interactions between individuals involving more than a few phrases in Yup'ik, original interaction appears in a left-hand column, with accompanying turn-by-turn translation on the right. In transcripts slashes (///) indicate speakers' overlapping talk and equal signs (=) indicate instances when speakers' statements followed quickly after one another without a pause. Gestures and researcher explanations appear in brackets.

To make the study accessible to Yup'ik educators and scholars, data within is presented in the phonemic orthography developed by the Alaska Native Language Center for local schools and universities. During the study, no one in Piniq used the diacritics in the phonemic Yup'ik orthography. I have left these out to leave the text accessible to local readers.

Choices about translations present another layer of interpretation in representing data and people. Yup'ik is typologically distant from English, and English translations that maintain Yup'ik word order, establishment of tense and frequency of evidentials can sound inarticulate in English. Following local conventions, tense and evidential constructions, and word order are translated and glossed within according to standard English discourse norms, excepting sections where I analyze and discuss relevant linguistic features.

2   Elders and *Qanruyutait* in Village Life

At the turn of the 20th century, community members in Piniq commonly described English as crucial for participation and survival in a dramatically changing world. The economic viability of Piniq depended upon integrating extensive subsistence practices with a global cash economy. International, federal and state regulations in English shaped local governance. Adults and youth actively consumed media in English. Youth were also schooled in a public educational system that strongly emphasized English language acquisition as the basis for academic and work opportunities. In some sense, then, English might be said to be dominating in its force.

At the same time, many community members expressed the centrality of local knowledge and resisted a sense of inevitable cultural loss during early language shift. A local language ideology valuing Yup'ik permeated young people's daily interactions in the remote community. Community members also underscored the importance of Yup'ik-speaking elders and elders' *qanruyutait* (*teachings*) within the social, ecological, spiritual and political terrain of the village, framing Yup'ik language maintenance in relation to *yuuyaraq*, a local knowledge system referred to as 'the Yup'ik way of life'.

Overviewing local beliefs about Yup'ik language maintenance and intergenerational learning, this chapter documents how adults in Piniq incorporated *yuuyaraq* within the everyday life of Piniq as they worked to foster self-determination and maintain community cohesion during times of rapid change. The chapter also begins to highlight how local youth in 2000 harkened to related local language ideologies, as well, in descriptions of their lives in Piniq.

Local Language Ideology

One of the most painful effects of language shift is the disruption that can occur between young people who speak primarily a nonheritage language and grandparents, or even parents who mostly speak a heritage language (Wong-Fillmore, 2000). For many Indigenous communities, such intergenerational disruptions also represent a potential loss of oral traditions that have served for generations as a means of passing on unique histories, knowledge systems and cultural practices.

By the mid-1990s in Piniq, most elders had learned at least some English through attending school for a few years. A few elders also used English for complex purposes such as running local stores or serving as village airline agents. However, most village elders were strongly Yup'ik dominant, and generally reserved their English use for interactions with non-Yup'ik-speaking outsiders. Community members also typically accommodated elders by speaking Yup'ik as a sign of respect. While in some instances elders tried to communicate with children in English, it was much more common for youth to try to use what Yup'ik they knew to interact with elders.

Villagers often referred to the Yup'ik of the elders as 'pure' Yup'ik – a Yup'ik that reflected knowledge of a largely self-reliant world before sustained contact and dependence upon the outside world. Even middle-aged adults who grew up speaking Yup'ik comfortably qualified their assessment of their own Yup'ik competence by stating that they did not know the 'hard words' of elders. For many community members, as well, elders' *qanruyutait*, 'wise words and instructions that provided moral guidance in the past' (Fienup-Riordan *et al.*, 2005: 3), also represented a 'cumulative knowledge on a timescale and spatial scale that no individual could match' (Lemke, 2000: 282).

As in other Yup'ik communities, adults described how *qanruyutait* and related forms of elders' instructions were 'teachings from the heart' shared out of love and caring for youth (Fienup-Riordan *et al.*, 2005). Adults also noted how this linguistic and cultural heritage had been only partially passed down to the generation of adults who attended boarding schools far from Piniq. Community members further expressed strong concerns that contemporary youth might lose access to elders' *qanruyutait* because of language shift (e.g. Wyman *et al.*, 2010a).

Community members including youth often discussed how elders' *qanruyutait* in Yup'ik were an important community resource, and described these teachings as elders' 'strong talk'. At the time of the study, community members were encouraged to share and to follow specific related socializing subgenres of *qanruyutait*, including *inerquutet* 'prohibitions' – sayings, teachings and stories about how *not* to behave, and the complementary genre of *alerquutet*, often referred to as 'prescriptions' – sayings, teachings and stories about how one *should* behave. As in other Yup'ik communities, elders' *alerquutet* and *inerquutet* ranged from specific advice about how to foster positive relationships with spouses, children, animals and the local environment, to specific advice and warnings about navigating and handling situations on surrounding lands and waters (e.g. Fienup-Riordan *et al.*, 2005).

As in many Yup'ik communities in the early 1900s, young men traditionally learned the system of how to behave and survive by listening to the advice and stories of elders in a *qasgiq* (*men's house*). Girls, on the other hand, learned from women in separate family dwellings (Fienup-Riordan, 1990). When community members changed to living in houses as nuclear families year-round, elders' advice changed to being *egmirte – passed on –* more within families, as opposed to communally. With the advent of new forms of schooling and media, elders' advice was also passed on more sporadically through a variety of informal and formal channels.

Very little of the elders' extensive knowledge of ecology, systems of navigation, strategies for resource harvesting or past cultural practices had been recorded at the time of the study. This created a general sense in Piniq, as in other areas of the Yukon-Kuskokwim Delta and Native Alaska, that when the current generation of elders passed away, thousands of years of orally accumulated knowledge and Yup'ik history would go with them. A related drive to record elders' knowledge and *qanruyutait* motivated multiple projects documenting elders' narratives in the Yup'ik region from 1980 to 2000.

Elders as Socializing Agents

In many ways, local life in Piniq centered on the sharing of *qanruyutait*. Community members and youth described elders in Piniq, as in other Yup'ik communities, as playing a crucial historical and contemporary role in social-izing youth (Fienup-Riordan *et al.*, 2005). The middle-aged generation of adults born in the 1940s and 1950s remembered hearing their parents and grandparents pass on advice at night before bed and especially in the morn-ing, when children were said to be most open to taking in *qanruyutait*. Multiple generations of community members also worked in creative ways to *egmirte- (pass on) qanruyutait*, and related concepts about teaching and learning in local venues and processes.

Community members described how the relationships between youth and elders were of special importance for sustaining practical and interpersonal kinds of knowledge surrounding subsistence, and how it was important for youth to learn to behave in certain ways around elders in order to learn *yuuyaraq*. Many non-Indigenous educators in Piniq ran into situations where silent students confounded them at first, or showed an extreme reluctance to take on new kinds of tasks. Later, we will consider how suppressive and disjointed forms of schooling helped produced children's silence in schools (Lomawaima & McCarty, 2006; Moses & Wigglesworth, 2008).

Community members, however, often interpreted children's silence in relation to a set of cultural expectations. As we will see, youth were socialized to take on considerable amounts of responsibility as they grew up in the local subsistence society. Many community members also described how Yup'ik young people were supposed to learn from elders and adults by being *takaryuk* (*respectful*). *Takaryuk* has no simple English counterpart, though it can be loosely translated in different situations as 'respectful', 'self-conscious' and/ or 'shy/embarrassed'. Considering community members' beliefs about the importance of acting *takaryuk* provides insight into ways young people were expected to learn from adults, and the ways in which young people were expected to demonstrate knowledge of Yupik, in particular.

Villagers labeled certain relationships as particularly *takaryuk*, and these relationships were often marked by avoidance of interaction and young people's silence. In previous generations, children had been expected to be *takaryuk* of their parents. Adults and some youth were also expected to act particularly *takaryuk* toward their uncles. A younger man in his late thirties, for instance, described how he was establishing himself as *takarnaqluni* (causing someone to show respect by being *takaryuk*) to his nephews and nieces by not saying anything to them. A man in his forties also called my attention to an everyday, patterned noninteraction one day as we spoke about fishing in passing out on the boardwalk. After an older man passed us on a four-wheeler without saying hello, the man asked me, 'Did you see that? Did you see how [Name] didn't say anything to me when he passed? He didn't say anything because he is my uncle so we don't speak to each other.'

Historically, young people produced extended Yup'ik with one another, and had their own gendered genres for traditional storytelling. For instance, older women remembered storyknifing, drawing in the mud with a knife while telling stories (deMarrais *et al.*, 1992). Yet, older men and women emphasized how, as youth, they were also generally expected to remain silent and still when listening to adults and elders, in particular, and to watch elders' mouths or to look down, versus meeting elders' eyes, to show that they were listening attentively. Men described remaining silent and not moving a muscle while paying attention to elders in the *qasgiq* (*men's house*). Women, as well, described how they were expected to remain still when they were instructed by adults at home, as in the following interview excerpt from Helen, a middle-aged woman, in 2000:

Helen: Anytime we (did) anything that they, that they don't agree with, they would [. . .] start talking to us, and we have to stop whatever we're doing and listen. Sit down and listen. We can't, it'll show disrespect if we keep on, like if I'm washing dishes, or cleaning house, or whatever I'm doing, I stop ... you know, stand or sit still to listen.

LTW: Um, umhmm.

Helen: That's paying attention. Paying respect.

Helen and others described how youth were expected to watch adults' mouths, paying close attention to what they were saying and concentrating in order to remember their teachings, echoing the words of many other adults in Piniq.

Elders and adults in Piniq also described how the meanings of elders' stories were supposed to become *mistuluteng* (*clear*, or *able to see from a distance*) when situations called for them in the future. As Elsie Mather, a well-known Yup'ik poet and scholar has described, traditionally youth were not expected to analyze elders' teachings, nor were elders expected to 'spell out or theorize' the meanings of stories. Describing her work documenting the oral narratives of one elder, Mather comments: 'We both knew that to ask many questions, especially of an elder by a young person, was one of the no-no's in our way of learning' (Mather, 1995: 16). Instead, youth were instructed to listen even without understanding, assuming that later they would make meaning or be touched by something they heard as understanding and knowing occurred over the course of a lifetime (Mather, 1995: 33; see also Fienup-Riordan *et al.*, 2005).

In Piniq in the 1990s and 2000–2001, many community members emphasized how young people should pay careful attention to adults and elders without interrupting when they were sharing *qanruyutait*. Adults also valued young peoples' receptive skills in Yup'ik and their abilities to follow directions. As in other Yup'ik communities, adults instructed youth to memorize the advice of elders, and to use *qanruyutait*, versus their own impulses, to avoid getting into danger, warning young people about the dangers of 'following your mind' (e.g. Fienup-Riordan *et al.*, 2005). On the surface, this message might seem to contradict the oft-stated goal of progressive education to help youth become critical thinkers in their own right. As community members pointed out, however, it was easy to become disoriented when navigating on the tundra. Ignoring *qanruyutait* from elders and adults could produce extremely dangerous results; remembering *qanruyutait*, in contrast, could be life saving. One mother described an incident where her teenage daughter became lost on her snowmobile traveling between villages. She attributed the problem to the young woman 'using her mind'. The daughter herself described how she got out of trouble when she remembered teachings from the school-based elders project described in Chapter 4, and was able to navigate home by the stars.

At the time of the study, adults also generally socialized children to be *takaryuk* by emphasizing how others were attending to young people's children's behavior, as will be elaborated in Chapter 5. Elders and middle-aged adults also warned that too much *cenirtaaq* (*visiting house to house*) would make children lose the appropriate stance of being *takaryuk*, and how later parents would be *tunriq*, or embarrassed by the misbehavior of their children. When my son, Jules, went through an early phase of being scared of people in Piniq, people excused the behavior by saying he was being appropriately *takaryuk*, and that if he was not, it would have shown that we visited around with him too much.

Most of the youth in the RS and GB groups acted *takaryuk* accordingly, remaining silent in local situations ranging from attending church to visiting someone else's house. Piniq was very social at the time of the study, and when young children attended feasts for birthdays or anniversaries of deaths, they generally visited out of sight of adults, playing in the back rooms of people's houses, or remaining quiet around adults. Young people also remained quiet around elders and adults in mixed-age public settings. At community meetings during the time of the study, for instance, adults in their forties and older generally discussed local issues, while many people in their twenties and thirties listened. At basketball games, as well, generally a few elders cheered loudest, mostly in Yup'ik, while only a few young people called out.

Youth sometimes complained that activities ranging from giving speeches, asking strangers questions or crossing in front of a crowd to go get something was 'too *takarnaq*' meaning that it made them too *takaryuk*, or self-conscious. Yet a person being *takaryuk* was not perceived as stemming from a lack of general confidence. In contrast, youth noted how their most confident and respected peers were often the most *takaryuk* around local adults. As we will see in later chapters, youth who were *takaryuk* around community members could also display very different behaviors in school.

At the same time, multiple parents of young people in the GB group also noted that youth in 2000 sometimes did not understand the expression of caring underlying adults' sharing of *qanruyutait*, misinterpreting the adults' *inerquutet* as *nunuq*, or scolding. One young father, for instance, described how his children reacted to adults' stern tones and countenances as they shared *inerquutet*:

> I try to pass them (the *inerquutet*) on, but when we talk to them, they
> think we are angry at them, from the tone of voice and the facial

expression. They misunderstand that, and they'll say, 'Daddy-*m nunuraanga (scolded me),'* when we tell 'em not to do this or that. My grandma said a person will only give advice if they love that person. [...] Even if we *inerquq (share prohibitions with)* our children, they think *nunuryukluteng (we are scolding them).*

Community members also commented on how certain types of relationships were becoming less *takaryuk* over time. Young men and women could be seen walking or hanging out and about in the community together, a change that some elders saw as violating social norms. Younger uncles were also less likely than older uncles to avoid interaction with nieces and nephews. Like adults, however, youth described and related Yup'ik language maintenance to the value of elders' teachings, and a subsistence way of life. Middle-aged community members also creatively incorporated elders and employed local forms of *qanruyutait* or strong talk into local institutions as a commonsense strategy for linguistic survivance, as we will begin to consider here.

Language Brokering, Linguistic Survivance and Institutional Power

Within the second half of the 20th century, as villages across the Far North and the Yup'ik region witnessed an influx of institutions, the increasing importance of related bureaucracies brought changing demands for bilingualism, biliteracy and literacy practices (Reder & Wikelund, 1993). The new demands of local bureaucracies also placed young men and women into new positions of leadership (Fienup-Riordan, 1990). As missionaries, teachers and government agents interacted with adults in Piniq, community members initially asked individual youth to interpret encounters in the church, school as well as over a radio system reaching the outside world. Some of these youth later became known locally for their gifts as adult community interpreters.

During the timeframe of this study, from 1992 to 2001, multiple community members in Piniq regularly negotiated the local 'developmental script' (Dorner *et al.*, 2008) described above, emphasizing respect for elders and the importance of local knowledge and related socializing genres, with 'the inherent complexity of communication in cross-cultural encounters' (Makihara & Schieffelin, 2007: 6) in a range of village institutions. In the 1990s and 2000, as elsewhere in the region, elders retained important positions as leaders within local bureaucracies in Piniq. Individuals born after the 1950s were also called upon to come up with new ways to adapt *yuuyaraq* as they proactively addressed local needs to maintain self-determination and a subsistence way of life.

This section documents the historical roots of bilingualism and biliteracy within the traditional council, the tribal court and the local church in Piniq, highlighting how local adults incorporated elders and elders' *qanruyutait* (*teachings*) into village institutions as a commonsense means of self-directing dramatic societal changes within village *contact zones*, 'social spaces where cultures meet, clash and grapple with each other, often in contexts of highly asymmetrical relationships of power' (Pratt, 1991: 33). As we will see, many of the resulting language socialization practices reproduced local language ideologies, underscoring the ongoing importance of elders and Yup'ik language maintenance, even as some institutions in Piniq like the local church also became sites of both language maintenance and language shift.

Traditional Council

In Alaska Native and American Indian communities, a focus on linguistic survivance can help illuminate how particular language practices are inherently part of what Vizenor refers to as 'the sure transmotion of sovereignty' (Vizenor, 1993: 23). During elders' lifetimes in Piniq, after the Indian Reorganization Act of 1934 was amended in 1936 to cover Alaska Natives, local governance changed dramatically from community decision-making to shared control among a locally elected 'traditional' council and district, state and federal authorities (Oswalt, 1990). In a number of key instances and in multiple less dramatic daily practices, community members faced the constraints of outside attempts to redefine local relationships, and turned to itself to handle local problems.

The Piniq traditional council took dramatic steps to counter government attempts to define local land ownership in corporate terms, for instance, with the passage of the federal Alaska Native Claims Settlement Act in 1971. Under the act, villagers born before 1971 were made shareholders, and village lands were owned as an asset of a village corporation (for reference, see Berger, 1985; Ongtooguk, 1986). When the village corporation failed to make a profit, however, villagers in Piniq transferred their lands to the traditional council in trust as part of a broader sovereignty movement in the 1980s (Oswalt, 1990).

Around the same time, village leaders decided to physically search incoming residents and visitors as they arrived at the local airstrip in order to enforce a local ban on alcohol and drugs. When visiting state employees such as eye specialists refused to allow themselves to be patted down by local residents, citing their US constitutional rights, the village chose to forego such services. The local search house dramatically cut local alcohol use, and in the late 1990s, council members were regularly asked to present their work at meetings of the Alaska Federation of Natives to help other villages.

As a result of Alaska Native conflicts with Alaska state authorities over federally granted subsistence and self-governance rights in the 1980s and 1990s, village leaders in Piniq were regularly put in the difficult position of having to argue for self-determination by using terms such as 'traditional' and 'customary', terms that were both recognized and constrained by outside legal agencies in preexisting power relationships (Morrow & Hensel, 1992). In cases where outside government agencies challenged village autonomy, often the community's case hinged on establishing traditional precedent for current actions. For instance, in one case, the local government attempted to banish a white resident suspected of drug dealing who refused to recognize the jurisdiction of the local court. The resident countered with a federal civil rights case against the traditional council, claiming he had been discriminated against as a white person. To avoid being found guilty, the council's legal case hinged on establishing historical precedent of the tribe's use of banishment as a 'traditional' method of local governance.

As an Alaska Native village that had only been federally recognized as a tribe in 1993, the government in Piniq existed in a legal gray area with very little set precedent for which kinds of community transgressions could be handled locally versus by state troopers or federal agents. While some early village leaders developed considerable English skills, many elders who spoke mostly Yup'ik maintained considerable local and regional power (e.g. Fienup-Riordan, 1990). The work of the traditional council also depended on regular demonstrations of linguistic survivance from younger bilingual adults like Thomas.

In the mid-1990s, Thomas was in his late thirties, and among the few people working in Piniq with some college education. As a bilingual broker, Thomas used his English skills to decipher the regular bulletins he received via fax about the potential effects of pending legislation on tribal self-determination and subsistence rights. He regularly wrote letters and made presentations in English to lobby legislators to help defeat or promote state and federal bills, often working in conjunction with elders. For eight years, Thomas was in charge of bringing grant monies into Piniq.

Thomas used Yup'ik to run the daily business of the traditional council, presiding over meetings and strategizing over lengthy discussions how to negotiate federal and state regulations in light of local concerns. As part of his work, Thomas also translated government documents into Yup'ik for elders, and council decisions and propositions into English for outside legislators, agency representatives, lawyers, and Native American/Alaska Native rights groups. In the interview below, I talked to Thomas about his job as a tribal administrator:

LTW: In the council, so you have elders who participate in the council as council members, and then you have people like your age who are the administrators.

Thomas: I think there should be a lot more participation by young people just because I think because, they're gonna be taking over. I mean, our elders are getting old, and you gotta learn how to take care of things the way they've been taking care of them [...] We need to have a lot of young people involved today. They need to be mentored into making sure our subsistence way of life is protected.

        ***

LTW: When you were first tribal administrator, how long do you think it took you to learn that job? Were there things that were hard about it in the beginning, or ...

Thomas: Yeh, there were some, yeh, I went through a lot of hardship for a while, because it was hard to me to understand things that I've never done before and it was hard to do things that I had never done before like putting together a grant application [...] college helped me to learn.

LTW: Um hmm.

Thomas: But the teachings from the elders, that's what's important, I think, that's the most important part. They make you learn patience. Not to hurry, not to do things in a hurried pace. I think that's what the young people here need to learn if they're going to keep going with their culture. They need to learn it in Yup'ik. I mean government-wise, tribal government-wise. The way I see it clearly is that we need to have a lot of young people learn a lot about the issues we face, the subsistence, the language. The cash economy, they need to learn to live with it. [...] The cash economy came from the Western Civilization, but I think those two can work hand in hand together for the benefit of our people to keep it going. And a lot of that I think is emphasized by our regional corporations, and the emphasis they give to that. [...] I think the villages need to recognize that, too. Through all that I think the tribal governments can go forward with that, they just need to keep it in focus. The

way to keep it in focus is to have more involvement by the
young people, try to learn these things from elders. (10/21/00)

Above, Thomas described how college helped him learn how to put together
grant applications, and many others in Piniq, as well, noted how grant writing was a relatively rare, yet particularly important form of literacy for creating local opportunities. As Thomas referred to issues facing the tribe, he also
emphasized the need of Yup'ik for subsistence, and English for dealing with
the challenge of maintaining subsistence in the face of 'the cash economy
coming on strong'. Thomas further stressed the active involvement of elders
in governance, and need for elders to mentor youth about tribal rights and
governance in Yup'ik.

This local logic linking the knowledge of elders with the importance of
Yup'ik language maintenance and self-determination becomes especially
clear if one imagines other ways that Thomas could have described his role
as a younger adult in the local government. Multiple members of the middle-
aged generation in Piniq at the time described how, unlike their parents, they
had grown aware and more likely to stand up for their rights using English
skills and literacy. Instead of highlighting how he himself used English literacy, advocacy and interpretation to run the local government, however,
Thomas stated that the younger generation needed to learn governance from
local elders in Yup'ik 'above all else'. Once one accepts Thomas's premise that
young people must learn local ways of managing tribal governance from
elders rather than from the bilingual middle generation, his assertion that
young people must learn about self-reliance and how to protect subsistence
in Yup'ik logically follows.

In 1998, Alaska state residents passed a law making English the official
language of governance in Alaska; almost immediately, representatives of
Yup'ik traditional councils and others challenged the law. In 2001, however,
Thomas commented that any such measure was unlikely to affect local governance in Piniq, given the extensive use of Yup'ik in the local traditional
council and the ways in which the council regularly pushed for self-determination on multiple fronts. He worried, however, about how the state measure
might impact funding for bilingual education in the local school.

Elsewhere in the interview, Thomas also expressed concern about the
ways he and young parents around him were finding themselves responding
to children's English use by talking to them in English, and emphasized the
importance of understanding both the content and emotional nuances of
elders' talk in Yup'ik. As we have seen above, adults like Thomas were very
actively passing on and adapting local knowledge in the local council through
their Yup'ik and bilingual/biliterate acts of linguistic survivance. In another

key local institution, the tribal court, bilingual brokers similarly worked to negotiate *yuuyaraq* with outside legislation.

Tribal Court

In Piniq in the mid-1990s, a number of adults in Piniq voiced a suspicion that state and federal government representatives did not care about local well-being. Many villagers also shared a perception that community members were not treated fairly in the Alaskan court system given cross-cultural differences and local teachings about how to handle unjust accusations. At the time, an Alaskan sociolinguist documented how differences in communication patterns and beliefs about questioning and evidence in Bethel courts were, indeed, leading to miscommunication and overincarceration of Yup'ik adults (Morrow, 1993).

In 2000–2001, village leaders in Piniq worked on a local tribal court system in an effort to proactively govern themselves and manage local–outside tensions over tribal jurisdiction. The head of the tribal court, Peter, described how the tribal court integrated traditional methods of social control and contemporary regulations:

Peter: The traditional system we have here, they follow their own system instead of following the procedures, well, there's some procedures that they have to follow, but in the past they'd rather do it the traditional way. And there's some controversies, classes, conflicts.

LTW: Like how would you describe the traditional way if someone has a problem, like stealing or drinking that they're trying to work with or,

Peter: Well, the traditional way is the elders get together and they talk with him. If that doesn't help they have to ban the person. They have to talk to him something like two or three times? If that doesn't help, they usually ban the person from the village. And it had happened quite a few times ...

Multiple interviewees, like Peter above, described elders' ways of 'strongly talking to' offenders repeatedly as a means of traditional governance. Village adults also contrasted such traditional practices as banishment with inefficiencies of the Western legal system, making a case for more locally controlled solutions to village challenges.

Peter described how he was 'blending' the Western approach to legal courts with more traditional forms of strong talk, laying out offenses and explaining penalties as a middle-aged village leader and bilingual broker. Peter went on to describe how two elderly court members would use different types of *qanruyutait* to underscore Yup'ik expectations for interpersonal relationships. One elder would strategically share specific *qanruyutait* laying out village norms for behavior. A second elder would then describe a possible negative future should the offender continue down a path of trouble.

Peter described how he called upon elders' *qanruyutait* to encourage juvenile offenders to reflect deeply on their actions:

Peter: I remember one young guy; he was in tears this last week.

LTW: What were you talking to him about?

Peter: Some violations here, you know. And I remember I told him some quotables from his grandmother, and I got into [Name]'s quotes. And I thought that young guy was very tough, but he was in tears.

LTW: You were quoting her ...

Peter: Sayings ... I was saying to that young guy what his grandmother used to say to me, and what [another elder, who served as a counselor in the school, described in the following chapter] used to say to us. Just short quotables, like proverbs.

LTW: Um hmm ... Do you remember any of them?

Peter: [Name]? I remember when she was living, she used to call me up to visit her. I remember she used to kiss me every time. And when I listened, she used to tell stories, tell stories, and then sometimes she used to say, [...] 'The laws, or the positive information, make(s) the person good or something positive from bad.' Something like that I remember. There's [Another elders]'s saying, I remember he told us that if someone tells you about your downfall, don't ... just receive it and try to improve it, try to improve yourself. If someone tells you about your laziness, don't hide it, just make yourself. Without any criticism, a person cannot learn.

In 2000 in the small community, adults were finding new venues and ways of embedding community means of disciplining youth, taking into account the emotional power of young people's personal relationships with elders past and present. Individuals like Peter harkened to elders' strong talk as well as the sayings of former elders in order to establish social control within a recognizable community framework, socializing youth through local government agencies.

The 'nature of survivance is unmistakable' in efforts to pass on 'native stories ... traditions and customs' (Vizenor, 2008: 1), such as community members' creative efforts to socialize youth in Piniq through the use of elders' *qanruyutait* in new village bureaucracies. Consideration of a very different setting, the local church, evidences how community members also used introduced spiritual institutions to underscore respect for elders and to foster community cohesion, further adapting local socialization practices in a dramatically changing world.

Church

In some Indigenous communities, conversion to Christianity may be strongly associated with ideological and emotional changes driving language shift (Dauenhauer & Dauenhauer, 1998; Kulick, 1992). In many Indigenous contexts, Christian missionary work and the creation of Bible materials foster new Indigenous writing systems and forms of Indigenous literacy practices (Hinton, 2001; Hornberger, 1997; Reder & Wikelund, 1993). Churches may also be sites where both Indigenous language maintenance and shift occur simultaneously, 'interwoven with the forces of modernization' (Hornberger & Coronel-Molina, 2004: 29) and global forms of media.

A local Moravian church had existed in Piniq for 60–70 years at the time of the study. Piniq community members participated and adhered to church teachings to varying degrees, yet by all accounts, the Moravian church was a central force in community life. Both church and subsistence practices heavily influenced weekly and yearly cycles of events. Villagers refrained from travel and work, including subsistence, on Sundays. Extracurricular activities in school, council meetings, and village basketball practices and tournaments were also scheduled so as not to conflict with weekly and annual church activities. In the late fall, winter, and early spring, church members from Piniq participated in an extensive exchange of songfests and church rallies, hosting hundreds of villagers from outside Piniq, and traveling in large numbers by snowmobile or plane for weekends elsewhere full of services and singing, gathering for food in people's houses, and nightly steam baths. In the summer, however, church activities tapered off as people left Piniq for longer days and stints of subsistence and commercial land-use practices.

New language practices in Indigenous churches commonly reshape thought, local identities and forms of power (Makihara & Schieffelin, 2007). Looking at early records of Moravian–Yup'ik encounters (Fienup-Riordan, 1991) and current spiritual practices in Christian Yup'ik communities

(Fienup-Riordan, 1990; Jolles, 2002), anthropologists highlight how traditional Yup'ik and Christian beliefs shared 'enduring principles and practices', such as deep respect for elders' teaching and persons. As in other village institutions, elders played a strong role in the church in Piniq. An official board of elders, elected yearly from the congregation, ran the daily life of the church, setting yearly schedules. Board members also sent representatives to district and national church boards, and issued local interpretations of doxa, such as a decision in the 1990s to uphold a ban on local dancing on religious grounds. In the church, elders further acted as social counselors, using Bible teachings to talk to people confidentially about social problems, and to teach about domestic life.

From 1992 to 2001, many traditional and Christian Yup'ik beliefs and practices existed side by side in Piniq, as in other Christian Yup'ik communities at the time (Fienup-Riordan, 1990, 1991; Jolles, 2002). As we have seen above, elders in Piniq shared *alerquutet* and *inerquutet*, describing the benefits of following traditional Yup'ik teachings and negative outcomes should youth veer from these teachings. In and out of church, multiple elders also offered advice about how to treat others and deal with life's trials, while discussing beliefs about the importance of following Jesus, their anticipation of Heaven, Judgment Day and the tortures of Hell in Yup'ik. A few community members expressed tensions around the ways that dramatic church-related changes had impacted the passing on of some local traditions. Adults and youth, for instance, described how outside missionaries had positioned specific local practices such as traditional Yup'ik dancing as antagonistic to Christianity. One parent also described how he felt unjustly critiqued for not passing on *qanruyutait*, when he himself had been socialized within the church, versus the *qasgiq*.

By the 1990s, however, community members had localized many church-related language socialization practices, and in many respects from 1992 to 2001 the church was a strong domain for children's ongoing exposure to Yup'ik. Young people were encouraged to participate in church regularly, and all multigenerational activities in 2000 were conducted in Yup'ik. In church services, young people listened to predictable directions, announcements and adults' lengthy sermons in Yup'ik.

At the time of the study, the local church in Piniq was also the strongest local domain for Yup'ik literacy. Youth encountered the Yup'ik Moravian writing system in church hymnals, schedules and notices, as well as local Bibles. Elders had considerable skills reading and writing the Moravian orthography, and extended Yup'ik literacy functions beyond the church. Community members translated public notices and newsletters into the Moravian writing system to involve elders in the political, economic and spiritual life of Piniq. Intergenerational community members also used the Moravian writing system in situated church literacy events such as singing hymns and reading prayers from texts (e.g. Heath, 1983). Even during language shift, very young children in Piniq memorized and recited *naaqer-kat* (*things to read/speeches*), lines of Bible verses in Yup'ik for individual performances in Christmas services, coached for weeks in advance by a pair of elders.

Villagers also localized English-language Christian media through bilingual practices in and out of the church. For instance, local choir members and church soloists actively consumed English videos, CDs and songbooks put out by media-savvy southern gospel groups like the Gaithers, and learned and performed new songs in English. If particular songs became popular, individuals would translate them into Yup'ik for soloists or village singing groups. As church songs were performed in intervillage religious songfests, adults from around the region also hand copied both Yup'ik and English lyrics from others into personal songbooks.

Through multiple practices, both Yup'ik and English church songs were imbued with new, situated meanings. Metaphors are often a vehicle for interpretation (Lakoff & Mark, 1980), and for the expression of Indigenous people's survivance (Basso, 1996; Vizenor, 2008). As in other Christian churches in Yup'ik villages (Fienup-Riordan, 2000), metaphors figured prominently in church discourse. Some popular church songs, for instance, compared life's struggles to familiar landscape-related metaphors such as storms passing over and river crossings.

Soloists commonly prefaced their performances with speeches in Yup'ik about how particular lyrics inspired them. Community members also performed songs to express caring for individuals facing life challenges including the loss of loved ones, or the sadness of an impending long-term departure from the village. Through repeated performance, Yup'ik and/or English songs often became associated with soloists, and/or individual community members who repeatedly requested the performance of particular songs. At times, the mere singing of specific church songs would move community members to tears, as they remembered beloved elders or family members who had passed on. During multiday wakes accompanying funerals, choir members also gathered in family homes to sing familiar Yup'ik hymns late into the night as a powerful, patterned expression of support.

By considering child-centered activities and young peoples' performances, however, we can also see how the church was also a site for linguistic accommodation of English. By 2001, Sunday school teachers used child-friendly English texts, comics, and/or coloring books to illustrate Bible stories, and used English to teach young children in Sunday school. Local youth and children usually chose to sing in English when singing on their own. Villagers were also increasingly consuming new types of Christian media flows in English. *Left Behind*, a movie by an alternative Christian movie company about Judgment Day, for instance, was popularly viewed on video in Piniq before a grassroots Christian media movement managed to get the film into mainstream movie theaters in larger metropolitan areas.

Within multiple local institutions in Piniq, community members negotiated a Yup'ik way of participating and belonging in a dramatically changing world. Adults integrated elders as leaders into new village bureaucracies as a means of negotiating dramatic political, social and spiritual changes. While the purview and emphasis in specific bureaucracies varied, within each of these local contact zones individuals also used Yup'ik for new functions, and linguistic brokering for fostering social cohesion in a bilingual world shaped by flows of regulation and information from the outside world. Yet such efforts were not without their challenges. As community members recognized rapid changes in local practices, they voiced concern about the potential loss of historically accumulated local knowledge.

Challenges getting by in the distressed, rural economy were also part of daily life, as villagers pieced together wage work and government funding with subsistence. Adults commented about how connected Piniq had become to the outside world, and how their Yup'ik way of life generally went unrecognized by mainstream politicians, policymakers and media pundits. Tensions over these struggles were never far from the surface in talk about Yup'ik language maintenance, and outside policymakers' ignorance about local life was a source of regular frustration for village leaders. In the face of these struggles, however, community members also used Yup'ik and bilingualism to shape vibrant forms of humor and local commentary, as we will consider here.

Linguistic Survivance and Humorous Commentary

Survivance can be discerned in the 'humanistic tease' and 'vital irony' (Vizenor, 2008: 1) in the face of pressures to conform to outside pressures and regulations. From 1992 to 2001 in many everyday instances, adults used bilingual jokes to comment on everyday issues like struggles over subsistence rights, the connection of the village to global or State regulations, and the global economy. Political and media figures, and media-related messages about global power were a common source of humor. Since much of what was portrayed in the media seemed so far from local life, and local life, in turn, was often rendered invisible in media portrayals, such jokes served as prime examples of the ways community members used language to assert an 'active presence over absence' (Vizenor, 2008: 1) in a globalized world.

The following jokes come from a New Year's Day celebration in 2001 in which community members packed the school gym for a day of games, humorous competitions and performances. For one of the performances, the annual MC for the events lined up four female elders on folding chairs to look as if they were sitting in a plane. He then proceeded to joke about 'what these elders did for their vacation'.

Joke 1:

Original:
Ciumek qanrutkeqatarqa [name of elder 1] a former Rock Star who performed with Tina Turner, Billy Joel and country singer Johnny Cash.
Win-*allrulliniuq ataucimek* Emmy, an Emmy Award, *tua-i-ll'* but now, she's devoting all her time to promote world peace.
Cali-ll' imkullrulliniuq, meeting-*aaryarturluni,* with Yasser Arafat plan meeting about the, the herring price,
Cali-ll' taum-wani atanrem assikelliniluki uqumelnguut nerellri, Cali-llu-gguq Alaska-*mun* move-*aryugluni tauna ataneq* in the year 2002.
That was [name of elder 1].

Translation:
First I'm going to introduce [name of elder 1], a former Rock Star who performed with Tina Turner, Billy Joel and country singer Johnny Cash.
She won *one* Emmy, Emmy Award, *but,* but now, she's devoting all her time to promote world peace.

She also was gone to a meeting with Yasser Arafat, plan meeting about the, the herring price,
Also that king liked the seal oil-soaked herring fish,
And also he says he wants to move to Alaska in the year 2002.
That was [name of elder 1].

Joke 2:

Original:
Tua-i-ll' [name of elder 2] recently got back from Washington D.C. where her and George W. Bush, *augna*

Translation:
Then [name of elder 2] recently got back from Washington D.C. where her and George W. Bush, *the presidential candidate,* they

imna atanrurteqatalria-gguq, they were discussing ways that they would raise the price of grass baskets, *mingkaat akiita mayurtengnaqlerkaita quyur, quyurtaallruut tamani.*
Cali-llu tauna President Bush-am-gguq, Bush- am qanrutellrua that he might be up here this spring to hunt for walrus with her friend.
Asverturyarturluni-gguq up'nerkaqu maavet taiciqsugnarquq, pissuryarturluni.
Cali-ll' mingqaarkanek taperrnarnek paqluteng-gguq maavirciiqut tayima up'nerkaqu.
Cali-llu-gguq umyuarteqluni pissurnayukluni unani,
Cali-llu piskuni-gguq uqiqurarkauluku.

That was [name of elder 2].

were discussing ways that they would raise the price of grass baskets, *they were having meetings over there to promote the price of grass baskets.*

And also that President Bush told her that he might come up here this spring to hunt for walrus with her friend.
He said he might be coming to here to eat some walrus meat this coming spring, to hunt.
Also, they will come here in the spring to check grass for basket-making.
And also he said thought he might go hunting down at the ocean,
And also when he catches something, they will have a seal party for him.

That was [name of elder 2].

Joke 3:

Original:
Tua-i-ll' una [name of elder 3] just got back from Savoonga Alaska, where she had to give up her Miss Alaska crown she held for 25 years.
Una-llu tua-i Oil of Olay! And other cosmetics companies have called her for promotions, but she says that politics revolve her ambition.
Augkunek-gguq narnircautnek imkunek-llu tepkeggninarqellrianek pillruyaaqaat, taugaam-gguq maa-i atanrurtengnaqellriani tamakuni calinguq.
That was [name of elder 3].

Translation:
And here's [name of elder 3] just got back from Savoonga, Alaska, where she had to give up her Miss Alaska crown she held for 25 years.
And this Oil of Olay! And other cosmetics companies have called her for promotions, but she says that politics revolve her ambition.
She said she bought some sweet scents and perfumes, but now she's working on the presidential campaign.

That was [name of elder 3].

Joke 4:

Original:
Tua-llu
[Name of elder 4]!
[Name of elder 4] just got back
from the Middle East.
Una-llu quyurtellrulliniuq
[pauses to read handwriting]
Oh! With Saddam Hussein,
tauna-llu-gguq quyurtellruuk,
meeting that was scheduled at
Goodnews Bay to discuss the
falling price of herring.
Iqalluarpiit akiit
mayurtengnaqluki
quyurtellrulliniuk tamaani.
Cali-llu tauna-wani cumigtelliniuq
[name of elder 4] *taum akian*
mayurtellerkaanek.
Upnerkaqu-gguq maa-i
iqalluarpak akia mayunrilkan,
fine-*arciqai taukut* herring-*aanek*
taukut kiputellret.
Yaah quyanarquci!

Translation:
And here's
[Name of elder 4]!
[Name of elder 4] just got back
from the Middle East.
She had a meeting with the
[pauses to read handwriting]
Oh! With Saddam Hussein, *she*
had a meeting with him, meeting
that was scheduled at
Goodnews Bay to discuss the
falling price of herring.
Trying to raise the price of herring,
they met over there.

And also he is very enthusiastic for
[name of elder 4] *to raise its price*
this spring.
He says if the price of herring does
not go up, he will fine *those herring*
buyers.

Yeah, thank you all!

Community members received the jokes above warmly, laughing at the speaker's skillful juxtaposition and commentary on local and global concerns. The jokes also highlighted the importance of elders as valued community members, while commenting on the kinds of relationships affecting local economies and subsistence. In the jokes, elders appear as high-profile leaders in the form of national and global economic policy brokers, as well as award-winning singers and beauty queens taking up global political activism. They fly about the world to meetings with political figures such as Yasser Arafat, President Bush, and Saddam Hussein, making and influencing decisions about local markets, such as raising the price of herring or the prices of grass baskets.

A commonplace historical theme and form of survivance in Indigenous stories has been the mockery of federal agents (Vizenor, 2008: 8). Jokes 1, 2 and 4 expand this theme by portraying world political figures as interested and receptive to local concerns. They care about local markets, and become locally socialized by consulting with elders, consuming Yup'ik food, and participating in subsistence. In joke 1, Yasser Arafat likes seal-oil-soaked herrings. In joke 2, George Bush says he might hunt for walrus with a local friend, and even go through a unique Yup'ik right of passage, receiving an *uqiquq* or seal party in his honor. In three out of four jokes, subsistence practices figure prominently.

In each joke, the MC also used switches into extended Yup'ik to heighten rhetorical effects as he cast the media and political figures within a Yup'ik portrayal of local life, and/or commented on local practices. In joke 1, the speaker switched from English to Yup'ik as he talked about Arafat eating seal-oil-soaked herring fish. In joke 2, the switch occurred as the MC described how George Bush might participate in local subsistence practices such as walrus hunting and collecting grass for baskets. In joke 3, the switch coincided with talk of the elder getting sweet scents, a reference to the general practice of women taking perfumed body lotions and sprays to their steam baths. In joke 4, the MC switched into Yup'ik as he turned to talking about an elder imposing a fine on commercial herring buyers for economic misconduct, in a local twist on the power of government representatives to fine local harvesters.

Like Yup'ik storytellers, the MC structured the overall poetic structure of the jokes with the use of connectives in Yup'ik, such as *Tua-i-ll' (then), cali-ll' (also), una-llu tua-i (and then this)*. The MC also repeated parts of the jokes, demonstrating a common use of codeswitching for emphasis, especially in sections describing elders meeting with political figures at the beginning of jokes 1 and 4. Overall, the MC mixed and juxtaposed Yup'ik and English for multiple effects, as he provided a public commentary on seemingly arbitrary mixes of media, political and economic power, as well as very real threats to local land-use activities in a globalized world. Simultaneously, we can see how the speaker also re-affirmed community members' respect and warm feelings toward local elders through a humorous performance crafted for his community.

Exceptions to Language Allegiance: Literacy and Subtractive Bilingualism

Within institutional contexts and daily life in Piniq, young people at the time of the study received strong messages about the roles of Yup'ik-speaking elders as local leaders and Yup'ik language allegiance. Local institutions and community practices supported the use of specific Yup'ik and bilingual practices, even if some institutions were beginning to linguistically restructure 'from the bottom up' as adults accommodated children's increasing use of English. Local creative commentary, as well, underscored recurring connections between elders, subsistence, self-determination and the use of Yup'ik.

One important exception to the community's overt allegiance to Yup'ik, however, could be found in the area of Yup'ik literacy. The following chapters document how the local introduction of a school-based Yup'ik writing system in the late 1960s inadvertently helped to create generational disruptions in local literacy practices. Community members generally did not use the school-based writing system for local purposes, and many saw Yup'ik literacy in the school-based system as redundant with English literacy. A young man in 2000, for instance, wrote that a local bilingual paper would be published in English and the Moravian orthography, but not the school-based orthography since everyone who knew the newer school Yup'ik writing system knew English. What he did not have to explain was how, with the exception of the elders and a small number of local language experts, most community members who attended upper elementary and secondary programs in English were more comfortable writing in English than in Yup'ik.

Orientations toward English use and bilingualism were also somewhat conflicted. Until the GB group were growing up in the mid-1990s, Yup'ik and English worked as indices of largely separate social groups in a racialized world. Everyone in Piniq spoke Yup'ik, and English was for interactions with *kass'aq*s (*white people/outsiders*) outside Piniq, and a small minority of local *kass'aq* teachers. Although the Yup'ik verb for speaking English – *qitevte* – translated into 'speaking any language other than Yup'ik, especially English' (Jacobson, 1984: 334), the Yup'ik noun for English – *kass'atun* – translated into 'like a white person, or outsider' and individuals were often described in everyday speech as 'speaking *kass'aq*' or speaking *white*, as opposed to speaking the Yup'ik language, *Yugtun* '*like a person*' or '*like a Yup'ik*'.

Adults wondered aloud, if youth were speaking *kass'aq* to one another and the adults around them, did it mean that they no longer wanted to be Yup'ik? Some adults also expressed concern that young people, by choosing to speak English, were trying to abandon an ethnic identity, with no promise of being welcomed into a world marked by racial inequality. As a grandmother told me one day, 'You know, Leisy, nowadays kids just want to be *kass'aq*, that's why they *qitevvluteng* (*are speaking in English*). But even if they speak *kass'aq* it's not going to make them *kass'aq*, you know?'

By 2000, many middle-aged adults used both Yup'ik and English skillfully and creatively. Yet, as villagers worked to maintain Yup'ik as the language of in-group communication, socialization and expression, local parents and youth who spoke English with one another also risked censure for 'acting *kass'aq* (*white*)'. Community members also increasingly assumed that young people could understand only English, and accommodated youth by speaking English to them. Subtractive notions of bilingualism, or assumptions that people could really learn one language well came out in multiple discussions of language and messages to youth. These tensions and ambivalences will be considered further in the following chapters.

Youth Commentary on Elders' Strong Talk, Subsistence and Local Stability

When I first began work as a teacher in Piniq, I was surprised to hear how many seemingly varied parts of village life were often talked about simultaneously, and how many topics would be linked with maintaining Yup'ik. In settings from school meetings to steam baths, talk about language shift brought up a seeming hodgepodge of topics that often included not only talk about elders and subsistence but also federal and state government intervention in local practices as well as general statements about changing food, weather, the changing behaviors of people in general, and young people in particular. Initially, I took such links among topics to be indiscriminate responses to the dramatic changes villagers had seen in their lifetimes.

The longer I stayed in Piniq, however, the more I began to see patterns in the links being made. Community relationships with elders, enacted through elders' forms of 'strong talk' in Yup'ik, as we have seen above, lay at the center of a local knowledge system and related beliefs about subsistence, learning, social relationships and local stability. This local knowledge system, in turn, provided the basis of local strategies for self-reliance in the face of globalization. Once aware of these links, I began to pay special attention to patterns in what first felt like disjointed sections of interviews with adults and youth (Briggs, 1986).

Evaluative talk and its effect in a community often embed a 'cultural framework, moral assumptions, and conceptions of person and notions of responsibility' (Irvine, 1992: 106–107). Young people in Piniq commonly identified learning from elders and participating in subsistence as the prime benefits of growing up in a Yup'ik village. Many youth also described Piniq as socially stable, and attributed this stability to their regular exposure to elders' teachings, as we see in the following interview as a high school student, Jack, responded to a question about intervillage travel:

Jack: I don't like to go to (*name of a nearby village*) cause every time we go we get stuck.
LTW: Do you know the people?
Jack: I guess this place is the best place to grow up and live.
LTW: What do you think makes this place the best place?

Jack: Well, you're near to the coast, I mean not too close, but the right
distance, and there's not too many drugs, like nobody rarely drinks,
and it's, like, what do you call, how should I say this, like *iniir-
inerquuteq (following elders' prohibitions)* like, disciplined or something.

LTW: I wonder what makes Piniq more *inerquuteq* than others.

Jack: I guess cause the elders always talk to them, the younger people,
like adults, or the teenagers.   (1/17/01)

When asked what it was like to grow up in Piniq, young men generally
responded positively, talked about the specific ecology and subsistence activities in the next breath, as Jack does above when he talks of 'being near the
coast', and references subsistence activities on the ocean. Young men and
women also commonly wove together references to subsistence, local stability, and elders' strong talk in descriptions of Piniq as good place to live. Jack,
like others, also described villagers as *inerquuteq*, which he loosely translates
as 'disciplined'. Above, Jack's quick succession of topics without bridging
argumentation, or *syntagmatic chaining* highlighted local language ideologies
(e.g. Hill, 1998) about the importance of the regular sharing of specific
socializing genres of *qanruyutait*, elders' teachings.

Relationships, Responsibilities, Subsistence and Having a *Piniq* Life

To explore young people's connections to *yuuyaraq (the Yup'ik way of life)*
in general and the Yup'ik language, in particular, throughout this book, we
will consider young people's relationships and gendered responsibilities in
local life. We will also build on the work of Northern scholars to conceive of
subsistence as 'a set of practices that are deeply embedded in specific sets of
social relations and ideas about how humans should relate to one another as
well as to animals' (Nadasdy, 2003: 63; see also Bodenhorn, 1990; Cruikshank,
1998; Fienup-Riordan, 2001; Frink, 2002; Hensel, 1996; Kawagley, 1995;
Morrow & Hensel, 1992).

The following interview underscores how young men's talk about
subsistence and their daily responsibilities as young hunters could lead to
reflections about changing social relationships and Yup'ik language
endangerment. At the time of the study, Piniq had no running water.
Households and community buildings, with the exception of the school and
teachers' housing units, used five-gallon buckets under sink drains to collect
wastewater, and other five gallon buckets, called *qerrun* or 'honeybuckets' in
toilet-like structures to catch human waste. As in other Yup'ik villages, adults

in Piniq socialized youth to help elders 'without pay', citing Yup'ik teachings that elders had the power of mind to influence the outcomes of hunting, as well as the quality of one's future (Fienup-Riordan *et al.*, 2005). One of boys' local responsibilities was to dump the buckets from under kitchen sinks outside, and to dump families' *qerrun* into dumpsters situated around the village, which village workers then hauled using ATVs to a holding lagoon outside the village, where the refuse was treated with chemicals.

Before the excerpt below, I was asking a group of four seventh grade boys about how they had learned about hunting, and what they had learned about being a good hunter. At this point in the interview, three of the students took a break and one, called Tom here, stayed on, saying he wanted to talk more about hunting.

Tom: I like to learn a lot about hunting.
LTW: Um hm? So your dad mostly teaches you, or Steve (another students' older brother), sounds like.
Tom: Yeh, I mostly dump honeybuckets before I go hunting.
LTW: Um hm.
Tom: I dump the elders' honeybuckets.
LTW: That helps?
Tom: ... yeh.
LTW: If you dump 'em what happens?

[the others come back, ask for a note, and leave again to run to the store]

LTW: So we were talking about the, you were telling about the elders, like you dump the honeybuckets before you go? And you can]
Tom: They tell us that we'll we'll be, we'll get, we'll start catching]
LTW: Um hmm?
Tom: Afterwards ... They say, someday, we'll catch a bird or something. They say that to us.
LTW: Umhmm? Like that elder tells you that?
Tom: They say someday you'll catch an animal.
LTW: Um hmm? I should tell Michael to do that, then he can get better at hunting. Then are there other things you're supposed to do or not supposed to do to be a good hunter?
Tom: Um ... bother girls? Or something?
LTW: Umhm?
Tom: Most of people are starting to do that ... or lost in some other/ cultures?/
LTW: /Hmm./
Tom: xxxx cultures. We're slowly losing our language.   (12/21/00)

Over the years in Piniq, I generally positioned myself as a nonskeptical learner, and when in the village, both my husband and I followed local conventions as well as tribal laws. In the segment with Tom, I, as usual, clearly positioned myself as open to and supportive of community beliefs by saying I would tell my husband to follow Tom's recommendations. Above, Tom brought up how he dumped honeybuckets before going hunting, alluding to local beliefs about the benefits of young hunters fostering relationships with elders through doing chores. Since I already knew of these beliefs, in the excerpt I also prompted Tom to spell out the underlying connections between helping elders and hunting. In response, Tom described how elders, in exchange for help, would speak to him of beneficial hunting outcomes.

When I asked if there were any other things Tom was 'supposed to or not supposed to do' to be a good hunter, Tom alluded to elders' teachings about young hunters refraining from having relationships with girls. He then moved to describing how some people were 'lost in some other cultures', disobeying these rules, and quickly followed with a statement about how the village of Piniq was losing Yup'ik. After this segment, a second student Mike returned, and I told him that Tom and I had been talking about dumping honeybuckets for elders before going hunting. Mike responded, 'It could really help, with their good gifts.' In a separate interview, a third boy who talked about moving away from Piniq described wanting to come back for visits 'to hunt and dump'.

In multiple interviews, boys commented on how their everyday chores were linked to elders' powers of mind to influence subsistence and life outcomes. In another interview, I talked with Tom and yet another young man, David, about when and how they learned to take on various responsibilities:

LTW: Dumping the *qerrun (toilet)*, how old were you guys?
Tom: Third grade, Grandmother would get up every morning. I didn't used to like (it), but now, I like it.
David: We do it 'cause elders' thankings are very strong.
LTW: How are their thankings?
David: They just say like this, *'Quyana'* (*Thank you*)
Tom: And then they say, sometimes they say like this, 'Someday you'll catch animal or bird'.
David: And then your life might (be) *piniq* (*good/strong*)   (4/2001)

Like adults, youth shape their responses for researchers within specific interactions. It is possible that Tom, David and others were telling me what they thought I wanted to hear as an adult who had worked on documenting elders' narratives with local language advocates. Yet unsolicited links such as these also demonstrated young people's awareness of the complex nexus of beliefs relating powerful local elders, intergenerational relationships, gendered roles and responsibilities, and subsistence, and how youth could use these connections to present themselves in a favorable light with adults. As we will see throughout the book, related beliefs about elders, subsistence and local knowledge, as well as young people's roles and responsibilities in the community underscored the importance of Yup'ik language maintenance in local language ideology.

Summary

As language shift became evident in Piniq in the 1990s and 2000, local language ideology in Piniq emphasized a strong, overt community language allegiance to Yup'ik. The primary reason many community members gave for keeping Yup'ik was to maintain relationships between young people and elders. Community members also described how the *egmirte-* or passing on of orally accumulated local knowledge was central to maintaining a Yup'ik way of life. Adults socialized youth to act *takaryuk (self-conscious, shy)*, and to listen and follow elders' *qanruyutait (teachings)*. Youth were taught to trust in their elders' teachings in Yup'ik, and to assume that importance of these teachings would become *mistuq-* evident over time, as needed. Adults also emphasized adherence to *inerquutet* and *alerquutet*, specific socializing genres of elders' talk, as a means for fostering personal discipline, positive relationships with humans and animals, safety in the subarctic wilderness, success in subsistence, and for having a life that would be *piniq* – strong and good. At the same time, adults expressed concern that youth were becoming cut off from elders, as well as the content and emotional power of *qanruyutait* as they increasingly spoke mostly English.

Essentialized views of Indigenous children as one-dimensional learners, or assumptions that Indigenous children can only learn in specific ways can cause teachers to lower expectations in the classroom, leading to the educational marginalization of Indigenous students (Deyhle & Swisher, 1997; Lomawaima & McCarty, 2006; Ongtooguk, 2000). By describing discourse norms around being and becoming *takaryuk*, and the local emphasis on *inerquutet* and *alerquutet* above, I do not mean to imply that young people in Piniq were only comfortable learning by being quiet, respectful, nonanalytic listeners, or that they only talked comfortably to one other. It is impossible to know how the discourse norms described above structured daily encounters in the past, what kinds of exceptions might have existed, or how such discourse norms changed over time (Ongtooguk, 2000). Further and importantly, as we have seen, local language socialization processes in Piniq were shaped by profound historical changes in government regulation, missionization, technological adaptation, and Indigenous activism in southwestern Alaska by the end of the 20th century. As we will see in Chapters 3, 4, 5, and 7, at the time of the study, there was more than one Yup'ik way of learning in and out of school.

Nevertheless, the data above evidences how multiple local adults sustained Yup'ik language allegiance and language ideologies in the face of dramatic changes by incorporating elders as respected leaders and creating new means of language socialization within rapidly proliferating bureaucratic spaces. The chapter also highlights the many creative and complex ways that local adults also used bilingualism and biliteracy to maintain a local 'Yup'ik way of life' over time, demonstrating linguistic survivance in the face of globalization pressures. As the youth commentary above demonstrates, in 2001, young people in Piniq were aware of the powerful ideological links between Yup'ik, elders, and subsistence within *yuuyaraq*, the Yup'ik way of life and knowledge system. Young men, in particular, also described their local roles as hunters in related, positive terms. At the same time, as adults began to wrestle with children's use of English, village institutions like the local church increasingly served as sites of accommodating children's English use. In Chapter 3, we will examine how the local school, another institutional contact zone with an explicit socializing mission, powerfully shaped young people's language socialization trajectories and local language ideologies, setting the conditions for rapid language shift.

3 Educators, Schooling and Language Shift

Education is 'arguably the most significant – if contested – domain for Native language use historically and today' (McCarty, forthcoming; see also Hornberger, 2008). Historically, oppressive educational policies placed extreme pressures on Indigenous languages in many places worldwide, influencing Indigenous language loss in individuals, families and communities (Battiste, 2008). Since that time, paradoxically, Indigenous communities have often turned toward using heritage language programs in schools in attempts to reverse language shift.

As we have seen in Chapter 2, schools are only one of many arenas in which individuals socialize one another to use language and socialize one another through language (Garrett & Baquedano-Lopez, 2002; Heath, 1983; Schieffelin & Ochs, 1986; Zentella, 2005). Nevertheless, as we will begin to trace in this chapter, educational policies, school practices, educators and related discourses are embroiled in individual, peer group, family and community language trajectories in important ways. Seemingly short-term decisions about school programs can also have long-term consequences for the maintenance of unique community languages and knowledge systems.

Yup'ik communities were historically subjected to early government attempts to silence Indigenous languages through English-only language policies in schools, and later attempts to disrupt young people's attachments to their communities through removal to distant boarding schools. As elsewhere, it is important take into account how such historical, overtly assimilationist forms of schooling reverberate across time, affecting language maintenance and language revitalization efforts today (McCarty, forthcoming). From 1970 to 2000, some of the most vibrant Indigenous language-speaking communities in North America seemingly embraced bilingual education, only to later witness rapid language shift (Krauss, 1997; Lee, 2009). With the exception of a few accounts from educators working in southwestern Native American communities (Holm & Holm, 1995; McCarty, 2002; Watahomogie & McCarty, 1997), what educators saw 'on the ground' in these schools and communities has not been documented.

Below we will briefly consider Piniq community members' diverse experiences with early forms of schooling, and throughout the book we will note how such experiences shaped community members' language ideologies and language socialization trajectories. In this chapter we will also focus below on the ways that later struggles over schooling during 30 years of national, local and regional bilingual education efforts helped set the specific conditions for language maintenance and shift in Piniq. The following interview segment with Julia, a longstanding Yup'ik teacher, underscores how children's language use in Piniq changed dramatically from 1970 to 2000 and how, in 2000, Piniq was rapidly moving toward language endangerment as a growing majority of children spoke very little Yup'ik:

LTW: When you came into the [Name of first bilingual program], what was the program like back then? It was run by the BIA ...

Julia: It was only Yup'ik, and the kids had only a half hour ESL by a ESL teacher. And she took the kids to that little house up there, the ESL group, and they'd do English. [The] second year [...] my son was one of the students. Not even one word in English. [...] [The teacher] would take the chair, she would say 'This is a chair, this is a chair'. They couldn't say that ... I keep thinking how those kids were. Even [though] I heard them, it's really hard to believe the kids were like that, no English.

LTW: Why, why is it hard to believe?

Julia: 'Cause these kids ... it's the opposite. When I say '*Una akumllaq,*' (*This chair*) They couldn't say it ... We ask them to speak Yup'ik, and they stop talking. When I ask them to be quiet, they keep talking, and when it's – the magic word is 'Speak in Yup'ik.' They stop talking ....

By listening to the voices of Yup'ik and non-Yup'ik educators in Piniq below, we will consider how educators struggled to make sense of the school's role in heritage language maintenance, as they wrestled with emerging dynamics of language shift. Importantly, we will further trace how a web of distant, as well as local actors, contributed to linguistic history in the making in Piniq.

Early School Orientations toward Yup'ik Language Instruction

Early schooling efforts in the Yup'ik region and Yup'ik literacy practices were intimately tied to Christian missionization and national efforts to explore and dominate Alaskan territory. Between 1781 and 1867, Russian orthodox missionaries started the first few schools in the region, simultaneously developing and promoting a Russian orthodox writing system. In the first 20 years of US Alaskan occupation, as part of broader proselytizing efforts, Catholic and Moravian missionaries extended schooling to a wider network of Yup'ik villages, developing additional church-based writing systems and materials, and teaching in Yup'ik (Krauss, 1980).

However, in 1885, Sheldon Jackson, a Presbyterian missionary who was 'adamantly opposed to the use of Native languages in education or religion' (Krauss, 1980: 19), became the first Alaskan Commissioner of Education. Shortly thereafter, Jackson gained control over most village schools serving Alaska Native students, and implemented an English-only language policy in a direct effort to eradicate Indigenous practices and ways of knowing. For roughly 50 years, teachers in many Yup'ik villages punished children for speaking their language in schools, and encouraged parents to speak to their children in what little English they knew (Krauss, 1980).

Community members from Piniq first attended school at a local federal Bureau of Indian Affair (BIA)-run elementary school in the 1930s, and many of the grandparents and parents of the Real Speaker and the Get By group members had painful memories of being punished for speaking Yup'ik. For the most part, however, schooling played a relatively minimal role in elders' overall education and socialization within their community (for a comparison with a similar generation of Navajo elders, see McCarty, 2002). Some elders reported how, when they were young, their parents did not place much stock in school learning. Whether students attended school often depended on how much they were needed at home, and many early school attendees stayed only a few years. Villagers at that time were semi-nomadic, and boys, especially, attended school for only a few months every year, between their time in fall camps for bird hunting and spring camps for hunting seals and birds. Girls, as well, were sometimes pulled out of school to help in camps, though they were more likely to stay and attend school. Most elders and adults in Piniq also continued to speak Yup'ik to their children.

The Boarding School Era

From 1947 to 1965, the only secondary school available to rural Alaska Native students was Mt. Edgecumbe, located across the state in southeastern Alaska. In 1962, a memorandum between the new state of Alaska and the federal BIA established Alaska's responsibility to provide a public elementary and secondary education for all state residents. While the state of Alaska provided money for high schools in white Alaskan villages, and high schools for white students in villages containing both white and Alaska Native residents, the state withheld similar high schools for rural Alaska Native secondary students. In the 1960s, as the number of Alaska Native youth seeking a high school education grew, the state of Alaska sent up to 2000 youth to boarding schools with American Indian students in Chilocco, Oklahoma, and Chemawa, Oregon. While individual students succeeded, students' overall educational outcomes were poor in these educational settings (Cotton, 1984).

In 1969, educational consultants from Virginia hypothesized that regional boarding schools in Alaska might put an end to isolated communities and subsistence economies by speeding Alaska Native assimilation, 'accelerat(ing) the breakdown of old village patterns', and developing 'rural folk into a disciplined and reliable workforce' (discussed in Cotton, 1984). Following the consultants' recommendations, the state of Alaska began to build in-state regional boarding schools for Alaska Native village students in Nome, Kodiak and the hub town of Bethel (Cotton, 1984). Over time, however, both the earlier program of sending students out to distant states and the later regional boarding schools came to be recognized as failed educational experiments. In 1971–1972, the Bethel High School program failed 96% of its entering class of village freshmen (Kleinfeld, 1973). Studies of regional boarding schools also documented the damaging effects of moving Alaska Native youth from family networks in small villages to dormitories in towns with higher rates of social problems, including high rates of drinking, vandalism, violence and suicide attempts among regional high school students (discussed in Cotton, 1984).

In the late 1970s, a study documented how teachers at St. Mary's, one private, small, Catholic boarding school in the region, succeeded in supporting Yup'ik students' well-being, leadership skills and later success in college by developing an overall school climate marked by clear, consistent educational goals, warm, caring relationships with students and a strong emphasis on students' responsibility toward supporting and helping others (Kleinfeld, 1979). Many of the Alaska Native leaders in the 1970s also attended Mt. Edgecumbe, which continued to serve as an educational alternative for youth from Piniq throughout the study within. Such examples stood out as exceptions from the boarding school period, however.

It is beyond the scope of the study to consider in-depth how community members in Piniq negotiated the historical educational shifts described above. Historical studies have shown how Native American young people's experiences in boarding schools have varied by particular school and time period, in relation to (1) young people's backgrounds before they came to school, (2) young people's ages when they first went to school and (3) the individual adults that youth encountered in school. In addition, young people's negotiations of the tremendous discrepancies between their lives at home and in boarding schools have historically been shaped by students' social interactions with peers, and how those peer interactions, in turn, were shaped by students' 'family, tribe, hometown, age, gender and personality' (Lomawaima, 1994: 56).

Some youth from Piniq attended boarding schools like Chilocco that gained notoriety for 'harsh and repressive' policies before World War II. Yet, as Lomawaima writes, boarding schools 'varied over time and over spaces as federal policies evolved, were interpreted by local staff, and were applied to ethnically and linguistically diverse students. Chilocco in 1935, with more than a thousand students drawn from Oklahoma, was a vastly different world than Chilocco in 1972, with 460 students, 61 percent from the Northwest, Alaska, the Southwest, and other distant states' (Lomawaima, 1994: xv). Youth from Piniq also attended different schools in different places.

Here, I can only point out a few of the ways that youth who went to boarding school later commented on their experiences as adults, and I approach this topic with caution. Nevertheless, community members' comments offer us glimpses into some of the ways boarding school experiences may have shaped local language socialization in Piniq. Multiple community members noted that their parents were reluctant to let them attend distant schools as youth. Women also recalled how they had disagreed with their parents over attending early boarding schools. In one interview, Julia remembered how she wanted to go to boarding school out of curiosity about the outside world, like some Alaska Native students and Native American students described elsewhere (Kleinfeld, 1973; Lomawaima, 1994). She also remembered her feeling of injustice when her own older brother was allowed to go, but she was kept home:

Julia: Yeh, we used to say, why send them if they didn't send us. Let us [go to] high school, they let them go.

LTW: Do you remember why you wanted to go?

Julia: I wanted to see uh, how it . . . we never go to other places, how it would be like to go to another place, and that was the *only* reason . . . to see how the outside is.

In another interview, Claudia reflected how her white teachers had strongly encouraged her to attend boarding school, and how she initially wanted to go, yet later came to appreciate her parents' decision to keep her home. The following interview segment starts as we discussed her parents' refusal to let her attend high school:

LTW: . . . and then when you graduated, you said that [the teachers] wanted you to go on to high school?

Claudia: *Ii-i (yes,)* they wanted me to go up to high school, but my parents didn't want me to go. And back then the parents were the law, heh heh heh heh heh. So even [though] we really wanted to, several of us didn't make it to high school.

LTW: In your group?

Claudia: Um hmm.

LTW: Looking back, are there things you'd say you gained or lost by not going?

Claudia: I'd say I gained, because I wouldn't – you stay in the village, then you become aware of how hard people are working to survive, survival? And getting along with each other, subsistence, stuff like that. And seems like the ones that went away for eight months out of a year, nine months? Missed lots, lots of good things going on in the village, and developed their early years somewhere else . . .

LTW: Um hmm.

Claudia: . . . in the Western world. And staying home we developed what we need to know to survive, does that make sense?

Claudia's words here about staying home and learning to appreciate how community members survived both physically and socially are striking given current thinking about Indigenous knowledge systems and data within. Scholars assert that Indigenous people's ability to survive in a challenging world has always been the ultimate evidence of the strength and adaptability of their unique community knowledge systems (Brayboy, 2008; Kawagley & Barnhardt, 2005; Lomawaima & McCarty, 2006). Multiple adults in Piniq who attended boarding schools commented how they had never been allowed to develop their own upper levels of knowledge of *yuuyaraq (the Yup'ik way of life)*, since they were cut off from elders and local adults as youth. In the following chapters, we will consider how later generations of youth who attended high school in Piniq learned community roles, responsibilities and related forms of knowledge as young adults within local learning trajectories.

Another woman from Piniq, in contrast, described how boarding school had forced her to stand up for herself, and how her experiences in boarding school influenced her ability to speak out about educational injustices back at home. Janet lobbied her parents to attend boarding school, then refused her parents' demands to come home so that she could receive her high school diploma. Janet also remembered how, after seeing only white elementary teachers in Piniq, she had been struck by the ways that school employees at Chilocco in the 1960s, 'even all the way up to the school superintendent', were Native Americans. As historians note, even the most oppressive boarding schools sometimes had the unintended effect of strengthening young people's pan-Indian identity and resistance to societal inequities (Lomawaima, 1994). Janet reflected, 'When we started going off to high school, leaving the village and going to certain places ... We learned to stand up for our rights, and that's where we learned to, not to be afraid to speak out ... I think (people) my age, we're more outspoken with *kass'aqs* (*white people*) because we know that's their way? And we know they understand.' Janet's words offer a glimpse into how young people's boarding school experiences may have shaped generational changes in linguistic survivance strategies back home.

A follow-up study with Alaska Native boarding school students found that 60% described their experiences positively, yet how others described very negative experiences including physical and sexual abuse, censored mail from home, alcohol and drug abuse by teachers and students and suicides, both at the school and later when the students returned home (Hirshberg, 2009). Throughout the boarding school period, Alaska Native parents, including parents from Piniq, wrestled with the myriad challenges of sending youth to distant high schools, and often brought their children home before they completed school. The return of 'adolescents' to Yup'ik villages for summer visits during the boarding school period and young people's later shift to staying home in the early 1970s also created new challenges, as communities adjusted to having older youth back at home after powerful community disruptions (Charles, 2009; Kleinfeld, 1973). More than one community member from Piniq alluded to lasting challenges from the boarding school era, mentioning how individual students faced extreme homesickness and prejudicial treatment in boarding school, and brought back damaging social habits.

As Yup'ik scholar Walkie Charles describes, the boarding school era marked the beginning of generational language shift in many Yup'ik villages that were already in sustained contact with the outside world, and villages where both very young children and youth attended boarding schools (Charles, 2009). For the most part, however, only older youth from Piniq and remote coastal villages attended boarding schools. At the turn of the century, adults who attended boarding schools were some of the most 'balanced bilinguals' in Piniq after growing up speaking mostly Yup'ik out of school during their childhood, and then being immersed in English for high school (for a comparison with early Inuktitut-speaking bilinguals in Canada, see Crago, 1992). Yet, as one woman noted, she and her peers were also more likely to borrow words directly from English into Yup'ik, instead of creating new words in Yup'ik or making borrowed English words sound Yup'ik through phonological incorporation like older community members (for a comparable example with Welland French, see Mougeon & Beniak, 1989). By 2000, with the exception of local elders, community members in Piniq commonly borrowed new words from English, rather than generating new vocabulary words in Yup'ik.

Nevertheless, in the 1970s, individuals from the boarding school generation became some of the first local educators in new elementary bilingual programs, alongside some of the youth who stayed home. In Piniq, the boarding school generation also generally grew up to raise Yup'ik-speaking children until the mid-1980s, as we will see below.

The Negotiated Promise of Bilingual Education

With the passing of the federal Bilingual Education Act in 1968, national legislators called for '"new and imaginative" programs that used children's native language while they used English' (McCarty, forthcoming). Building on fledgling Indigenous self-determination and bilingual education movements elsewhere, Alaska Native community members and others worked to lay the groundwork and advocate for a historic push to introduce bilingual education into public schools for Alaska Native students. Linguists from the University of Alaska, for instance, consulted with Yup'ik individuals and developed 'a single (writing) system for the whole Central Yup'ik language area' for use in the schools, hoping to use 'the good points of each church orthography', and 'accurately represent the language', so that Yup'ik writing 'would be easy to learn and use' (Jacobson, 1995: 447).

In 1971, Alaska also passed a law requiring every school with 15 students or more with a dominant language other than English to provide a 'bilingual-bicultural education program'. The Alaskan bilingual education law defined 'bilingual-bicultural education programs' as 'an organized program of instruction in elementary or secondary education which is designed for children of limited English-speaking ability, uses English, the child's primary language, or both as a means of instruction, allows children to progress effectively through the educational system, and which may include elements of culture inherent in the language' (Coon, 1979, cited in Morrow, 1990). Villages gained decision-making powers over local schools, and four elementary schools in the Yup'ik region began to pilot the first Alaska Native bilingual education programs under the BIA.

In 1974, the landmark Supreme Court Lau vs. Nichols case lent further support for the bilingual education movement in Alaska. However, the Lau case left the door open to future debates over educational approaches for bilingual students (Crawford, 1995). The revised federal Bilingual Education Act that same year introduced a definition of bilingual education supporting use of a student's heritage language in school only until the student could perform on grade level in English. In federal policy, 'the centrality of the goal of English proficiency was clear; bilingual programs were not aimed at developing or advancing the capacity to use a language other than English' (Ruiz, 1995: 72).

From the very inception of bilingual education in the Yup'ik region, community members and educators held multiple, sometimes conflicting, conceptions about the purpose of Yup'ik bilingual programs (Iutzi-Mitchell, 1992; Morrow, 1990). Even though the schools offered Yup'ik language instruction, early programs in Alaska, as elsewhere, were designed to transition students to English instruction as quickly as possible (Lipka *et al.*, 1998; Marlow, 2004). Witnessing language shift within certain areas of the Yup'ik region, however, many Yup'ik elders, educators and parents also hoped that any amount of 'Yup'ik in the schools', would help maintain the Yup'ik language and culture for the future (Morrow, 1991). At the state level, as well, policymakers sometimes saw local heritage language education programs as 'promoting the survival of Native language and cultural knowledge, alongside with English language and Euro(Anglo)-American cultural knowledge' (Iutzi-Mitchell, 1992: 31).

Like school-based Indigenous language programs elsewhere, Yup'ik bilingual education programs initially faced tremendous challenges, demanding a 'host of mutually reinforcing corpus and language acquisition tasks' (McCarty, 2008: 166; see also Fishman, 2001; Hornberger, 1997, 2008). From 1970 to 2000, Yup'ik educators and others worked to build capacity for the new programs through program, material and professional development efforts. Later in the 1980s, bilingual education evolved into an ongoing consultative process (e.g. Wyman *et al.*, 2010b) involving regional and local school boards, school district administrators, local principals and community members. District and local administrators presented villages with the choice between (1) Yup'ik as a language of instruction for up to three years of transitional elementary schooling, (2) English as a core language of instruction, with some minimal Yup'ik use in grades 1–3 and (3) English as a sole language of instruction.

As late as the 1980s, a large majority of Yup'ik students and community members in the 22 villages served by LKSD indicated on surveys that they wanted at least equal amounts of Yup'ik and English taught in local schools (54% and 62%, respectively), and a substantial portion of students and community members wanted more Yup'ik instruction than English (16% and 12%, respectively). In contrast, 64% of the mostly white certified teachers at the time wanted the school to offer more English than Yup'ik instruction, and 12% wanted only English instruction (Morrow, 1990). In spite of these overall patterns of racialized differences, some Yup'ik community members voiced loud objections to bilingual education, while individual white educators also became advocates of extending local bilingual educational programs to support Yup'ik language maintenance.

As different players with varying goals saw their interests converge on the use of *some* heritage language instruction in local schools, early transitional programs that exited children into English after only a few years of heritage language instruction became popular in the Yup'ik region, like elsewhere in the United States and the Canadian Far North (Morrow, 1990; Ruiz, 1993, 1995; Usborne *et al.*, 2009). Linguistic transfer theories – theories upholding the idea that heritage language instruction could support language development in a second language – provided the ideological 'common ground' for those wanting to focus on developing English and those wanting to support bilingualism and/or Yup'ik language maintenance in the Yup'ik region.

By 1973, 17 village schools, including the school in Piniq, were utilizing Yup'ik as a primary language of instruction in grades K–3 under the Primary Eskimo Program (PEP hereafter) (Marlow 2004, citing Reed 1974). When bilingual education started in Piniq, some community members worried that teaching Yup'ik in school would hinder children's development of English. Many others, however, saw the immediate benefits of instructing students in Yup'ik after their own painful experiences with English submersion.

A small group of adults from Piniq were trained to be teachers and learned the new, school-based writing system, and within five years, Piniq had what was considered in the region to be a model bilingual program at the time. In a model that became institutionalized in Yup'ik- and Inuktitut-speaking areas of the Far North (Taylor & Wright, 2002), Yup'ik educators taught all core subject areas in Yup'ik to students from grades K–3, with a half hour a day of English as a second language instruction. Students switched into an almost all-English program at the fourth-grade level.

The New Local High Schools

Not long after the beginning of bilingual education in Piniq, the demands of Alaska Native parents across the state led to the famous Molly Hootch civil rights case, putting an end to the inequity of the boarding school system for Alaska Native youth. Following the case, villagers in small remote villages determined by public vote whether to have a small high school built in their village, or to continue to send their children to distant boarding schools. Expressing hopes that their children would learn traditional skills and values, and also know how to live locally after high school, villagers within most Alaskan villages chose to build small local high schools (Cotton, 1984). Below, the woman who acted as a community interpreter for the meeting in Piniq describes the powerful moment:

> Everybody (was) really excited about getting a high school in Piniq so young people wouldn't have to leave Piniq for nine months to go to school somewhere for four years. And everybody was *really* excited about it, and a whole bunch of people from the district office came and the superintendent and all of the school people (came). And they asked me to translate for them, and I was more than happy to do it because that's what we really needed, a high school, or something so the kids could stay home.

Not long thereafter, almost all youth in Piniq began staying home to attend high school. Local educators found themselves with the relative freedom to determine the nature of the elementary and high school Yup'ik program, but also the challenge of creating secondary programs, materials and Yup'ik instructional methods from scratch with few secondary Yup'ik teachers. The new high school in Piniq added Yup'ik literacy classes for one hour a day grades 9–12. By the early 1990s, teachers offered one-hour 'language maintenance' classes to grades 4–12, as did many schools in the region.

Persistent Questions about Bilingual Education, Yup'ik Literacy and Linguistic Transfer

In addition to conflicting views of the purpose of bilingual programs in the region, the first decades of bilingual education in the Yup'ik region were marked by a general confusion about when and how Indigenous literacy should 'transfer' into academic English language skills. The introduction of the new Yup'ik unified writing system facilitated the networking of Yup'ik educators, and the inclusion of both the Yup'ik language and local knowledge in schools throughout southwestern Alaska (for overviews of some of these efforts, see Lipka *et al.*, 1998; Wyman *et al.*, 2010a). However, efforts to develop upper levels of Yup'ik literacy through the early-exit bilingual programs with minimal secondary maintenance classes were challenged by constraints both in and out of school.

Since the emphasis on English literacy skills far outweighed students' experiences with Yup'ik literacy development in local K–12 schools, youth felt more comfortable writing in English as secondary students. The school-based Yup'ik writing system was also slow to move out of the schools into community life, where adults had already started using church-based writing systems for personal letter-writing and institutional communication. Adult community members from Piniq and elsewhere primarily learned the school-based writing system when they needed it for teaching in schools. In the region overall, only a small portion of adults initially received training in the new school writing system, creating a new Yup'ik literate elite (Fienup-Riordan, 2000). As in other Moravian villages, some villagers in Piniq expressed resentment toward the school's use of the new phonemic writing system, and a related ambivalence toward bilingual education programs (e.g. Harrison, 1981).

In the 1980s students in the Yup'ik region, like many students elsewhere at the time, were also abruptly 'transitioned' out of bilingual programs into all-English instructional environments after only a few years of heritage language instruction. Questions about the year after students exited transitional bilingual programs, and how students should transition into English classrooms generated confusion and contention in many places in the United States including the Yup'ik villages of LKSD (Williams & Rearden, 2006). In the 1980s, leading bilingual scholars demonstrated how bilingual development was additive, and how literacy instruction in one language could support academic literacy development in a second language under supportive schooling conditions (Cummins, 2000). Bilingual education advocates in the Yup'ik region, as elsewhere, used related theories and findings to convince community members that instructing Yup'ik-speaking students in their 'first' or 'dominant' language could support their 'second language' development of English, and overall academic skills.

Well-designed studies of immigrant and Indigenous students in North America have continued to support this claim (Romero-Little & McCarty, 2006; Thomas & Collier, 2002), demonstrating how students who receive instruction primarily in a heritage language in grades K–3 and at least 50% of their upper elementary instruction in a heritage language perform as well as comparable groups of peers in English programs by middle school, and outperform peers by high school. Studies of transitional programs in Canadian Inuit communities have also shown that students receiving only a few years of primarily heritage language instruction in elementary school may outperform peers attending English or French programs by the third-grade level, and generally outperform their peers in high school (Taylor & Wright, 2002; Usborne *et al.*, 2009).

However, bilingual students may also need time before the additive benefits of heritage language instruction become evident on tests (Cummins, 2000). When students in transitional bilingual programs are tested in English after only a few years of instruction, they may initially appear to be behind grade level (Thomas & Collier, 2002). Further, children face additional challenges when they undergo abrupt shifts from heritage language programs taught by minority educators to English programs taught by white outsiders. Exposure to minority teachers as role models and heritage language instruction in bilingual schools helps empower minority students by fostering their self-confidence and self-esteem (Cummins, 2000). A group of educational researchers in Canada found that Inuit children who were in early heritage-language education programs with Inuit teachers developed more positive views of themselves and peers than Inuit children enrolled in dominant-language kindergarten classes. Yet, in a later study, the researchers documented how Inuit children's self-esteem dropped when they were abruptly transitioned from classrooms with Inuit teachers to classrooms with white teachers, complicating the ways in which students' academic skills evidenced themselves in classrooms (Bougie *et al.*, 2003).

Andrew, one of the first students to attend the Yup'ik program in Piniq, remembered crying and being terrified of transitioning into the English program. As a young child, Andrew heard of elders who were whipped for speaking Yup'ik in school, and feared bad grades and not being able to finish assignments in English. He remembered, 'there were lots of us who would rarely speak in English in front of anyone, even if the teacher wasn't there. *Qitevtellerkaq takarnaqluteng (speaking English made us feel self-conscious)*, but only in front of very close friends we would practice our English.'

Questions about how students should 'transition' in grade 4 from a Yup'ik into an English classroom also resounded within Piniq in the early 1980s, as one veteran educator reflected:

There was a misunderstanding by the grade level English-speaking teachers from elsewhere about the instructional level of students entering the 4th grade English classroom from the Yup'ik PEP program. Teachers believed that students should be able to do 4th grade work, and there was no training for teachers about how to transition students into an all-English classroom at the 4th grade level. Teachers, thinking that the kids were supposed to be able to work at a fourth grade level, said, 'Well this program's not working.' [...] They didn't necessarily train the administrators what the program was all about, [either], so the new administration [came] in, [did]n't really know the goals and aims of the program, and that [made] a difference, too.

When a new administrator took over the leadership of the school in Piniq, the combination of a short-term principal from outside the community and ongoing concerns about the transitional fourth grade year led to longstanding consequences for school programming and community language maintenance in Piniq, as we will see.

The Decision to Scale Back Bilingual Programming

Strong individuals from inside and outside communities can play a 'considerable role in influencing local language use' in Yup'ik villages (Morrow, 1990: 193). Educational leaders also open and close important 'windows of opportunity' for supporting bilingualism in small village schools (Mohatt & Sharp, 1998), even though these leaders rarely receive training in language development. In the 1980s, Lucas, a new white administrator in Piniq, had a significant impact on a pivotal choice concerning the use of Yup'ik as a primary language of elementary instruction. According to educators in Piniq, Lucas had four English-speaking children of his own, and seemed opposed to placing them in Yup'ik programs. School district administrators from the time also observed that multiple Yup'ik villages changed from using Yup'ik to English as a primary language of instruction after Lucas's stint as local principal.

Lucas lobbied against using Yup'ik as the language for teaching early literacy and math in the local school in Piniq, expressing concern over the transitional fourth grade year. In 1983, the village switched to the 'bilingual-bicultural' program model, scaling back the use heritage language instruction in elementary school. Under the new program, students received literacy and math instruction in English; Yup'ik was relegated to a secondary place in the curriculum.

Parents are often unfamiliar with the details of various bilingual program models offered in schools (Bayley & Schechter, 2005). Parents in endangered language communities in the Yup'ik region and elsewhere may also falsely assume that (1) any school support for an endangered language will enable language maintenance, and (2) children must be schooled primarily in a dominant language to acquire that language, and consequently support programs that offer only small amounts of heritage language instruction (May & Hill, 2005; Wyman *et al.*, 2010b). In the 1980s, the community members in Piniq may not have realized that in the new 'bilingual/bicultural' program, students would receive core instruction in English. If community members did realize how the new program would shift the focus of the elementary program away from Yup'ik literacy development, they may not have been overly concerned or even thinking about possible effects on Yup'ik language maintenance. After all, community members had maintained Yup'ik as the main language of home and local communication in the face of direct school attempts to eradicate Yup'ik, as well as the disruptive boarding school years. Children in the 1980s were coming to the school speaking Yup'ik, as were most children in surrounding Yup'ik villages. While a very few families spoke English to children at home, these children seemed to be picking up conversational Yup'ik from peers.

Yet Piniq had become increasingly connected to the outside world since the 1970s when bilingual education was first adopted. Within the new linguistic ecology, the program change contributed to vicious cycles of *reduced resources for* and *increasing doubts about bilingualism* both in and out of school, as we will see below and in the following chapters.

Setting the Course for School Programming

The change back to English as a primary language of elementary instruction set the course for school programming in Piniq for the next two decades. As we will see below, for a brief period, local educators tried to take a step back toward using Yup'ik as a primary language of instruction after language shift became apparent by implementing a dual-language program. From the 1980 to 2000, however, the overall percentage of Yup'ik instruction in the elementary program never exceeded 50% for grades 1–3, and students never received more than one hour of Yup'ik language instruction a day for 'language maintenance' after third grade.

Directly following the change in the school program, white certified elementary teachers replaced Yup'ik-speaking teachers as the primary teachers of grades 1–3. The early Yup'ik educators who had been the main elementary teachers teaching Yup'ik content area classes moved into other supportive positions in the school. Two Yup'ik educators gained teaching certificates and became secondary classroom teachers. Julia, the early Yup'ik teacher quoted in the beginning of the chapter, worked first as an elementary 'associate teacher' supporting a certified white teacher in the classroom, and then moved on to become the local kindergarten teacher for decades. Another Yup'ik educator worked as an associate teacher in the new bilingual-bicultural program, working alongside a white teacher to present academic concepts sequentially in English and in Yup'ik in the 1980s. Both the white teacher and Yup'ik associate teacher from the time reported that presenting ideas across languages helped students gain access to content knowledge.

Later, in 2000, another certified white teacher described how a Yup'ik aide's language brokering helped students' conceptual understanding and connection to schooling during language shift:

> I can tell that even if I talk about this from now until the end of the year, they're not going to get the concept. So, I could have ... I will say, '[Name of bilingual aide], come here. Will you please teach this to the children?' She will come in, speak in Yup'ik and teach the kids. And, then I will come back and re-teach. And, it's like, 'Ah' – the lights go on. We just see lights going on and the kids are excited and they go, 'Oh, yeah!' And, it's not with every kid, but those kids who are special or proficient in the Yup'ik. And, it's been wonderful! And, just having her in the classroom and she can say things to the kids that I, as a professional teacher cannot. And, she can speak in Yup'ik to the kids and it seems to get them in the heart more than if I said something to them sometimes. It's more effective.

When bilingual aides used their linguistic repertoires and relationships to get to students 'in the heart' and connect learning to community life, their spontaneous explanations and acts of interpretation made class material accessible to students. However, simultaneous translation of classroom material does not promote heritage language maintenance (García, 2009). Even in cases where associate teachers and aides served as coteachers, Yup'ik remained in a subordinate status, used primarily as a means to help students understand lessons in English. Since students in Piniq were only expected to develop early literacy skills in English, Yup'ik educators also deemphasized Yup'ik literacy instruction. Only a few community members were trained in the school-based Yup'ik orthography, and by 2000–2001 bilingual aides expressed confusion about whether they were even allowed to teach Yup'ik reading and writing.

How teachers positioned aides within the school hierarchy over time varied tremendously, as well. Local noncertified Yup'ik educators who were treated as coteachers one year found themselves repositioned as low-level aides grading papers with a different certified teacher in the same classroom the following year. In one instance, a certified teacher even directed a local aide to remove her Yup'ik materials from the classroom completely, stating that they had no place in school.

In the 1990s and in 2000–2001, the small number of Yup'ik-speaking certified educators often made connections to local life while explaining concepts in English and Yup'ik, creating additive spaces for bilingual discussion. The Yup'ik teacher in the seventh grade classroom in 2000–2001, for instance, regularly made opportunities for students to connect academic questions and assignments to local knowledge, whether by asking to students to discuss and write about current issues facing Piniq, or folding local history into everyday assignments. Another Yup'ik high school teacher in 2000 shared how he used Yup'ik to get across complicated concepts in math. As we will see in Chapter 6 on the Get By group, Yup'ik educators built on local *qanruyutait (teachings)* and metaphors to stress local values, and to connect youth to local knowledge in extracurricular activities.

Still, many local educators' efforts were challenged by the complexities of language shift itself. The 'ideological and implementational spaces' (Hornberger, 2008) for connecting youth to Yup'ik and local knowledge were also constrained within a school structure heavily weighted toward outside educators and mainstream educational curricula.

Language Shift Begins

Shortly after the local bilingual program was scaled back, elementary Yup'ik educators noticed seemingly subtle changes in children's peer culture. The Get By group, whom we will consider in detail in Chapters 6 and 7, were the first children to be instructed primarily in English in their elementary years after the program change described above. They were also the first children in Piniq to use primarily English as a peer language. As one Yup'ik elementary educator who left the village and later returned described, 'Even in the short three years [we were gone], we came back and heard kids playing in English, and we'd never heard that before.'

Some elementary Yup'ik educators began to raise awareness of possible language endangerment in the mid-1990s. At the time, however, it was still hard to believe that Yup'ik was in danger. Almost all older youth and adults in the village used Yup'ik as their language of everyday conversation. At least a third of all children in Piniq were coming to school speaking Yup'ik fluently. Many others had Yup'ik productive skills.

By 2000, however, educators at all levels of the school noted with alarm the decreasing numbers of students coming to school speaking Yup'ik comfortably. In fall 2000, after I stated my interest in learning how youth were using Yup'ik and English, a high school teacher gave the following overview of the rapidly changing linguistic situation:

> Well, I can tell you right away that the young people these days don't hardly speak Yup'ik. You're only going to hear them speaking English to each other. It seems like the last group that really spoke Yup'ik to each other was the group you taught like [Real Speaker student] and them. Nowadays kids speak pidgin Yup'ik and pidgin English. They can't speak either of them well – they don't know how! The 7th through even the 10th graders *qitev-luteng* (*are speaking in English*) all the time. I tell them to speak in *Yugtun* (*Yup'ik*), and they'll try for a while, then they will start whispering to each other in English again. When I say '*Yugtun* (*in Yup'ik*),' they are quiet.

At the elementary and secondary level, local educators expressed increasing concern about students' changing uses of Yup'ik, and confusion about students' hybrid forms of Yup'ik and English talk.

'It's Not Yup'ik and It's Not English'

Contemporary language shift settings are complex heteroglossic environments, in which students' forms of mixed language use evidence both students' language shift and their remaining strengths as heritage language learners (McCarty, forthcoming). Yet schools are not set up to young people's linguistic repertoires or translanguaging practices in dynamic settings of heritage language maintenance and shift (Jaffe, 2007; Jørgensen, 1998), let alone to build heritage language fluency from students' emerging mixed codes. Within Piniq, Yup'ik educators noted and expressed increasing concerns over students' changing Yup'ik use and codeswitching. As one bilingual aide stated in 2000, 'It's as if they're stuck in between Yup'ik and English, and when I see the language they are using, it makes me want to cry. It's not Yup'ik and it's not English.' As another aide reported:

> Sometimes I have to read their journals three times in English to understand what they are saying. They have broken English and broken Yup'ik, it's sad. [As she says this, she gestures, using one set of fingers as English and the fingers on her other hand for Yup'ik]. It's like they're lost, they're right in there [interlocking both sets of fingers]. For instance, with the Yup'ik they'll say '*meqsaryugnaunga?*' that's not a word. They're trying to say, 'Can I have a drink of water', and they should be saying '*Meqsar-tur- yugnaunga?*'

In the aide's example, we gain a glimpse of young people's remaining heritage language strengths in Piniq at the time of language shift, and a glimpse of the ways in which young people's new Yup'ik forms appeared to violate longstanding rules of Yup'ik use for adults. The young person's request was only missing one verbal postbase, yet the missing postbase would roughly equate to missing a verb for older, fluent Yup'ik speakers:

Student: *Meq-sar-*-yugng-aunga*
Translation: *Water-go-*-can-I*
Gloss: Can I go water?

Adult: *Meq-sar-tur-yugng-aunga*
Translation: *Water-go-drink-can-I*
Gloss: Can I go drink water?

Chapters 5–7 document how students' hybrid forms of language use evidenced ongoing processes of language shift, students' linguistic survivance, and remaining possibilities for bilingualism. However, rapid changes in children's incoming Yup'ik proficiencies presented tremendous challenges even for experienced Yup'ik teachers.

Working with Children's Eroding Language Competencies

Local parents, teachers and administrators described one woman, Annie, as an expert, creative and highly competent first-grade teacher. By 2000, Annie had also served as an educator in Yup'ik villages for over a decade. Annie regularly designed locally based curriculum units and lessons, tailoring her classroom practice to build on community funds of knowledge (Moll, 1992). Annie also confidently mapped lessons to meet district- and state-mandated curricular learning goals. Annie's classroom commonly hummed with student activity, and the first-grade students in Piniq achieved for decades under Annie's encouraging and watchful eye.

In 2000, however, Annie noted how increasing numbers of students were coming to school seemingly not knowing Yup'ik. In an interview, Annie also described how she had been forced to adjust her locally based science and social studies units to focus on Yup'ik language development:

It is hard. They aren't even remembering basic vocabulary. Like in science, I got different kinds of rocks, and I have them do classification – they usually love classification, putting rocks into different kinds. And I showed them the kind *'teggalquq'* (*rock*) and nobody knew it so we learned the word *'teggalquq'* (*rock*). And we went over it and we talked about how their moms use them to sharpen their *uluaqs* (*semi-circular knives*), and they use them in the steamhouses, and they knew the word. Then a couple months later I showed them the rock and said, 'Remember we talked about this kind of rock? Who can tell me what this rock is?' And the closest they could come was *'teggliq'* – some kind of metal.

Annie was even more troubled by the ways children in her class were having difficulty following basic sentences, and the ways that some students were having trouble making Yup'ik sounds, especially *q*, and *rr* the back velar stop and related fricatives. As Annie noticed, 'The throat sounds are the hardest. One student will just make a garbled sound *piciatun* (*any old way*) until he gets to the ending, like this [makes random sounds] – *rtua* (*I am*) ... That must be how Yup'ik sounds to him!' she said with disbelief.

Annie and other veteran teachers also noted how peer dynamics were further driving language shift among young children. As we will see in the following chapters, in 2000, some youth maintained relatively strong Yup'ik skills, given uneven and wide-ranging processes of language shift. Among older youth, Yup'ik also held status and strong Yup'ik speakers commonly used their Yup'ik in front of their peers. However, elementary teachers struggled against the influence of peer culture as relatively strong Yup'ik-speaking children started to 'cloak' (Mendoza-Denton, 2008) their Yup'ik skills and speak mostly English in class. As Julia, the local kindergarten teacher, described:

Julia: Even some, like [names a child], her first language is Yup'ik, [yet] she wouldn't speak to other kids in [Yup'ik], she wouldn't try it, even [though] her Yup'ik is very good, she won't ... I guess she might be afraid they might not understand her.

As language shift progressed, Annie, Julia and others felt little control over children's language use with one another out of school. Annie, for instance, described seeing two young children chatting in English as they hung up their backpacks getting ready to play at one child's home. Knowing that one of the children was a strong Yup'ik speaker, and the other came from a family actively trying to use Yup'ik at home, Annie asked the children in Yup'ik, 'Why are you talking in English? We are Yup'iks, you should speak Yup'ik.' 'They just looked at me,' she sighed.

As teachers witnessed rapid language changes and children's increasing use of English, they expressed increasing concern about the future of Yup'ik. As Annie stated, 'If these kids do not learn now, they are not going to be able to pass the language on to their own children.' Noting how language shift was shaped by multilayered sociolinguistic dynamics, however, teachers also expressed confusion about the role of the school in reversing language shift, and increasing concerns that parents might be passing the responsibility for teaching Yup'ik to the school.

Yup'ik in the Broader Sociopolitical Context of Schooling

Since the 1990s, international research on bilingual education has highlighted how schools must attend to and counteract broad power-laden assumptions in society by placing extra effort, time and positive emphasis on the language of minority groups, and by creating an overall environment that sends strong messages about bilingualism as additive in order to foster bilingualism in minority languages (Cummins, 2000). Considering Piniq, we can see how the overall sociopolitical organization of language and schooling worked against Yup'ik language learning from 1970 to 2000. Yet, we also see how gains in creating culturally and linguistically responsive schooling were possible, even if they depended on continuous negotiations at the levels of school-community discussions, teacher and curriculum development, and classroom pedagogy (Lipka *et al.*, 1998).

As late as 2002, school districts in Alaska recruited 70–80% of certified teachers from outside the state (Alaska Advisory Committee to the US Commission on Civil Rights, 2002), and the average village teacher in the school district serving Piniq stayed for 2.3 years. Yup'ik certified teachers were a minority within the certified staff in Piniq, and Yup'ik noncertified staff members were not included as school decision-makers. Between 1990 and 2000, the school in Piniq suffered tremendous instability at the administrative and secondary level as rotating groups of mostly white administrators, upper elementary and secondary teachers came and went. At one point, the school had six administrators in four years. Another year, the staff ran the school for three months without an administrator. More than one new teacher never got off the plane from Bethel, deciding not to teach in a remote village during the 45-minute ride over the tundra from the hub town, leaving school staff scrambling for a replacement. Multiple outside educators made their disconnection to the village evident by leaving Piniq the day that school got out for summer break. In 2000, when the school year began, the school had no high school math teacher. Two local Yup'ik educators, having seen similar disruptions multiple times, told me, 'We'll survive,' even as they worried about having no teacher in a core subject.

As rotating groups of mostly white teachers came to Piniq and adjusted to village life, some teachers continued to bring with them strong deficit assumptions about Indigenous peoples and schooling. Below, one teacher responded to an interview question about 'things she wished she had known as an incoming teacher':

Teacher: And, another thing and this is kind of weird, but when I first
came out here, I had these ideals that … Oh, boy! I'm great and
I'm going to change these people to be good! I'm going to
change them in my way. And, then after my first year, I
realized, hey, wait a minute! I don't want to change them. I
don't want to change … their ways are per - they've been doing
these ways for thousands of years. I don't want to change
them. I want to help them to be the best they can be. And, that
means a combination of Yupik and English. It's not, 'I'm going
to change them to be the best English people they can be!'
LTW: Uh … hmm.
Teacher: No, that's not what success is, success is being the best they
can be. And, that's a combination of both cultures.

Other teachers came to Piniq eager to learn about the strengths of the local community and to connect school learning to students' lives, yet wrestled with community feelings that the school did not go far enough to recognize local knowledge and practices in rural Alaska. As teachers made beginning ventures into community life, they often began to realize just how much their students knew to navigate the local social and physical landscape as young adults. Teachers also expressed deep frustration at the school's inability to provide relevant instruction, and related this struggle to their secondary students' disengagement and low attendance patterns, as the following teacher describes:

The attendance, there's just no connection in the kids' minds of the attendance and what they're getting out of school. It shows how important they think it is, I think, or how much they're getting out it. And, that might be an even sadder thing if they feel like they're getting so little out it that they don't mean to come ever. We need to look at what we're teaching. [She starts to discuss *Wuthering Heights*] I had them write a summary of the story, what happened. And, I had 10 questions of the test and the last question, 'Why do you think LKSD requires this as a text?' And, they all looked at me and they're like, 'What is the answer?' I said, 'Because I don't know.' [laughs]. And, we all tried to come up with a reason. And, my theory is that, location-wise, it does deal with isolation and the feeling of being outside of the town and being part of ... and, living way outside, kind of like, Piniq to Bethel. We made that comparison ... it's a classic and we got the master plot and we found which one it fit. But, I had trouble coming up with a reason why they picked it.

Multiple outside teachers commented on the stress of adjusting to Piniq, describing how students voiced resentment toward white teachers and tested them to see if they would stay. One teacher, for instance, noted how he had never considered his own whiteness before coming to Piniq, yet how, in his early days in Piniq, 'not a class went by when I wasn't made aware of being a *kass'aq.*' In 2000, another white teacher compared his first year teaching in the village to 'breaking rocks' saying, 'You don't know why you are breaking rocks, but if you break enough rocks, and people decide you are there and are going to break rocks or do what you are going to do, then there is a real tolerance that you are really in it for good.' He stated that, during a non-local teacher's first year in Piniq, the teacher was doing most of the learning in the classroom, and that if the teacher could make it through, he would gain something precious and a deeper view of himself. At the same time, the early negotiating and dealing with 'each kid on his own level' was not a very efficient process, 'in fact it's very inefficient in terms of the stress of the individual and the time it takes.' Such learning cycles were tremendously inefficient for Piniq youth as well (Jones & Ongtooguk, 2002).

Outside teachers' struggles were compounded by cross-cultural miscommunication. Cultural 'mismatches' related to eye contact, wait time and interactional patterns have been extensively documented in Native American, Alaska Native, Inuit and Yup'ik communities. Teachers who are not from communities can learn, over time, to adjust their teaching styles to facilitate communication with students (Cleary & Peacock, 1998; Crago, 1992; Deyhle & Swisher, 1997; Lipka et al., 1998; Mohatt & Sharp, 1998). Some teachers, like myself, benefited from 'crash courses' in cross-cultural communication as Yup'ik educators and community members patiently explained how, for instance, spotlighting individual youth might backfire in the classroom. Other teachers learned (or did not) to pick up interactional 'cues' through trial and error themselves as part of their initial, very steep learning curve as teachers in another culture. Jacob, a self-described 'loud, talkative, verbose' white teacher, for instance, described how he learned to tell when his communication style was really 'rubbing people the wrong way' as community members frowned or abruptly walked away from him. Another white teacher described how she had initially tried to force children to answer her verbally and look her in the eye before she learned to extend her wait time when expecting answers, and to note when students raised their eyebrows for 'yes', or looked down when listening.

White teachers' challenges adjusting to village teaching were further exacerbated by their experiences as non-Yup'ik speakers in a Yup'ik-speaking village. Teachers from outside the community often expressed strong reactions to Yup'ik as a language marked by voiced and voiceless fricatives, back velar sounds, and long, agglutinated 'words' representing English sentences. In the 1990s and again in 2000, local community members and students highly praised teachers who tried to learn Yup'ik, even if some also laughed at teachers' efforts at pronunciation. Through minimal or nonexistent attempts to learn Yup'ik, rotating groups of outside teachers subtly and not so subtly positioned Yup'ik as an unnecessary and/or impossible language to learn.

Non-Yup'ik-speaking teachers were not able to use Yup'ik as a medium of instruction, or to spontaneously tie young people's discussions or comments in Yup'ik into overall classroom learning. These teachers' everyday interactions could also easily close spaces for students' Yup'ik use. For instance, during a class observation in 2000, two GB students attempted to use Yup'ik to discuss an assignment with each other in small group work. When the classroom teacher interrupted the boys' discussion of the assignment simply to make a passing comment in English, his interruption inadvertently ended the boys' use of Yup'ik for the rest of the class.

In a district-sponsored strategic planning process in 1994, community members requested that teachers use culturally relevant approaches throughout the curriculum. When white teachers worked with local educators and/or community members to position local knowledge as a resource, they could make spaces for Yup'ik in the classroom. For instance, in the mid-1990s, a fourth-grade teacher and two longstanding Yup'ik paraprofessional educators wrote and received a grant, then worked together to develop a thematic unit around collecting mouse food from the tundra. The educators developed related writing tasks in Yup'ik and English, and were pleased with the ways students took on increasingly sophisticated types of writing in English and Yup'ik in the unit.

Given the high amount of administrative and certified teacher turnover, however, as in many other Alaska Native communities 'for the most part, (outside) teachers (did)n't get close enough to Alaska Native culture to understand it well or to use it as a meaningful context for instruction' (Jones & Ongtooguk, 2002: 501; see also Mohatt & Sharp, 1998). Secondary youth in Piniq were generally the most adversely affected by the resulting inconsistencies in school leadership and overall educational disjunctures. While older students praised some white teachers, they also loudly complained about their frustration with others who were not 'understandable', in some cases storming out of classes, boycotting single classes, or dropping out of school in frustration. At one point in the 1990s, a group of high school youth asked student council members to deal with the breakdown of classroom management in a secondary math class, to no avail.

Multiple local adults showed an extreme patience and willingness to socialize and teach new teachers about the community, inviting individuals to their homes, local events, and along on subsistence trips. Other community members voiced historically rooted suspicions that all white teachers viewed Yup'ik students through deficit lenses. As one grandmother commented, 'You know, the *kass'aq* teachers think they are up here, [raising one hand high in the air], and the Yup'ik children are down here [placing her other hand low].' Community members also sometimes loudly voiced deep frustrations with individual teachers. At multiple points between 1992 and 2001, community members pressured teachers and principals who were seen to be discriminating against youth or incompetent to leave Piniq. In the spring of one particularly turbulent year, it looked like I would be the only returning teacher from the 5th–12th grade. In multiple contrasting cases, white teachers respectfully learned about the community, and developed positive relationships with parents and students. Community members expressed disappointment when they saw these educators leave, more than once stating, 'Just when the kids were beginning to open up to him/her, he/she left.' Within multileveled negotiations, school leaders also played a large role in setting the direction of the school, as we consider below.

Educational Leaders and Everyday Language Policymaking

Administrators' everyday types of educational decisions, in particular, could swiftly and quietly undermine the Yup'ik program, or, alternately, open spaces for linguistic survivance. The principal in 2000, for instance, decided not to substitute bilingual aides. Thus, whenever the aides were needed elsewhere, as in the weeks of individual testing in Yup'ik, or were out sick, the Yup'ik program would grind to a halt. Seemingly small decisions about allocation of school space also worked as another form of hidden administrative language 'policymaking', and were indicative of the changing status of Yup'ik in the school. Between the years 1992 and 2001, consecutive administrators moved the Yup'ik classroom from the main building to a portable building outside. Later still, the Yup'ik teacher was asked to travel from classroom to classroom while Yup'ik schoolbooks were stored in a girl's shower stall.

Nevertheless, the potential for administrators to use their influence to open important windows of opportunity for Yup'ik and community knowledge remained. Both secondary and elementary students could benefit tremendously when individuals were able to connect academic learning to local knowledge, community members and concerns. In response to two school shooting incidents in the region in the late 1990s, one administrator in Piniq hired Andrew, a respected counselor and influential elder in the village, to talk to the students regularly in a newly created position of 'elder consultant'. According to educators, Andrew was particularly adept at adjusting his Yup'ik for various ages, using simplified Yup'ik for younger groups to make his teachings more accessible. In school, Andrew talked to students about the past, sharing *inerquutet* and *alerquutet*, the socializing genres described in Chapter 2. Multiple students, teachers, and staff members described how Andrew's efforts and presence improved the school's learning environment. As one youth commented,

> He talked to us about that [a school shooting that had taken place in the region], and before he started, everybody, most students were like, *anaguteq* or mischievous. [Then he] started talking to us and changed the whole school.

When Andrew passed away suddenly and unexpectedly in school, however, as one student put it, 'it hit us so hard.' Staff and students were wracked with grief, and the program was discontinued. At two other times between 1992 and 2001, administrators appointed well-respected secondary certified Yup'ik teachers as 'Dean of students' with leadership responsibilities at the secondary level. In both cases, the educators used their connections to the community and the students to provide stability and leadership within a struggling school. Yet, when both men moved on, one to a position in another village, and another to well-deserved retirement, student–teacher dynamics of miscommunication and distrust intensified once more.

Certified Yup'ik educators either made up a small minority, or were not part of the secondary staff from 1992 to 2001.

Experimenting with Programming and Wrestling with Theories

As elementary educators increasingly became aware of language shift in the late 1990s, they tried to research and adopt a dual language immersion program. Visiting a school in Anchorage, elementary educators from Piniq saw how bilingual educators worked with Spanish-speaking immigrant students and English-speaking students, and how teachers separated their days into distinct blocks for Spanish and English. Back home, certified educators and aides in Piniq attempted to implement dual language instruction in grades 1–3, offering half a day of Yup'ik instruction and half a day of English instruction. However, when the educators tried to implement Yup'ik math instruction, as one teacher described, parents' complaints 'started pouring in':

> I tried to do math in Yup'ik, but I couldn't because the young parents these days who supposedly know how to read the new Yup'ik system couldn't read the instructions in Yup'ik to help with the math problems . . . they couldn't do it, so now I do it in English.

Given the ways that bilingualism takes time to develop, dual language programs for two to three grades are generally insufficient. In cases where imbalances of power exist between majority and minority languages, special emphasis must also be placed on supporting minority languages in order to counterbalance societal forces (Baker, 2006). Many Indigenous heritage language programs start in early grades and add additional grade levels one at a time to build stronger program models over time. Within the constraints of the original transitional program in Piniq, however, the balance of instruction remained tilted toward English. When educators tried to reestablish Yup'ik as a primary language of instruction in core academic subjects, they also ran into challenges stemming from the historical attempt to introduce a new Yup'ik writing system within a K–3 transitional Yup'ik program.

As educators began to struggle with the uneven dynamics of language shift, folk versions of early linguistic transfer theories also constrained their efforts to consider how the school might be used to reverse language shift. The following words come from an interview with an administrator that I discuss at length below, and were spoken repeatedly in one form or another by many educators in the 1990s and 2000–2001:

> The students we are getting are not first language Yup'ik speaking students. Well, I should revise that; some are testing just over the first language Yup'ik speaking mark and others are testing just over the English speaking mark. So do you create a bilingual program to teach Yup'ik? Or a bilingual program to teach *in* Yup'ik?

Confusion resounded in many local backstage discussions of bilingual education program choices. As one long-term, locally influential educator repeatedly pointed out, none of the bilingual program models offered by the district seemed to match the uneven nature of early language shift. In the 1970s and 1980s, educators had focused on the ways that Yup'ik-dominant students should 'transition' or 'transfer' their 'first' or 'dominant' language skills into their 'second language' – in this case, English. Yet, in the 1990s and 2000, as children's language began to shift unevenly, educators asked, 'What do you do when some of the children speak mostly Yup'ik, other speak mostly English, and others don't show a preference for Yup'ik or English?' When previously self-explanatory terms for childrens' language competences suddenly no longer appeared to make sense, the educational theories that provided the groundwork for dramatic moves forward in bilingual education in the 1970s also constrained educators' efforts to understand how the school might be used to develop bilingualism in a rapidly changing linguistic ecology. Increasingly, teachers asked, what *is* the students' 'language dominance', 'home language', 'first language' and/or 'second language' anyway?

Contrasting Policies and Testing Regimes

With the passage of the federal Native American Language Act of 1990/1992, Native American and Alaska Native communities earned the right to use, maintain and teach their ancestral languages. In the mid-1990s, a small charter school in the Yup'ik regional hub town of Bethel also became one of the first schools to work toward reversing Alaska Native language shift through a strong bilingual education program (Baker, 2006). Starting with a single kindergarten class and building grade by grade, year by year, as other Indigenous language revitalization efforts have done, educators in the school taught children who came to school speaking English almost entirely in Yup'ik using immersion methods through grade 4, and provided 50% of academic instruction in Yup'ik through grade 6 (Aguilera & LeCompte, 2007).

In 2000–2001, however, just as language shift was becoming widely recognized in Piniq, discussions of how the school might be used to reverse language shift became further constrained by a dramatic educational policy shift as Alaska moved toward implementing a new statewide, high-stakes graduation exam in English: the High School Graduation Qualifying Exam, or HSGQE. From 2002 to 2007, as the HSGQE was implemented in Alaska and high-stakes benchmark tests in English related to federal No Child Left Behind legislation were implemented nationwide, many schools in the Yup'ik region, like schools serving Native American and immigrant students elsewhere, scaled back heritage language instruction and/or witnessed community divides over heritage language programs (McCarty, 2008; Menken, 2008; Wyman *et al.*, 2010a, 2010b).

As preparation for the HSGQE began to define the goals and activities of the local school in Piniq in 2000 and 2001, the tenuous and unequal balance between Yup'ik and English in the school capsized toward English mainstream education. Certified teachers poured their efforts and most of their free time, including many weekends, into learning how to implement a new standards-based district education system to get ready for high-stakes testing in English. School–community meetings focused on explaining the new regulations and what high-stakes testing in English would mean for students' progression through school. White teachers generally ran these meetings, often covering topics at high speed in English. As we see below, the meeting in which the HSGQE was first introduced, in particular, evidenced a near complete breakdown between the school and the community, as policymakers and local educators delivered new sets of authoritative and coercive regulations. The following description was reconstructed from notes taken during the meeting in the fall of 2000.

The meeting had been rescheduled multiple times due to low turnout, yet with door prizes such as 50 gallons of gas, free lunches, and a drum of diesel fuel, this time the lunchroom that doubled as a gym was full of community members. All school staff attended, except Helen, a Yup'ik teacher who had gone home to take care of a sick relative. The principal started the meeting by applauding one Yup'ik teacher for an award for being the district's Native Youth Olympics coach of the year. He then introduced the certified and classified school staff, calling them, 'The best staff I've ever seen in the bush.'

Jacob, the white Dean of students, then took over, commenting how hard it would be to fill the shoes of a previous Dean, a longtime and well-respected Yup'ik educator. Jacob handed out a discipline rubric with a complex layout of levels of behavior problems, actions and consequences printed in English on the front and the back of four sheets of paper. Jacob described in English how students could get slips of paper called POPS ('power of positive students') for good behavior, while community members silently flipped through the pages of the rubric. Earlier, the aforementioned coach told me that according to a respected elder, giving students too many rewards loses their respect, so he did not give out the slips. Another Yup'ik teacher said he had only given out one in two years.

Jacob started going over the discipline rubric, then described a sheet of district attendance rules in English, speaking fast. At one point, a parent interrupted the presentation, shouting from the second to last row, 'You need a translator. It's too long. I can't understand you – you need a translator.' Jacob responded, 'Yeah, I know, we really wanted to have a translator here, and I thought Helen was gonna translate, has anybody seen her?' The principal went out to look for her again as Jacob asked, 'Can anybody else translate?' None of the six Yup'ik school staff sitting in the audience, all fluent Yup'ik and English speakers, moved.

Jacob went on, handing out additional flyers in English on the HSGQE, the new high-stakes end of high school exam. Number 12 on a flyer about 'Frequently asked questions about the HSGQE' stated that unspecified accommodations would be made for students who were 'Limited English Proficient' (LEP). The majority of students were classified as 'LEP', though no one asked related questions or commented on possible accommodations.

After Jacob covered the sheets quickly in English, the audience sat silent. Looking weary, a school board member gave a short talk in Yup'ik about how parents needed to help their kids and come up to the school, 'even just to read a book to the elementary students'. The meeting ended shortly thereafter with no further comment. On my way home, a local grandmother remarked, 'That was too much *kass'aq* (*English/white*) meeting, too much in *kass'aq* (*English/white*).' She then joked, 'They need to slow down and say, "Hell-*o* . . . people . . . of . . . Piniq!"' humorously comparing the school meeting to movie portrayals of Indigenous people's initial encounters with Western explorers. Later, I asked one of the Yup'ik educators why no one volunteered to translate. 'I don't know,' he replied, throwing me a wry look, 'How do you translate "discipline rubric" into Yup'ik?'

Other school–community meetings underscored how the ever-present 'language question' could also obscure deep educational equity issues, as we will see in the following section.

School–Community Talk about Language and Achievement

Scholars of bilingualism and bilingual education have noted that discussions about language can sometimes serve as a smokescreen, keeping educators and community members from discussing broader equity issues in education and society (Zentella, 1997). In Piniq, community members' assumptions that Yup'ik was holding students back from achieving in English often came up when community members searched for explanations for low standardized test scores. In one meeting in 2001, for instance, when a teacher presented a set of students' test scores, it was noted that the math scores were particularly low. In small rural schools, the performance of single teachers can have strong effects on student learning, since students take classes from the same teachers multiple years in a row, commonly in multiple subjects. In 2000 and 2001, students and parents had complained that the local math teacher had given students worksheets to complete on their own, without tracking student progress. Other educators also spoke angrily about their colleague's damaging impact on local youth. One teacher stated that she hoped that high-stakes testing and a new district teacher accountability system might prevent such inequities in the future. In the interview below, Kelly, a high school student, described how she had disengaged from schooling out of frustration with the teacher:

LTW: You said you don't like school.
Kelly: Have to wake up early to go to school, and I'm a junior now and I don't know how to do math. That's why I hate school, cause I didn't learn that much. I'm learning though, slowly, finally.
LTW: What happened there? Sounds like there are a bunch of you having a hard time in math.
Kelly: Our teacher, or our former teacher we had for, like, four years or so, maybe five, he just sat there and waited for us to ask him for help. And we didn't ask him that often because he wouldn't explain, he wouldn't really .... *explain* it, just tell us how he got the answer. Then the last year he was here, he sat there and waited for retirement, so, we didn't really learn anything. (4/3/01)

Some students from Piniq who had tried to attend post-secondary institutions quickly became discouraged and dropped out as, like other Alaska Native youth, they were faced with paying university tuition for remedial math courses (Jones & Ongtooguk, 2002).

As we will see in Chapter 6, the five students who 'made it' to graduation in 2001 were all strong Yup'ik-speaking youth, unlike their school-leaving counterparts. When the low math test scores were presented in public, however, the first comment from the audience came from an elder who wondered aloud in Yup'ik whether the scores reflected students' difficulty learning in English since they spoke Yup'ik. A Yup'ik teacher responded to the elders' question by starting a discussion in Yup'ik about local purposes for maintaining Yup'ik, yet, after a few minutes the white teacher in charge of the presentation cut short the discussion, moving onto the next item on the agenda. The elder's assumption that Yup'ik undermined students' academic achievement remained in the air, while the impact of the math teacher in question was never publicly discussed. A potential opening for addressing damaging assumptions about bilingualism and achievement was also pre-empted because it did not come in the right slot in the agenda, and was not understood by the educator running the meeting. Ironically, earlier in the same meeting, community members were invited to 'discuss' the local language program in Piniq. The topic had been covered at high speed in English, however, spawning little comment.

Framing and Facilitating Community Language Program Choices

From 1990 to 2001, Piniq continued to have the local 'choice' of determining its bilingual program. In 2000–2001, most parents chose to have local educators conduct home visits with children in Yup'ik for a temporary home literacy program. On periodic teacher-designed community surveys, a majority of parents indicated that they wanted 'more Yup'ik than English' in the local bilingual program. Some community members and local educators lobbied to return to using Yup'ik as the primary language of academic instruction in the local elementary program. Other community members were understandably reluctant, however, given the unstable school situation. Still others expressed lingering doubts about whether Yup'ik would 'hold children back' from learning English. Many critiqued the school's seeming inability to meet the educational needs of secondary students, in particular.

Educators from outside the community expressed confusion as they witnessed local divides over language program options and a community grappling with language shift. Consecutive administrators, as well, expressed confusion about how they should be facilitating community decisions about language programming. Administrators commonly stated that it was 'for the community to decide' local language programs. At the same time, we have seen how the structure of school meetings could open up, yet also constrain such discussions.

The excerpt from an interview with a local principal below further evidences how dominant, negative societal discourses about bilingualism (May, 2005) shaped some educators' understandings of the tensions around local program decisions, and discussions of the school's role in language shift and language planning. [Note: The principal's statements are numbered for reference in the discussion following]:

LTW: I'm curious what perspectives you've heard on the language issue, because I've heard a lot from the people who want to keep the language [program], but I've also heard that there are those in the village who are advocating against.

Principal: From what I've seen it's about 50–50. Like in anything, even the presidential election, you've got your 10 percent who are dead set against it, your ten percent who are for it, and then the rest are split in the middle somewhere.

(1)   There are social reasons for wanting Yup'ik. There was a policy against Yup'ik, and I've never seen anyone hit for speaking Yup'ik, but that happened here, and if you've ever been slapped for speaking Yup'ik, you can bet that person's going to want Yup'ik.

(2)   Then there's another group of parents who see that there's an end of high school exam, the HSGQE, and that test's in English. If you went to China the test would be in Chinese, that's just the way it is. And that group says they want their kids to get as much English as possible.

(3)   Then there's a third group who says the group can do [Yup'ik First Language] and transition into the second language later, and if they get a firm base in their first language, they transition [those skills]. I don't know if I agree with that or not.

(4)   But one thing I do know is that this is an issue that needs to be decided by the community and the parents. My role is to present the information that is given to me, it is not my role to dictate, and I mean that very sincerely. [Here the principal described how he generally followed the recommendations of the local school board]

(5)   With the bilingual plan of service, I brought some teachers in to talk to the [school board], I gave them the information, and I refused to make a recommendation. In this issue, I am simply the facilitator and the expediter. Because like I said earlier, this is a complex issue.

(6)   From an economic standpoint – that's jobs! And from the social standpoint, you have the people who were slapped. And as a social and community issue you have who is advocating which position, and then there are the different families. It's much more complex than [unintelligible], and you can go to any school in LKSD and in any one of the communities [where the language] is viable, language is an issue. The ones where language is not an issue are the villages where the language died, there it's not an issue.

(7)   And whether the language lives has a lot to do with the power behind that language. When you're conducting business in that language, that language is going to be strong.

The overall point that the school principal was trying to make in this lengthy interview segment, that schools, *on their own*, cannot maintain or reclaim community languages without community support, is well established in the literature on reversing language shift (Fishman, 1991, 2001; Hornberger, 2008). At the same time, as we have begun to trace above, schools are embroiled in community linguistic ecologies. Misinterpretations of fourth-grade students' linguistic practices led to the scaling back of the local bilingual program in Piniq in the 1980s. Directly following this change, language tip quickly took hold among youth in Piniq. As we will see in Chapter 5, parents' home attempts to pass on Yup'ik in 2000 were also being undercut as their children entered school in English. At the time of this interview, language was indeed a school–community issue. Assumptions about programs and everyday talk about language and achievement, however, obscured local meanings and practices of bilingualism, the school's historical and contemporary role in language maintenance/endangerment, continuing possibilities for bilingualism, and broader issues of educational equity.

In statement 1 above, the principal sympathetically alluded to historical schooling inequities related to Indigenous language use. In general, outside educators in Piniq knew that to talk about Yup'ik was a 'hot spot of history' – a subject that risked bringing up painful and powerful memories of the kinds of abuse historically experienced by elders and adults in school (Wyman & Kashatok, 2008). By framing people's reasons for wanting to maintain Yup'ik in terms of historical abuse, however, the principal placed linguistic inequities in an unfortunate, but distant past, while overlooking contemporary reasons for Yup'ik language maintenance. In contrast, community members including youth commonly spoke of Yup'ik as a part of a broader Indigenous knowledge system, as a local resource for fostering social cohesion, and as a useful resource for contemporary self-determination efforts. Local parents rarely directly linked past abuses to their personal motivations for speaking or not speaking Yup'ik. As we will see later, the one parent who directly linked abusive experience to subsequent language choices at home spoke English in an attempt to protect her children from experiencing the linguistic discrimination she faced in school.

In the principal's statement 2 above, we also see how everyday school logics posited high-stakes testing in English as a natural outcome of national citizenship (Crawford, 1995; Ruiz, 1995). The principal declared that, 'If you went to China, the test would be in Chinese'. The idea that federally recognized Alaska Native tribes, as sovereign nations in a state-to-state relationship with the US government should have a say in the purpose of schooling, or the types of language used and assessed in schools, was noticeably absent from this statement, as was recognition of national legislation such as NALA mentioned above, or multilingual education efforts in countries elsewhere at the time.

In statement 3, the principal voiced doubts about the linguistic transfer theories, stating, 'Then there's a third group who says the group can do YFL and transition into the second language later and if they get a firm base in their first language, they transition (those skills).' With the rejoinder 'I don't know if I agree with that or not,' the administrator distanced himself from the key tenet of international research and linguistic theories supporting additive views of bilingual education – that time spent learning a heritage language builds up overall language skills, and is therefore not time wasted on development of English. Between the 1990s and 2001, multiple principals in Piniq qualified their description of bilingual development theories similarly. To imagine what this statement might have looked like, we can contrast it with the words of another principal from a high-achieving school in LKSD who would regularly assure community members about the possibilities of bilingualism, reportedly stating, 'We have a thousand years of research telling us that teaching a child in his or her first language will help them learn English.'

Like the principal above in statements 2, 6 and 7, educators commonly talked of Yup'ik and English in *utilitarian* terms, what individuals could use language *to do* in the present or future. This discussion most often led to statements about youth needing English for jobs and college, as well as the power of English for use in government and economic institutions. Language policy scholars have pointed out how such instrumental arguments about majority languages can obscure existing and potential future functions of minority languages. They also note that *all languages* have identity-linked and emotional, as well as functional, purposes, even if majority language speakers may not often think about how they value and appreciate their language for reasons that extend beyond functional uses in society (González, 2001; May, 2005; Ruiz, 2009).

Around the time of this interview, the principal above gave a graduation speech citing institutions like the church, the traditional council, the school board and others 'as part of the support for the students and the school', declaring that in all of his years as principal, he had 'never seen a more caring, concerned community'. Chapter 2 documents how adults in Piniq used Yup'ik and bilingualism in local religious and government institutions, reproducing strong local language ideologies about the importance of Yup'ik. Multiple school principals noted the power of these local institutions (some resentfully, others respectfully). Few, however, recognized the bilingual practices and socialization processes used in these spaces.

In statement 6 above, the principal described language program choices as an 'issue', only for villages where Yup'ik was still spoken. Stating, 'Once languages die it's no longer an issue,' the principal framed language endangerment as a passing concern, one that the community would eventually simply get over and move beyond.

My intention in examining one administrator's statement at length is not to lay blame on a single individual in a complex educational system. All of the assumptions in the administrator's statements above were voiced multiple times, by multiple players, over the course of the school trajectory detailed above. Many of the principal's assumptions, and related discourses equating schooling in English to educational achievement, economic advancement and citizenship were also commonplace in dominant society at the time, and regularly expressed in debates about language rights in the United States and elsewhere (May, 2005; Ruiz, 1993).

It is important to note, however, how competing sets of ideological assumptions about language shaped systemic constraints in the local school, and diminished students' opportunities for developing bilingualism in early language shift. The first set of assumptions – rooted in the local historical experience of oppressive school-based English-only language policies – centered on the idea that students could only really learn one language well. The second set of assumptions – rooted in later, localized versions of theories used to initially justify bilingual education for Yup'ik speakers – supported the notion that students could learn two languages well, but *only* if they had acquired their heritage language at home before coming to school. In the following chapters, we will further trace how these varying ideologies and contingencies shaped local language socialization processes and the rapid sociolinguistic transformation in Piniq.

Summary

As we have seen above, historically rooted, ongoing struggles to improve Alaska Native and language minority education shaped local language programs in Piniq, and the ways in which human, linguistic and economic resources were deployed over time within the local school. After early, damaging forms of oppressive English-only schooling and experiences with boarding schools, local community members developed new forms of Yup'ik language instruction and gained local high schools along with others in the region. As bilingual education gained a certain amount of traction in the Yup'ik region from 1970 to 2000, transitional forms of elementary bilingual programs represented a major achievement on the part of Yup'ik educators and non- Yup'ik allies working to develop linguistically and culturally responsive education. They also represented a highly negotiated 'middle ground' in contested community schools staffed largely by outside educators and administrators subject to broader national- and state-level policy constraints.

For decades, educators worked within the constraints of these programs, and from the 1970s into the mid-1980s, local teachers in Piniq used Yup'ik as the main language of instruction through third grade. The overall amount of English in the school far outweighed the use of Yup'ik K–12, and educators wrestled with the challenges of understanding the instructional and social needs of students moving from Yup'ik programs taught by local Yup'ik teachers into English programs taught by a rotating cast of white outsiders. Early attempts to introduce a new Yup'ik writing system in a program that exited students into English instructional environments after only a few years of Yup'ik instruction also inadvertently created later challenges for developing Yup'ik literacy and heritage language instruction during language shift.

Nevertheless, the early use of Yup'ik as a primary language of instruction in elementary grades did help 'stave off' language shift to some extent as Piniq became increasingly connected to the outside world. When educators and community members scaled back Yup'ik language instruction within the local school in the early 1980s, language shift rapidly accelerated. Within a very short time period, elementary educators witnessed dramatic changes in young children's language of peer culture. Five years later educators throughout the K–12 school struggled with students' increasing use of English. Educators also began to notice increasing amounts of children coming to school already speaking mostly English. In the following chapters on families' and young people's language socialization trajectories in Piniq, we will trace how the reduction of English instruction in the local school, along with additional societal changes such as increases in migration, transformed language socialization processes out of school.

As we consider schools in contexts of dramatic sociolinguistic and educational change, it is crucial to consider what historically accumulating, dynamic fluxes mean for educators on the ground. As we have seen above, longstanding and talented local educators faced tremendous challenges as they tried to understand how various language programs and school practices were shaping children's rapidly changing sociolinguistic worlds. Systemic instabilities and inequities, and later, the implementation of a high-stakes assessment system in English, repeatedly constrained their efforts. When commonplace educational theories and bilingual program models did not appear to match the complexities of students' bilingual practices, school and community discussions of achievement also reproduced damaging assumptions about bilingualism.

Still, as we have also seen, from 1990 to 2000, every educator in the school made a difference, and possibilities for learning and developing bilingualism remained, even as educators in Piniq struggled to understand widespread and rapid language shift. Yup'ik educators' everyday acts of linguistic survivance helped students integrate academic and local knowledge. In some instances, Yup'ik and non-Yup'ik educators in local study groups also developed locally based curriculum together, supporting young people's biliteracy. An administrator's decision to create a counseling job for a talented local elder in one instance, and two administrators' decisions to place strong Yup'ik secondary teachers in positions of leadership periodically calmed the turbulent high school and supported students' learning. As we will see in the following chapters, bilingual students themselves also continued to demonstrate linguistic possibilities as they navigated a contested school space.

In the epilogue, I discuss how crosscurrents of Indigenous language reclamation and standardizing educational reforms continued to play out in the Yup'ik region over the decade following this study. First, however, we will continue with the story of Piniq, tracing how young people's and families' language socialization trajectories intersected with the school trajectory above directly before and during language shift.

4 The 'Last Real Yup'ik Speakers'

Yup'ik youth exist at the crossroads of multiple sets of discourses casting them as inauthentic, resistant to schooling and/or culturally confused. Often Alaska Natives are portrayed as previously noble, original ecologists, who have been corrupted by modern society and are now deeply troubled (Fienup-Riordan, 1990). This literature adopts the historical focus of anthropology on authenticity by positing 'traditional', versus contemporary, Indigenous peoples' practices as worthy of study and mention (Cruikshank, 1998; Smith, 1999). The continuum of cultural value is then mapped onto existing tribal members, with the most current generation portrayed as the most contaminated by the modern world.

Related assumptions about authenticity also extend to academic language ideologies. Linguists have historically privileged elderly speakers and community members who grew up speaking only one language as idealized 'native speakers' (Kramsch, 1997); for much of the 20th century, linguistic theories also underscored commonplace 'one-people/nation, one-language' assumptions about the links between language and group identity. Currently, however, linguists are somewhat at odds with themselves when it comes to characterizing languages and speakers. Many linguists celebrate languages as dynamic, emergent systems, highlighting the agency of speakers who creatively mix languages and critiquing the 'monolingual bias' in previous scholarship. Yet when a language appears endangered, other linguists characterize language change and language mixing as a sign of decay and loss.

Bilingualism studies must make sense of this confusion, identifying which types of language change and bilingual practice might be 'natural' benefits of knowing and using more than one language, and which forms of bilingualism evidence language shift and endangerment (Allen, 2007; Henze & Davis, 1999). Since youth are often in the forefront of linguistic change and innovation regardless of a language's vitality, and community members and scholars examine intergenerational differences for signs of language shift, bilingual young people's linguistic practices are also most likely to be cast as problematic.

Faced with entrenched achievement gaps, educational scholars, as well, have characterized Alaska Native youth as deficient and alienated (Deyhle & Swisher, 1997), or 'caught between two worlds', even as their definitions of those worlds have varied (Henze & Vanett, 1993). Literacy researchers have speculated that Alaska Native youth feel ambivalence toward academic literacy, since it symbolizes distance from community adults who are knowledgeable, yet 'marginally literate in school-like practices of literacy' (Erickson, 1984: 539, discussing Scollon & Scollon, 1981). Yup'ik educational scholars have asserted that Yup'ik youth enter and leave schools 'confused and disoriented' since they perceive, yet do not understand traditional ways or discourse patterns, and schooling represents a knowledge system that has yet to be integrated with Indigenous knowledge (Kawagley, 1995: 111; see also Mather, 1995).

Very little research, however, documents how Indigenous youth negotiate societal discourses and learning experiences in and out of school. This chapter examines how youth in Piniq who later came to be identified as 'the last Real Speakers of Yup'ik' (the RS group) actively worked out what it was to be Yup'ik, rural, young men and women in the late 20th century. Situating the Real Speakers' linguistic practices in relation to shared and unusual language socialization trajectories, the chapter considers how youth in Piniq established Yup'ik as an everyday language of local peer culture, even as changing school programs, patterns of migration and language ideologies set the conditions for the Get By group's rapid 'tip' into English. Highlighting young people's movement within a distributed linguistic ecology, the chapter also evidences how Real Speaker group members used Yup'ik to connect to a regional, as well as local, youth culture on the cusp of a local language shift.

By considering the trajectories of a group of young men I call the young *nukalpiat* (*real hunters*) in more detail below, we will see how some youth grew to distrust schooling and vocally resist English as they (1) experienced the educational instabilities and challenges described in the previous chapter and (2) took up local responsibilities, gender roles and concerns about language endangerment. Further comparison of how the young *nukalpiat* and their peers integrated wide-ranging symbolic resources illuminates how youth interpreted shared histories and their positions within a unique, Indigenous subsistence society. Significantly, by tracking RS group members into their lives after high school, the chapter highlights school-community disjunctures and changing dynamics during early language shift.

'Everybody Spoke Yup'ik'

As was commonly noted, the Real Speaker group was raised speaking predominantly Yup'ik until they went to school. They also received most of their elementary instruction in Yup'ik until fourth grade. In stark contrast to later youth, RS group members like Stephen below described how his peers took speaking Yup'ik for granted while growing up:

LTW: Describe your experience learning Yup'ik.
Stephen: No, I learned it when I was growing up, heh, I didn't have to learn it, it was in my blood already ... Yup'ik is the only language I speak for couple years, maybe six years, or longer.
LTW: Do you remember the first time you heard or/
Stephen: /xxx/
LTW: /Oh/ sorry?
Stephen: No, I never heard anybody speak Yup'ik for the first time ... Probably what I'm trying to say is nobody, everybody spoke Yup'ik when I was growing up so it was just like a person learning his or her language. (phone interview, 1998)

Claiming that 'I didn't have to learn it,' 'it was in my blood already', and 'It was *just* like a person learning *his or her* language,' Stephen emphasized a strong, natural connection to Yup'ik, and how commonly his peers spoke Yup'ik. Likewise, Daniel, another RS youth, described how he had used Yup'ik with local adults and peers, and viewed English as a language for talking to outsiders:

LTW: When you grew up, what language did you use?
Daniel: Only times I spoke English was when I spoke to my teachers, when I spoke with their kids, teachers' kids?
LTW: Um hmm?
        ***
Daniel: I never spoke English to my age group growing up, maybe today, maybe today, little bit, but not, like all these.
LTW: Do you think it's changed since you got out of high school, the proportion of Yup'ik and English you use?
Daniel: Uh, not really, no. Just talk it to, well actually, yeh, talk it to younger people.
LTW: Um hmm?

Daniel: Starting, I don't know, few years after us, there was, uh, kids, kids younger than us, when we were in school, who would speak English, you know.

LTW: Um hmm?

Daniel: And in a way we thought, even [when] we were in school we thought that kids in the future aren't gonna speak any Yup'ik, and today it's ... taking part, it's taking place right now, as we speak.   (7/27/01)

Like older community members, RS youth described how Yup'ik and English worked as indices of largely separate social groups and worlds when they were children. By time the RS group was in high school in the mid-1990s, however, they were aware that younger groups were increasingly speaking English with community members as well as outsiders, and discussed the possibility of language endangerment. Nevertheless, the RS group's own peer culture remained strongly grounded in Yup'ik.

'Every Day a Different Story'

In the mid-1990s, there was little to no evidence that young people's changing attitudes toward Yup'ik might be causing a language shift. In contrast, RS youth generally voiced strong Yup'ik language allegiance, echoing local themes of respect for elders, and the importance of community knowledge and self-determination presented in Chapter 2. RS youth also *used* Yup'ik as the dominant language of peer culture, sharing a rich expressive life in their heritage language. RS youth joked together, replayed events from daily life, discussed TV shows, told ghost stories and retold elders' stories in Yup'ik when hanging out in study halls or on school trips. During sports seasons, RS youth also used Yup'ik to talk about eligibility for travel to other villages for tournaments. During the tournaments, students used Yup'ik to talk about other teams, tease one another about potential and real relationships with students from other villages, and recap exciting moments from games.

Out-of-school RS youth additionally used Yup'ik as they learned to participate in family and community life. Young people's local responsibilities generally increased as they grew up in a vibrant subsistence society, and by high school many young men missed days of school and spent time with adults and friends in key hunting seasons, catching as many as 78 ducks over a weekend. Young women's work substantially increased, as well, as they juggled after school and extracurricular activities with preparing birds and/or skinning and butchering spring seals.

Any time of year, but particularly during heavy periods of subsistence, youth shared stories of their situated learning of *yuuyaraq* (*the Yup'ik way of life*), the local knowledge system of their community, recapping their experiences for one another. Below, another RS youth highlights how hunting stories played an especially prominent role in boys' peer culture in the mid-1990s:

> I remember couple times we would tease people like they don't hunt, or, at school. Like when we were in school, seems like they would always talk about hunting trips like Joe, Jeff, and they always, *every day*, different boat story, different hunting story ... (4/5/01)

As elsewhere, not all youth in Piniq took up widely available local gender roles in the same way (Eckert & McConnell-Ginet, 2003). Roughly 20% of the young men in the RS group, for instance, did not hunt; from observations, these youth generally lay low during hunting seasons. Hunting, however, was highly visible and publicly valued in Piniq, as in many circumpolar Inuit communities at the time (Frink, 2002). Among young men in particular, hunting prowess was rivaled only by athletic prowess for garnering status within local peer culture.

RS young men further associated Yup'ik language use with hunting. Responding to a question about local domains and activities for Yup'ik language use, for instance, Stephen from above initially stated, 'We *always* speak Yup'ik when we're hunting, we never talk English.' Stephen quickly clarified, however, noting how he found himself accommodating younger people's English use, like Daniel above:

> Or, we'd rather speak our language than speaking English, but when we're speaking with other younger kids we gotta use English cause that's what they know better. If we speak Yup'ik they won't understand, uh ... it's becoming most of the kids now.

Like the adult community members who found themselves using English with children in local institutions such as the church and school, many youth in the RS group began to assume that children understood more English than Yup'ik.

'And I Still Don't Know How to Write It'

Multiple Indigenous groups develop and introduce new writing systems within school programs in attempts to increase the status and functions of Indigenous languages, and/or to support students' overall academic development. Such efforts are often necessary components of broader language planning efforts, yet in educational settings where children spend roughly 10,000 hours developing literacy in English, attempts to develop Indigenous language literacy through minimal language programs sometimes fails to produce mass literacy, or affect students' Indigenous language literacy use beyond graduation (Hinton, 2001).

The introduction of new writing systems in schools can also have the unintended effects of disrupting existing local literacies and creating linguistic insecurities in Indigenous language speakers. As we recall from Chapter 3, the RS group learned academic literacy in Yup'ik through grade 3, then shifted abruptly into English language programming with an hour a day of Yup'ik through grade 12. A few years out of high school, Stephen described how his Yup'ik literacy skills remained weak:

Stephen: And I *still* don't know how to write ... make a story with, heh, writing Yup'ik, 'cause it'll take forever to write, try and figure the writing out, so ...
LTW: Hmm.
Stephen: It's hard to read Yup'ik, uh, words, when I see them in the paper. Takes me a long time for, for me to understand the way they're written, cause ... hmm, I'm pretty used to reading in English.   (1998)

Stephen went on to state that reading in the church-based Moravian writing system was easier than reading the school Yup'ik writing system for him, since he could 'just read' in Yup'ik along with others when they were reading or singing in church. However, Stephen also described how he and his peers could not read the Moravian writing system 'very well' like local elders.

By the time RS youth reached high school, their cumulative experiences reading and writing in English so far outweighed their experiences with Yup'ik literacy that students who were clearly stronger Yup'ik speakers were more comfortable readers and writers of English. When presented with district books with Yup'ik and English translations on opposing pages in high school, Stephen and his peers chose to read English versions of texts, like many other Yup'ik-speaking youth in the district at the time. When given chances to write in English or Yup'ik for school newspaper articles, youth mostly chose to write in English, claiming that writing in Yup'ik would be 'too hard'.

While RS youth spoke mostly Yup'ik to one another, Yup'ik literacy had almost no role in peer culture:

1 **LTW:**   How would you say the way you speak and write and read compares to the other people your age?

2 **Stephen:** Uh, we don't do that, that's, heh, we just talk to each other in Yup'ik ... well, uh, everybody in my age, whoever knows how to speak Yup'ik we talk to them, but we don't write to each other in Yup'ik at all, cause we have more important things to do like, play Nintendo .../heh heh/

3 **LTW:**   /HEH HEH heh heh heh /heh heh.

4 **Stephen:** /heh heh/

5 **LTW:**   But if you had to leave someone a written message, what would you leave it in?

6 **Stephen:** In English, for my friends, cause it'll be faster and just stick it on somewhere and it'll be done, instead of trying to write it in our language/ xxx/

7 **LTW:**   /is it the xxxx/

8 **Stephen:** since that other person might ... they would say that I misspelled this thing and do another thing ... heh heh heh.

9 **LTW:**   Is that pretty much the same for the people your age? That they would write more English?

10 **Stephen:** Yeh, cause that's, that's the way we're taught to make money and nowadays everything's for money so we gotta learn English very good.

11 **LTW:**   Um hmm

12 **Stephen:** Our language is slowly disappearing, or whatever, fading away.

Above, Stephen underscores the distance between Yup'ik literacy and young people's lives by jokingly ranking Yup'ik writing as 'less important' to him and his peers than playing Nintendo video games – an activity that adults sometimes critiqued as a young person's 'waste of time'. Stephen's statements also showed how youth in Piniq were aware of how societal discourses commonly place English and Yup'ik 'in opposition, as though one cannot be both successful in the larger society while also maintaining Native language and cultural lifeways' (Lee, 2009: 308).

In the mid-1990s, RS youth and local adults often described English as a necessary language for 'getting a job' or 'going to college'. In response to my question about his group's tendency to write in English, Stephen stated, 'that's the way we're taught to make money and nowadays everything's for money so we gotta learn English very good' in line 10, placing responsibility for his peer group's use of English versus Yup'ik literacy on schooling and societal forces emphasizing English as a language of social mobility in a cash society.

By quickly shifting from talking about the need to use English for work to talking about how Yup'ik was 'slowly disappearing' and 'fading away' (line 12), Stephen also linked school's emphasis on English to local language shift and endangerment. Like many others at the time, Stephen voiced the growing assumption that biliteracy was unlikely in the face of such outside pressures.

Tellingly, Stephen also imagined how his peers might criticize him if he tried to write Yup'ik, and expressed doubts about his own abilities to spell Yup'ik words correctly in the school-based Yup'ik writing system (line 8). Above, Stephen contrasted the relative ease of 'just' writing in English, versus Yup'ik (line 6) and 'just' speaking, versus writing, Yup'ik (line 2). While Stephen's descriptions echoed most of his peers', the following section documents how some youth in the RS group were already expressing insecurities about even speaking Yup'ik. Parsing how unusual types of childhood experiences did and did not lead to such insecurities, we can see how translocal processes were already reducing some children's opportunities for learning to speak Yup'ik, and how youth negotiated these changes within local peer culture.

Learning from Unusual Trajectories

It might be easy to assume that youth in the RS group simply learned Yup'ik from their parents. Considering the cases of three RS youth whose parents spoke to them in English, however, we can see how school and peer language socialization supported children's overall use of Yup'ik, even as schooling's reverberating effects were already disrupting intergenerational use of Yup'ik at home within a small number of families.

In the mid-1990s, it was rare to witness parents communicating with high-school-aged youth in English. A few community members, however, remembered how parents of one local family had been among the first to speak English to their children. In an interview in 2000, Anna, the mother of this family, talked about how her childhood experiences in school shaped her subsequent decision to speak English to her children:

Anna: I had bad experiences going to that classroom the first year, going through school that first year, with the teacher. I d[id]n't understand what she was saying and then she'd get really mad about something and ... shove me to the corner, butt my head to the corner to stay there.

LTW: *Qaa. (Really?)*

Anna: I didn't understand what she was saying, but ... I could tell by the way she was handling me that she wanted me to stay there. And they used to get, the teachers used to get physical, they used to physically abuse us.

LTW: Hmm.

Anna: And it wasn't ... We'd tell our parents, but they'd tell us nothing to do about it, or, there was no law, or, nothing to [do], for protection. So when I started having kids I told my husband, 'I want to raise my kids so they know English first, [to] speak, know how to speak English good, so when they go to school they can understand what the teacher is saying.' So I raised all my kids Yup'ik – I mean, English first language. Then when they started going to school or playing with kids, they start[ed]. They picked up Yup'ik right away, learned it right away, but it was easy to for them to go back to English. And I guess I'm doing the same thing with my grandchildren. But ... we speak Yup'ik and English to them so even [if] they don't speak it, they understand.

The reverberating effects of oppressive school language policies and related, painful memories of physical and emotional punishment are a major force of language endangerment worldwide. Many Indigenous and non-Indigenous parents have attempted to protect their children by speaking the language of oppressors at home (Battiste, 2008; Krauss, 1980; McCarty, forthcoming; St. Denis, 2003). Like multiple adults in Piniq, Anna described how her parents had been unable to protect her from physically abusive teachers in a school marked by strict adherence to English-only language policies. Anna also shared how her fear that her children would encounter similar abuse led her to speak to her children in English.

Nevertheless, community members responded to their shared experience of linguistic abuse in varying ways in Piniq, as in other Native American communities (Lee & McGaughlin, 2001). Anna's choice to speak English to her children was relatively unusual for the time in Piniq. Her family's experience also highlights how children's language socialization experiences in school and with peers shaped the overall effects of parents' initial home language socialization choices. As Anna described, her children became productive Yup'ik speakers once they attended school in Yup'ik and entered a local peer culture where children spoke mostly Yup'ik with one another. Anna's youngest child Ethan was in the last group of children in Piniq to receive Yup'ik as a primary language of instruction before the local school scaled back its bilingual program in the 1980s. As a high school student in the mid-1990s, Ethan spoke Yup'ik regularly and comfortably. He also spoke Yup'ik fluidly with adults and local elders.

At the time the RS group was growing up, a small number of white teachers had married into Piniq. Children in these families, as well, had peers and relatives who spoke to them in Yup'ik, like Ethan above. The principal of the local school supported the use of Yup'ik as a language of instruction for all children, and non-Yup'ik teachers organized Yup'ik as a Second Language class for their children. Those who stayed in Piniq used Yup'ik regularly in local peer culture as older youth.

Thus, the small minority of children in the RS group who were not socialized to speak mostly Yup'ik at home seemingly 'picked up' Yup'ik as they got older. The large majority of RS youth who spoke Yup'ik at home facilitated these children's Yup'ik language development through local Yup'ik youth culture. The use of Yup'ik as the primary medium of academic instruction in the local elementary school, as well, helped sustain young people's use of Yup'ik with one another in the dynamic local linguistic ecology.

Migration, Mobility and Linguistic Survivance in a Regional Linguistic Ecology

In a globalized world, many Indigenous peoples experience forms of dislocation across national borders, with effects on the language use of Indigenous children, families and sending communities (Hornberger & Coronel-Molina, 2004; King & Haboud, 2010). Other Indigenous communities consume global flows of media and goods, while community members physically move within more regional patterns of migration. In this section, we will begin to situate local youth culture and the community of Piniq within a regional linguistic ecology made up of relatively small and autonomous, yet interconnected, Yup'ik villages, the regional hub town of Bethel and larger urban centers of Anchorage and Fairbanks by considering varying forms of RS group young people's migration.

During the 1980s, adults left Piniq temporarily to take advantage of jobs and education elsewhere. Mothers and fathers finished degrees in Fairbanks or Anchorage, bringing their spouses and young children with them. Other parents chose to leave older children in the care of aunties, cousins, and/or grandparents, so as not to move youth during high school. Alternately, couples split temporarily as individual parents left to pursue post-secondary education and extended family members helped support spouses with younger and older children who remained in Piniq. Increasing numbers of second-language Yup'ik speaking adults married into Piniq, as well, to raise children where they could have relationships with elders, practice subsistence, and grow up in a strong, safe community.

The back and forth movement of young couples between their home villages for the first few years of marriage further shaped children's language learning trajectories. Although young men married into other villages, it was more common for young women to move to partners' villages. Young women often reported difficulty 'getting used to' new villages, and spent weeks at a time visiting their home villages until their oldest children started elementary school.

Young children also flowed to and from Piniq through adoption. In the 1990s, rural Yup'ik villages had birthrates among the highest in the nation. Throughout the study, young children in Piniq and other Yup'ik villages were often treated as a life-giving resource to be shared (Fienup-Riordan, 2000). Siblings and cousins gave children to relatives who lost a child through tragedy, relatives past childbearing age, and/or families with all boys or all girls. Adopted children also commonly maintained ties to their original parents in Piniq and elsewhere.

Out of the RS group members who lived in Piniq as high school students from 1992 to 1995 (*n*. 45), nine students (17%) spoke mostly English and stood out as exceptions among their high school peers. Each of these youth had lived as children in a town or village where children spoke English to one another for at least one year, and their experiences demonstrated how even relatively short childhood immersion experiences among English-speaking peers and schools using English as a language of instruction could disrupt young people's later use of spoken Yup'ik. As older youth, child migrants in the RS group reported that they had lost the ability to speak Yup'ik comfortably because of early childhood experiences in English-speaking places.

Yet many child migrants who returned to grow up as part of the RS group in Piniq developed bilingual competences as they reentered a local youth culture in Yup'ik, as we see in the reflections of Michael, a young man who moved as a child with his mother and siblings to an English-speaking village, then back to Piniq after three years:

LTW: Do you remember what it was like when you came back here?
Michael: Yeh, I couldn't understand anything everybody was saying, I mean, they'd say something and I'd just look at them and try guess what they were saying, but … the longer I stayed here, the more I started to understand, and now I understand most of what they're saying. It was difficult at first, but I got used to it.
LTW: So you came back when you were eleven right before junior high?

Michael: Yep.
LTW: And then in high school could you understand? Like, when you guys were hanging out, what did you speak?
Michael: Joe and them were always speaking Yup'ik and I'd always just sit back and try guess what they were saying, and then I started catching onto it. That's how I learned what they were saying because they'd always speak Yup'ik and I started to pick up slowly, slowly.   (4/6/01)

Michael and other child migrants in the RS group described how they received little linguistic accommodation from Yup'ik-speaking peers when they moved or returned to Piniq, and how they struggled for years to speak Yup'ik comfortably. There were obvious differences between these youth and their peers, and when they were expected to listen to the extended Yup'ik discourse of adults, youth like Michael and his younger sibling relied on the spontaneous translations of other students to follow along. Nevertheless, many child migrants were socialized over time to use Yup'ik listening and token speaking skills according to local discourse norms. From observations in high school, Michael and his younger sibling used Yup'ik receptive skills to 'go with the flow' of peer life in Yup'ik. They also caught and laughed at jokes, listened to stories about daily life, were popular students, and participated easily in school activities in Yup'ik.

However, another child migrant in the RS group, Mark, described a more challenging reentry into local life:

Mark: We lived in Anchorage for a while ... I still did speak Yup'ik, I still do, I understand and speak. I think pretty much everybody started to not care if anybody speaks English and Yup'ik cause I still understand and speak it. They don't bother me about speaking Yup'ik now no more.
LTW: They used to?
Mark: Yeh, *every* day, like everybody, like, very ... very much discriminating against English. I don't know, it's just weird, just weird, the way they talk to you just because you're speaking ... English they think you're ... I don't know, somehow.
           ***
LTW: In your group, in high school, did you speak English, like how did you use language compared to them?
Mark: I spoke to my friends off and on, like Yup'ik, English, Yup'ik, English, that's the way I speak. Not just this you know, I'm not just Yup'ik, [laughs]. I feel comfortable with English instead of

Yup'ik cause it's harder for me to know Yup'ik. I just know simple
Yup'ik but not advanced Yup'ik. Not like advanced Yup'ik, just
simple words, and if they use advanced Yup'ik I ask them right
away, 'What is this?' and they look at me like they're puzzled,
'You don't know that?' And I say 'Yeh, I don't know that much
of Yup'ik.' I just know a lot but not very a lot.

**

LTW: Did it ever cause any problems with your friends, or?

Mark: Nope, my friends accept me the way I am. I just don't like the
older generation to like put me down on that, like, they should just
accept people the way they are, if they learn it, they learn it. And
it should stay with them for the rest of their lives. [...] This Native
tongue will never fade, once you learn it as a kid it will never fade,
just stay in your heart. And I don't know why some people just, I
don't know, just put you down just cause you're speaking English.
And it feels like a crime sometimes, you know? [laughs]

Above, Mark describes the challenges he faced as a child migrant and heritage language learner relocating to Piniq from Anchorage in the 1990s as the
community began to voice concerns about language endangerment. Mark also
describes how he used Yup'ik to position and reposition himself within peer
interactions over time. As someone who knew 'a lot, but not very a lot' of
Yup'ik compared to his friends, Mark's vocabulary comprehension and overall
Yup'ik competence was lower than that of his peers. Using both Yup'ik and
English, Mark also faced intense, everyday scrutiny, and regularly had to
explain why he knew 'simple, but not advanced' words in Yup'ik.

We additionally see how heritage language learners may express resentment when they feel like community members and peers are 'putting them
down', treating them like linguistic 'criminals' for speaking English, especially when they themselves are wrestling with the historical reverberations
of circumstances beyond their control. We also gain insight into the ways
both increasing migration and changes in schooling set up increasing linguistic accommodation, with implications for the 'tip' into English in local peer
culture. In the mid-1990s, Mark attended school with the last group of RS
youth to receive primary instruction in Yup'ik, yet ended up graduating with
the first class of GB youth to receive instruction in English. Unlike the slightly
older Michael above, Mark describes how, during his time in high school,
'pretty much everybody started to not care if anybody speaks English and
Yup'ik', and peers and adults stopped 'bothering' him 'about speaking Yup'ik'.

In the mid-1990s, individual youth also moved to Piniq to get away from
challenging individual and community circumstances, bringing with them

wide-ranging linguistic competences and stances toward local life. The next section considers how youth in Piniq negotiated such people-flows in local youth culture.

Older Youth Migration and Linguistic Negotiation in Local Peer Culture

In urban centers and some rural villages, Alaska Native youth are exposed to disproportionately high rates of violence, alcohol-related abuse, and suicide. In the mid-1990s, Piniq had a reputation as a safe, dry, traditional and religious village, and parents sent or brought individual youth to Piniq as a way to foster their well-being. Youth themselves also chose to come to Piniq to stay with cousins or distant relatives as they dealt with deeply challenging life experiences. One young woman who I will call Bertha, for instance, decided to come to Piniq as she grieved the suicide of her brother in her home village. As Bertha reported, 'I didn't want to have school at [Home village] cause it would bring back so many memories.' Moving to Piniq, Bertha stayed with relatives for a few months. She also encouraged her cousin to join her, as she described in an interview in 2001:

LTW: And [Cousin] followed you?
Bertha: No, [Cousin] came after, [Cousin] came after me, like couple of weeks after he came. 'Cause there was so many things going on in [Home village] and it's close to Bethel. I asked him to come, too many drugs and alcohol going on over there ... parents ... school kids.
LTW: Um.
Bertha: So I asked him, I was buggin' him to come here and have school, 'cause there's hardly any here. So, when I asked him, he said he d[id]n't know. So I kept on ... pushing him to come here. So he came.

Bertha and her cousin spoke Yup'ik fluently, were welcomed by their local cousins and classmates in Piniq, quickly joined the local basketball team and participated in subsistence. Later, Bertha married into Piniq and raised her children locally, where she hoped they would develop respect for elders and be safe.

In a few contrasting instances, RS group members gave Yup'ik-speaking youth from other villages a hard time, emphasizing Yup'ik dialectal differences. Such instances most often arose as specific power plays between local and nonlocal youth, and were only salient for a short period. English-speaking youth without productive or receptive Yup'ik competences, on the other hand, faced more longstanding challenges as they entered local life and tried to negotiate language differences, especially if they came from urban areas. Local girls, for instance, initially criticized a girl from an urban area who participated actively in class discussions, as someone who 'act(ed) *kass'aq (white)*' or 'too loud'. In a very different and unusual case, two English-speaking brothers with distant local connections moved to Piniq to 'stay clean' while awaiting a trial for theft, after getting expelled from schools in urban areas of Alaska. The brothers boasted loudly in English of gang affili-ations and interpersonal violence, were largely met with silent rejection from local youth, and left Piniq after a few tense months.

On the cusp of language shift, youth culture in Piniq remained grounded in Yup'ik and local village practices, yet young people were not simply main-taining and reproducing patterns of intergenerational Yup'ik use with Yup'ik-speaking peers. To be sure, RS group members built on shared local childhood language socialization experiences as they spoke mostly Yup'ik with one another in local social networks. However, youth were also continuously reinforcing local norms around the use of Yup'ik as an unmarked language, interactionally 'owning' the local space in Piniq (e.g. Blommaert *et al.*, 2005) as they encountered flows of Yup'ik-speaking youth, English-speaking youth with Yup'ik receptive skills, and English-speaking monolingual youth from other villages and urban spaces.

When RS group members themselves traveled out of Piniq for school-related activities, they also used Yup'ik to connect to a regional network of Yup'ik peers and to negotiate diverse contact zones, as we will consider here.

Yup'ik as an In-Group Code Away from Home

During regional academic and sports tournaments, multiple Yup'ik village teams flew to the regional hub town of Bethel, and temporarily occupied the social spaces of hub town youth as they spent weekends in the local high school. Such trips provided opportunities for youth to interact in Yup'ik and/or English with family members in Bethel. RS youth from Piniq also generally enjoyed meeting, competing against and socializing exten-sively with youth from other villages. Youth from Yup'ik-speaking coastal villages including Piniq used Yup'ik to trace overlapping social and family networks, to share jokes and stories, and to tease one another.

Shopping in larger stores and visiting restaurants in Bethel provided rare opportunities for Piniq youth to interact in English with non-Yup'ik adults besides their teachers. These situations could also sometimes be uncomfortable, as village students were watched closely in stores, as if suspected of shoplifting, and as waiters in restaurants grew visibly impatient with students who took time deciphering menus, asking multiple questions. Youth from Piniq could also be sensitive about competing against English-speaking, mostly white students on the large hub town high school sports teams. Overall, Piniq youth interacted minimally with white adults and students from Bethel on these trips, using Yup'ik instead to make comments to one another in asides and jokes.

When traveling out of the Yup'ik region, as well, RS group members used Yup'ik as an in-group code. During the summer of 1992, when I was a counselor for a University of Alaska Fairbanks Upward Bound program, an RS group member and his friends from Yup'ik villages used Yup'ik extensively, prompting other Alaska Native students to speak longingly about the usefulness of Yup'ik as a secret language, and how they wished they knew their heritage languages. The Yup'ik basketball coach reported that RS group members from Piniq also used Yup'ik as a secret language to shout directions at one another in front of an opposing Inupiaq team during a basketball game in Anchorage. According to the coach, the Inupiaq youth responded by mocking the Piniq youth, making up nonsensical responses with exaggerated Yup'ik (or perhaps shared Inupiaq) sounds.

Yup'ik in the Local Contact Zone of School

Attending a secondary program run almost entirely by non-Yup'ik-speaking white administrators and certified teachers, youth used Yup'ik as an in-group code for negotiating racialized dynamics of schooling. Youth generally encouraged white teachers to learn Yup'ik, as a way to position themselves as respectful learners in the community (e.g. Cleary & Peacock, 1998). The unusual nonlocal teachers who were willing to make mistakes, get teased, and still persist in learning enough Yup'ik to 'get by' in community life often received strong positive responses from students, as well as from community members. However, in the 1990s, RS youth had never seen an outsider learn Yup'ik beyond simple survival statements.

Most RS group members described how they initially learned English through school, taking English as a second language classes a half hour a day as children, then switching to an English-language program in fourth grade. By high school, most youth could switch easily into conversational English to address teachers, or to speak to a small handful of non-Yup'ik-speaking youth. When relaxing, students told me about village life, dramatic events, shared jokes, and debated current events in conversational English, often incorporating 'village English' patterns and Yup'ik discourse makers, such as *Aren* (*I mean*, said when correcting a verbal slip-up), *Icugg'* (*You know*), -*Qaa?* (*Really?*), *Kaca'a* (*'You're in a hot spot!'*), and borrowed Yup'ik terms for subsistence, spirituality and emotional stances.

With help, most students also wrote and shared personal stories and essays, memorized and gave speeches, and earned proficient scores on district writing assessments in academic English. Tapping into shared backgrounds and lifelong relationships, as well as varying language competencies, youth often helped one another access academic knowledge and meet requirements in English. Youth also spontaneously interpreted for one another from English to Yup'ik as they made sense of teacher explanations and unfamiliar assignments.

Often, RS youth used Yup'ik to enliven the everyday moments of schooling, sometimes forcibly inserting social exchanges into classroom discourse (e.g. Rampton, 2006), making side comments in Yup'ik ranging from descriptions of what was going on outside the window to general statements, as in the case of one student who often declared *'Kaigpaa!'* (*I am hungry!*) loudly in the middle of class before lunch. Students also joked with one another about teachers' appearances, actions and strange preferences in Yup'ik asides.

Periodically, students also used Yup'ik to share critiques of school assignments, and/or how they were 'pissed off' at teachers, as in the case of a student who loudly exclaimed, *'Nekanaqluni!'* (*Darn it how frustrating!*) to classmates when I asked her to rework a challenging assignment in English. In a few instances, individuals used Yup'ik to help one another cheat on tests. At other times, students vocally tested the fragile linguistic boundaries of school authority, making public remarks in angry tones in Yup'ik around teachers, or speaking Yup'ik directly to white teachers in front of classmates, waiting to see what teachers would do. In such instances, especially when students included the term *'kass'aq'* (*white/English*) in their remarks, non-Yup'ik-speaking teachers would be left in the tricky situation of wanting to assert authority in a situation they could not fully describe. While the word *kass'aq* could mark a negative stance toward white people, the word could also be used in more neutral ways to mean 'outsider' or 'nontraditional'.

If teachers focused on what they imagined students said even in the most seemingly clear-cut moments of student opposition, their claims often sounded more and more like linguistic paranoia in racialized contact zones (Haviland, 2003; see also Blommaert *et al.*, 2005). Parents who remembered being abused in school for speaking Yup'ik were understandably suspicious about vague teachers' claims. In extreme cases, some teachers tried to ban the word *kass'aq* from classrooms, claiming that its negative connotations made it a racial epithet. However, simply suppressing talk about race and forcing students to become 'colormute' (Pollock, 2004) did not make underlying tensions go away.

Individual adults and youth sometimes used Yup'ik to guard the boundaries of local Indigenous knowledge systems so that white outsiders would not misunderstand local beliefs and practices. One local teacher, for example, warned his students never to translate certain topics related to Yup'ik spiritual beliefs into English; in the elders project described below, local educators also worked together to decide which topics would be appropriate for translation. RS group members also used silence when they experienced confusion and/or expressed passive forms of resistance when requests from teachers 'crossed the line' into threatening the legitimacy of community knowledge. Many teachers working as outsiders in schools serving Alaska Native and Native American communities can recall instances when curricular assignments have collided head on with Indigenous beliefs and knowledge systems (Cleary & Peacock, 1998). During my first year of teaching, in one such instance, a ninth- and tenth-grade class ground to a halt when I moved from working on Greek myths to introducing the related, district-required writing assignment for the unit.

Indigenous place names often harken to specific local experiences and stories, and can be important forms of evidence in land-claims negotiations in Alaska and Canada (Basso, 1996; Cruikshank, 1998). In the mid-1990s, secondary Yup'ik language teachers in Piniq often centered their curriculum on local knowledge by teaching youth the local Yup'ik names of various traditional camps, river channels and land forms. In a district-mandated English assignment in my classroom, in contrast, students were asked to come up with a 'myth' or origin story explaining a local landmark or natural phenomenon. When I introduced the assignment, youth in my class became quiet. Slowly, one young man began to ask questions. If we called something a myth, didn't that mean it wasn't true? They were supposed to simply make something up about a local landmark? As I tried to articulate the reasoning behind 'making something up' about a local place or natural phenomenon, I began to realize how the assignment threw into question the validity of local stories as community knowledge. Later, when I worked with youth and local adults to document elders' narratives including origin stories, I gained further insight into the ways the assignment challenged the authority of community members to determine the meaning and truth behind local narratives, by comparing them to dismissed stories in Greco-Roman history.

In school, many RS group members voiced deep concerns about the potential loss of Yup'ik knowledge and language, especially as elders passed away. The following section shows how some youth also developed a particularly antagonistic stance toward learning English within troubled trajectories at school by considering the experiences of a group of youth that I call the 'young *nukalpiat*' or *real hunters*.

The Young *Nukalpiat*

The high school youth in the RS group had wide-ranging English speaking and literacy skills. Within one class of juniors and seniors, for instance, students' English reading levels varied from third to 10th grade levels, even though most students had stayed together in local classes since kindergarten. Considering the school experiences of a group I call the 'young *nukalpiat*', we can see how students' academic development and English language learning were undermined when young people's in and out of school learning trajectories led them toward profoundly different types of relationships, identities and orientations toward knowledge systems. We also see how the school instability and tensions documented in the previous chapter negatively impacted students over time.

By the time I met the young *nukalpiat*, some were identified as high achievers in school. In interviews, these students attributed their academic achievement to having relatively young parents who both 'pushed' them to do well in school so that they could go on to post-secondary training and also included them in local opportunities to learn subsistence. Many others, however, had stood out for years as particularly difficult to motivate academically. Tracing the young *nukalpiat*'s trajectories of schooling illuminates a history of inconsistencies in approaches to school challenges and failure under unstable school leadership. Chapter 3 documents how RS youth as children had been transitioned abruptly from Yup'ik to English instructional environments at the fourth-grade level, and how outside teachers who expected students to be able to immediately transfer skills from Yup'ik into English expressed confusion about this year. Some RS group members like Stephen above described a smooth transition into the English instructional program. Individual *nukalpiat* who had been particularly *takaryuk* (*shy*) as children, however, shared memories of running away from school in fourth grade. In elementary school, almost all of the *nukalpiat* were also held back a grade or two due to low school performance and/or excessive absences.

The overassignment of youth to special education classes and the underenrollment of youth in gifted and talented programs is an entrenched challenge affecting Alaska Native education, as well as the education of other underserved minority populations in the United States (Deyhle & Swisher,

1997). In the young *nukalpiat*'s elementary years, outside administrators changed every few years. Many young *nukalpiat* were in and out of the principals' office, and then assigned to Special Education classes, which some passively resisted by refusing to go.

Over time in the community, many of the young *nukalpiat* grew into responsible and skilled hunters, taking on increasing learning challenges and responsibilities within their families as food providers. As older youth, most of the young *nukalpiat* adeptly demonstrated *takaryuk (respectful)* stances out of school, and expressed respect for local Yup'ik teachers, village leaders and elders. The local secondary Yup'ik teacher treated the young *nukalpiat* like upcoming leaders, and recognized how many of the young *nukalpiat* possessed local knowledge, maturity and strong Yup'ik skills.

However, many nonlocal teachers and administrators also positioned the young *nukalpiat* in school over time as 'at-risk' youth, infantilizing and distrusting them in similar ways to 'burnouts' elsewhere (Eckert, 1989). The divide that these students experienced between their in and out of school lives fed what at times became an intense distraction with the world outside the window, as Charlie, one of the young *nukalpiat*, remembered in 2001:

Charlie: When I worked on papers, like when I started reading?
LTW: Um hmm?
Charlie: I'd think of hunting, on my mind, even though I was reading that one, thinking of going out hunting 'Oh man, it's a beautiful day out there.'   (6/18/01)

While Charlie's comments above might seem like the comments of any young person who daydreams in class, his interest in life outside was more than just a pastime. Hunting fit into a celebrated and recognized community role for young men, and a historical tension between boys' subsistence activities and schooling that had existed for generations. Some older villagers, as well, described hunting as something the young men should be learning, critiquing how, when students focused on school, they simply graduated to 'do nothing'.

The young *nukalpiat* became, over time, the least likely to conform to school authority. The year before I met the young *nukalpiat*, they had been separated into a motivational program where they built a kit airplane. The kit plane project was intended to teach the *young nukalpiat* vocational education and academic skills in one long thematic unit with a concrete goal. The popular program stood out as the highlight of the group's school experience, culminating in a trip to an airplane show in the Lower 48. At the same time, videos from the project showed students quietly working in a shop. When students were mainstreamed into regular classes with a separate English as a Second Language class, their former teacher expressed happy surprise at one *nukalpiat*'s ability to exchange daily greetings in English as an eleventh-grade student.

During basketball season, 'making the team' temporarily motivated some students to attend school and complete enough work to obtain the minimal C average. Like many other students, however, when the season was over, many of the young *nukalpiat* went back to focusing on their lives out of school. At times members of the young *nukalpiat* complained that they were not being taught calculus, showing an awareness of how teachers' low expectations had already constrained their opportunities for gaining academic knowledge. By the time they reached their final years of high school, many of the *nukalpiat* also resented and distrusted school, making overt anti-English statements, and deeply questioning the relevance of school knowledge for community life. Some claimed a local elder had told them that school was 'brainwashing them' to be like *kass'aq*s (*white people*).

District data from 1999 showed that students from Piniq were generally not achieving on standardized tests, and also how boys were scoring significantly lower than girls, as in all of Alaska, starting in third grade. Locally, many of the young men who were underperforming in school performed in the locally sanctioned arena of subsistence. To be sure, some non-Yup'ik-speaking young men in the RS group also took up conflicting stances toward school-based literacy practices and hunting. Once, as I extolled the wonders and importance of reading and how students might read out of school, one such student called across the classroom to a strong Yup'ik speaker, 'Yeh, Steve, I always take a book in the boat when I'm hunting, don't you?'

It would be simplistic to claim that young *nukalpiat*'s own conflicting stances toward local knowledge and academic literacy directly caused the achievement gap of local youth, or the young men's disengagement with schooling over time. As we have seen in Chapter 3, the school in Piniq was an unstable, contested space in which rotating groups of outside educators struggled to see the connections between schooling, local strengths, and local needs, like many teachers in small rural schools and teachers in Indigenous schools elsewhere (Cleary & Peacock, 1998).

Many of the young *nukalpiat* themselves also voiced strong feelings that their opportunities in school were being negatively impacted because of racialized tensions that manifested themselves in specific interactions in specific classrooms with specific educators, as I repeatedly witnessed when angry youth transitioned into my own classroom. In the mid-1990s, multiple young *nukalpiat* bound beliefs about language, maleness and their local orientations into a discursive system that was decidedly antischool and anti-English.

Nevertheless, the young *nukalpiat*, like others, also demonstrated complex, hybrid forms of linguistic survivance in a global world.

Moving Beyond 'Two Worlds' Views of Yup'ik Youth

The pictures in this chapter, drawn by one of the young *nukalpiat* who was a respected local artist, illuminates commonly recognized local performance domains for young men in local peer culture at the time, and how these domains tied to both a collective past and present.

It would be easy to view Figures 4.1 and 4.2 as simply split into separate modern and traditional worlds; both figures feature men split in half, with one half of wearing a hunting *qaspeq*, and the other half holding a basketball dressed in basketball shorts and shoes. In each drawing, one side of the figure also displays traditional clothing and practices, wearing a *piluguk*, for instance, a traditional sealskin boot, as opposed to the Sorrels or 'Bunny boots' used by Alaska pipeline workers and by most local men at the time.

Figure 4.1 Man with mountain

Figure 4.2 Man with dance mask

Through allusions to traditional Yup'ik spirituality, the drawings above also demonstrate how some of the *nukalpiat* had an interest in past practices that were no longer openly discussed in the village. In Figure 4.1, the human's bird wing visually references the ability of shamans to turn into animals. Figure 4.2 includes a Yup'ik dance mask split into two, with half of the mask appearing as a basketball, though as described in Chapter 2, Yup'ik traditional dancing had been banned in Piniq since the time that elders had converted to Moravianism.

However, at the time of the study, being a hunter and being a jock were integrated parts of contemporary male life in Piniq. Basketball was the ultimate local performance domain, fostered through school sports and popular village and intervillage tournaments. Young people's interest in basketball was also fed by their consumption of NCAA and NBA-related cable broadcasts, magazines and clothing. As we will see in the following section, the young *nukalpiat* also actively integrated media portrayals with local narratives and experiences, as they made sense of their histories, identities and stances as local hunters, as well.

Media Consumption and Local Alignment

In far-flung rural places, media has a very visible influence on Indigenous young people's lives and language use. Veteran teachers in Piniq recalled how initially community members watched early TV stations with the sound off, yet how, when VCRs became widely available in the 1980s, teachers had to develop new policies for dealing with interpersonal aggression when young children began to imitate kung-fu movies with one another (see also Condon, 1987). In the mid-1990s, global media was highly evident in young people's peer culture, and in and out of classrooms, youth made regular reference to media characters, movies and TV specials. Over the course of a month in the spring of 1995, for instance, seventh- and eighth-grade youth watched video-tapes of the popular Disney movie *The Lion King* repeatedly; their humming and singing of related songs ran as an undercurrent in classrooms and extra-curricular activities. In contrast, many older youth rode multiple musical trends in youth culture in the early 1990s by listening repeatedly to famous bands' breakthrough albums such as Nirvana's grunge album *Nevermind*, and the heavy metal album *Metallica*.

At times, young people's use of media refrains evidenced the strange juxtapositions that mark the flows of commercial media into local spaces in a globalized world, as in one instance when youth and some adults broke into the Atlanta Braves' controversial Tomahawk song and gestures to cheer on a local basketball team. Yet, young people's media use in Piniq, as elsewhere, did not have a straightforward homogenizing influence on Indigenous youth and languages (Langlois, 2004), but also evidenced how young people take up new forms of media as they create globally connected, yet localized peer cultures in relation to specific communities, circumstances and alignments (Deyhle, 1998; Alim *et al.*, 2009). Throughout the 1990s and 2000–2001, many youth in Piniq who donned the latest global youth style and actively consumed movies and music showed great interest in community knowledge, and continued to take up local roles, responsibilities and stances as members of a subsistence society.

Significantly, youth also used media in ways that showed their ongoing interpretation of their position as Yup'ik youth. Older youth in the RS group, for instance, used jokes to indirectly critique media portrayals of Indigenous peoples – as when one high school student teased a friend by inserting her Yup'ik name into lines from an ad for the Disney movie *Pocahontas*. The young *nukalpiat*, as well, used media resources to (1) frame and perform local identities; (2) develop shared understandings of history; and (3) make sense of their collective relationship to the outside world as Yup'ik, circumpolar Inuit, young men, and hunters. While RS group members rarely described themselves as related to Native Americans elsewhere, they commonly identified with a pan-Inuit identity, expressing interest in 'other Eskimos' elsewhere. RS group members also synthesized local narratives with media representations to make sense of colonization in the Far North and contemporary challenges to community self-determination. A class of the *nukalpiat*, for instance, tried to help me put tensions with outsiders into historical perspective by showing me *White Dawn*, a movie about a group of white whalers who are rescued when stranded by a group of Baffin Island Inuit only to be killed eventually for their tendencies toward violent, uncivilized behavior. In the movie, the Inuit reflect sadly on the ways outsiders brought interpersonal violence into their peaceful society. While the young *nukalpiat* knew and were proud of stories about famous Yup'ik warriors from the 18th and early 19th century, they used the movie to bolster assertions that life among Yup'ik people was socially more stable before contact with *kass'aqs*.

Some of the young *nukalpiat* also used jokes to interpret and comment on the distance between local and media portrayals of male strength, leadership and power. The young *nukalpiat* described how local male elders who had lived in sod houses in the days before snowmobiles and outboard motors performed impressive physical feats in the past, such as running fast enough to catch a fox and jumping to dodge arrows, and sometimes wondered aloud what it would be like to hunt by *qayaq* or travel long distances on foot over the tundra. Youth also shared stories of elders' experiences, expressing respect for local elders' knowledge of how to face potentially life-threatening situations in the wilderness, while remaining calm and aware of ones' circumstances. One running group joke involved a set of codenames for male elders, including 'Steven Seagal', 'Bruce Lee' and 'Rambo'. The joke underscored the young men's respect for the elders while contrasting the elders' local ways of commanding respect and controlling emotions to movie portrayals of male power as fast-paced interpersonal aggression and hyperbolic rage.

Youth also drew on media representations as they interpreted controversial subsistence issues. Researchers in the Yukon-Kuskokwim Delta describe the challenges Yup'ik youth and adults face as they position themselves vis-à-vis subsistence practices, given conflicting ideologies of cultural and ecological preservation. According to Yup'ik ideology, animals offer themselves to hunters when they deem hunters worthy; hunters recognize the animals' offering by taking and treating subsistence foods and by-products respectfully; and both male and female members of households assure that animals will return to offer themselves again through actions such as helping elders without pay, sharing subsistence foods with others in need, working diligently and treating others well. Yet the ideology of harvesting animals and fish in order to sustain animal populations runs directly counter to Western scientific notions of restricting harvesting activities to maintain game and fish populations for the future (Fienup-Riordan, 1990; Hensel, 1996).

Stories of Yup'ik men shooting at the floats of Fish and Game helicopters so agents cannot land and issue citations are commonplace in the Yukon-Kuskokwim region (Hensel, 1996: 77). In a highly publicized case in the early 1990s, as well, two Yup'ik boys from one village were arrested for hunting a musk ox out of season after they had consulted and received elders' permission for the hunt and shared the catch according to Yup'ik norms. The judge ruled against the boys' claim that they were practicing allowable 'traditional and customary' subsistence practices, since musk ox were not typically found in the particular area. Overall, the case demonstrated how Indigenous youth, as well as adults, can be caught when subsistence rights are granted based upon static legal definitions of 'authentic' Indigenous practices (Morrow & Hensel, 1992, see also Nadasdy, 2003, Patrick, 2005).

In a study of subsistence discourse in Bethel, Hensel quotes one Yup'ik young man's expression of confusion in the face of conflicting ideological discourses of sustainability, 'I feel guilty if I shoot and I feel guilty if I don't shoot' (Hensel, 1996: 79). In contrast, the young *nukalpiat* in Piniq vocally positioned themselves as aligned with community on the issue of subsistence rights. Like many Yup'ik adults in and out of Piniq, the young *nukalpiat* spoke of resentment over government regulation of subsistence. In one related, memorable instance, a young *nukalpiat* described the pictures he had seen in a TV broadcast about the large numbers of swans who had died as development destroyed their habitat in the Lower 48. The young man loudly critiqued how Yup'ik people were restricted from taking birds that had been part of their subsistence practices for generations, when people elsewhere were primarily responsible for the birds' endangerment.

English Styleshifting and Schooling

Many of the young *nukalpiat* expressed strong concerns about English as a language that was 'taking over Yup'ik'. Youth also used humorous style-shifting into nonacademic varieties of English as they negotiated tensions in schooling. One related example comes from early in my teaching when I asked youth to write dialogue for personal hunting stories in English. After pointing out that such dialogue would normally take place in Yup'ik, a young man responded to the request by inserting mock southern English into the assignment, having Yup'ik hunters refer to one another with humorous names such as 'horse-nabber'.

In another such instance, I asked two young men to work with each other on getting more voice inflection and hand gestures into English speeches for a district competition. The two youth worked at the end of the hall, reciting their speeches simultaneously and walking around one another in a circle. As they humorously egged one another on, they moved into performing exaggerated hip-hop influenced English features like intonation, pitches and gestures, experimenting with new ways of expressing emotion without caving to school-related demands to adopt an academic emotional style associated with white teachers.

In an interview six years later, one of the young men described how he and a few close friends at the time experimented with appropriating ways of speaking from 'Def Comedy Jam', a cable TV show that helped spread the Hip Hop movement in the early 1990s by highlighting the performances of African-American comedians. In many places worldwide, Indigenous and non-Indigenous youth currently use Hip Hop language to develop new resistance vernaculars and to publicly comment on racism and societal inequities (e.g. Alim *et al.*, 2009; Mitchell, 2004). The subgroup of young *nukalpiat* were the first to pick up on the global linguistic flow of Hip Hop in Piniq, yet these youth denied requests to perform their new, media-inspired style for peers and local adults.

Creating Spaces for Bilingualism and Biliteracy with the Real Speakers: The Elders Project

While youth everywhere experiment with new forms of language and integrate multiple forms of knowledge, a large body of research also demonstrates how Native American and Alaska Native students benefit from culturally responsive curriculum grounded in community knowledge (for reviews of this literature, see Castagno & Brayboy, 2008; Demmert & Towner, 2003; Deyhle & Swisher, 1997). In the spring of 1993, four elders in Piniq passed away in short succession – deeply saddening RS group members, and raising students' concern about the loss of local knowledge. Against the backdrop of students' grief and longing for connection to local elders, and some students' deep anger and resistance to schooling, the local Yup'ik teacher and I initiated an effort to bring community funds of knowledge to the heart of the secondary Yup'ik and English language curriculum.

The project initially focused on fostering and supporting student inquiry, while bringing students into regular contact with elders to document *qanruyutait*. In the 'elders project', students interviewed elders about traditional stories, the kinds of *inerquutet* and *alerquutet* described in Chapter 2, as well as elders' personal memories and village history. Teachers including myself also used class discussions, group work, regular anonymous surveys, and individual written reflections in Yup'ik and English to solicit students' input on the content and structure of classroom learning, and plans for distributing resulting work.

RS group members' Yup'ik skills were generally high enough that youth in the RS group could listen to extensive *qanruyutait* (*teachings*) from elders, summarizing or even translating what they heard with few errors with help on the occasional word. Once adult community members helped students and elders negotiate discourse norms of interviewing, students also later conducted interviews with elders on topics of personal interest ranging from suicide as a historical and cultural phenomenon, to the community's relatively recent adoption of Christianity.

Over time the project grew to involve 10 local adults and 45 elders. Yup'ik educators helped students transcribe narratives in the school-based phonemic Yup'ik writing system. Local community members helped document elders' narratives in the Moravian Yup'ik writing system, and take interview transcripts back to elders for their approval or editing. At the end of the first project year, students, teachers and I used a new computer word processing program to produce a homespun book of elders' narratives in the two Yup'ik writing systems. The book included students' English translations of elders' narratives, students' written comments about things they had learned, found difficult or found interesting in the project, and their thanks for elders' participation. The following year, a student teacher noted that the book was being used in classrooms throughout the K–12 school.

Local teachers and I continued to develop new pedagogical approaches to 'teaching through the community' (Moll, 1992), as students collected and documented local elders' narratives. Youth sometimes voiced linguistic insecurities given differences between their own Yup'ik and the Yup'ik of elders, and the challenges of writing in Yup'ik, yet also carried out biliterate academic tasks. Youth spoke mostly Yup'ik with one another in small groups, and English with me in large group discussions, for instance, as they strategized how to solicit additional information to turn a contemporary oral narrative from a local adult about a hunting incident into a junior and senior play. Drawing on multiple parts of their bilingual and biliterate repertoires (or 'continua of biliteracy' as described by Hornberger, 2002), youth then moved back into Yup'ik to draft further questions and reinterview local adults. As a teacher, I positioned individual hunters as resources for small groups of students, then asked each group to generate scenes and dialogue based on their shared knowledge of related subsistence practices. Youth used Yup'ik and English to plan the local performance; actors worked with a local college graduate to practice the play in Yup'ik and English, and other students wrote short speeches thanking elders for sharing their knowledge about subsistence. The students then used Yup'ik to perform the play for local audiences.

Like other educators building on community funds of knowledge at the time in immigrant and Native American communities, Yup'ik educators, community members and I worked to position local knowledge as historically accumulated, yet also dynamic, adaptable and situated within particular activities and social relationships (González et al., 2005; McCarty, 2004). We also situated our work within the tribal self-determination efforts described in Chapter 2. In 1995, for instance, a district writing assessment prompt required youth in one of my English classes to write a formal essay discussing tribal jurisdiction. To contextualize the question, youth read and discussed daily news reports of a controversial case involving two Tlingit young men whom tribal leaders had disciplined in a traditional manner by banishing to a remote island. They also used minilessons on related vocabulary, and short writing exercises to scaffold discussions of related issues. Youth in the class then invited council leaders to talk with us in Yup'ik about local efforts to establish jurisdiction over nontribal members living Piniq, and compared these efforts to the Tlingit case. Eventually, each student in the English class produced the required academic essay in English for the district's writing assessment, many receiving high marks for an assignment that would have stumped them a year earlier.

During the two most active years of the elders project, students used information from local interviews to complete academic assignments and compete successfully in district academic competitions in Yup'ik and English. Their work fulfilled Yup'ik and English curriculum goals, and the elders project had a number of positive side effects, the most striking being the collaboration among educators, and high numbers of community members participating in schooling. Through my involvement in the project as a teacher-researcher, I learned how to provide students with different types of scaffolding and options so as not to falsely assume that every student would respond to 'experience near' assignments in the same way (Wortham, 2006). Over time, as I made regular opportunities for students to build on local knowledge and increasingly involved local adults in classroom and extracurricular activities, it also became easier to engage students in mainstream curricula, as previously challenging youth seemed to move beyond defensive postures toward nonlocal knowledge and academic English. A number of the young *nukalpiat*, on the verge of feeling pushed out of school altogether, finished and graduated from high school.

For a short time, participation in the elders project transformed some students' experiences of secondary education, as the reorganization of 'curriculum, pedagogy, and social relations promoted students' active participation in identity and knowledge construction, within an inclusive view of biliteracy' (Hornberger, 2005: 164). By changing 'narrow, unproductive and damaging relationships between teachers and students, schools and families, and students and curriculum' (González *et al.*, 2011), Yup'ik colleagues and I also temporarily improved the academic outcomes of RS group members, as students increased their willingness and ability to engage in sophisticated types of learning and biliteracy events, and 'planful thinking' (Heath, 1998, 2008) about connecting classroom and community goals.

The efforts above did not miraculously fix the ongoing dynamics of distrust between the school and the community, or fully make up for tremendous gaps in some students' academic skills. Nevertheless, the markers of success above were welcome relief given ongoing turbulence and profound discontinuities in the local high school. The efforts also helped create the conditions for students who were struggling with schooling, as well as their relatively high achieving counterparts, to integrate social and academic learning in a contested school space. When my colleagues and I zeroed in on language shift with the RS group, however, we quickly ran into challenges understanding the rapidly changing sociolinguistic setting.

Making Sense of Language Endangerment

In the mid-1990s, as the awareness and discourse of language endangerment gained prominence worldwide and community members expressed concerns about language shift, I and my colleagues attempted to tailor our youth action research to address these concerns at the request of the local traditional council. RS group members read about Indigenous language endangerment and revitalization efforts in the United States and Alaska through newspaper articles and scholarly papers (Krauss, 1980). Youth also interviewed a scholar of language endangerment over the phone, and wrote letters and surveys to youth elsewhere, inquiring about language use, shift, and maintenance efforts in other Alaska Native villages. For the first time, some RS group members became aware of some of the political struggles surrounding language education in Indigenous communities elsewhere.

Teachers and I experienced what others found later elsewhere: Indigenous youth may eagerly take up local language activism when they are exposed to language issues (Lee, 2009; McCarty et al., 2009). Like the overall elders' project, the unit on language shift and endangerment engaged youth in the feeling of 'doing something' meaningful to their community. Many of the students' comments from the time echo a sense of active involvement, and a view of Yup'ik as a link to histories, struggles for lands, self-determination, and a unique community identity (Smith, 1999: 73).

At the same time, the effort was more challenging than broader attempts to connect students to community funds of knowledge. Students, colleagues and I struggled to make sense of the ways language use was seemingly influenced by multiple local, individual, and familial contingencies and societal phenomena. While some youth in younger groups on the project were strong Yup'ik speakers, Yup'ik teachers also noted how the first group of youth to receive English, versus Yup'ik, as a primary language of instruction needed considerable extra help interacting with elders and making sense of elders' talk. Youth in the younger groups also offered changing explanations for their own decreasing use of Yup'ik compared to their peers; a student from one of the younger classes I taught was the first youth I knew to claim he did not speak Yup'ik 'because my best friend when I was young didn't speak it'. In the following chapter, we will see how multiple processes in and out of the school were already dramatically undercutting local attempts to maintain Yup'ik.

The RS Group's Post-Secondary Trajectories

Relationships of trust between students, communities and schools are shaped within the relatively short-term relationships between students and particular teachers. They are also earned over time, depending on the ways that schooling appears to 'pay off', or not, in community members' lives after high school (Erickson, 1987). Tracking what happened to the RS group living in Piniq in their early years after high school demonstrates how school performance did not necessarily lead to post-secondary success or jobs in a depressed village economy, and how, at the time of language shift, local work required bilingualism.

Alaskan education scholars have documented rural high school students' challenges transitioning to college (Barnhardt, 1994). While some RS youth went right on to post-secondary training out of school, most decided to 'take a year/some time off' between high school and post-secondary training. For many, the year off turned into a few years, at which point they were absorbed in village life or had young families of their own. In the following interview, a young woman describes how instability in secondary school staff impacted her own and her peers' ability to figure out the maze of scholarship and college applications.

LTW: Did you think about going to college right after high school?
Julie: Yeah, I thought about it. But, it looks like we didn't have any help, somebody to push us to fill out some papers, some scholarships. Because the teachers change, I mean. Like, every year, new teachers come and old teachers go, something like that. And the teachers change and the principal.

Some youth worked their way back into the school orbit to get help completing applications, and approximately a third of the students in the RS group tried some form of post-secondary education, though half of these students left post-secondary programs before completing them, many after a semester or two. Some students described how negotiating the social activity and heightened academic expectations of an impersonal college setting away from home was particularly challenging. Three students had successfully completed post-secondary training programs by 2001. Of these three, one was back in the village taking care of his grandma, a second was living in another village and a third was living in Bethel.

Often young men from Piniq expressed interest in attending post-secondary vocational training, with the hopes of coming back as skilled laborers. One RS youth had trouble passing an entrance placement test for a vocational program. Another young man entered a program for diesel engine training, but did not complete the program. The youth was mechanically adept, highly familiar with snowmobile engines and had learned quite a bit about airplane mechanics in the earlier kit plane project. Still he described how in his classes 'the talking was too fast, and the instructor assumed we knew about cars.' After a few students left the program before completion, the admissions officer began to tell others that he wanted 'no more drop-outs from Piniq'.

Gender and Work after School

Researchers using surveys to document migration and aspirations of young adults in rural Alaska assert that 'women, like women in rural areas all over the world, are voting with their feet', moving away from arctic and subarctic Alaska Native villages at higher rates than Alaska Native men and aspiring to careers that would lead them toward urban centers (Hamilton & Seyfrit, 1994). In high school, young women in the RS group were generally more vocal than young men about leaving Piniq. Nevertheless, in 2001, roughly two thirds of both RS young men and women lived in Piniq, and another 10% followed partners to surrounding Yup'ik villages.

Alaska Native women in rural villages are more likely to hold full-time and paper and pencil 'pink collar' jobs, since men generally take less prestigious jobs that will not interfere with subsistence (Bodenhorn, 1994; Hensel, 1996). Since women's subsistence work processing birds and seals could be done at night at home, this made it easier for women to hold school jobs than men, who needed to be ready to go out for full days in fall and spring, dependent upon on contingent seasonal and daily weather patterns. In 2000–2001, 50–60% of the RS young men and young women who stayed in Piniq had some form of wage employment. Women, however, were much more likely to hold full-time work, and young men were much more likely to participate in part-time commercial resource harvesting, as we see in Table 4.1. Women tended to hold a disproportionate number of jobs in institutions that were directly controlled from outside the village by work schedule regulations, such as the school and the Post Office.

Table 4.1 Employment of RS and GB youth living in Piniq

RS and early GB group N = 75	Young women (31)	Young men (44)
In any kind of paid work	18 (58%)	21 (48%)
In year-round work	12 (39%)	6 (14%)
Part time work (any kind)	6 (19%)	15 (34%)
In commercial resource harvesting (herring fishing, cannery work, salmon fishing in Bristol Bay, collecting wood for local sale, etc.)	1 (3%)	8 (18%)

In other village institutions, jobs were distributed more evenly according to gender, though young RS men held a larger percentage of positions related to community authority and commerce, and young RS women were more likely to occupy jobs related to caregiving and education. In 2001, almost half of the RS young women with full-time work in Piniq were involved in education, as opposed to one young man. In contrast, half of the young men in full-time work were in management positions in other village institutions, though these jobs were difficult to get. Young men often combined part-time work in construction and/or commercial resource harvesting with subsistence types of work that required little school or post-secondary training, yet built on local knowledge.

The biggest and shared challenge to finding wage work in Piniq for all RS group members was the low number of paid positions in the distressed rural economy. In 2000–2001, more than 70% of village residents in Piniq earned less than the minimum wage, and less than 30% of residents worked all four quarters in 1999. Some RS youth complained about the ways local council members gave hiring preference to workers who needed to support families, and how this made it hard for youth to establish themselves as economically independent before they became responsible for children of their own. Some RS youth found wage work through family and friend networks. Local employers reported that they hired youth for their personal qualities, as opposed to school performance, and a number of the young *nukalpiat* group members were chosen for positions of responsibility in local institutions based on their knowledge of the community, maturity level, and their general trustworthiness.

Subsistence after School

Young men and women joined new social networks and participated in new subsistence activities as they entered the mixed economy after high school. For young men who oriented toward subsistence and village life, hunting continued to involve a challenge-filled trajectory of learning alongside experienced adult mentors. One young man who peers referred to as a *nukalpiaq* (singular of *nukalpiat*) described how he continued to learn crucial knowledge of the environment 'every day' by participating in subsistence activities with older men. During a winter with particularly fast-melting ice, for instance, he had learned to identify patches of ice where his snowmobile might plunge through into water. Two years later, similar conditions sent six snowmobiles to the ocean floor, though fortunately no one was hurt.

For young men who remained in Piniq, hunting also remained an important local activity, as Michael, the following speaker describes:

LTW: If a guy, I'm trying to think of what's cool in high school, if a guy doesn't hunt, most guys hunt, huh.
Michael: Yeah.
LTW: Like all of 'em⸮
Michael: Yeh, I mean, you gotta find food for your family and can't always go to the store. I mean, almost everybody has two or three chest freezers⸮ You know they just stock up on food, my gram she's got like four or five of those.
LTW: Wow.
Michael: 'Cause, um, every year we keep on trying to stock up on everything, depending on the season, 'cause like every year there's bird time, it's ptarmigans, eiders, geese and fall time it's ducks and geese, but you know, like, it's different kind of geese there in fall time and spring time, [Here he goes into detail about differences about fall and spring bird-hunting.]   (4/6/01)

Michael described how young men needed to hunt as local providers for their families, since the quality of the fresh meat from the tundra was superior to the highly processed or mass-produced foods available in the freezers of local stores, and the small local stores sometimes ran out of meat. When low-paying local jobs directly conflicted with subsistence, often subsistence won out. For instance, in 2000–2001, a national Americorps program offered the promise of a living allowance and a college credit of $5000 to volunteers who would work eight hours a day, five days a week at the traditional council. For the eight young adults from the RS who tried Americorps, however, the opportunity to work for less than living wage in rural Alaska for a year did not seem worth giving up subsistence activities. The position had yet to be completed in 2000–2001.

Many young men were able to generate some cash income by combining seasonal construction work with commercial resource harvesting. Some young men's restricted opportunities for post-secondary education, however, left them particularly vulnerable to the ebb and flow of commercial resource harvesting and legislative grant monies. Young men who did not orient strongly toward subsistence were most likely to float between jobs in the hub town of Bethel and local life, or to work in the school. RS youth with low Yup'ik skills, in particular, bounced between service jobs in Piniq and elsewhere.

Young men and a few young women reported that they were attracted to the National Guard for the opportunities to experience other places, and/or to be a 'part of something bigger'. At the time Piniq had a particularly successful National Guard with a respected local community member for a sergeant, and multiple RS young men and women who barely or never completed high school ended up joining the National Guard. Like low-income minority youth elsewhere, youth in Piniq were also aggressively pursued by military recruiters. Mark described how a recruiter called and persuaded him to join the military with promises of help with health benefits, college and getting a house:

Mark: I was thinking of benefits, especially. They said they would help me go to college through this thing the GI bill; they said they would help pay 75 or over, so that's a great benefit, the military will help you for college. I think that's all I wanted to go to the army for was for college.

LTW: So how was it when you got involved?

Mark: [Laughs, hard.] Very hard. Recruiters are very persuasive, but then they turn around and don't help. My drill sergeant said you've been suckered.

When I asked Mark to reflect on his comment that he had been 'suckered', he said that he had felt that way in the hard times. Yet Mark, like other interviewees, also went on to describe how the military offered a powerful learning experience, through which individuals could realize their physical and mental stamina, while taking on new types of risk and performance over time. In Chapter 7, we will continue to see how for young men, in particular, subsistence offered similar opportunities, while school, most often, did not.

It is difficult to generalize the RS group members' 'life after high school' in Piniq. Individuals broke every pattern mentioned above, and such simple patterns do not adequately portray the dynamic flow of young people's lives after school. Over 14 months in 2000–2001, as I tried to track the RS group members' trajectories, some youth decided to try post-secondary education eight years out of high school, while others left programs. Youth gained and lost jobs though local programs that were created and folded, and moved to and from other villages, hub towns and urban spaces, as they pieced together a life. A few youth also started families of their own, and flowed between Piniq and their partners' home villages.

However, as I followed up with former students in Piniq in 2000, two points became increasingly clear. First, local adults continued to socialize older youth to use and value Yup'ik during early rapid language shift. Second, jobs in local institutions demanded that youth negotiate new, challenging positions as linguistic and cultural brokers, using bilingual and biliterate competences other than those most commonly emphasized in school, as we will consider below.

Maintaining and Activating Yup'ik Use in Local Life

After high school, many RS youth reported that they maintained or increased their Yup'ik use as they entered community life. Some young *nukalpiat* gained local management jobs, and a number of these youth reported that they generally stopped using English after getting out of school, with the exception of when they ordered things over the phone. When the cable TV show 'Def Comedy Jam' went off the air, some of the early experimenters stopped using Hip Hop-influenced English, remembering this practice simply as something funny from their school days.

Joining adult communities-of-practice, youth became increasingly aware of the ways their own spoken Yup'ik evidenced rapid language changes preceding language shift. Individuals, for instance, commented on the differences between their own speech and that of elders, and noted that adults 10 years older than them used 'difficult words' they could not understand right away. One strong Yup'ik speaker from the RS group, for instance, reported that he was sometimes good-naturedly teased for being a 'dumb Yup'ik', when he did not know words used by slightly older peers. Nevertheless, the RS group continued to use Yup'ik for a life's array of purposes with minimal difficulty with one striking exception: when they encountered young children who were using mostly English, as we have seen above.

As RS group members entered everyday life and interacted regularly with local adults, three young men who had been too insecure to speak Yup'ik in school activated Yup'ik productive skills and started to speak Yup'ik in interactions with peers as well as adults. Another child migrant, Graham, describes how he and another youth 'tipped back' after apparent childhood language loss, as they chose to suddenly start speaking Yup'ik as adults:

Graham: Couple years ago I just started speaking Yup'ik. Not that much though.

LTW: How'd you start, or . . .

Graham: Me and my best friend, he told me we should start speaking Yup'ik to other people and I was like, OK, and so I started, I talked to my dad in Yup'ik, and I started talking it to my friends. Some of them they never ever heard me speak Yup'ik.

LTW: Like who?

Graham: Like (names two friends) and

LTW: When they heard you what'd they do?
Graham: They were like 'Wow I never heard you speak Yup'ik, I never heard you talk Yup'ik before.' And, uh, they were ... pretty amazed, somehow.
LTW: Like in what way?
Graham: In a good way, surprised.

          ***

LTW: I wonder why [friend's name] all of a sudden wanted to speak Yup'ik. That was couple years ago?
Graham: No I think it was last year, last summer.
LTW: Was he out of school, or?
Graham: He was out of school. I don't know, I guess he just wanted to. Cause he told me that when he was little he used to speak Yup'ik, and I guess that's why he wanted to, and cause we're both really Yup'iks.   (7/30/01)

Graham went on to describe how, compared to his peers, he did not understand 'some words or probably most words' when elders' shared extended Yup'ik discourse in stories or church sermons, guessing that 'If I lived here all my life, I'd probably be very fluent'. When asked if he could tell a short story in Yup'ik about something he did the day before, Graham replied that it 'would be kind of hard', clarifying, 'I just say things I know in Yup'ik and mostly in English ... in Yup'ik it's little by little, the way I talk.' Cases like Graham and his friends were unusual in the study, yet spoke to both the potential and challenges of redirecting individual language trajectories in young adulthood. Such cases further demonstrated how youth who positioned themselves for years as nonspeakers could reposition themselves, taking up new stances as Yup'ik speakers as they moved across the school–community boundary in Piniq.

Below, we will further consider how youth performed complex acts of linguistic survivance as they transitioned to new roles as bilingual brokers in village and regional institutions.

Linguistic Survivance and Local Work

Of those 26 young adults who held jobs in 2001, only a few had what young people would call 'decent jobs'. These jobs most often targeted the social and cultural needs of the village, were funded by grants and administered through the new bureaucracies, and generally involved additional training in the form of workshops or classes out of Piniq. Two young women, for instance, held jobs as early childhood literacy educators in a federally funded program. One young man headed a local Cultural Preservation Program documenting the knowledge of elders. After gaining recognition for his strong Yup'ik skills in a college language class, another youth was hired and trained by the Regional Corporation to work as a 'Culture Coordinator' running elders' camps during summers for school students around the Yukon-Kuskokwim Delta. Another young woman worked as an Indian Child Welfare Worker, and a fourth young woman worked for the tribal court as a translator and scribe.

RS group members who found local wage work relied on Yup'ik and English to fill their new roles, demonstrating linguistic survivance as linguistic and cultural brokers in village institutions. Many of the RS youth who went on to work within the local government described the awkwardness of trying to take on the voice of authority as young people in a village where they were related to everyone. Some described the tension of negotiating conflicts over tribal, state and federal jurisdiction. One RS group member, for instance, described how he had been stressed as a young tribal police officer when some of his relatives thought he had helped state troopers forcefully take a family member to court in Bethel. As some community members expressed anger that the Tribal Council did not handle the case locally, the young man clarified his noninvolvement in the case, resigned from his job and repaired relationships with his family.

As bilingual brokers working in social services positions, other youth worked with elders as locally accepted counselors to negotiate the challenges of exercising state policy and authority. As the local Indian Child Welfare Worker, for instance, Susan was responsible for helping families in cases of alleged neglect or abuse. Susan received training on family and child protection law, intervention strategies, and learned the guidelines under which the state of Alaska would intervene in local cases. Yet, Susan also described how she sometimes felt embarrassed and awkward counseling families, since she was not an experienced parent. The RS group member who held the position before her had resigned, saying it was too stressful as a young adult to give advice to older people about family issues.

To deal with this stress, Susan called on elders to step in as counselors and asked them to tell parents about how they raised children and dealt with domestic issues in the past. In other instances, RS group members described how they used commonplace local sayings to help socialize young people as part of their new jobs. One young woman who worked as a scribe for the tribal court, for instance, described how she told juvenile offenders, '*Yuut tangvagaatgen (People are watching you)*', when she was asked to speak to young people in court cases.

When I asked young adults from the RS group with jobs in village institutions to reflect on their high school education, some critiqued how they felt ill prepared for local jobs. Individuals expressed how they wished they had learned more about writing reports in English for funding agencies. Other youth expressed how they wished they had learned more Yup'ik, since many found themselves working with elders. Many youth with and without jobs noted how crucial it was for traditional council members to be able to write grant applications. Noting the challenges of making federal and state regulations accessible to community residents, still others noted how they needed to be able to translanguage both between Yup'ik and English and between bureaucratic English and local English to do their jobs.

Within individualized language trajectories out of Piniq, other youth were increasingly exposed to dominant discourses challenging local assumptions about the importance of Yup'ik maintenance and bilingualism/biliteracy. Below, once again, we will consider the case of Mark.

Ideological Crosscurrents and Linguistic 'Resistance' after High School

Within some Indigenous communities, local messages about the importance of maintaining ancestral languages are so commonplace, embedded in everyday interaction and linked to powerful local relationships and activities, that they serve as an *alternative hegemony* – a set of beliefs that is not commonplace or accepted in dominant society, yet accepted and rarely challenged as the unmarked local norm (Kroskrity, 1998; Meek, 2007). Multiple youth commented on the need to learn English, and local beliefs about the importance of Yup'ik clearly contrasted with the messages youth received through school and the media. However, young people from Piniq rarely directly countered the powerful discourse linking respect for elders and local knowledge with Yup'ik language allegiance described in Chapter 2.

In many Indigenous communities today, youth voice deep connections to their heritage language, yet simultaneously wrestle with strong ideological countercurrents from broader society (Lee, 2007, 2009; McCarty *et al.*, 2006, 2009; Tulloch, 2004). When Indigenous youth have not had enough opportunities to learn their heritage language and feel criticized by community members for not speaking those languages, they may also voice both sympathy for and resentment toward local language advocates.

Mark, who described his experiences as a child migrant and in the military above, was the one young person in the study to openly challenge local discourses about the importance of maintaining Yup'ik. Before the following interview excerpt, I asked Mark whether the pressure he had experienced to speak Yup'ik as a youth 'inspired, demotivated, or had no effect':

1 **Mark:**   It didn't have an effect on me. But it inspired me, I guess, to keep this. They're just paranoid, I guess, to lose this language. I can see how much they care about speaking Yup'ik. And, uh, I always tell 'em 'I'm Yup'ik and I'm proud of it.' The language, once you speak it and you use it since you were a little boy, you will never lose it. It inspired me I guess to teach it to my little kids, if I have kids someday.

2 **LTW:**   But they seem paranoid?

3 **Mark:**   Yeh, they just care about the language, I guess.

4 **LTW:**   How important do you think it is to have Yup'ik to be Yup'ik, do you need it to be Yup'ik, or?

5 **Mark:**   Yes, you need a language to be Yup'ik, but you don't have to speak it to be Yup'ik, 'cause it's just a language. And . . . I don't understand why our Yup'ik language is so important, especially how it's gonna help, how, how is Yup'ik gonna help out if . . . if you got a job. Let's say you got a job out there, somewhere in the 48's. Nobody speaks Yup'ik, and you know so much Yup'ik and a little bit of English, how's that gonna help? That's how I see it, you know, 'cause jobs nowadays, you can't just live here and have a job all your life here in Piniq. It depends on who you are, I mean, but you could if you want to, but it gets *boring*. So you gotta try something out there and your employer might not speak Yup'ik. And if you know so little bit of English, is he gonna, is he gonna fire you because you know so little? And I guess they just don't know how important English is.

6 **LTW:**   The people who are pushing to speak Yup'ik, or?

7 **Mark:**   Yeh, cause they've lived here in Piniq most of their lives. They don't work out there. And I could see lots of elders or people who speak nothing but Yup'ik having a problem speaking to people who speak nothing but English to them out there in Bethel or close by Anchorage. And you need to have a translator. I think I know why they want us to speak Yup'ik so much, I'm not pretty sure, but this is what I think: They quit school since they were eighth grade. Eighth grade is when some people quit school. They never had high school. My grandmother quit school when she was in third grade. And I

think that's why, they didn't go to school and they want to speak Yup'ik more. And there's this other woman who use to abuse 'em for speaking Yup'ik.

8 **LTW:**   Hmm.

9 **Mark:**   Yeh, that's why I think they want to keep it.

10 **LTW:**   Because they were abused for speaking it?

11 **Mark:** Yeh, they were at that old building, and they, my grandmother went there and they used to get abused for speaking Yup'ik, and they had a hard time, a rough time … But, um, and it's just, they haven't experienced the outside world yet, and to them it's very important because they are Yup'ik. And there's nothing wrong with that, I think there's nothing wrong with that.

Parts of Mark's statements above are striking examples of what one might expect to find a young person saying in a village facing rapid language shift, particularly when Mark talks about not needing Yup'ik and describes English as a key to future jobs. Yet, Mark stood out as an exception in his peer group. Here again, by considering unusual cases, we can consider how youth negotiated local language ideologies as they developed particular local identities, alignments and individualized linguistic repertoires in relation to life circumstances over time. In Piniq, some families held higher status than others, and in high school, Mark often complained the village was 'prejudiced' against his family. Mark participated peripherally in hunting, yet also spent his free time trying out making up rap lyrics and sharing them with a few close friends.

After challenges finishing high school, as we saw above, Mark joined the army. He later worked in a cannery, then moved to Anchorage for a while before running out of money. In striking contrast to his earlier descriptions of feeling like he 'didn't know a lot' of Yup'ik, Mark described proudly how he had crossed styles (Rampton, 1995), mastering the 'slang' used by African-American friends in the military, at the cannery, and in his urban apartment complex in Anchorage. He also compared himself to another local Yup'ik friend from Piniq who had also become friends with African-Americans in the army, but had not been able to cross as easily. When Mark returned to Piniq, he used his new style and wore clothing associated with urban gangs in Anchorage. Locally, Mark was subjected to rumors of gang activity – rumors which he cited as yet more evidence of village prejudice.

It is likely that multiple layers of Mark's life experience – including Mark's position in the community, his local experiences as a relatively weak Yup'ik speaker among his peers, as well as his later experiences and expected departure back into a broader society where monolingualism in English remained valued and expected – shaped the ways in which Mark's interview segment above was 'shot through' with questions about the usefulness of Yup'ik and assumptions about the impossibility of bilingualism. Yet, as we consider Mark's statements about his personal connections to Yup'ik, his expressed sympathies for community language advocates' concerns, and his recognition of his grandmother's experience with linguistic oppression in school above, we also see how Mark's responses were further 'shot through' with strong local discourses valuing Yup'ik, and how Mark's relationships and life experiences continued to orient him toward community members and concerns.

In interpreting the 'ideological cross-currents' (McCarty *et al.*, 2006) and Mark's complex interactional shifts above, we must also keep in mind how individuals negotiate moment-to-moment encounters, orienting toward institutional discourses in particular places, at particular times, with particular people (McDermott & Tylbor, 1995). Specifically, we must remember the very unusual context of the interview itself, as Mark interacted with me – a researcher and former English teacher who had parroted societal and school-based assumptions about the importance of English for jobs, while echoing local community members' expressed concerns about language endangerment.

Summary

In one important way, the RS group members were, as the community described, the last 'real speakers' of Yup'ik in Piniq at the time of the study: they were the last group to use Yup'ik as a general peer language. Yet, on the cusp of language shift, young people in Piniq actively integrated multiple and varied types of linguistic resources, learning experiences, life circumstances and ideologies in ways that challenge typical binary descriptions of Indigenous youth. They also complicated stereotypical notions of Alaska Native youth as passively 'caught' in a cultural crossroads, and romantic assumptions about youth as especially prone to resistance.

In the mid-1990s, youth took up locally available gender roles as they regularly shared stories in Yup'ik with one another. Young men, in particular, used talk about hunting in Yup'ik to mark Yup'ik identity, and to ideologically align themselves with community knowledge and local struggles for self-determination vis-à-vis state regulating agencies. Over the course of challenging school trajectories, some of the young *nukalpiat* (*great hunters*) also bound respect for elders and participation in subsistence with Yup'ik language allegiance, overtly anti-English stances and subtractive views of schooling and bilingualism.

Yet, for young people in the Real Speaker group, using Yup'ik was not necessarily a straightforward gesture of local solidarity, nor was speaking English necessarily an act of buying into a different, dominant society. Like bilingual youth elsewhere, RS youth localized global linguistic practices and styles, even while Yup'ik remained their general peer language. And resistance – what was the true resistance? Was it to be found among the young *nukalpiat* who voiced opposition to the *kass'aq* world, taking pot shots at English as they expressed resentment toward outside teachers and Fish and Game agents? Many of these young *nukalpiat* tied Yup'ik to the past and subsistence, and English to a shared history of linguistic oppression and an overall distrust of schooling. However, it could be argued that the same young *nukalpiat* were also orienting toward a local knowledge system that existed before colonization, rather than expressing resistance (Morrow, 1996). As they made sense of history and their connections to circumpolar Inuit elsewhere, the young *nukalpiat* synthesized local narratives with global media images, moving across languages. A subgroup of the young *nukalpiat* were additionally among the first youth in Piniq to dabble with a nonlocal, non-*kass'aq* English as they secretly appropriated media-related Hip Hop language.

Was resistance more easily identifiable in the case of Mark, who began writing rap lyrics in high school, then later crossed to pick up what he called 'slang' from African-American friends? Over time, Mark distanced himself from Piniq mentally and physically, participating in diverse social networks and adopting a style of dress that community members associated with urban gangs elsewhere. Mark also voiced resentment toward the 'village prejudice' he experienced as a minimal Yup'ik speaker and a member of a marginalized local family, making it easy to consider his stylization as the development of a new personal 'resistance vernacular' (Mitchell, 2004). Yet Mark voiced the same logics of English as necessary and Yup'ik as backwards found in dominant society and an English-only movement elsewhere (Crawford, 2000; May, 2005). Further, both the young *nukalpiat* and Mark voiced binary assumptions about the need to choose between Yup'ik and English, reinscribing historically rooted assumptions about bilingualism as impossible.

Considering the words and experiences of Yup'ik-speaking and non-Yup'ik-speaking RS youth, we see how young people were grounded in localized, gendered and even individualized alignments right before youth culture tipped into English in Piniq. On the cusp of language shift, youth also expressed multiple, ambiguous forms of linguistic survivance within the small community. While many youth in Piniq oriented toward mass-produced media, forms of music and dress, and some experimented with nonlocal and nonacademic Englishes, the same youth also localized new styles in varying ways for contradictory purposes.

To understand how emergent identification processes and forms of survivance did and did not contribute to the rapid sociolinguistic transformation of Piniq, we must analyze young people's everyday linguistic practices in relation to longer-term individual, peer group, family and community trajectories. As we have seen, the majority of the RS youth remained in surrounding villages after high school. Social networks, more than school-based skills, determined who received scarce local jobs, and those who received 'good jobs' used bilingualism and biliteracy to broker varying power relations and discourses in village institutions. As RS group members left school and moved full-time into the adult life of Piniq, many reported using more Yup'ik than in high school; a few individuals also uncloaked linguistic competences, activating receptive skills to speak Yup'ik. Not surprisingly, youth who spoke the least Yup'ik and were the most marginalized within Piniq, like Mark above, were most likely to move away and challenge community discourses about the importance of Yup'ik maintenance. Even these youth, however, voiced ideological crosscurrents when discussing language endangerment.

Between 1992 and 2001, RS group members also evidenced, witnessed and participated in the beginnings of rapid sociolinguistic transformation in Piniq. In 1995, individuals who had moved from or back and forth to English-speaking places felt insecure about speaking Yup'ik with peers. Most RS youth also expressed linguistic insecurities about writing in Yup'ik. RS group members' youthful experimentation and stylistic performances in English played little direct role in language shift. Nevertheless, many RS youth who spoke Yup'ik with peers and older adults reported using more English with children in Piniq in 2000–2001 'since that's what they understand nowadays'. In the following chapters, we will further trace how changes in schooling, migration, language socialization and language ideologies drove the 'tip' into English among the following group of GB youth. We will also trace how GB youth culture emerged as a driving force of language 'tip' in Piniq, transforming family and community language use in its wake.

5   Family Language Socialization in a Shifting Context

On the 2000 census, 91% of Piniq community members reported that they used a language other than English – Yup'ik – at home. Yet, as we have seen, many educators in the local school questioned these figures. Looking at the dropping Yup'ik test scores and diminishing Yup'ik productive skills of young children entering school, educators quickly pointed out that the census figures did not distinguish whether children were *exposed to* Yup'ik, or *spoken to* in Yup'ik. Educators also worried that parents were no longer speaking Yup'ik to children at home, and shifting the responsibility for Yup'ik language maintenance to the school.

If the educators' assertions were true, their fears were well founded. Other populations have put resources into formal schooling in an endangered language with little impact on everyday linguistic practices of young people. Language shift scholars also warn that heritage language programs in school can backfire if community members assume that youth are learning their heritage languages at school and stop using heritage languages in intergenerational communication in nonschool spaces (Fishman, 1991; Krauss, 1980). Yet, there were problems with these assertions. First was the assumption that parents either simply *did* or *did not* speak Yup'ik to children at home. As we will see below, during early language tip in Piniq, a very small number of families spoke only English, more spoke only Yup'ik, but an equally large number of families spoke both Yup'ik and English at home.

By making assumptions about parents' choices, educators also underestimated the degree to which (1) school practices intersected with community language practices; and (2) youth themselves shaped emerging patterns of language socialization and language shift. Historically, language acquisition studies have focused primarily on how adult caregivers shape young children's language use through one-on-one interactions. However, as studies of language socialization and human development demonstrate, young people's language use develops through multilayered and multidirectional processes. Individuals, including small children, contribute to developing patterns of socialization, even as they learn through their participation in contexts and activities (Garrett & Baquedano-Lopez, 2002; Heath, 1983; Rogoff, 2003; Schieffelin & Ochs, 1986). The language 'choices' of children can also profoundly shape parents' attempts to maintain Indigenous languages at home.

In light of these findings, scholars are reconceptualizing how parents, children and older youth coconstruct family language use in response to changing language learning opportunities and language ideologies in Indigenous communities (e.g. Kulick, 1992; McCarty et al., 2009). In this chapter, we will look longitudinally at emerging patterns of family language use in Piniq, using quantitative and qualitative data to tease apart and examine individual, sibling, peer and family language socialization trajectories during language shift. Section I compares profiles of families with children in the Real Speaker (RS) and/or the Get By (GB) group, situating these profiles historically in relation to changes in school language programming and migration discussed in previous chapters.

Section II looks more closely at parents' on the ground experiences and acts of linguistic survivance as they tried to maintain Yup'ik as a home language during early language shift. By considering the cases of two families, we will see how siblings socialized one another, undermining and/or supporting parents' initial choices to teach their children Yup'ik. By situating each family within their respective extended families, we will also document how parents' and children's everyday language choices accumulated across nuclear families over time, shaping language shift and pockets of Yup'ik language maintenance during the community's rapid 'tip' into increasing English use.

Importantly, throughout the chapter, we will see how changes in local peer culture and related forms of sibling and peer language socialization strongly mediated parents' home language maintenance efforts, as wide-ranging pressures and doubts about bilingualism began to transform the village linguistic ecology as a whole.

Section I: Diminishing Resources, Emerging Contingencies and Ongoing Choices

Family decisions about home language use are not one-time decisions. Studies of immigrant families demonstrate how family-level decisions for heritage language use 'must be constantly reaffirmed, often in the face of opposition ... even in areas where conditions seem to favor language maintenance' (Bayley & Schechter, 2005: 45) such as communities where adults commonly use a heritage language. Within contemporary Indigenous communities, as well, such decisions must be constantly reaffirmed, as families negotiate changing language learning opportunities and assumptions about language within complex, dynamic linguistic ecologies.

Chapter 3 documented how, between the RS and the GB groups, the local school changed the primary language of elementary instruction from Yup'ik to English, and how, very shortly after this change, adults noted how school-aged children in the GB group used increasing amounts of English with one another. Yet, educators also noted how growing groups of children were speaking mostly English before they came to school, while other small children and school-aged youth continued to speak Yup'ik regularly and comfortably.

Based on students' school assessment data and observations in 2000, families of GB youth could be categorized into three groups: (1) 'strong Yup'ik-speaking', families in which all children used extended Yup'ik discourse with family and friends, and family members generally restricted English use for encounters with non-Yup'ik-speaking individuals; (2) 'non-Yup'ik-speaking', families in which no children spoke Yup'ik; and (3) 'Yup'ik-and English-speaking', families in which some siblings spoke Yup'ik comfortably, and some spoke mostly English. In 2000–2001, the breakdown of these groups was roughly as shown in Table 5.1.

In Table 5.1, we see little evidence that families in Piniq were simply choosing to speak English to their children. In contrast, even as Piniq's shift to English became increasingly apparent community-wide, the number of families in which all children spoke mostly English was very small. All children spoke Yup'ik in roughly half of the families in Piniq. In another group of families, some children spoke Yup'ik comfortably, while others spoke mostly English.

Table 5.1 GB families

Type	Number	%
Strong Yup'ik-speaking families	34	51
Yup'ik and English-speaking families	25	37
Non-Yup'ik-speaking families	8	12
Total number of GB families overall	67	100

Such broad family classifications, however, obscure the ways that adults and children were negotiating shared and varied language-learning opportunities within social relationships over time. Longitudinal studies within immigrant communities highlight how life's varying circumstances affect wide-ranging types of individual and family bilingualism (Valdés, 1996; Zentella, 1997). By further disaggregating the data above, we will see how families' experiences with home language maintenance and shift in Piniq depended upon particular constellations of individuals within both nuclear and extended families. We will also begin to trace how the school's change to English instruction, increasing migration and reverberating changes within sibling and peer interactions began to strongly influence the outcomes of parents' attempts to maintain Yup'ik at home.

Strong Yup'ik-speaking families: Sibling and peer language socialization as an 'acid test' for heritage language maintenance

In Piniq, during rapid language shift, local adults, educators, and youth took note of younger families with multiple children who spoke Yup'ik, and young children who spoke Yup'ik, since these families were becoming the exception. In the 34 strong Yup'ik-speaking families, parents spoke Yup'ik to each other; parents spoke Yup'ik to the children; children responded to parents in Yup'ik; and children spoke Yup'ik to one other. More often than not, children from strong Yup'ik-speaking families spoke Yup'ik with friends in their peer groups, as well. As we will see in later chapters, GB aged youth from these families often used Yup'ik as a language of status in front of their non-Yup'ik-speaking peers, even as they sometimes accommodated peers by speaking English. Young children from these families, in contrast, sometimes hid their Yup'ik skills from peers in 2000, as we will see below.

From the outside it might have appeared as if the strong Yup'ik-speaking families were merely reproducing Yup'ik language socialization practices of yesteryear, or that parents were using the same language socialization practices that they had used with the RS group members a few years prior. If such was the case, all one would have to do to support language maintenance would be to look at what these families were doing right, and reproduce these patterns within younger families and the community at large to stem language shift. However, as we will see below, in 2000, all Piniq families were increasingly affected by changes in the local linguistic ecology.

While there were lessons to be learned from parents in the strong Yup'ik-speaking families, by distinguishing between (1) families with multiple children and families with one child; and (2) families whose children spanned the RS and GB group versus families whose children were GB group and younger, we can begin to understand the multidirectional nature of language socialization and families' emerging challenges during rapid language shift. Table 5.2 further demonstrates how younger families with multiple children GB age and younger, in particular, were impacted by the 'tip' into English in local peer culture.

Roughly a fifth of all strong Yup'ik-speaking families in 2000–2001 were families in which single children lived with either an older parent or a grandparent. The few children in these families generally learned Yup'ik well in a sustained dyad with an elderly relative. Community members working to learn languages with only a few speakers currently use similar dyads to foster heritage language learning within one-to-one relationships with elders, as in the Breath of Life workshops described elsewhere (Hinton, 1994). Recent research on immigrant bilingualism in urban settings, as well, shows how grandparents who are caregivers serve as key resources for developing children's knowledge of their heritage language and culture, even as grandparent–child relationships are coconstructed intergenerationally across multiple languages, literacies, activities and types of knowledge (Kenner *et al.*, 2007: 238).

Families' main challenge in early language shift, however, lay in sustaining Yup'ik as the language of intergenerational communication with multiple siblings. In general, as we will see below, during early language shift, children's sibling and peer language socialization had a large influence on parents' efforts to maintain Yup'ik at home.

Transitional RS and GB families

As we can see in Table 5.2, roughly a third of the strong Yup'ik-speaking families were transitional families, or families with older children in the RS group. In four such families, single youth in the GB group represented the last members of a large family of RS children. While from the outside it looked as if parents in these families were successfully maintaining Yup'ik, even some

Table 5.2 Strong Yup'ik-speaking families by subtype

Subtype	Number	% of strong Yup'ik-speaking families
GB families with a single child	6	18
Transitional families, with RS and GB children	11	32
GB families with multiple children	14	41
Unclassifiable	3	9
Total	34	100

of these parents spoke of increasing pressures on Yup'ik home language maintenance, as Janet, a parent with RS and GB aged children described:

LTW: When your kids were small, you spoke to them in Yup'ik and English or Yup'ik then English.

Janet: Yup'ik. When they were small they didn't really learn English till they started going to school. I didn't really believe in raising my kids speaking English.

LTW: Why did you, do you remember why you thought you wanted them to be raised in Yup'ik?

Janet: I didn't really think about it, like I didn't know how bad our language was going to be dropped, later on, and I didn't think to raise them speaking English, cause I was raised speaking Yup'ik. [...] With the older boys, it was all Yup'ik. They spoke in Yup'ik all the time. But speaking didn't mean they could understand everything. Like, if I asked them to do something, or talk to them, if they didn't understand what I was saying I would have to translate it into English, and then they would understand what I was saying. Even if I spoke Yup'ik all the time, they didn't really have a good comprehension of the Yup'ik language. They still don't. [She gives an example of a command they wouldn't understand, discussed below]

LTW: To you it seems like English is more understandable?

Janet: Yah to them, sometimes. Not all of it, though. They can understand a lot of it because they grew up with us speaking Yup'ik, but now their generations, starting with [Name of first sibling in the GB group] maybe? They speak, most of the kids they speak to them in English. Our Yup'ik language is shot. So, so, sad, it's really sad.

LTW: What do you think made it change like that?

Janet: My generation, there were some people who wanted to bring up their kids, well, I guess from watching TV, reading books, you know just about everywhere else they go, speak in English. And I guess nowadays speaking in English is faster than speaking in Yup'ik.

LTW: Hmm.

Janet: For them to understand.

LTW: Hmm, faster somehow.

Janet: Faster in comprehension.   (3/17/01)

As Janet describes above, and as we saw in the previous chapter, when RS youth were growing up, after experiencing historical abuse for speaking Yup'ik in school, the mother in one early family began to speak English to her children, as did a small number of white teachers who married into Piniq. Yet, most youth in the RS group spoke Yup'ik at home until they went to school. Almost all young people in the RS group used Yup'ik as a first language. Families were not particularly conscious about maintaining boundaries between Yup'ik and English. Parents occasionally switched to English while speaking to their children, although Yup'ik remained the primary language of the home. When the RS group were children, the idea that the Yup'ik language might, in the words of Janet, be 'dropped, later on' was far from parents' minds.

As members of the Real Speaker group, Janet's older children received early instruction in Yup'ik, and then transitioned into English classrooms after third grade. Janet's story in one form or another was voiced repeatedly in the study, especially among younger families. Parents started out speaking in Yup'ik to children, doing what came naturally to them as Yup'ik speakers who had been socialized in Yup'ik. Later, when children who received school instruction in English came home evidencing bilingual skills, however, when faced with instances of intergenerational miscommunication, parents tended to assume the problem stemmed from Yup'ik language comprehension. Janet described how she found herself sometimes accommodating her children in English.

Elsewhere in the interview, Janet also described how she found herself adjusting to ongoing changes in her children's Yup'ik language use. Many Indigenous languages have specific and elaborate deictic forms for indicating direction. In Yup'ik, an elegant demonstrative system of pronouns, adverbs and related verb stems meaning 'to go (in some specific direction)', marks a highly tuned orientation to the speaker's surroundings (Woodbury, 1993, 1998; Wyman, 2009). In multiple interviews, community members and youth commented on young people's loss of the Yup'ik demonstrative system right before and especially during language shift. Mark, the RS youth quoted in Chapter 4, for instance, called demonstrative pronouns 'hard to understand' 'strong words'. An elder from a third family described how her granddaughter could not understand simple requests involving Yup'ik demonstratives, and how, as a result, she had started using her minimal English, versus Yup'ik, with her.

Here Janet described how she struggled with her RS children's seeming noncomprehension of Yup'ik demonstratives:

Janet: With my kids Wes and Charlie, when they were growing up they always spoke Yup'ik and I always spoke Yup'ik to them until they went to school. Once they started school they couldn't fully understand what I said, like if I said *'Tauna mayurrluku ingna-llu* *acianun elliluku'* (*Put up that one near you and put the one over there away from both of us under it*), I had to translate [. . .]

LTW: So what happened if you asked Wes and Charlie to do that, can they do it?

Janet: They can do it, but they don't understand the concept. I have to talk slow, like [Pointing] *'Ingna book-aq'* (*that book there away from both of us*), *tangvagcellua* (*making them look at me*), [Pointing to something else] *'Ingna-llu acianun elliluku* (*and put that over there away from both of us, under it*).'* I have to point and talk very slow. If I say it in a moderate speed they'll say '*Ca? Ca piluku?*' (*What? Do what to it?*) *Waten pirraarlua* (*I do like this first*) [Pointing].

By the time Janet's younger children in the GB group entered kindergarten, the primary language of local elementary school instruction was English. As Janet and her husband socialized their GB children, she noticed dramatic changes in local peer culture, and became concerned about how 'our Yup'ik was (being) dropped', stating 'our Yup'ik language is shot'. She also increasingly assumed that 'nowadays' English must be 'easier' or 'faster' for children's comprehension.

Janet and her husband continued to speak Yup'ik to their children, and each of their children tested as fluent Yup'ik speakers in school, used Yup'ik at home, enjoyed close relationships in Yup'ik with grandparents, and used extended Yup'ik comfortably with peers. Yet, as Janet's youngest children reached adolescence, she commented: 'It's like we are being suckered into speaking English with them when we should be forcing them to speak to us in Yup'ik.' Janet's feeling that she was getting 'suckered into' speaking English with her children against her will was shared by other parents in families with youth in the RS and GB group, as well as parents in younger families with all GB youth.

Nevertheless parents, adults, older RS siblings and siblings' friends in transitional families spoke Yup'ik to younger GB children. Younger GB children in these families also spoke Yup'ik comfortably later as youth. The only transitional families in which younger siblings did not speak extended Yup'ik comfortably in 2000 were four families who had migrated to and from, or simply from English-speaking places.

Sibling and peer language socialization within nuclear and extended families

Commonly, the eldest children of bilingual families develop relatively strong heritage language skills through one-on-one interaction with caregivers (for a review of related research, see Shin, 2002). Recent studies in immigrant communities, however, have documented how older children, upon reaching school age and receiving instruction in another language, socialize younger siblings to start speaking that language before they reach school age (Fishman, 1991; Shin, 2002; Wong-Fillmore, 2000). Scholars have also noted similar birth order effects in contemporary Indigenous communities where children are schooled in English (McCarty, 2004).

Birth order had little impact on RS group members' language use. Yet, shortly after the school reintroduced English as the primary language of elementary instruction, younger families increasingly began to evidence common patterns of family language shift elsewhere. In the Yup'ik- and English-speaking GB families who remained in Piniq, oldest siblings generally developed good productive spoken skills in Yup'ik and used these with friends. Younger siblings generally maintained a strong base of Yup'ik receptive skills, and could 'get by' with adults by following Yup'ik directives, and responding to Yup'ik questions with relatively simple, and/or predictable Yup'ik phrases. However, younger siblings in GB families also spoke mostly English, infrequently used extended utterances in Yup'ik, and described linguistic insecurities around speaking Yup'ik.

Researchers strengthen their analyses of resource distribution within Yup'ik villages by considering groups of related nuclear families (Fienup-Riordan, 2000), and this generalization holds for the distribution of families' linguistic resources for heritage language maintenance. Fourteen of the strong Yup'ik-speaking families with school-aged children in 2000 (41%) had multiple children all the age of the GB group or younger. In the large bulk of these families, peer language socialization within extended families supported heritage language maintenance, as we see in Table 5.3.

When the GB group was growing up, early peer socialization clusters – regular friendship networks of children beyond siblings – increasingly predicted whether young children would speak Yup'ik comfortably with peers later on as older youth. While children were generally discouraged from 'visiting around too much', children in many families spent much of their free

Table 5.3 Nontransitional GB strong Yup'ik-speaking families with multiple children

Subtype	Number
With Yup'ik-speaking cousins	11
From a strong Yup'ik-speaking village	2
Unclassifiable	1

time growing up visiting with or being watched by cousins. During early language shift, such chance groupings of cousins had a strong mediating influence on parents' attempts to raise their children as Yup'ik speakers. The young children in the large majority of strong Yup'ik-speaking families with multiple children in the GB age range were in Yup'ik-speaking cousin clusters. A small number of families had moved to Piniq from other strong Yup'ik-speaking villages with older, Yup'ik-speaking youth.

Increasing migration

As Chapter 3 documents, before the 'tip' toward English in local youth culture, a small number of parents began to speak English to RS children. Elementary schooling and a local peer culture in Yup'ik helped those individuals seemingly 'pick up' and speak Yup'ik later as older youth. A small number of RS children also migrated back and forth to English-speaking places. These youth, in contrast, generally described how they felt too insecure to speak Yup'ik upon their return to Piniq. They also did not use extended Yup'ik later as older youth with peers.

During the 1980s, increasing numbers of children flowed back and forth to English-speaking places with parents. Increasing numbers of adults who grew up in English-speaking places married into Piniq, as well, raising their children locally so they could learn subsistence, live near family, and grow up in what was often described as a safe village setting. Between the RS and GB groups, the percentage of students affected one or both of these two kinds of mobility increased from an average of 17% to close to 35% per grade level. Thus, language socialization patterns miles away, and refracting effects of language shift elsewhere in the region increased pressures on local language socialization practices in Piniq, just as the local school scaled back its use of Yup'ik instruction.

Migration did not impact all families the same way. When children and young people in transnational immigrant communities migrate to heritage language speaking countries, they often strengthen their heritage language skills (Zentella, 1997). Movement back and forth to strong Yup'ik-speaking villages shaped pockets of Yup'ik language maintenance in Piniq during language shift. Following district efforts to support bilingual education, a number of villages also increased Yup'ik language instruction in the 1990s, providing Yup'ik as the main language of elementary instruction through at least grade 2 (Wyman et al., 2010b). For Yup'ik children who spent time in strong Yup'ik-speaking villages and/or stronger Yup'ik language programs elsewhere, family migration extended children's opportunities for learning Yup'ik beyond the physical boundaries of Piniq.

Mothers in two of the strongest Yup'ik-speaking young families in 2000–2001, for instance, were sisters from a strong Yup'ik-speaking village who brought their young children home for more than two weeks roughly every other month. During these trips, the cousins from Piniq socialized primarily with other cousins who spoke Yup'ik. When they returned, their children also sustained their Yup'ik by playing with one another.

Even relatively short stints to villages with strong Yup'ik-speaking peer cultures and Yup'ik school programs could increase young children's use of spoken Yup'ik with peers, as will see in family 1's case below. Unlike learners connecting to countries with stable heritage languages, however, children and youth from Piniq migrated to and from villages in an Indigenous region where language shift was already well underway, and children spoke Yup'ik in roughly one out of four Yup'ik villages by 1995 (Krauss, 1997). While many Piniq families had ties to strong Yup'ik-speaking villages, it was more common for families to travel to the English-speaking hub towns of Bethel or the larger city of Anchorage for work or education.

Above, we have seen how parents' choices to maintain Yup'ik at home were supported by some form of sibling and/or peer language socialization in Yup'ik in almost all of the strong Yup'ik-speaking families with multiple children, and children in the GB age group. The unusual language socialization trajectories below, on the other hand, evidence how multiple language learning contingencies together shaped unique children's and families' experiences over time.

Considering unusual language socialization trajectories in light of multiple contingencies

In some ways, the many types of people flows, and family circumstances playing out in permanent and temporary caregiving situations made Piniq an ideal place for considering how multiple contingencies jointly shaped children's bilingualism within atypical, as well as typical language socialization trajectories. In one case, a middle child in an otherwise strong Yup'ik-speaking family had lived with a parent in an English-speaking town for a few years as a young child, then moved back to live with his grandparents in Piniq. The child's siblings, who had stayed in Piniq, used Yup'ik confidently with adults and peers. In 2000–2001, however, the child who had moved away described feeling too insecure to speak Yup'ik with his peer group, and used mostly token amounts of Yup'ik framed in English discourse with friends.

In contrast, a younger sibling in one family, Jill, showed particularly high skills in Yup'ik as a result of a temporary move to a strong Yup'ik-speaking village elsewhere. When it was discovered that Jill's grandmother had cancer, three-year-old Jill was sent to live with extended family members in a neighboring village to keep her company. Jill maintained close ties with her nuclear family, calling her siblings and parents every night over a marine radio system. When Jill missed her siblings, she visited Piniq for a few weeks, returning to the other village when her grandmother missed her. During her visits home, Jill's family pointed out how Jill had become a stronger Yup'ik speaker than her older siblings, who asked Jill for Yup'ik words when they interacted with me in Yup'ik.

By considering multiple contingencies within atypical cases, we can also see how specific friendship groups affected how much Yup'ik individuals in the GB group 'picked up' over time after moving to Piniq from English-speaking places. One GB brother and sister who were close in age had lived in Bethel for a few years. In an interview in 2000, their mother, Kendra, described how she had tried to go to college, but had a hard time after having written only one paper in high school. When Kendra lived in an urban area, she thought that speaking English would help her children in school. After moving back to Piniq and witnessing Yup'ik-speaking youth doing well in school, Kendra regretted speaking in English to her children, and stated that she would enroll them in Yup'ik immersion if she could. Kendra reported that her daughter picked up Yup'ik from friends when she returned from spending her first few years in Bethel. Some of those same youth dated her daughter's return to Piniq as the point when they themselves switched into English. Her older brother, on the other hand, returned to friends who spoke mostly English. At the time of the study, he had yet to pick up the Yup'ik tokenism regularly employed by his younger sister.

In the following chapters, we will focus further on GB young people's linguistic negotiations in local youth culture. In Section II, however, we will continue to document the reverberating effects of schooling and a changing local peer culture within family life. Specifically, we will look more closely at how parents negotiated sibling and peer language socialization in a rapidly changing linguistic ecology, making evolving choices about home language practices.

Section II: A Closer Look into Family Language Socialization

During early language shift, parents made ongoing language socialization choices, negotiating heterogeneous sets of linguistic resources, emerging patterns of language use and assumptions about bilingualism as their children interacted with siblings and peers in extended family networks.

Many also took active steps to socialize their children to interact with adults in locally acceptable ways, and maintain Yup'ik. Only some parents, however, were able to sustain Yup'ik as the primary language of home life over time. Community members also had questions about linguistic boundary maintenance during language shift as they witnessed adults' and children's hybrid linguistic practices.

Family 1

Jeff and Megan, the parents of family 1, described wanting their children to know Yup'ik. When their first child, James, was born, they also became locally known for their efforts to speak only Yup'ik to James. At the time of the study, Yup'ik children were commonly expected to be potty trained before they started talking, and were not expected to speak extended Yup'ik productively before age three, before which time they were considered *ellangumanrituq* 'he/she is not aware'. By the time James was two, he responded appropriately to predictable adult-initiated greeting routines and questions with young Yup'ik children (e.g. Crago *et al.*, 1993). When an adult or elder said '*cama-i*' (*shake hands*), for instance, James would present his hand quietly, as was expected. When James was 3, during a visit, Megan also displayed his Yup'ik by asking '*kituusit?*' (*what's your name?*) and *kitugaa* (*what's his/her name?*) pointing to his younger brother.

Young bilingual children commonly start codeswitching by inserting single words and phrases, often as tags or exclamations, into utterances, especially in cases where languages have very different grammatical systems like Yup'ik and English (Reyes & Ervin-Tripp, 2010; see also Allen, 2007). While Jeff and Megan spoke to James primarily in Yup'ik, they noted how they themselves sometimes incorporated words in English:

LTW: And was he learning English around the same time, or that came later.

Megan: That came later. I don't know what made ... either it was me, because I would say things like 'look' or yeh, mostly 'look', and when I did that Jeff would say not to say it in English, say it in Yup'ik instead. But I don't know, I guess I was used to saying small words in English like 'look' or 'don't' or 'no' stuff like that.

Home language socialization in Inuit communities, as elsewhere, has been influenced by school language uses over time (Crago *et al.*, 1993). Numbers and colors follow different systems in Yup'ik and English (for a description of the Yup'ik numerals, see Lipka *et al.*, 1998). They are also related to societal messages about early school readiness skills and quotidian interactions in schools. Locally, in Piniq, community members commonly described how these systems were 'easier' in English, and Megan used English with James as she taught him numbers and the names of colors. While Megan taught James to recognize the Yup'ik used in another predictable greeting for small children at the time, *'qavcircit?'* (*how old are you?*), James responded with English numbers, like many other children in Piniq.

As we see Megan's statement above, even in cases when parents used only very minimal amounts of English, their own codeswitching could leave them wondering about the possibilities of Yup'ik language maintenance, and how they themselves might be contributing to family and community-wide language shift. However, as we will see below, such minimal uses of English for tags, content words, and colors and numbers did not in and of themselves lead to family language shift.

In addition to paying attention to their own interactions with James, Jeff and Megan also asked others to speak to him only in Yup'ik. This effort, however, proved to be more challenging. Multiple studies have demonstrated how even very young bilingual children are attuned to the language preferences of the speakers around them, and how children learn not only from their parents, but also from their 'siblings and peers how to make use of both languages in conversation and with whom' (Reyes & Ervin-Tripp, 2010: 68). Megan and Jeff restricted James' physical movement within the village, adhering to Jeff's mother's teaching not to *cenirtaaq* (*visit around*) too much. They also made a house rule that James' older cousins, Emily and Johnny, had to speak Yup'ik when they came over to play.

Although Emily and Johnny's parents spoke to them primarily in Yup'ik, they were younger siblings in a large family. As we will see, Emily and Johnny spoke predominantly English, though they understood and could speak 'survival Yup'ik' to get by with adults. As a slightly older GB youth, Emily also sometimes used codeswitching for rhetorical purposes.

In spite of Megan and Jeff's overt requests and guidelines for home language use, James adopted a pattern where he would switch to whatever language he thought his peers used more by age 3. As Megan reflected in an interview:

When he (James) was growing up, his cousins were mostly around, too, and they were speaking mostly in English? The cousins, what, when I think about it, to this day, I think to this day, because of Jeff, when the cousins would come around he would tell them to speak Yup'ik, and they'd become pretty good in Yup'ik, the cousins ... and they became good in Yup'ik and he (James) became good in English.

Around the same time, Jeff noted how James was picking up English phrases from the TV. In a phone conversation, he described the influence of TV and videos on James, 'My son is monolingual Yup'ik,' he told me, 'but will talk English because Buzz Light Year spoke it. If that's how easy it is for my son to acquire that medium, imagine how easy it is in a house where the family speaks English!'

Nevertheless, James' parents still socialized him as a Yup'ik speaker. By the time James was four, Megan reported, he 'was pretty good at telling stories, like maybe about his dreams, or what happened, or what he remembers in the past. He could speak in sentences.' James also continued to use Yup'ik as his main language at home, showing a keen awareness of the language preference of his parents as well as his peers and characters on TV (e.g. Shin, 2002).

Entry into school as a family turning point

Jeff and Megan's temporary success fostering James' home Yup'ik use changed when James entered kindergarten and began to intensely experience the influence of English-speaking peers, as Megan describes here:

> And then he went to school. And then, when he was in kindergarten, he spoke more English, and then English became stronger since then. From kindergarten through ... when he got into first grade, we would try to encourage him to speak Yup'ik, but he didn't want to because his classmates are speaking English and he didn't want to do that. I mean, he even said it like, 'No, I'm not gonna do that because of this person.'

Families in immigrant and Indigenous communities report the entry of an oldest child into school as a common tipping point in family language shift (McCarty, 2002; Shin, 2002; Wong-Fillmore, 2000). Scholars have also documented how elementary programs in nonheritage languages may have a subtractive effect on children's development of their heritage language, as well as second language development. For instance, one study tracked young children's language development in an Inuit community in the Eastern arctic over a period of three years. Separate groups of children in the study received K–2 instruction in Inuktitut, English or French. Children in the study who received Inuktitut instruction in their elementary years emerged with stronger skills in their heritage language as well as the dominant language. Starting the *very first year of school*, children in same community with the same incoming proficiency in Inuktitut also varied in their Inuktitut conversational proficiency and academic language development. For *each of the three years of the study*, the Inuktitut language gap increased between the groups of children receiving Inuktitut versus dominant language instruction (Wright *et al.*, 2000).

These findings mirror the scholarly literature on the subtractive effects of dominant language programming in Native American communities (Romero-Little & McCarty, 2006). In one Navajo study, for instance, students who received English language instruction actually scored *lower* on assessments of heritage language as fourth graders than they had as incoming kindergarteners, as well as lower on English tests than their counterparts with Navajo immersion instruction (Holm & Holm, 1995, reported in McCarty, 2004).

As researchers note, however, it is difficult to disentangle school, community and peer effects on language development. When James entered a school language program in English, he became best friends with another English-speaking child. James was also old enough to spend more time out of the house with Emily and Johnny, his English-speaking cousins. Thus, he was exposed to both more English in school and more English within peer interactions. Of course, in Piniq at the time, as we have seen, those peers, as well, were being instructed in English.

James' 'tip' into English within his individual language socialization trajectory also increased his younger siblings' exposure to English in the home, as we will consider here.

James and Ben: Sibling influence and family language shift

When James was two, his younger brother Ben was born, and their little sister, Ricky, was born two years later. When I started regularly observing family 1, James, Ben and Ricky were ages seven, five and three. Jeff and Megan described Ben's early attempts at speech as *pikagteq* – a Yup'ik term for speakers who make common developmental mistakes mispronouncing words, such as failing to distinguish front velars from back velars (e.g. using k sound instead of the hard back velar, q), or to distinguish velar voiced and voiceless fricatives (g and gg,) from corresponding voiced and voiceless back velar fricatives (r and rr).

In the fall of 2000, at age 5, Ben generally responded with a range of avoidance behaviors when Jeff and Megan asked him to speak Yup'ik. He often chose not to respond to Megan and Jeff's requests, and many families had stories of younger children remaining silent when they were told '*Yugtun*' (*speak in Yup'ik*). Since remaining silent could be interpreted as *takaryuk* (*shy/respectful*) behavior, commonly, parents let it pass. At other times, Ben simply responded with a silly sound (e.g. 'Pbbbt') and a laugh.

Megan and James described how Ben's early development of Yup'ik was not as strong as his older brother's:

Megan: Seems like Ben … (was) not very good in Yup'ik even when he was growing up. Because when Ben started speaking, James was speaking more English, and they spent most times together, and seems like Ben was learning more English than he was Yup'ik .

Megan described how James started out borrowing single English words into Yup'ik statements, a pattern common among strong Yup'ik-speaking adults and children, as we have seen already and as we will continue to see below. The word ending, –(a)q, is used for turning Yup'ik verb bases into stand-alone words, and for attaching Yup'ik morphology onto English words (Jacobson, 1995). In 2000, like many other children and youth who spoke mostly English in Piniq, Ben often codeswitched by borrowing one Yup'ik cognate into an otherwise English sentence, using the –(a)q ending to bring new hybrid Yup'ik 'words' into English statements, as we see in this example:

Ben: Man, Jules keep on … *uqla-q.*
Translation: Man, Jules keep on … *'to make messy'* –(a)q
Gloss: Man, Jules keeps on … *making a mess.*

At age five, Ben mostly played with his siblings and cousins, and he always wanted to play with his big brother. When James was at school, Ben would wait for him, periodically asking Megan:

Ben: Ma, how time James *taqa-q*?
Translation: Ma, how time James *'to finish'* –(a)q?
Gloss: Ma, what time does James finish?

At age seven, James noted his daily influence over his younger brother's use of English. The following discussion with James, Ben, Megan and me took place as we ate ice cream one Sunday night at their grandmother's house:

LTW: How did you learn Yup'ik?
James: From growing up.
Megan: *Waten, (Like this)* I learned Yup'ik from my family, from my friends.

LTW: How did you learn English?
James: I was born.
LTW: How did Ben learn English?
James: From me! [pointing to himself] He copied me.

Above, as would be expected, James has only vague ideas about how he developed his own language skills. Nevertheless, he was quick to point out how his own use of English shaped his brothers' language use.

Much of Ben's language input came from interacting with older children, or attending to snippets of conversations between family members. The following excerpt was one of many instances where Ben tried out his older brother's words as James talked with Megan. These repetitions were most often in English, as in the following interaction, when James tried to get a glass from a high cabinet while Megan watched and Ben ate nearby:

James: Man, I'm thirsty.
Ben: Man, I'm thirsty.
James: [getting up on the counter] I can hardly get them, look [going after the glasses]
Ben: I can hardly get them, look.
Megan: James, *atraa!* (James, *get down*!) [laughing as she gets the glasses from the cabinet] It's hard enough for me.
Ben: It's hard enough for me.

Above, we can see how Ben used selective repetition, repeating everything James and Megan said in English, except for Megan's Yup'ik command. In 2000, Jeff and Megan were also expressing concern about 3-year-old Ricky's language development.

Ricky

Jeff and Megan referred to Ricky as a 'tomboy', and described how she would not put up with anything from her older brothers. When James and Ben tried to roughhouse with Ricky, she would yell back at them, making her parents laugh at her feisty behavior. Like her brothers, Ricky could understand questions and commands in Yup'ik. At age 3, however, she mostly used single Yup'ik words or short statements, like Ben. Jeff and Megan complained it was hard for them to understand her language, and to even know whether Ricky was trying to speak Yup'ik or English, though they assumed she was speaking English.

The chart below highlights patterns in Ricky's typical utterances in fall 2000:

English utterances	Yup'ik utterances
I gonna pee on you	*Taitai (Come)*
My dish, my cup	*Kiiki (Hurry up)*
It's hide in there	*Taisgu (Give it to me)*
It's always going in there	*Aug'a (Get out of the way)*

Overall, parents' and teachers' biggest concern was how quickly Yup'ik children seemed to lose confidence and skills 'creating' in Yup'ik as an agglutinating language beyond formulaic utterances. As we see above, Ricky could use English words and word order to create new meanings. In contrast, her Yup'ik utterances tended to be short directives that were commonly heard in caregiver–child talk.

Parents' codeswitching in interaction with children

Codeswitching is common among many bilingual adults, and can demonstrate high levels of linguistic skill and creativity, as we saw with the New Year's Day jokes in Chapter 2. Yet, codeswitching in bilingual communities and homes can also sometimes obscure how nonheritage languages can crowd out spaces for heritage language learning within accumulating face-to-face interactions over time (Kulick, 1992; Lanza, 1997). In cases where language shift is closing spaces for heritage language use community-wide, codeswitching in parent–child interactions can also reduce children's opportunities for trying out heritage language vocabulary and grammatical constructions, especially in cases where the overall grammatical frame for language use is changing from a heritage language to a majority language among children, as in the Piniq case (Baker, 2006; see also Myers-Scotton, 1998).

Megan would direct requests to Ricky solely in Yup'ik, yet she would also commonly use the –a(*q*) ending above to inflect English words with Yup'ik postbases and word endings. The excerpt below and similar examples demonstrated how the use of English loans for everyday words was commonplace among caregiver speech to children, and how children were encouraged to interpret and reproduce patterned codeswitching under the guise of 'talking Yup'ik'. At the same time, as we see below, children could also subvert parents' and others' attempts to support Yup'ik maintenance in such exchanges, responding with a minimal English answer or action. [Note: Original interaction appears on the left, translations on the right.]

1 **LTW:**	Ricky *qavciqsit?*	Ricky *how old are you?*
2 **Megan:**	How old-*arcit? Qavcircit?* Show-*aqerru.*	How old *are you? How old are you?* Show *her.*

3 **Ricky:**	Noo=	Noo=
4 **LTW:**	=*Qavcircit?*	=*How old are you?*
5 **Megan:**	*Qavcircit?* Show-*aqerru unatevkun Qavcircit?*	*How old are you?* Show *her with your hand. How old are you?*
6 **LTW:**	*Qavcircit?*	*How old are you?*

[Ricky holds up some fingers]

7 **LTW:**	Yeh? Wow …	Yeh? Wow …
8 **Megan:**	*Elpes-mi, waten, waten* 'two'.	*How about you, like this, like this* 'two'.
9 **Ricky:**	ahh	ahh
10 **Megan:**	'Two-*aartua', Waten piqaa,* 'Two-*aartua'.*	'I'm two' *Do like this,* 'I'm two.'
11 **Ricky:**	ooo …	ooo …
12 **LTW:**	Two-*aartuten?/*	*Are you two?*
13 **Megan:**	*Waten,* 'Two'	*Like this,* 'Two'
14 **Ricky:**	Two	Two

In the above example, in line 2, when Ricky did not respond to the common greeting for young children, Megan clued Ricky in about the question by exchanging 'how old' for the base in Yup'ik *qavci-* (*how many*), attaching the second person Yup'ik interrogative ending –*rcit*, followed by a repetition of the whole phrase in Yup'ik. Megan directs Ricky to show her age, this time inflecting the borrowed English verb 'show' with an imperative ending –*qerru*.

After Ricky answered the question by showing her fingers, Megan repeated the request again, trying to get Ricky to inflect an English number as if it were Yup'ik ('two-*aartua*') (line 8–10). I followed along, repeating the statement as a question with a second person ending (line 12). However, perhaps because I had responded to her fingers in line 7, Ricky finally responded with simply the number in English.

Yup'ik, English, and codeswitching in play with siblings

At the time in Piniq, children were generally expected to come up with their own activities. Like many others in Piniq, Jeff and Megan also followed a pattern of nonintervention in the children's play. Locally, the negative term 'ptarmigan mother' alluded to the tendency of female ptarmigans to aggressively defend their eggs, and local adults described how such actions robbed children of important learning opportunities for getting along with peers. Jeff, Megan and other community members explained how, according to Yup'ik beliefs, if a parent stood up for a child too much, protecting him or her from older siblings or peers, that child would then come running for help anytime he or she ran into a problem. Jeff stated that siblings would also get along better in the long run once they learned their place in the pecking order.

Parents and others loosely monitored toddlers, sometimes encouraging them to 'share- *aqerru*'. At times when their children's arguments erupted into loud complaints, Jeff and Megan sometimes intervened with general admonishments to 'Nice-*arluku*' (*Be* nice to *him/her*) or, especially in the case of conflicts between James and Ben, '*Tua-i ingkuuk!*' (*Enough, you two over there!*'). Most often, though, older children, or groups of mixed age children, including toddlers, were typically left alone, and James, Ben and later Ricky's play was self-directed while Jeff and Megan attended their own business.

The following excerpt took place as James, Ben and Ricky played in the family living room one afternoon. James and Ricky used a video camera, although whenever Ricky went to look through the eyepiece, James turned the camera off, making it impossible to see. Ben was playing with cars in the background, yet he also monitored James and Ricky's interaction and participated indirectly with comments.

1 **James:**	[to LTW] I let her think she's broke-ing it.	[to LTW] I let her think she's broke-ing it.
	[James turns it off again as Ricky tries to look through the viewer.]	
2 **Ricky:**	Huh? [whining] Haaa haaa haaa	Huh? [whining] Haaa haaa haaa
3 **James:**	Oh, go home.	Oh, go home.
4 **Ben:**	Oh aahhhh! Hoh hoh hoh hoh who who who	Oh aahhhh! Hoh hoh hoh hoh who who who
	[James turns the camera on for a minute]	
5 **Ricky:**	[Looking through the camera] Mine!	[Looking through the camera] Mine!
6 **James:**	[Turns it off again, moving his hands away] *Piksaitaqa.*	[Turns it off again, moving his hands away] *I never did it.*
7 **Ricky:**	[howling in anger] AAAAAAAHHHHHH!	[howling in anger] AAAAAAAHHHHHH!
8 **Ben:**	Who who who	Who who who

 9 **James:**   [Turns it on] fix-*aq-aqa*   [Turns it on] *I* fixed *it.*
10 **Ben:**   Fix-a-*qa-qaaaa.*   *I* fixed *iiiiiiiit.*
               [Ricky looks through the viewer, able to see]
11 **Ricky:**   Yes!   Yes!
               [James turns the video camera off again]
12 **Ricky:**   Hey! [complaining]   Hey! [complaining]
               AAAAH   AAAAH
               [James and Ricky now both yelling]
13 **James:**   How come he like   How come he like
               to play with it⸮!   to play with it⸮!
14 **Ricky:**   /... that⸮/   /... that⸮/
15 **James:**   /You know/   /You know/
16 **Ben:**   How come he like to   How come he like to
               play with it, how come   play with it, how come
               he like to play with it,   he like to play with it,
               how come he like to   how come he like to
               play with IT!   play with IT!

In the segment above, although he was ostensibly doing his own thing, Ben echoed and mimicked James' English statements and Ricky's sounds, voicing parts of previous words repeatedly (e.g. line 16, and 'hoh hoh hoh' in line 4 after James' statement 'go home'). We also see how Ben repeated James' use of Yup'ik, with the exception of James' one complex Yup'ik utterance (and claim to innocence):

James (line 6):   *Pi-ksait(e)-aqa*
Translation: 'To do' – 'to have not V'd' – word ending (1st singular subject to 3rd singular object transitive indicative)
Gloss: *I never did it.*

The few times Ben repeated Yup'ik grammatical frames from James, these statements typically included English words combined with beginners' attempts at postbases and endings in Yup'ik, as in 'fix-*aq-aqa*', I *fixed it* (correct would be fix-*ar-aqa*) line 9, which Ben exaggerated by extending the final vowel sound in line 10.

Most often, however, the children's interactions with one another were almost entirely in English, with single Yup'ik words appearing in an English frame. Above, we also see how James used a dialect of English common to the Yup'ik region at the time locally referred to as 'village English' (Jacobson, 1984), using 'let' in line 1, as in to 'make' or 'force' someone to do something, and substituting 'he' for 'she' in line 13. In line 16, Ben imitated his brother's use of the 'village English' feature.

Children's codeswitching in the face of demands to 'Yugtun' (speak Yup'ik)

In 2000–2001, Jeff required that his children speak to him in Yup'ik. James could fill this request relatively easily, and often had everyday conversations in Yup'ik with his dad. In one instance, James received directions from his dad in Yup'ik as he learned how to use a computer game. He also made simple requests (e.g. *come with me*, or *show me how to do it*) in Yup'ik, issued simple complaints (e.g.) *'Pisciigatua'* (*I can't do it*), and made suggestions *'Ampi uternaurtukuk'* (*'Come on, let's go home'*) in Yup'ik, showing how he could interact and make himself understood in new situations in Yup'ik.

Like James, Ben used simple, everyday Yup'ik requests with Jeff such as *'Maligcugamken!'* (*I want to go with you!*). In his attempts to get Jeff's attention, Ben also sometimes used English words to cover vocabulary gaps, attaching simple Yup'ik endings to English words to negotiate Jeff's expectation that the children speak Yup'ik. In the following example, Ben tried to get Jeff to scold James during a game:

Ben: Dad, James-*aq* cheat-*arta!*   Dad, James- (*Yup'ik marker*) cheats!

Often James and Ben's attempts to speak at least some Yup'ik would produce the desired effect of earning their father's quick focus. It is difficult to know to what extent James and Ben thought they were successfully 'speaking Yup'ik' when borrowing single words, word endings or codeswitching. Bilingual children often use codeswitching as a communicative tactic (Baker, 2006; Reyes & Ervin-Tripp, 2010). Anecdotal evidence from parents suggested that other young children would try out beginner types of codeswitching, inserting a single word or word ending into English utterances when asked to speak Yup'ik, as in one mother's example:

We speak to her and the other kids in Yup'ik, but they answer in English. Only the oldest can speak Yup'ik. The other day I told Suzy to go tell her Dad that the *akutaq* (*berry and Crisco mixture locally referred to as 'Eskimo ice cream'*) was done, and she came back and said, 'Mom, I said it in Yup'ik!' *'Qaillun?* (*How?*)' 'Dad *akutaq* done,' [laughs].

The mother also described how her daughter tried attaching a common Yup'ik first person to third person possessive ending to a single English word in response to another request to speak Yup'ik:

The other day she said, 'My mom's playing Nintendo,' so I said *'Yugtun.'* (*'In Yup'ik'*) 'Mommy-*qa* (*my* mommy) playing Nintendo.' She also said, 'Dad's in the room.' I said *'Yugtun'* (*'In Yup'ik'*) She said, 'Daddy-*qa* (*my* daddy) is in the room.' When we ask her to speak in Yup'ik, she says, 'I can't.'

Another parent described how, in response to a request to *'Yugtun' (speak Yup'ik)* her young child used the same ending to make a common phrase 'my mother', while also randomly applying additional –*(a)q* endings to make other English words sound Yup'ik:

> The other day she came running in saying, 'Mom, I want a banana, can I have a banana, can I have a banana?' I said, *'Yugtun' ('In Yup'ik')*. She said *'Aanaqa (My mom)* can-*aq* I-*aq* have-*aq* banana-*q*?' [laughs].

Through codeswitching, children sometimes tried out emerging hypotheses about Yup'ik and English as typologically distant languages as they negotiated their parent's requests to *'Yugtun' (speak Yup'ik)*. However, while parents commonly requested that children *'Yugtun'* in Piniq, such creative attempts on the part of children were relatively uncommon. More often, children simply responded to requests to speak Yup'ik by answering in English, or not at all.

Moving in and out of Yup'ik use

James and Ben were most likely to try to produce Yup'ik with their father, who more consistently refused to answer unless they spoke to him in Yup'ik. Jeff's busy schedule meant that he was only infrequently around, however, and the children spent most of their time with Megan. Jeff himself also dropped the Yup'ik requirement periodically, sometimes when talking about something exciting with his children, or, more often, in the name of expediency. In one instance, Jeff made a last minute decision to allow James to come on a boat ride, but the boy needed his raincoat. After Jeff and Megan tried to tell James to get it in Yup'ik, they resorted to telling him in English in an effort to hurry, Jeff noting to me, 'The [Yup'ik] word for raincoat is too long.'

Megan used both Yup'ik and English with the children, maintaining general requests and directives in Yup'ik, and using Yup'ik or English for more lengthy explanations. As we have seen above, however, when speaking Yup'ik, like others her age, Megan often used English words within Yup'ik statements, in a form of codeswitching common in Piniq, the Yup'ik region and Inuktitut-speaking areas elsewhere (Allen, 2007).

In spite of Jeff and Megan's growing perception that Ben and Ricky, especially, were stronger English speakers, they most often scolded all three children in Yup'ik, even in cases where expediency was required. When

Ricky teetered on the edge of a couch, for instance, Jeff and Megan ordered: *'Atraa! Igteqatartuten!* (*Get down! You're gonna fall!*)'

Megan and Jeff also comforted the children in Yup'ik (e.g. Zentella, 2005), as in the following excerpt, which starts when Jeff, James and Ricky were examining the video camera from the example above:

Jeff:	*'Taaki, 'taaki, James.*	*Let me see, let me see, James.*
James:	Hey, it's hard.	Hey, it's hard.
Jeff:	[talking about a video camera part] Look, *twist-aumassiiyaagtuq, u man'a* wire.	[talking about a video camera part] Look, *it's too twisted, this here* wire.

[James doesn't listen and the video camera starts falling off a tripod]

Jeff:	*Igtuq,* hey!	*It's falling,* hey!

[Jeff turns the video camera and it brushes Ricky's eye.]

Ricky:	[howling] HAAA / HAAA HAAA, HAAA HAAA HAAA/	[howling] HAAA / HAAA HAAA, HAAA HAAA HAAA/
Jeff:	*'Taaki, akleng,* look *ellinaurput wavet, wavet, tua-i, kitak tua-i, una-qaa. Wani.*	*Let me see, I'm sorry,* look *we'll put it to here, to here, enough, ok enough, this- huh? Here.*
Ricky:	[still crying]	[still crying]
Jeff:	*Niitelarta wani, camun pia.*	*This thing for listening right here, where does it belong?*

[Ricky quiets down as she watches Jeff screw a piece back on the camera]

Using biliteracy to support Yup'ik maintenance

During the time of the study, the school district was pushing reading extensively, and an early childhood literacy program distributed small, locally relevant books in Yup'ik. At the same time, given the state of adult literacy in the school-based Yup'ik writing system, some parents complained that the Yup'ik words in children's books were too long to read. Others found that they could more easily translate books from English.

Jeff and Megan read their children books, often translating English books into Yup'ik. Such sessions were striking examples of how Megan used extended Yup'ik to engage Ricky in literacy. Below, we also see how such biliteracy events (Reyes, 2006) could serve as focused interactional spaces for promoting children's listening and speaking skills in Yup'ik. The following example starts as Megan read Ricky one of her favorite books in English, and spontaneously translated into Yup'ik:

1 **Megan:**	*Tua-i-llu-gguq angqa-* ball-*arlutek.*	*OK, and it says they are* *playing* ball.
2 **Megan:**	*Mikelnguut-gguq* ball-*aq* *kauvagkatni,* one Little critter-*aam nevpaggluku.* *Alinglutek. Tuai-gguq* *xxxx*	*It says when the children* *hit the ball,* one little critter *broke it. They were* *scared. Then it says,* *xxxxx*
3 **Ricky:**	xxx¿	xxx¿
4 **Megan:**	um hm.	um hm.
5 **Ricky:**	*Una* ball-*aq*¿	*This the* ball¿

[Turns the page and they are playing ball]

6 **Megan:**	*Yep. Waten, 'angqaq*¿*'*	*Yep. Like this 'ball*¿*'*
7 **Ricky:**	*Angqaq*¿*', Ma,* one-*aq*¿	*Ball*¿ *Ma, the* one¿
8 **Megan:**	Yep ... *Tang waniwa*	Yep .... *Look right here*
9 **LTW:**	*Cauga*¿	*What is it*¿
10 **Ricky:**	xxxxx	xxxxx

[Megan shrugs her shoulders with an 'I don't know' expression, then
turns to a picture where the friends are playing hide and seek in the
backyard]

11 **Megan:**	*Caugat makut*¿ *Panik, huh*¿	*What are these*¿ *Daughter, huh*¿
12 **Ricky:**	*Naguq.*	*Grow*¿
13 **Megan:**	Yep, *Nauguuk.*	Yep, *the two are growing.*

[pointing to a picture of a Critter hiding behind a tree].

14 **Ricky:**	It's <u>hide</u> in there	It's <u>hide</u> in there
15 **Megan:**	*Waten, 'iirutaaq'*	Like this 'hide and seek'
16 **Ricky:**	*Iiruvqaq*	*Hiding*
17 **Megan:**	*Um hmm ... Tua-i-llu* *iterlutek* house-*amun* *aquillenilutek* friend-*aa,* friend-*aara-gguq* Bozo Builders set-*arluni ....* Train- *anqerrluni-llu.* *Ayagaqluni cukpiarluni* *wavet- gguq tuaten* *yaaq(xxxx)* *ayaqpagaqluni.* So cool ... *Piugtuten*¿	*Um hmm ... And then* *the two go into the* house *and when they are* *playing* friend-aa, *his* friend *it says has a* Bozo Builders set ... *He* *also has a* train. *It could* *go really fast to here, and* *like that it's really going* *way over to there xxx.* So cool ... *Do you want to*¿
18 **LTW:**	*Wiinga-llu, piyugtua.*	*Me too, I want to.*
19 **Megan:**	*xxxxx*	xxxxxxxx

20. **Ricky:** Leisy-*m una* me-ya-*qaqa* house-*aq enii-waa-qa-qa*.

Leisy-*'s this* me-ya *it's mine* house *her house* waa *it's mine.*

21. **Megan:** Hm. [to LTW] She said something about Leisy ... Leisy-*m una*

Hm. [to LTW] She said something about Leisy ... Leisy's *this*

22. **Ricky:** mm Leisy xxxxxxxxx *enii*

Leisy xxxx *her house*

23. **LTW:** Leisy-*m enii*¿

Leisy's *house*¿

24. **Ricky:** xxxxxxx *Una enii enii*

xxxxxxx *This her house her house*

25. **Megan:** So cool .... [pointing to the picture]

So cool .... [pointing to the picture]

26. **Ricky:** xxx

xxx

Megan's reading of the story contains embedded assumptions about literacy (Heath, 1983). The first most obvious assumption was that reading together has a place at home. Megan asked Ricky comprehension questions, paused for predictions and accepted comments from Ricky about the book, though the comments were not necessarily expanded or picked up on.

Throughout the reading of the story, Ricky was engaged, looking at the pictures, making comments and listening closely to her mom's translation. In a number of instances, Megan asks Ricky comprehension questions about the story in Yup'ik, and Ricky attempted to respond to some of the questions in Yup'ik, as in line 12 when she guesses about a plant that is growing.

As in other examples, Megan also borrowed key English words into her translation, modeling the increasingly common local pattern of codeswitching by attaching Yup'ik postbases and endings to key words such as 'friend', 'train' and 'little critter' to incorporate them within a Yup'ik frame. Ricky, as well, codeswitched in some of her answers, such as '*Una* ball- *aq*?' (*This* ball?) (line 5). At other times, Ricky made guesses in English (line 14).

Looking above, it is difficult to know how much Ricky understood various Yup'ik postbases or endings. Yet, when Megan modeled Yup'ik responses to her own questions, Ricky tried to repeat them with prompting (lines 6, 7 and 15, 16). Over enough failed attempts to get comments accepted in English or a mix of Yup'ik and English, Ricky tried to make a more complicated statement in Yup'ik about, likely, seeing a train set similar to the one in the book in my family's house. In line 20, Ricky uses a Yup'ik ending to mark a possessive subject, –*m* (e.g. Leisy-m, or Leisy's), and also inflects the word 'house' in Yup'ik correctly (*enii- her house*), using a common demonstrative, *una* (*this*) to point to the picture of the train set.

Jeff and Megan's efforts translating stories into Yup'ik had also already become more complicated with James. 'From an early age, bilinguals can identify differences between languages and begin making hypotheses about how print is associated with sounds in different languages' (Reyes & Azuara, 2008, discussed in Reyes & Ervin-Tripp, 2010). When James began to learn how to read, his parents reported that he started to get annoyed when his parents translated English books into Yup'ik. By the time he was 7, James wanted to figure out instead how the words matched the letters he was learning in school.

Socializing children to be takaryuk

Families undergoing language shift do not only experience loss, but also find ways to maintain continuities across potential intergenerational disruptions (Garrett & Baquedano-Lopez, 2002). Jeff and Megan, for instance, used multiple, common strategies for socializing their children to be aware of community expectations, and to behave *takaryuk* (*respectful/shy*) accordingly. Jeff and Megan sometimes told their children in Yup'ik to 'be *takaryuk*', as in one instance when James looked into our refrigerator for some juice and Jeff scolded him. Local understandings about what made such instances '*takaryuk*' were often implied.

Megan and Jeff also interpreted and directly labeled their children's reluctant or shy behavior as instances of being *takaryuk*. Megan, for instance, often stated that she wished her children would get used to playing outside rather than playing Nintendo games. In one visit, she happily reported to me that James had joined a group of unknown children playing outside with slingshots. Ben wanted to join them, and put on his coat, but then came back in and started to play inside again. Megan, seeing him return, asked him '*Takarnaqsiyaagtuq- qaaǂ*' (*It causes one to be too takaryuk, huhǂ*) to which Ben did not reply.

Most commonly, however, Megan and Jeff socialized their children to act *takaryuk* by projecting the sense that other people were attending critically to situations when they wanted to change their children's actions. For instance, one time when Ricky complained about something and frowned in front of my husband and me, Megan scolded her, saying 'Look, *tangvagaatgen*' (*they are watching you*). Often, when my family and I visited friends in Piniq, parents would either say '*Tangvagaatgen*' (*They are watching you*) or tell their children in Yup'ik that '*Next time you want to go to their house they're not going to want to have you.*'

It is possible at these times that community members were tapping into local, historically rooted beliefs about white outsiders as especially likely to scrutinize and critique local practices. Yet, Jeff and Megan commonly projected such criticism onto others, as well. Out on the boardwalk one time when Ben complained about wanting to ride his bike, Megan told him *'Aatavet niicugniaten'* (*Your dad is listening to you*), referencing Jeff, who was out of sight in a nearby food storage house. When the boys were rolling down a dirt hill on a walk and Megan wanted them to stop, she told them (in Yup'ik) *'Look, you're getting dirty, those kids when we walk home are going to think you look funny.'* Other families used this strategy as well.

In one interview, Megan described how she thought that *takaryuk* behavior might hold her children back in certain contexts, and how she did not want the children to be afraid in new situations. In daily observations, however, Megan and Jeff used the strategies above to socialize their children in light of community behavioral expectations. In the following section, we see how James, Ben, Ricky and their cousins all combined Yup'ik receptive skills, productive skills and their knowledge of how to act *takaryuk* to 'get by', as they grew up 'within earshot' of Yup'ik (e.g. Pye, 1992) around extended family members.

'Getting by' within extended families

Megan and her sister-in-law, Auntie M., often shared caregiving duties, dropping cousins off at each other's house, and Emily and her young siblings often visited James and Ben. During these visits, Megan and Auntie M. commonly discussed their daily lives and work at home, and shared stories about their families. The adults typically spoke uninterrupted in Yup'ik to one another, talking to the children briefly in Yup'ik to ask questions or issue directives.

When visiting at James, Ben and Ricky's house, Emily, their slightly older cousin, would honor James and Megan's general request to speak Yup'ik in their home by remaining quiet, or answering and asking simple questions and making requests with simple Yup'ik phrases, such as *Nauwa_____?* (*Where's _____?*), *Cauga _____? (What's_____?), Piyugngaunga? (Can I?)* -*mek piyugtua (I want ____).* When she visited with her young brother, Andy, she would also watch him, asking Andy basic caregiving questions in Yup'ik such as *Qerrutaaten? (Are you cold?), Nerellruuten? (Did you eat?), Piyugtuten? (Do you want?).*

One of the many afternoons when I visited Megan, Emily's mother and a third sister-in-law joined her. Over coffee, *akutaq* and crackers, the three mothers and I talked about a range of village events in Yup'ik, while James, Ben, Ricky and their cousins all played quietly in the background. For the two-hour visit, almost all of the adult conversation and comments to children were in Yup'ik. The mothers addressed children with Yup'ik questions, '*Nanta* sister?' (*Where's* sister?) and '*Neryuumiituten-qaa?*' (*Don't you want to eat?*). The children answered briefly, or, in some cases did not respond. When given no response, the mothers would leave the children alone, and go back to their chatting. Over the course of the visit, the moms also periodically intervened in the children's playing, directing, 'Shar-*araaten tuniu*' (*He's sharing with you, give it to him*), and '*Nipesgu*' (*Turn it off*). Early in the visit, Ben played quietly with cars, and started instructing his younger cousins, saying, 'You guys are a team, I'm on a team.' Auntie M. noted Ben's language use, and told him, '*Yugtun qalarten*' (*Talk Yup'ik*). Ben looked back at her. For the next 10 minutes or so, Ben played silently, then went to another room to play Nintendo with older cousins.

After their game finished and the children were scolded in Yup'ik for getting into some seal-cleaning materials, James, Ben and their cousins indirectly asked permission to go outside by standing near the door and getting dressed in coats and boots. Emily's mother, seeing them, asked '*Caciqsit?*' (*What are you guys going to do?*). When Ben answered, 'Play outside,' his mom Megan called '*Kitak, ani!*' (*OK then, go out!*). Seeing that a very small cousin planned to join them, Auntie M. directed, '*Anenrilu, qusertuten*' (*Don't go out, you have a cold*).

After about twenty minutes, we heard the crying sounds of Ricky, who had fallen in a puddle surrounded by snow outside. Megan brought Ricky inside, pulling off her wet shoes and pants in the arctic porch. While Ricky howled 'Cold, cold, cold' Megan declared, '*Tua-ll' assirtuten*' (*Ok, you're good*), then Ricky entered and cried on the chair for a minute. Auntie M. asked her 'Sleepy-*rtuten?*' (*Are you* sleepy?). When Megan reentered the house she tried to quiet Ricky, saying 'Cry-*anrilgu*. Cold-*anrituten*' (*Don't cry. You're not cold*).

In this short visit and in instance after instance in Piniq, young children were immersed in a background of adult interaction in Yup'ik. They also remained quiet around visiting adults, simultaneously fulfilling community expectations about respectful behavior, while avoiding instances when they might be called to task for not speaking or responding to questions in Yup'ik. Adults asked children periodic questions in Yup'ik, and at other times incorporated English words into Yup'ik questions as they cared for them, though if the children gave no answer, most often adults dropped the questions. The children generally followed directives in Yup'ik, but also answered requests from the adults to speak Yup'ik by remaining mostly quiet, or using basic Yup'ik. More often, however, James, Ben and Ricky and their cousins played together unsupervised, out of the view of adults in back rooms or outside.

Socializing cousins through creative play

In Piniq, as children got older and parents were busy with subsistence activities, preadolescent groups of cousins spent days loosely watched by grandmas and aunties. James, Ben and Ricky often played with their cousins, Emily, Johnny and younger siblings. The children were always welcome to eat at relatives' houses, and at any time they might be found consuming new forms of media together, checking out cable TV cartoons, watching their favorite movies, or playing video games. In these instances, like others, younger children observed and imitated their older siblings. At age one and a half, for instance, Ben played with James' video game, imitating James' hand motions on the controls while watching the introductory sequence over and over on a TV screen.

Weather permitting, children also spent long hours outside coming up with their own games. In late winter, children skated or sledded down snow-drifts that could reach to the tops of local houses. In the spring and summer, children's stretches of time out of adult view extended. In early May, the sun began to stay up until 11:30 PM; the world started to melt, and the local terrain changed rapidly from snow-covered to spotted with melting puddles and deep mucky roads for ATVs. Groups of children went out after school with rubber boots, engaging in popular past-times like using cast-off plywood or debris to raft over impermanent ponds scattered across Piniq.

When school let out for summer, children commonly played out on boardwalks near relatives' houses, when they were not accompanying adults on long berry picking trips. Each day the scenery provided new opportunities. Children flew kites made out of plastic bags and string on windy days. For a while, a daily trip to check for mail at the post office provided a chance for James, Ben and their cousins to throw rocks in channels of water from melting snow, or to play in mud. A week later as the water subsided, the same trip involved a stop to scrape dust from the local road into piles with sticks, and throw dust at playmates. Two weeks later, James, Ben, Ricky and their cousins' games changed again to throwing rocks. As the boardwalks emerged in larger sections in June, parents bought bikes and scooters from local stores or Bethel. Children across Piniq tried them out on boardwalks, using debris to create paths and jumps.

Language socialization studies have recently begun to demonstrate how children foster shared understandings of local relationships and practices through role-playing and creative play (Meek, 2007; Paugh, 2005). In their spontaneous games, children in Piniq often practiced subsistence. A group of boys played duck hunting with sticks for guns in an old abandoned boat. In mid-May, little boys went together to the outskirts of the village with slingshots to catch small migratory birds and practice hunting, while their older brothers started walking out onto the tundra to catch ducks and geese. Older girls watched the tundra emerge from under the snow, waiting for the time to head out with friends for long days of egg hunting on the village outskirts. In Chapter 7, we will look more closely at how older youth shaped their language use as they became increasingly involved in subsistence and household responsibilities.

On one post office trip, Emily led James and Ben in throwing an elaborate pretend *uqiquq* (*seal-party*). *Uqiquq*s historically were used for distributing seal meat from a boy's first catch to local women. In many Yup'ik villages in 2001, women threw *uqiquq*s to honor a wide range of subsistence-related rights of passage, such as a girl's first berry or egg gathered from the tundra, or a boy's first catch of a bird or seal. While preparing for *uqiquq*s, women from Piniq would shop in Anchorage stores and send home boxes of household goods such as Tupperware, hand towels, soaps, cooking utensils and plastic cups, larger gifts like plastic laundry baskets, and candy for children. On a windy day in spring, summer or fall, the woman hosting the *uqiquq* would then spontaneously announce the event over handheld village marine radio systems connecting local homes. Other women across the village would then drop what they were doing and gather at the designated spot, laughing and joking as they stood together, trying to catch goods as they were thrown into the air (for more background on *uqiquq*s, see Fienup-Riordan, 1991).

Children, including Emily, James and Ben, participated peripherally in many *uqiquq*s, playing together on the outskirts of groups of women, and moving closer to the action when hosts would throw candy for children. On the day in question, the children and their younger cousins also demonstrated how children were keen observers of adults' gift exchanges. On an open spot of tundra, the children imitated local women, throwing special 'gifts' of large chunks of mud to 'grandmas' in an imagined front row of an imagined crowd of women. They then threw mid-sized chunks of mud around in a circle, and smaller handfuls of mud further out 'to stop the whining of people in the back' of the invisible *uqiquq* participants. Through their creative play, the children spontaneously interpreted previous observations of women's common gestures and strategies in *uqiquq*s, reinforcing local messages about the importance of attending to others with a special emphasis on respect toward elders. Although the children's fantasy *uqiquq* took place almost entirely in English, it also demonstrated the children's awareness and ability to keenly imitate community practices as a form of shared learning.

Children in bilingual communities may develop more sophisticated uses of bilingualism as they grow older even in cases where they never learn to speak heritage languages fluently (Zentella, 1997). In the following section, we will see how GB youth also used codeswitching for creative purposes as they shared stories with young children.

Learning to codeswitch for creative effect

In a study conducted in the late 1980s, researchers documented how Yup'ik girls in multiple villages reinforced knowledge of kinship terms and nicknames, and fostered a sense of group solidarity through telling stories to peers and young children while drawing with knives in the mud. The researchers also noted how girls' stories included many scary stories from movies and TV shows, as well as other kinds of traditional and contemporary stories (deMarrais *et al.*, 1992).

In Piniq in 2001, middle-aged women remembered storyknifing. Younger women no longer told stories using knives in mud, yet ghost stories regularly traveled among networks of friends and family members. In multiple cases, young people's renderings of these stories illuminated the ways in which youth drew upon local features and experiences, as well as their bilingual competences to creatively localize media narratives.

One afternoon, for example, while playing with Play-Doh at this researcher's house, Emily shared a number of ghost stories with her cousins James and Ben. In one story, a health aide visited an empty house, where a spooky voice said *'Wantua'* (*I'm here*). A second story focused on a woman ghost in a traditional dress near a broken snowmobile out on the tundra.

Emily also shared the following popular story about a doll that came to life and tried to kill a spoiled girl. Five separate youth shared versions of the story with me in the spring of 2001, though each teller elaborated the story and the words of the doll character differently. Emily, who spoke mostly English, shared the following highly localized version of the story with James and Ben, codeswitching into Yup'ik for multiple commonplace rhetorical purposes (Note: translations appear italicized in parentheses, and gestures in brackets below):

Emily: Um, there was this girl and her father, it was in Alaska and it's true. They went to, maybe Bethel? To go Christmas shopping. It was December something. They went to go Christmas shopping. This girl saw a big huge doll? She liked it. Then she went,

'Aani, uumek piugtua (*Mom, I want this*).'
'No *akitussiyaagtuq* (No, *it's too expensive*).'
'Ehh, *piyugaqa!* (*I want it!*)'

Her father was looking for a gift for his mom, then she kept on stamping on the floor, then she was *qisteq*'ing (*having a fit*). Then her father went up, it was upstairs? Then both of them were *takaryuk* (*embarrassed*), so they just bought it.

She went to school, it was on a weekend, then she went to school? When she went school? She didn't – after school she came home? After school she used to always bring friends after school, then this time she didn't? Then, when her mom, her mom said like this:

'*Ciin aipaqinricit* friend-a, *aipaq-an?* (*How come you are not with a* friend, friend, *your friend?*)'
'*Naam, ak'a aipamek pingertua.* (*I don't know, I already have a friend.*)'

She went to her room, she locked it? She played with the doll, then the doll went like this? [Eyes wide open] and then went like that to her, the girl [Pretends to put her hands to someone's neck in a strangling gesture.] Then her mom and dad went to – they were both teachers? They went to a meeting? The auntie was babysitting and the, she was in the living room. And then the, that, girl unlocked it before he went like this? [Grabs]. Then the girl went like this? With her leg on the door [Motioning kicking]. Her auntie went like this, she looked back, she went to go check the girl. It was locked cause of the ... the doll? She was going like this? [Pounding] then she took an axe and she broke it, the door, and went '*Uitasgu!*' (*Leave her alone!*) Then the doll went like this '*Pikaqa*' (*She's mine*).

Then, and then the auntie said like this, and then the auntie took the axe and – but not on the sharp thing, she was just going like that [gesturing holding the handle] – When the doll was going to take the axe away, she, he dropped the girl, then, the auntie took the doll. Then the girl went to their auntie's house, quickly? Then, the auntie called, told the grandma, then, no, then the auntie called the priests and the polices to go take the, and told them the story real fast? She was out of breath? Then, when ... she told the priests and the polices to take a tank of gas and matches and lighters to burn the house and the *doll*. They did that? And then ... um, the doll went like this, it was, like, screaming? And crying? Somehow like that, and then he said, the doll went like this: '*Ciin-mi teguksaitaqa*, um, *augna* girl-*acuayaaq?*' ('*Why, then, didn't I ever take her,* um, *that little* girl?') Then the auntie told the grandma, and that's it.

LTW: Ehh, sca-ry.
Emily: It's true, and I know one.
James: Was that, was that doll <u>real</u>⸮
Emily: <u>Yep</u>. It was sleeping⸮ Sleeping for a while⸮ Then its eyes open
          and it woke up, the doll went like this [Sitting up]. When the
          girl went back, the doll went like this [Opens eyes wide]. *Iirpak*
          (Big eyes).

The plot above could have easily come from the media; when I asked Jeff about the story, he laughingly remarked, 'Sounds like a Chuckie movie,' referencing a series of blockbuster horror movies about a haunted doll. Yet, above we also see how Emily localized her story through embedded details and commentary on the emotional states of characters, as well as through Yup'ik voicing. The story takes place during a familiar activity, Christmas shopping in the hub town of Bethel. Aunties as babysitters and local grandmas' houses as places to go for help provided locally familiar frames of reference. Emily's choice of the final descriptive word, *iirpak* (*big eyes*), as well, reflected children's common ways of describing the eyes of *kass'aq* visitors to Piniq at the time. The characters' feelings in the hub town store, the father scolding the girl for not controlling her emotions, and Emily's use of related emotion words in Yup'ik (e.g. *takaryuk- shy, qisteq – act like one is going to wail*) also resonated with local socialization patterns.

Above, Emily used more extended Yup'ik to voice the main character's interactions with adults and the evil doll. Emily's Yup'ik had a few small but noticeable errors, the most obvious being the use of *'aani' (mom)*, in the first quote when the character addressed her father. This was likely a performance error, given the commonplace use of kinship terms for mother and father in Piniq.

Emily also made two errors in transitive interrogative endings, using a second person intransitive, versus transitive, interrogative ending as the mother asks, *'Ciin aipaqinricit friend-a, aipaq-an*⸮' (*How come you are not with a friend, friend, your friend⸮*), and substituting a noninterrogative transitive first to third person ending for the appropriate interrogative counterpart as the doll asks, *'Ciin-mi teguksait-aqa' (Why didn't I take her⸮*). These instances more likely evidenced Emily's relative exposure to specific forms in local talk and her limitations as a heritage language learner. In 2000 and 2001, adults in Piniq commonly used second person intransitive interrogative endings with young people, and youth themselves commonly used first to third transitive endings. However, transitive interrogative endings came up much less frequently in village interactions, and adults hardly ever used first person transitive interrogative endings with youth.

James and Ben did not remark on Emily's language use, although in other instances they would be quick to ask '*ca²*' (*what²*) if they did not understand their cousins. Instead, they followed along quietly, then focused on verifying Emily's story. As we see above, both older youth and young children in Piniq continued to develop their bilingualism during language shift, even if many were not developing Yup'ik fluency. Youth who spoke mostly English also learned to use and interpret Yup'ik/English codeswitching as a resource for rhetorical emphasis (e.g. Zentella, 1997), as they creatively entertained one another, localizing media flows.

At the same time, James, Ben and Ricky spent most of their time interacting together in English with one another and their older cousins. Their peer group formed one of many, and many young parents, including RS group members, struggled to maintain Yup'ik at home, given the daily face-to-face influence of cousins, neighborhood children or even a single playmate who spoke English regularly with their children.

Activating Yup'ik in a different village

In 2001, Megan and the three children spent a month away from Piniq in her home village, where James and Ben attended a Yup'ik first language school and socialized with Yup'ik-speaking cousins. After the visit both children used markedly more Yup'ik with peers and family in Piniq. As a younger sibling, Ben's increased willingness to try to speak Yup'ik was especially pronounced. When asked to speak Yup'ik, Ben used more complex phrases in 'survival Yup'ik', such as the following question used for asking permission, '*Pi-yugnga-unga²*' (*Can I²*).

Ben also further developed his codeswitching competences by adding simple Yup'ik postbases and word endings to English verbs, as we see in this example, which starts as James, Ben and a friend asked for permission to play a video game:

1	**James:**	We want play Rainbow Six.	We want play Rainbow Six.
2	**Ben:**	Can we²	Can we²
3	**Megan:**	You guys will be scared.	You guys will be scared.
4	**James:**	We won't.	We won't.
5	**Megan:**	You might have bad dreams tonight.	You might have bad dreams tonight.
6	**James:**	It's just a game.	It's just a game.
7	**LTW:**	*Cakucimek²* Rainbow 6²	*What kind²* Rainbow 6²
8	**Megan:**	*Yugtun qanrraartek.*	*Speak it in Yup'ik first.*
9	**James:**	xxxx Rainbow 6²	xxxx Rainbow 6²

10 **Megan:**	*Assircaarluten.*	*Be good.*
11 **James:**	Yeh … please.	Yeh … please.
12 **Megan:**	Ben, *Yugtun qanrutaanga.*	Ben, *speak Yup'ik to me.*
13 **Ben:**	Um, play-*aryugngaaput* Rainbow Six?	Um, *can we* play Rainbow Six?

In another conversation, Megan noted how she self-consciously tried to speak Yup'ik when she was out and about with her children, feeling like community members looked down upon parents for speaking English. My use of Yup'ik in line 7 likely tripped Megan's awareness that I was observing the interaction above, and Megan switched into using Yup'ik, requiring that James and Ben speak Yup'ik in order to get the desired game (line 8), equating Yup'ik use with 'being good' (line 10). In line 13, we also can see how Ben incorporated the English verb 'play', into a Yup'ik morphological frame, correctly adding postbases and an accompanying word ending inflected for a plural subject:

Ben:	play-*ar-yugnga-aput*
Translation:	play-*a(q)-'be able to V' - 1st person pl.*
Gloss:	*Can we* play?

While the statement above would be considered beginner's Yup'ik, Ben's increased willingness and ability to use simple verbal postbases and word endings were striking, given how quickly young children in Piniq were switching to simply inserting single Yup'ik words into English utterances.

James also improved his Yup'ik during his time away, as he spoke Yup'ik regularly with cousins and friends and developed writing skills in a Yup'ik elementary program. Yet, the children's subsequent changes in language use after returning to Piniq demonstrated (1) how young bilingual children are sensitive to interlocutors and changes in setting, and alter their language use accordingly (Reyes & Ervin-Tripp, 2010); and (2) how young children play agentive roles producing language ideologies and emergent language policies within their peer groups and families (Gilmore, 2010). Back in James' class in Piniq, only a couple of children spoke Yup'ik regularly, and they rarely used Yup'ik in front of one another, as we saw in Chapter 3. Only five months after the family's return to Piniq, James complained that he could not speak Yup'ik because the back velar stop –*q* 'hurts my throat'. He also said that he would not speak Yup'ik because, 'Tommy doesn't speak Yup'ik,' referencing a popular boy in his class.

Shifting practices and assumptions

In family 1's case, a set of common experiences and assumptions meant the eventual accommodation of children's English. The first assumption was that Yup'ik was 'hard', especially when it came to teaching school-related preliteracy skills such as the words for colors and numbers. As James entered school, he became self-conscious about his own Yup'ik use, used increasing amounts of English like his peers, resisted his parents' attempts to use Yup'ik and used English to socialize his younger siblings. As Jeff and Megan's doubts about Yup'ik language maintenance increased, they began to assume that English would be expedient or easier for James to understand. Through their overall use of English, and use of English in codeswitching, Jeff and Megan also inadvertently accommodated their younger children's English use, reducing the Yup'ik language learning opportunities of James and their younger children over time.

Yet, during family language shift, Jeff and Megan creatively found ways to demonstrate linguistic survivance, passing on key community expectations for children's socialization, such as how to interact respectfully with adults by listening to Yup'ik directives, responding to simple Yup'ik questions, and acting *takaryuk* when appropriate. Ben, Ricky and their cousins developed receptive and some productive competences in Yup'ik, awareness of unique community practices, and generated creative language uses with one another. The group of cousins also learned how to use their bilingualism to 'get by' with adults according to local discourse norms.

Considering family 1, we also see how family language shift could potentially be disrupted and reversed. When Megan moved her children home to another village, James, Ben and Ricky's receptive skills were activated as the children were exposed to increased Yup'ik language learning opportunities within a Yup'ik school program, and when children played with Yup'ik-speaking peers. Back in Piniq, however, Jeff and Megan faced multiple challenges as they attempted to counteract the pressures of English language instruction in school, and sibling and peer language socialization in English. As parents, they had initially been intent and actively involved in teaching their children Yup'ik. Over time, their children had a hard time producing extended Yup'ik at home, and did not produce extended Yup'ik with peers.

During early language shift, increasing numbers of families in Piniq 'tipped' into using increasing amounts of English over time as wide-ranging pressures shaped peer interactions within their children's networks of siblings, cousins and friends. Nevertheless, as we will see below, some families found new ways to support Yup'ik language maintenance, mobilizing sibling and peer networks to support heritage language maintenance during the early, uneven phase of community language shift.

Family 2

The mother of family 2 and her husband Joe were strong advocates for 'keeping our language going'. Jenny wrote an impassioned newsletter to the community urging parents to speak Yup'ik and pointing out how elders' Yup'ik vocabulary was rapidly being lost. As a long-time school aide, Jenny also attempted to persuade parents that if they spoke Yup'ik to their children, their children would be able to both speak Yup'ik and achieve in English.

Jenny was aware how school district personnel were urging parents not to codeswitch with children, and Jenny and Joe created firm boundaries around the use of Yup'ik in their home. They also actively shaped ways that their older children spoke to their youngest son, Willie. Yet, in the encounter below, described in field notes, Jenny described and demonstrated how she faced multiple challenges separating Yup'ik and English language use, given ongoing Yup'ik language change and codeswitching during rapid language shift:

I am sitting with Jenny on some benches in the front hallway of the school, watching the high school boys play ball through the door to the gym. Periodically people are passing as they check with the front office, or head off down one of the adjoining school hallways. Jenny is there with her four year old Willie. I ask Willie how old he is in Yup'ik, '*Qavcircit?*' Willie doesn't respond though Jenny asks him to '*Kiuluku*' (*Answer her*). Another woman comes in and asks the boy '*Kituusit?*' (*What's your name?*) Again, he doesn't respond. Jenny starts telling me how they've been trying to speak to him only in Yup'ik:

'It's been hard to try to speak to him in only Yup'ik. Because we're so used to the English words for objects, like "spoon-*amek*, fork-*amek*" (spoon-*ablative modalis case marker*, fork-*ablative modalis case marker*). I had to tell my girls, too, because they would say things like, "Mommy go see-*rru*" (Mommy go see-*optative ending*). And I had to tell them they need to use Yup'ik words. We had to work on them. And the parents need to realize that we have to speak Yup'ik.'

At this point Willie goes and tries to get something from the candy machine. Jenny tells him '70 cents-*anqertuq*' (*it has* 70 cents) then turns to me, 'like that, '70 cents'. We could say it in Yup'ik, but it's so long. There are lots of words like that, sometimes I say them to him and they're so long I wonder if he's going to remember them. Like the words for colors. He gets *kavirliq* (*red*) and *tungulria* (*black*), but we tried the word for orange, or *cungagliq* (*green*) and he doesn't get them. We went over them and I tried to teach them. But we parents need to realize we are speaking English.

Right then, Lillia, Jenny's daughter in the GB group appears in the hall. Jenny asks her: '*Malrugnek kangiranqertuten-qaaỉ* (*Do you have two quarters?*)' Lillia throws Jenny a funny look, and then asks 'What's *kangiraq?*'

'Quarters.' [Jenny turns to me] 'See?'

One of the janitors who maintains the school comes out of the gym declaring, 'Bathroom check-*alaranka*' (bathroom check-*I always do it to them*)

'Or like that,' Jenny says to me. '<u>check-*alaranka*</u>.'

The janitor sits down with us and says, 'Yep, kids these days, they always wanna take a short-cut.' Jenny responds, 'No, it's <u>us</u>. The parents, because when a baby is born, it doesn't speak a language. I blame the parents.'

Like Jenny above, multiple sets of parents claimed that it was easier to use English for new words, since Yup'ik words were 'too long'. When providing examples, adults would almost always identify lengthy neologisms, such as the word for quarter in Jenny's example above, or Jeff's raincoat example earlier. As one middle-aged adult commented: 'It all started with our generation. Sometimes using English just seems so much easier.'

Jenny's example of her daughters' use of 'Mommy go see-*rru*,' and the janitor's phrase, 'bathroom check-*a-lar-anka*' (bathroom check – *always doing-first person subject to plural third person object transitive ending*), also demonstrates how community members sometimes attached Yup'ik word endings to multiple English words appearing in Yup'ik word order, as they tried to maintain Yup'ik. Codeswitching is common among bilingual populations, and can show the natural tendency of bilinguals to creatively draw upon wide-ranging linguistic resources in everyday talk. Yet, in examples like these, we see how codeswitching could also obscure the ways that English was creeping into interpersonal interactions, potentially robbing children of opportunities to acquire Yup'ik vocabulary and a sense of how to use Yup'ik morphology.

During rapid language shift, Jenny and her husband taught their older children to avoid codeswitching with Willie, so that he could hear Yup'ik consistently. Jenny and other family members also pretended not to understand Willie when he spoke in English, and kept one another from moving back and forth from Yup'ik to English (e.g. Lanza, 1997). In a second family with RS and GB youth, parents included their older, RS group-aged Yup'ik-speaking children in an effort to teach a young adopted child from an English-speaking village to speak Yup'ik. Like other children, the boy was also socialized into subsistence practices and eventually became one of the strongest Yup'ik speakers among his GB peers.

Many villagers and youth remarked how Willie, age four in 2000, stood out as a 'really good' Yup'ik speaker as a young child. The following section further documents Lillia and Willie's strengths as Yup'ik speakers in a context of rapid language shift.

Willie

It is beyond the scope of the study to detail the language acquisition of the strong Yup'ik-speaking children in Piniq. In 2000–2001, Willie was also known for being shy in general, was already aware of *takaryuk* situations, and rarely talked around me. Over the course of a summer, however, I worked with Jenny's GB-aged daughter Lillia to consider Willie's language development. Lillia taped herself interacting with Willie as she read to him, used Play-Doh, played video games and walked around Piniq. The data sample is small, and reflects the unusual nature of the work. Yet, it also demonstrates dramatic differences between children's language use in family 1 and family 2.

Children are highly attuned to words that are used frequently in their environments, and often borrow these words as part of their repertoires. Jenny reported that initially it was somewhat difficult to avoid borrowed English words in statements to her children, though over time, it got easier the more she did it. As many people including older youth noted, Willie also used Yup'ik words that young speakers often replaced with borrowed English words, such as *ciilrak (helicopter)*. Below, we will also see how Willie used a range of unique Yup'ik features that were quickly disappearing along with the shift to English.

Orienting toward multiple worlds in Yup'ik

Willie's multiple, overlapping worlds supported his Yup'ik use. As part of a church-going family, Willie often sat quietly through lengthy Yup'ik church services. He also sometimes sang in Yup'ik as part of the intergenerational group described in Chapter 2. In one session taped by Lillia, Willie sang along to a taped church hymn, 'Shall We Gather at the River' in Yup'ik, sounding out pieces of lengthy Yup'ik agglutinated phrases.

Later in the session, Lillia and Willie played a video game, and as we see below, even the children's interactions around media could serve as opportunities for using unique Yup'ik features. The segment starts as Lillia gives Willie advice how to move his character on the TV screen, gaining points by gathering objects while avoiding dangerous obstacles and characters.

[Words with asterisks are discussed below, underlines indicate emphasis]

1	**Willie:**	*Kiiki, *ayagluten.*	*Hurry up, *go on.*
2	**Lillia:**	**Nauggun *ayagluniⵁ*	*It's going through whereⵁ*
3	**Lillia:**	No!	No!
4	**Willie:**	*'taaki.*	*There it is.*
5	**Lillia:**	*Aqumluten* xxx	Sit down xxx
6	**Willie:**	Whew.	Whew.
7	**Lillia:**	*Kita. *<u>Maaggun.</u>*	OK. **<u>Through here.</u>*
8	**Lillia:**	*Kitak *<u>tauna</u> teguluku.*	OK now, take **<u>that one</u>.*
9	**Willie:**	*Caⵁ*	*Whatⵁ*
10	**Lillia:**	**Tauna.*	**That one.*
11	**Willie:**	*Caⵁ*	*Whatⵁ*
12	**Lillia:**	**Tauna-wa. Tauna tegusqaa.* *Kitak, *ayagluten.*	**That one, of course. Take that one. OK, leave.*
13	**Willie:**	**Una-wa* and *Unaⵁ No⸮*	**This oneⵁ And this⸮ Noⵁ*
14	**Lillia:**	**Ayagluten, kiiki!*	**Leave, hurry!*
15	**Willie:**	**Nauggun. Lookⵁ*	*<u>Through whereⵁ</u> Lookⵁ*
17	**Lillia:**	**Tuaggun pivkenak!*	*Not through *that!*
18	**Willie:**	**<u>Uuggunⵁ</u>*	**<u>Through hereⵁ</u>*
19	**Lillia:**	*No, *uuggun.*	*No, *through here.*

In video games, players must solve problems and develop strategies as their characters move through visual spaces, experiencing new challenges and reacting to increasingly complex dynamic circumstances (Gee, 2003). Audiotaped data limits us to considering the siblings' talk without visual context. Nevertheless, we see that Willie followed instructions and asked multiple questions to produce spatially situated meanings using the Yup'ik demonstrative system described above.

The siblings used demonstrative pronouns repeatedly, often combining these with the common postbase *–ggun* (*through*) as Lillia helped Willie navigate paths and obstacles on the screen. (Note: Definitions of Yup'ik demonstratives come from Jacobson, 1984: 653–654):

Ex. 1   (lines 8, 10, 12) *'Tauna/taukut'* *That/those* that are visible, located near the listener, not moving.

Ex. 2   (line 7) *Maa-ggun- 'Through here'*, from *maani*, an adverb used for an extended entity located near the speaker, moving in spatial orientation and in sight.

Ex. 3   (lines 18–20) *U-ggun 'through this'* from *una- this*, used for more restricted or still entities that are near the speaker and visible.

Willie also used related question forms to solicit spatial information, including:

Ex. 1   (line 15) *Nau-ggun, 'through where?'*

Willie and Lillia additionally used a related verb for directional movement:

Ex. 1   (line 1, 14) *ayag- 'to leave'*

Commonly, community members in Piniq named new media as a contributing factor in Yup'ik language shift, and many local adults noted how children's and young people's morning and nightly exposure to the Yup'ik *qanruyutait* (*teachings*) described in Chapter 2 decreased after the introduction of TV to the remote community. However, as we have seen above, within families who were able to establish strong patterns of regular face-to-face Yup'ik use, interactive media use could also prompt opportunities for children's use of unique linguistic features in Yup'ik directives, questions and descriptions.

Siblings generating complex Yup'ik statements in interaction

As we have seen, during rapid family, peer group and community language shift, many children in Piniq voiced and demonstrated insecurities about using even commonplace Yup'ik postbases and word endings. In the brief interchange below, we gain further insight into Lillia and Willie's unusually high level of Yup'ik use for children at the time. Before the following interaction took place, I loaned Lillia some Play-Doh and asked her to play with Willie while taping him. Lillia and Willie made a cake together, using toothpicks for birthday candles and pretending to blow them out. Below, Lillia tried to keep Willie from mixing colors, causing Willie to initiate an extended discussion of the unusual origins of the Play-Doh:

1 **Willie:**	*Icugg kenermek, angniq anutiiq.*	*Remember lighting the candle, happy birthday.*
2 **Lillia:**	*Tua-ll caluten?*	*Then what do you do?*
3 **Willie:**	*Kiiki. Cupuuraaq. Kiiki!*	*Hurry up. Blow. Hurry up!*
4 **Lillia:**	*Pisciigatut pikenritaput.*	*They can't, they are not ours.*
5 **Willie:**	*Ca, ca pikenricia?*	*What, what's not mine?*
6 **Lillia:**	*Ukut-*	*These-*
7 **Willie:**	*Pikaput? Una taugaam pikaput? Kiami?*	*Is it ours? But is this ours? Then whose?*

8 **Lillia:**	*Aug'um* boy-*acuaraam.*	*That little* boy's
9 **Willie:**	*Kia,* boy-*acuaraam?*	*Whose, that little* boy's?
10 **Lillia:**	*Icugg, aug'um.*	*You know, that one.*
11 **Willie:**	*Nalluaqa. Nalluaqa.*	*I don't know. I don't know.*
12 **Lillia:**	*Kass'ayagaam.*	*The little white boy's.*
13 **Willie:**	*Elliin avgutaanga?*	*He's sharing with me?*
14 **Lillia:**	*Cakuciuga mingua?*	*What color is it?*
15 **Willie:**	*Kia taitellruagu?*	*Who brought it?*
16 **Lillia:**	*Wiinga-*	*Me-*
17 **Willie:**	*Naken?*	*From where?*
18 **Lillia:**	*Eniitnek*	*From their house*
19 **Willie:**	*Waten,* Will-*amun*	*Like this, tell* Willie *to*
	avgutesqiu. Kia-llu	*share with him? And*
	una pikau?	*whose is this?*
20 **Lillia:**	*Kass'ayagaam.*	*The little white boy's.*
21 **Willie:**	*Kepurpek'naki!*	*Don't cut them!*
22 **Lillia:**	*Caqatarcit-mi?*	*What are you going to do then?*
23 **Willie:**	*Neriki?*	*Eat them?*
24 **Lillia:**	No*, natermun piaqunaki.*	No*, don't put them on the floor.*

As in the previous excerpt, Lillia and Willie used Yup'ik comfortably with one another above, staying in Yup'ik even in instances of miscommunication. Given rapid changes in children's language use at the time in Piniq, their interaction also demonstrated Willie's confidence in his ability to create complex meanings by 'gluing together' Yup'ik verbal cognates, postbases and word endings encoding information about subjects, objects and transitivity. As he tried to work out why the '*kassayagaq*' (*little white boy*) he'd barely met might share Play Doh with him, Willie followed local discourse norms, letting word endings do the work of establishing subjects and objects except in cases of special emphasis (line 13, line 19). Willie also used multiple forms of Yup'ik word endings, showing his unusual command of Yup'ik morphosyntax for the time:

Ex. 1 (line 15) *Kia taite-llru-agu?*
Translation: *Who 'To bring'- past tense- (3rd person subject to 3rd person singular object interrogative ending)*
Gloss: *Who brought it?*

Ex. 2 (line 13) *Elliin avgut(e)-anga.*
Translation: *He 'To share'- (3rd person singular to 1st person singular object indicative ending)*
Gloss: *He is sharing with me.*

Ex. 3   (line 19) *Waten, Willie-mun avgute-sq(e)-iu¿*
Translation: *Like this,* Willie-*to share- to want one to* V- (*3rd person singular
                  to 1st person singular interrogative ending*)
Gloss: *Like this, he wants to share it with* Willie¿

In the examples, Willie correctly completed statements and questions by
distinguishing between indicative and interrogative transitive word endings
encoding information about subject, object and number. In examples 2 and
3, Willie used the Yup'ik cognate for the verb 'to share'- versus incorporating
the more commonly used English word at the time. In example 3, Willie also
uses a verbal postbase -sq(e)- to create a compound verb.

While many aspects of culture translate across languages, Woodbury
documents how form-dependent expressions such as the demonstratives discussed above and verbal postbases encoding emotional stances often do not
get translated when Cup'ik adults share stories in English (Woodbury, 1993,
1998). In a later example from the Play-Doh session, Willie combined a postbase, -kayag-, loosely translated as 'to V of the darned one' (Jacobson, 1984:
464) within a complex statement:

Ex. 4   *Ang(e)-kayag-i-uq*
Translation: *'to be big'-'to V of "darned" one'-'becoming'- (3rd person singular
                  subject indicative ending)*
Gloss: *The darn thing is getting big.*

Notably, Lillia first translated the example above as simply 'it is getting
big', leaving out Willie's use of -kayag- to mark a negative stance, as would
be predicted by Woodbury (1993, 1998).

Fluent Yup'ik speakers mark tense relatively infrequently in extended
discourse, using tense-neutral, dependent subordinative endings extensively
(Jacobson, 1995). While Yup'ik-speaking adults and strong Yup'ik speakers
in the GB group regularly used subordinative forms in 2000, other youth
rarely used the commonplace endings. At age 4, Willie was already gaining
the sense of how to combine direct tense markers with subordinative mood
endings to mark tense in extended Yup'ik discourse:

Original	Direct Translation	Gloss
Elagyam caniani aqumgallruunga.	*I sat in the food house's next to place.*	*I sat by the food house.*
Aqumluni	*He sitting*	*He sat*
Nangerluni	*He standing*	*He stood*
And (name)-aq.	*And (name).*	*And (name).*

Above, Willie established the tense of the narrative in the first sentence, using a verbal postbase *-llru-*. Willie then used the subordinative, tense neutral *-luni* to construct the narrative. Willie also described his location as *'elagya-m caniani'* meaning literally, *'in the food house's next to place'*, using the Yup'ik possessive marker *-m* correctly in combination with yet another demonstrative, *cani- 'area beside'*.

As we have seen above, the parents in family 2 limited their codeswitching and tried very consciously to speak to their children solely in Yup'ik. As parents of RS youth, as well as GB youth and young children, Jenny and Joe were also able to garner their older children's support in socializing their younger children to speak Yup'ik. As younger children in the family, both Lillia and Willie were comfortable interacting in Yup'ik, using special vocabulary and a range of linguistic features that were quickly disappearing in the community. A broader family network of Yup'ik language advocates with Yup'ik-speaking young children also supported Jenny and Joe's efforts to maintain Yup'ik at home, as we will consider below.

Supporting heritage language maintenance through children's networks in extended families

While many families shared common challenges maintaining Yup'ik during early language shift, exceptional cases pointed to remaining possibilities for bilingualism. In 2000, younger children from most families with second-language Yup'ik-speaking or non-Yup'ik- speaking parents spoke basic Yup'ik words and phrases, but were not comfortable expressing themselves fully in Yup'ik. By considering one former child migrant's family we can see how the common one-parent, one-language strategy for raising bilingual children (described in Baker, 2006; King *et al.*, 2008; Lanza, 1997) could work to counter language shift *if* the parents involved had the support of other adults and children's Yup'ik-speaking peers.

Paul, the father of one strong Yup'ik-speaking family, had spoken Yup'ik as a young child in another village, yet stopped speaking Yup'ik at age 3 when his family moved to a town where he was immersed in English. In 2000, Paul combined listening skills in Yup'ik and basic Yup'ik to 'get by' with adults in Piniq, and was a valued community member. In a taped interview, Paul also expressed his support for his children learning to speak Yup'ik, sharing his perspective on bilingualism:

LTW: You've lived places where there are lots of Yup'ik people, like [Names a place] but they didn't speak Yup'ik, like, from your perspective, why do you think you'd want them to learn it or why do you think it's important?

Paul: It gives them more of an opportunity to get a job, cause nowadays certain jobs are requiring it, both Yup'ik and English. So I think that would be a big plus if they knew both of them.

Paul hoped that raising his children as Yup'ik/English bilinguals would open future job opportunities, and later in the interview, Paul commented how more certified local teachers might help increase the use of Yup'ik in school. Paul's nuclear family was also in a group of related families, including Jenny's, who were making a sustained effort to speak only Yup'ik at home. Paul supported his in-laws' efforts to raise their children as Yup'ik speakers, learning and using Yup'ik commands with his children, even though he mostly spoke to them in English. His children spoke only Yup'ik with their mother and a grandmother who lived close by; Paul's youngest child played with Willie regularly in Yup'ik; and an older Yup'ik-speaking cousin from the same family group was Lillia's best friend. Like Jenny's children, Paul's children all became strong Yup'ik speakers at a time when Yup'ik use was dwindling among older youth, and rarely heard among kindergarten children in Piniq.

Strong Yup'ik-speaking families had varying reasons for wanting to maintain Yup'ik. Some described Yup'ik as an inherent part of Yup'ik identity, and many mentioned the importance of raising children to be able to speak with elders. Some who were familiar with linguistic transfer theories described how they wanted their children to benefit academically from being bilingual. Not all strong Yup'ik-speaking families were working consciously on avoiding English loan words in their talk to children. Yet, in each of these strong Yup'ik-speaking families with multiple children, younger siblings benefited from having at least one close young peer who spoke Yup'ik; in 2000–2001, I only knew one case of a younger sibling maintaining Yup'ik into early teenage years without a friend, usually a close cousin, who also spoke Yup'ik. Without support for Yup'ik maintenance within their peer group, older children who initially developed along the lines of the strong Yup'ik-speaking families above much more frequently spoke English to younger siblings and peers, like James above.

Within urban settings dominated by English, multiple parents have strategically supported their children's heritage language development by setting up enclaves of families and/or structured playgroups so their children could play with other children learning a heritage language at home (e.g. see Fishman, 1991; King *et al.*, 2008). What is striking about the Piniq case, however, is how quickly, within a remote, rural community where adults continued to speak to one another predominantly in Yup'ik, such family and peer enclaves began to either 'make or break' parents' attempts to help their children learn how to speak Yup'ik comfortably.

Summary

As we have seen above, during the early, uneven and rapid phase of early language shift in Piniq, community and family members in Piniq were not simply choosing to speak English to their children. Instead, multiple changes combined to unevenly erode young people's overall resources for learning Yup'ik. Young people's changing peer dynamics also reverberated through social networks, rapidly driving subsequent individual and family shifts to English.

Looking longitudinally and comparatively at how individual, peer group, and family language trajectories intertwined within the broader linguistic ecology of Piniq, we can see how family and community language maintenance relied on the support of peer language socialization, and how multiple contingencies emerged as partially determining whether individuals learned and maintained Yup'ik. Further, we can highlight common patterns within community members' deeply uneven experiences of Indigenous language maintenance and language shift.

Individuals had tipping points, and oldest children were most likely to start using predominantly English once they were old enough to attend the primary English domain of school and to play independently with friends. Families had tipping points toward English use, and these tips in many cases became most pronounced as a family's one or two oldest children went to school, started using English, and then began to influence the language learning of the younger siblings. The community had a tipping point, and after the GB group became adolescents, adults increasingly began to assume that young children who spoke in English needed to be spoken to in English in the name of comprehension and expediency.

Researchers impact the situations they study when they try to enter homes to observe family interactions (Rogoff, 2003; Smith, 1999). My presence in family 1 through direct participation over time and in family 2, through work with an older sibling setting up situations for eliciting language, meant that I did not observe either family under 'normal' circumstances. Yet, even taking this into consideration, we see how the language socialization patterns in the two families intersected with the Get By group in varying ways, with implications for heritage language maintenance.

Both families made conscious choices and dedicated efforts to teach their children Yup'ik. In family 1, the young parents started out successfully teaching their oldest child Yup'ik, and even consciously tried to create a home–peer nexus to support peer socialization in Yup'ik. Once their oldest child James attended school in English and played more independently with cousins from another Yup'ik-and-English-speaking family, however, his perceived switch to English dominance presented challenges for the parents as they tried to maintain Yup'ik use with their younger children. Over time, family 1 started using common emerging patterns of mixing Yup'ik and English, as parents increasingly accommodated their children's use of English. The parents in family 1 maintained expectations that their children would understand basic Yup'ik, and socialized their children into communal discourse norms such as the practices around being and becoming 'takaryuk'. As within many families, however, increasing doubts about bilingualism combined with eroding Yup'ik resources in children's peer networks, producing rapid family-level language shift.

One way to approach the question of what, if anything, families could be doing differently was to look at the remaining strong Yup'ik-speaking families. In general, the parents of GB youth had to pay much more attention to their everyday language use than parents of the RS group in order to maintain Yup'ik in the home during community language shift. By 2000, parents in many young, strong Yup'ik-speaking families also wrestled with questions about language use, and adopted family language policymaking strategies that had been unnecessary and unheard of even 10 years earlier. Some parents established firm boundaries between Yup'ik and English, limiting codeswitching in the caregiver talk of adults and older siblings, and pretending not to understand English (e.g. Lanza, 1997). The parents in strong Yup'ik-speaking families generally modeled consistent Yup'ik use and maintained high expectations for their children's Yup'ik 'response-ability' (Holm et al., 2003). They also generally shared a firm belief in additive bilingualism, and maintained confidence that learning Yup'ik would not ultimately hold their children back from learning English in the face of growing community doubts about the possibilities of bilingualism. Children from these families were some of the highest-performing students in their classes.

The varying family language socialization trajectories in Piniq also depended on whether parents were able to take advantage of and/or develop pockets of young Yup'ik-speaking peers to counter the accumulating effects of schooling, migration and a shifting youth culture within the dynamic local setting. While maintaining firm boundaries around Yup'ik, the parents of family 2 enlisted older RS siblings, as well as a group of young, Yup'ik-speaking cousins from another family to play with Lillia and Willie in Yup'ik. Their Yup'ik language maintenance strategies worked, and their children could use Yup'ik postbases and endings to communicate comfortably in Yup'ik with peers and adults at a time when increasing numbers of youth in Piniq were expressing linguistic insecurity and only using token amounts of Yup'ik.

Trying to pull apart caregiver–child, child-to-child and child-to-parent influences may at first seem like a chicken-and-egg question. Did the children speak Yup'ik in their peer and sibling networks when their parents maintained Yup'ik in the home, or were parents able to maintain Yup'ik in the home when they had the help of peer and sibling networks? As we have seen above, all of these interactions played a role in steering family language socialization trajectories toward Yup'ik language maintenance or language endangerment. By the time the Get By group was growing up, the village linguistic ecology had rapidly changed to the point that unless parents made a sustained choice to speak Yup'ik to the children and became increasingly involved in adopting strategies for maintaining Yup'ik at home, children in the Get By group could not just 'pick it up' from their friends and the school as they had only a few years prior. Sibling and peer networks of Yup'ik-speaking children undoubtedly supported parents' efforts to sustain Yup'ik as a main language of home life in earlier generations. Yet the importance of lateral language socialization became highly evident once the change to English instruction in the local school, increasing migration and subsequent changes in local youth culture decreased children's overall resources and opportunities for learning Yup'ik in the village as a whole. As youth culture 'tipped' into English, this change also became a driving force of family and community language shift.

Educators were right: in 2000 and 2001, many families were accommodating their children's English, assuming that once the oldest children went to school they understood English better. But what many educators were not noting is how many of these families had originally succeeded teaching their oldest children Yup'ik, and how school practices were implicated in families' challenges maintaining Yup'ik. The importance of both school instruction and peer culture for family heritage language maintenance might be potentially discouraging for local community members working to counter language shift. As we have seen in Chapter 3, the local school in Piniq was a contested domain often marked by tension as rotating groups of outside administrators, teachers and national policies heavily influenced everyday school practices. As we have seen above, young people's everyday interactions with one another were also the hardest interactions for adults to influence, especially as children reached school age, when they spent more time in the English domain of school and much of their time in unsupervised play.

Nevertheless, as we have also seen above, during rapid language shift, children and youth who seemed to speak mostly English were still what researchers call 'emergent bilinguals' (Reyes, 2006) – young people with bilingual competences who used these competences in interaction with others around them, and whose bilingualism and biliteracy could be further developed under the right circumstances. In the following chapters, we will look closely within the peer culture of older youth, seeing how GB group members negotiated varying language socialization experiences with one another, demonstrating linguistic survivance in the rapidly transforming linguistic ecology.

6 The 'Get By' Group

As previous chapters document, in 2000–2001, Yup'ik was the main language of adult life in Piniq. Adults sent youth strong messages about the links between speaking Yup'ik and maintaining a unique identity. In village institutions and local work, community members used bilingualism to shape local self-determination efforts. Almost all families started off speaking Yup'ik to their children, and the oldest children in most families spoke Yup'ik with peers and adults. Children in roughly half of the families in Piniq also used Yup'ik with one another, and the school in Piniq had a Yup'ik program.

Nevertheless, the village of Piniq was beginning to experience a sea of sociolinguistic change and rapid language shift, as young people's language practices served as a focal point for vicious cycles of reduced resources for and increasing doubts about bilingualism. When a nonlocal principal made negative assumptions about young people's opportunities for developing bilingualism, English took the place of Yup'ik as the main language of elementary instruction before the GB group entered school. Increasing adult, child and youth migration to English-speaking urban and village spaces, as well, contributed to young people's increasing insecurities speaking Yup'ik, even as some migration to strong Yup'ik-speaking villages shaped pockets of children's Yup'ik language maintenance and use.

As eldest siblings entered school and played with peers in English, their increasing use of English set off waves of linguistic accommodation within young families. As parents increasingly tipped into using English in local homes, they also further reduced the Yup'ik language learning opportunities of young children. Some families, however, were working together to successfully maintain children's use of Yup'ik in networks of young cousins and playmates.

Within this chapter, we will consider how youth themselves interpreted, experienced and negotiated the countercurrents described above, given the dynamic language learning opportunities, language ideologies and linguistic practices around them. To understand young people's changing positions in a rapidly transforming linguistic ecology, in Section I, we will listen to young people's insights about individual and family language socialization trajectories. We will also consider some of the many ways in which youth continued to use Yup'ik to 'get by' with nonlocal and local adults, and young children.

In Section II, we will look within youth culture itself in order to highlight continuities and changes between the GB group and the slightly older RS group from Chapter 4, and to see how strong Yup'ik-speaking GB youth interacted with growing groups of youth who spoke mostly English. Importantly, we will also begin to detail young people's individual and collective acts of linguistic survivance as they faced a very specific challenge: the challenge being the first group to speak mostly English in a setting of heritage language endangerment.

Section I: 'Kassauguci-qaa?' ('Are You Guys Whites?')

In an interview in 2001, David, a member of the Get By group, described how adults sent youth in Piniq strong messages about language and identity. He also noted how easily young people could circumvent adults' calls to speak their heritage language:

LTW: Who do you use Yup'ik with?
David: My gram. Well, most elders.
LTW: Are they understandable to you?
David: Sometimes. Like it's starting to disappear, Yup'ik language? And *kass'aq* (*white/English*) language is starting to appear.
LTW: Hmm.
David: That's why people tell us ... to speak in Yup'ik. They say *'Yugtun. Kassaunrituten.' (In Yup'ik. You're not a white person).* Joe? Jenny's husband? We were playing football yesterday? He told us *'Yugtun. Kassauguci-qaa?' (In Yup'ik. Are you guys whites?)* Asked if we're *kass'aqs* (*whites*) and we started speaking like, it ...
LTW: You started speaking, in Yup'ik?
David: [Raises eyebrows, meaning 'yes'] And then when he got- you know people? When they're there? When they're not there we do whatever we want, we speak whatever we want. If that person told us to speak Yup'ik, who told us to speak Yup'ik, is coming? We *canguallaq* (*pretend we are not doing something*), like, if we're

doing something bad? Whenever we see 'em come, like, [we] let
someone be a lookout or something?

LTW: Um hmm?

David: We're doing bad stuff and then he comes, that person says he
comes? We lighten up, settle down, try not to be loud.

At the time of the above interview, unlike many of his peers, David
tested high on school measures of Yup'ik fluency, used Yup'ik at home and
could use Yup'ik easily within the everyday life of his community.
Nevertheless, David's description of the pick-up football game underscores
the challenges facing local adults who tried to influence young people's
everyday language use with peers, and resulting intergenerational tensions
during language shift. As David noted, adults tried to directly encourage
youth to maintain Yup'ik as a language of in-group communication, most
often by directly telling youth to '*Yugtun*' (*speak Yup'ik*), and/or accusing
youth of 'wanting to be white' when speaking English. Youth were easily
taught that by speaking English to community members, versus *kass'aq*
(*white*) outsiders, they were, in the words of David above, 'doing something
bad'. Youth in the first group to speak mostly English were also keenly aware
of ongoing language shift and language endangerment. At the same time,
Yup'ik-speaking youth in Piniq could '*canguallaq*' (*pretend to not do something
bad*), in David's words, using Yup'ik or simply staying silent around adults,
while using English with one another out of local language advocates'
purview.

In spite of community members' fears and commonplace assumptions
about youth in shifting communities, however, there was very little evidence
that David and his peers were distancing themselves from being Yup'ik, or
orienting toward English as a language of status, commerce and/or a global
youth culture. Rather, in contrast to David's own offhand referral to speaking English as 'doing whatever we want', as we will see in this chapter, youth
culture became a driving force of language shift in Piniq *in spite of* the ways
youth themselves expressed heritage language allegiance and made considerable
efforts to use and maintain Yup'ik as part of a unique Indigenous knowledge
system.

Making sense of language loss and endangerment

Like RS group members before them, individual youth in the GB group
noted in 2000–2001 how the deep imbalances in school instruction and
staffing described in Chapter 3 were undermining intergenerational
communication in Piniq. One boy I'll call Christopher, for instance, directly

linked the linguistic disjunctures within his family to the need for changes in schooling in the following interview segment:

LTW: If there was something you could change about Piniq, what would you wanna change?
Christopher: English teachers.
LTW: Yeh?
Christopher: Into more Yup'ik teachers. That way my brothers and sisters can start speaking Yup'ik.

Christopher went on to express concerns about the ways in which his younger siblings were speaking in English to his grandparents, who mostly spoke Yup'ik and could only understand them 'once in a great while'. As the oldest child in a family of multiple children, Christopher could speak easily with his grandparents, yet his younger siblings could not.

Other GB group members noted how peer influences, as well as schooling, shaped their own and their younger siblings' language use. In one interview, a high school girl Mary described how she grew up speaking Yup'ik until school started, and she started playing mostly with an English-speaking peer. As one of the oldest children in her family, Mary developed strong bilingual competences, and continued to use Yup'ik with her parents at home. Yet Mary described how her younger sister shifted from speaking mostly Yup'ik to mostly English within a short period after entering school:

My younger sister, she started speaking and understanding [Yup'ik] before she turned one [...] She spoke Yup'ik mostly, and then like me school started. Then she started speaking English mostly. And then she met her cousins, and found out they exist and they started playing with them, and those cousins of ours spoke English mostly, so she learned from them.

Mary went on to note that her younger siblings understood, but had a hard time speaking Yup'ik; within the GB group it became common for younger siblings in young families to self-identify as non-Yup'ik speakers, or to claim that they could not speak Yup'ik well. Unlike the GB youth above who critiqued the influence of schooling on their families' attempts to maintain Yup'ik, however, many GB youth shared brief, seemingly self-explanatory stories of the ways their personal tips into English and insecurities speaking Yup'ik were caused by childhood migration or specific friendships with English-speaking peers.

Amy, another GB youth, moved to Piniq after living in Anchorage as a child. Calling herself an 'English girl', Amy described how her parents spoke to her in Yup'ik, yet how she 'spoke English all the time even when they're saying Yup'ik stuff'. Nathan, another child migrant, and Mike, a youth who stayed in Piniq, described how they shifted from speaking Yup'ik to speaking mostly English as young children. The following interview segment occurred after I asked the two boys what Piniq might be like in the future:

1 **LTW:**   What kinds of things will be the same, what kinds of things will be different?

2 **Nathan:**   Our Yup'ik language might be the same, or might be different, I don't know.

3 **Mike:**   I heard one village lost their language.

4 **LTW:**   What do people say about, like, Yup'ik and English?

5 **Nathan:**   When I used to be small, I used to speak Yup'ik language, but when they were [inaudible] we lost that language.

6 **Mike:**   Me, too.

7 **Nathan:**   When I played with ... when my mom brought me to Anchorage, I forgot how.

8 **Mike:**   Me, I forgot how from uh, playing with a boy who talked English too much. When I try speak Yup'ik I speak it wrong.

As they talked about the future of Piniq, other villages' experiences and their individual language learning trajectories, Mike and Nathan partially articulated connections between their personal experiences and community language endangerment. Describing how they once knew and spoke Yup'ik as children, the boys noted how they stopped speaking Yup'ik after specific life experiences, such as Nathan's stint in a distant city (line 7) and Mike's friendship with an English-speaking peer (line 8). Narrating their language trajectories and linguistic insecurities about 'speaking Yup'ik wrong', above, Nathan and Mike also voiced seemingly straightforward outcomes of unexpected life events.

However, simple descriptions of teenagers 'losing' language and culture obscure the deep societal inequalities and historical processes that contribute to dramatic changes in Indigenous communities (St. Denis, 2003). In Mike and Nathan's statements, we also see how youth themselves can inadvertently naturalize linguistic insecurity, language loss and endangerment as logical outcomes of single experiences and relationships, overlooking how longer-term processes shape their identities as Indigenous language 'forgetters'. As Lemke notes, 'the formation of identity, or even fundamental change in attitudes or habits of reasoning, cannot take place on short times-cales. Even if short-term events contribute toward such changes', emergent longer-term processes and the effects of subsequent events 'make these changes count' towards human development (Lemke, 2000: 282). The ongoing project of developing and enacting personal identities, as well, 'requires integration across timescales: across who we are in this event and that, at this moment or the other, with this person or another, in one role and situation or another' (Lemke, 2000: 283).

The formation of young people's identities as heritage language 'speakers' or heritage language 'losers and forgetters' similarly depends on how young people's linguistic interactions are set up, negotiated in the moment, and then followed up in long-term processes. Stories like Mike's of how specific personal friendships 'caused' personal language loss became common in Piniq only after changes in schooling and migration eroded young people's collective resources for learning Yup'ik, and local peer culture started tipping into English. Growing up within earshot of Yup'ik, children and older youth also continued to develop bilingual competences and bilingual ways of getting by in the local setting over time.

'Getting by' and linguistic survivance in the community

Contextualizing young people's self-descriptions with ethnographic observations provides a more nuanced picture of young people's bilingualism during language shift. Often, youth in the first generation to speak a nonheritage language as an unmarked peer language in communities retain considerable receptive skills and basic productive skills in their heritage language, though such skills can be difficult to locate and measure (Dorian, 1989; Valdés, 2005). In the GB group youth like Nathan, who moved from Piniq to urban areas or non-Yup'ik-speaking villages and then back again, and youth like Mike, who stayed in Piniq, but expressed linguistic insecurities about speaking Yup'ik, typically spent years picking up receptive skills in Yup'ik. Youth like Amy, who moved in their upper elementary years to Piniq from an urban area and subsequently stayed in Piniq, also developed bilingual ways of getting by locally, even if their Yup'ik comprehension skills remained at a basic level.

In daily life, most youth in the GB group could follow village happenings in Yup'ik. Youth reported that they regularly listened to the VHF marine radio system described in the previous chapter that villagers used to make general community announcements, locate one another and discuss the logistics of subsistence. Most GB youth were also adept at 'getting by' in Piniq using simple statements and phrases in Yup'ik, even as growing proportions of youth reported that they could not comfortably 'create in the language', and did not appear to know how to use more than simple Yup'ik morphology. Nathan, for instance, used basic Yup'ik at home with siblings who never left Piniq as well as grandparents, aunts and uncles, after returning from his stint in Anchorage. Amy reported how she, too, used Yup'ik to speak with her grandmother and aunties.

In 2000–2001, multiple GB group members also interpreted for older community members. Mary from above served as a bilingual broker when elders needed to write personal checks in English, and helped translate a local elder's announcement that he wanted to run for village president. Like local adult interpreters, Mary noted the linguistic challenges of translating from Yup'ik to English given the differences in Yup'ik morphology and English word order. Yet even minimal Yup'ik speakers like Mike who had grown up in Piniq helped interpret short, predictable interactions between elders and white teachers.

Like many other youth in the first group to use mostly English, Amy, Nathan and Mike also used Yup'ik to 'get by' in village institutions. In church, GB group members followed predictable Yup'ik announcements, directions in choir practices and instructions for annual events like the extensive round of Christmas caroling. Young people like Amy who moved to Piniq as older youth from urban areas reported difficulties following Yup'ik sermons in church and understanding teachers' Yup'ik use in school. Still, many youth like Nathan and Mike who spent years in Piniq reported that they could understand extended Yup'ik discourse. In the following section, we will consider how youth used their bilingualism to negotiate interactions with adults in the local school.

'Getting by' with adults in school

Endangered languages often serve as powerful, in-group, boundary-marking resources for both those who speak and those who rarely speak the languages in everyday life (May, 2005; Mougeon & Beniak, 1989). As in the RS group, strong Yup'ik-speaking GB youth used Yup'ik to figure out assignments with one another, and to talk about everyday events. Strong and even relatively weak Yup'ik speakers also used Yup'ik as an everyday resource for sharing critiques, comments, jokes and insults out of the linguistic purview of the mostly white nonlocal teachers. During an after-school study hall, one strong Yup'ik speaker flirted with a girl in Yup'ik, asking her if she wanted to marry a white teacher sitting nearby. 'Eww!' she laughed back at him, smiling. While waiting in a long line for ice cream at a sixth-grade sleepover, a former child migrant who usually spoke English complained loudly about the teachers running the event, calling out *'Cukaipagceci!'* (*You guys are so slow!*) In interviews, youth described how they used Yup'ik to make comments about teachers' breath, and to curse at one another without getting in trouble around white educators.

GB youth also regularly used Yup'ik to get by in very different ways with local educators in school. The seventh-grade group in 2000 spent their day with a Yup'ik-speaking homeroom teacher who often spoke Yup'ik in class. The teacher enjoyed talking to students about local history, and made multiple efforts to connect students' lives to the curriculum. When conducting highly standardized textbook assignments in English, the teacher also maintained the daily patter of the classroom in codeswitched Yup'ik and English. Strong Yup'ik-speaking youth often spoke Yup'ik fluidly with the teacher. Youth who spoke mostly English also used simple phrases in everyday classroom interactions, calling to the teacher, *'Taqua'* (*I'm done*), *'Ak'a pillruanka'* (*I already did them*), and *'Cataituq'* (*he's/she's not here*).

Some individual Yup'ik educators used mostly English in extracurricular activities, yet used Yup'ik with strong Yup'ik speakers. Other local language advocates tried to directly encourage students' Yup'ik use. As the girls' basketball coach, Jenny commonly shouted directions in Yup'ik like the following, noted during a pickup game before a tournament, *'Maliggluku,* stay with him!' *'Ullagluku!* (*check him!*)' *'Eggluku!'* (*Throw it in!*), *'Cukaitessiyaagtuten!'* (*You're too slow!*) *'Nutga!!'* (*Shoot it!!*) In one practice, Jenny tried to require girls on her team to speak nothing but Yup'ik, though the effort lasted for one day.

GB youth were accustomed to following stretches of extended discourse in local activities. Many youth, for instance, participated in an after-school activity called Native Youth Olympics, or NYO. Elders used versions of NYO events traditionally to maintain strength, balance and flexibility during the long winter months. In the contemporary school-sponsored version of NYO, youth competed in events such as high kicks and jumps, and the 'seal hop', where students lay on the floor, then hopped as far as possible on their knuckles and toes, holding their bodies off the ground. Youth also competed for individual medals and team trophies in intervillage tournaments, and spots on a district team for statewide competition.

After-school activities commonly opened spaces for local adults to socialize youth about working together and handling emotions, using *qanruyutait* (*teachings*) in school discourse. Talking about a previous NYO tournament, the coach had described how he was 'kind of embarrassed' when one of the players did not do as well as he had hoped, and had visibly thrown his arms down in frustration. The coach went on to say, 'I never talked to this team about it, but it's not the Yup'ik way to show your frustrations. You are not supposed to, like, stand up for yourself, but to take it. I need to find some time to talk to these guys about it.'

The following bilingual talk, given to approximately 40 GB youth ages eleven to eighteen years old during a practice in Piniq, highlights how local adults fluidly and skillfully mixed Yup'ik, English as well as additional symbolic references in extended discourse aimed at youth. In the beginning of the talk, the coach discussed his search for a girls' chaperone, and his strategy for choosing students for an upcoming tournament in a mix of Yup'ik and English. The coach then discussed the previous incident with the frustrated athlete, using his bilingualism and local knowledge to underscore cultural expectations for behavior (Yup'ik is marked by italics, and English translation follows the excerpt):

Original:
Taugaam Alan-*aaq* pick-*arciqaat,* (name of village)-*mi* first-*aareskan taugaam. Taugaam,* state-champ-*aarullruuq* two years in a row. *Tua-i* pick-*aryugngaluku. Taugaam,* um, *waniw' tua-i nallunriraa* beat-*arciuleq.* Beat-*arciungerpeci-wani qenengluci piarkaunrituci.* Just because somebody beat you, you don't *qenngeq, Qenngarkaunrituci.* Accept-*ararkaugaci* defeat-*aq assirtuq.* Beat-*aqaci kia imum-wani,* learn from it. *Tua-i* control-*ararkauguq.* Learn to control yourself. Beat-*aqaten kia imum.* You're not taking first place in tournament, and you get beat in a tournament, don't get mad, don't show it ... Work harder ... *Tuaten piarkaugut qenertarkaunritukut* don't *tengluaq* the floor ... *Tuaten piarkaugukut, elitarkaugukut,* Beat-*arciuyuunani kina yuuyuituq. Wall' kina imna* error-*aamikun, elicetuuq.* All through life ... like in hunting. *Tua-i nani navgikuvet,* it's part of life, learn from accidents. *Tuaten ayuquq.* Work hard-*arturluni taugaam, elicarauguq.* Work hard-*aq* even in education. Homework-*arturarrarkauguci.* NYO trip-*aryukuvci* homework-*arturararkauguci. Icugg' tua-i* don't quit on anything.

Translation:
But they'll pick *Alan only if he gets* first *at* (name of village). *But he was* state champion two years in a row. *So, they are able to* pick *him. But he now knows how it is to be* beat. *Even if you are* beat*en, you aren't supposed to be getting angry.* Just because somebody beats you, you don't *get angry. You are not to get mad. You have to* accept defeat, *it's good. If someone* beats *you* ... you learn from it. *You are to* control *yourself.* Learn to control yourself. *If someone* beats *you,* you're not taking first place in tournament, and you get beat in a tournament, don't get mad, don't show it ... Work harder ... *That's what you should do, we are not to get angry,* don't *pound* the floor ... *We are supposed to do that, we should learn. No one will ever live without ever getting* beaten. *Or anyone learn from his* error. All through

life ... like in hunting. *So then wherever if you have a breakdown of your snowmachine*, it's part of life, learn from accidents, *that's the way it is.* Work*ing* hard *all the time is the way to learn.* Work hard, even in education. *You guys have to do your* homework *all the time. If you want to go on a* NYO trip, *you have to do your* homework all the time. *You know*, don't quit on anything.

Above, we can see how the local coach, like many local adults at the time, assumed that the GB group could understand common vocabulary in Yup'ik and English, Yup'ik morphology and English word order. The coach also expected youth to follow commonplace Yup'ik verbal postbases used for marking tense (e.g. *–ci* for simple future and *–llru* for simple past), and postbases commonly used in issuing directives (e.g. *–kau, have to V* in 'accept-*ararkaugaci'*, *'you have to* accept'), and Yup'ik word endings encoding 1st, 2nd or 3rd person, singular, dual or plural subjects and objects, and verb transitivity/intransitivity. The coach also used complex statements combining connective mood endings and establishing dependent clauses such as *-kuvet, if/when you* and *-kumta, if/when we.*

As we have seen in the previous chapter, at age 4, Willie from family 2 had already acquired and started to combine many of these same Yup'ik postbases and endings. During language shift, adults also commonly expected youth to interpret multiple agglutinated Yup'ik phrases in relation to one another, as in the statement from above, 'NYO trip-*aryukuvci* homework-*arturararkauguci'* (*If you guys want to go on the* NYO trip, *you guys have to do your* homework *all the time*).

In the latter section above, we also see how the coach socialized youth in relation to local discourse norms. The coach used tense-neutral, dependent subordinative endings (*-luku, -luni*, etc.) extensively, marking tense infrequently, following norms for extended Yup'ik discourse and storytelling. Through his patterned use of connectives like *tua-i* (*so then*) and *taugaam* (*however*), the coach further created a locally recognizable poetic structure for his talk.

As the coach spoke, he repeated phrases in Yup'ik and English for emphasis. In many places, he also inserted one English word in Yup'ik sentences, following patterns of codeswitching similar to strong speakers of Inuit languages elsewhere (Allen, 2007). In many other instances, however, the coach moved fluidly between English word order and Yup'ik morphology, blending Yup'ik and English frames within single statements. The coach further moved into discussing *qanruyutait* (*teachings*) about maintaining control of emotions in public, emphasizing the importance of self-discipline by repeating related points in Yup'ik and English multiple times. Using a local analogy about a risky situation in hunting – snowmobiles breaking down and/or running out of gas – the coach highlighted cultural expectations for how to handle stressful situations and learn from accidents.

The youth in the practice followed the speech intently without asking clarification questions, following local expectations for listening to adults. Watching GB youth get by with local adults in similar situations, it was often difficult to know when youth might be using their awareness of the local context and following adults' borrowed English words to figure out predictable meanings (such as the relationship between homework and the upcoming NYO trip in the statement highlighted above). Yet, at many points in the overall talk and above, listeners would need considerable Yup'ik receptive competences to discern the coach's meaning, such as the coach's broad statement about life and learning, *'No one will ever live without ever getting beaten. Or anyone learn from his* error,' spoken primarily in Yup'ik.

Multiple local adults who found themselves speaking mostly English with their young children and grandchildren voiced the concern that their English-speaking children and grandchildren would not be able to 'really understand them' when they grew older. In light of these tensions, the coach's talk served as a strong expression of linguistic survivance. During early language shift, adults creatively negotiated the expectation that youth would connect to important local teachings through Yup'ik use. Youth also worked to get by with local adults.

Yup'ik literacy and linguistic insecurity

By upper elementary and secondary grades, students' Yup'ik literacy lagged far behind their English literacy competences. Nevertheless, teachers tried to use Yup'ik literacy to support the learning of locally relevant curricular content. In the mid-1990s, the school district worked with elders to developed themes for a secondary curriculum based on *yuuyaraq* (*the Yup'ik way of life*). Upper elementary and secondary Yup'ik teachers had few classroom materials, yet gamely tried to follow the curriculum. Each sixth-grade class, for instance, started with the students reciting a statement about Yup'ik values. In high school class brainstorms, as well, teachers asked students how to be *takaryuk*, and recorded students' answers in Yup'ik on a classroom poster. Class assignments commonly covered subsistence terms in season. Teachers also read to students from the few available books, including the materials produced by RS youth and educators in the elders project described in Chapter 4. The high school Yup'ik teacher who had been involved with the earlier project, however, noted that she had to simplify the Yup'ik morphology when she read the elders' narratives aloud to GB students.

During rapid language shift, teachers also struggled to involve students with wide-ranging Yup'ik competences in class interactions (e.g. Jaffe, 2006). In the Yup'ik classes observed, students sat according to their comfort level speaking Yup'ik, with the stronger Yup'ik-speaking students in the front, minimal Yup'ik speakers across the back, and the few non-Yup'ik speakers out on the side. Teachers asked group questions, moving along as strong Yup'ik speakers called out the answers.

Individual youth who had spent early childhoods around English-speaking children faced particular challenges following Yup'ik instruction, and developed a range of coping behaviors in school. Amy, for instance, described how she couldn't understand very much in Yup'ik class, and how she would ask her teacher if she could get water, go to the bathroom or fill in word searches to pass the time. When I asked Amy about her experiences in the seventh-grade homeroom, she also reported that she watched other students so she could know what to do without calling attention to herself.

When it came to Yup'ik reading and writing assignments, teachers and students struggled even more. In the seventh-grade class, for instance, only a couple of the strongest Yup'ik speakers would respond to teachers' requests to read aloud in Yup'ik. When the Yup'ik teacher asked students to write the names of animals in one class, even strong Yup'ik-speaking youth complained loudly about how 'hard' it was, and asked if they could write in English. In the sixth-grade class, students more willingly attempted to write in Yup'ik, though their results were slow at best. In one class observed, student interaction in Yup'ik only picked up when the aide in charge was asked to temporarily step outside the room, and a group of boys dove behind a bookshelf to form a circle on the floor to tell one another hunting stories, strikingly, in Yup'ik.

In a few instances, white teachers attempted to support students' bilingualism by offering students opportunities to write assignments in Yup'ik. However, such efforts inadvertently called to the fore students' limited opportunities for developing Yup'ik academic literacy in a school setting that systemically undervalued Yup'ik, and related linguistic insecurities (see also Dauenhauer & Dauenhauer, 1998). Ellen was one of the younger children from a strong Yup'ik-speaking family, a confident and popular young woman with students and school staff. Ellen spoke Yup'ik at home and with adults out and about in the village. Yet, when the time came for Ellen to give her valedictorian speech at graduation, she chose to write the speech in English. Her teacher reported that Ellen was worried about making mistakes in Yup'ik in front of an audience.

Sandra was another strong Yup'ik speaker from the GB group who reportedly felt challenged when she was asked to transfer her everyday

Yup'ik-speaking skills into academic assignments. Julia, the local kindergarten teacher remembered Sandra as one of the strongest Yup'ik-speaking children in her class. As an older youth, Sandra used Yup'ik with peers and as she fulfilled multiple local responsibilities such as helping her grandmother, running activities in church and babysitting nieces and nephews. When Sandra returned as a senior to interview her former kindergarten teacher for a school newspaper article, Julia agreed on the condition that Sandra interview her in Yup'ik. Sandra never completed the interview, reportedly telling Julia, 'I can't.' 'I *know* she can,' Julia sadly asserted.

Yup'ik literacy and contradictory expressions

In a public mixed message about the desirability, but difficulty of academic Yup'ik speech and literacy, a high school girl wrote an emotional letter to the school paper in 2000, encouraging her peers to speak Yup'ik. In the letter, the youth spoke of how she had gone into a classroom and seen first-grade children saying the pledge of allegiance in Yup'ik, and how she doubted that her peers could do the same. The article appeared in English.

Within Yup'ik classrooms, writing assignments could present opportunities for students to express overt allegiance to Yup'ik literacy. However, even these expressions could inadvertently mark Yup'ik literacy as difficult in a setting where youth and adults felt like inexperienced users of the school-based phonemic orthography. In a Yup'ik class, for instance, one student boasted of finishing an assignment quickly. Another student responded, 'that's cause you did it in *kass'aq* (*white/English*).' In her comment, the student overtly critiqued the first student's choice to use English instead of Yup'ik writing, using the stigmatized label '*kass'aq*' (*white*) for English. Simultaneously, the student also highlighted how writing in English was generally easier than writing in Yup'ik for GB youth.

The first student, a minimal Yup'ik speaker, tried to counter the insult using token Yup'ik, stating, 'Well you did it *paciatun* (*any old way*).' His comment backfired, however, when the class picked up on his mispronunciation of the common Yup'ik word *piciatun*, and teased him. The Yup'ik teacher rallied to his aid, saying 'Me too, when I read *piciqsia*, I read it *pacaqsia*; I was *takaryuk* (*embarrassed*).' Her sympathetic comment, as well, underscored assumptions about the difficulty of reading in Yup'ik, and related feelings of linguistic insecurity.

Nevertheless, in another setting, some of the same youth voluntarily chose to read and write in Yup'ik. In the local church, Sunday school students were given the weekly choice of copying down and reading a Bible verse in front of the full Sunday school using the Moravian Yup'ik writing system or English. The time I observed the seventh-grade class, the students who had complained loudly about how writing in Yup'ik was 'too hard' in school vocally chose to write their Bible verse in the Moravian orthography in order to distinguish themselves from the sixth-grade group who generally read the same verse, but in English. Since students' Sunday school literacy practices were typically short, bounded exercises, youth easily helped one another fulfill the expectations of these Yup'ik literacy events by copying from one another and reading as a group.

Section II: Negotiating a Bilingual Peer Culture

According to school-based assessments and observations, within most secondary classes in 2000–2001, a majority of students spoke mostly English. Within many classes, a third or less of the students used Yup'ik postbases and word endings comfortably. Yet, GB youth did not stigmatize or put down one another for being heritage language speakers like youth in some other Indigenous North American communities experiencing shift (Lee, 2007; Pye, 1992). In contrast, strong Yup'ik-speaking students in the GB group expected listeners to share receptive skills in Yup'ik. They also commonly made Yup'ik comments and jokes as they entered groups of English-speaking youth, without overt comment from their peers. Like their RS predecessors, these youth used extended Yup'ik discourse to talk about anything from speech contests to basketball games.

Comparing students' peer-directed uses of Yup'ik and social standing within local peer groups further highlighted how Yup'ik remained a language of status within the GB group in 2000–2001. Class presidents, student council members and prom queens and kings in the GB group were generally strong Yup'ik speakers who used extended Yup'ik discourse with peers. Strong Yup'ik-speaking students were also commonly chosen as team captains for organized team sports and spontaneous intramural games, as well, though these individuals were also star athletes so it would be too simple to attribute their status to language use.

Subgroups of youth used Yup'ik to varying degrees, and among different class groups one could find pockets of strong Yup'ik speakers using Yup'ik with one another. By analyzing the practices of subgroups in light of young people's individualized trajectories, we can further consider how youth negotiated uneven language learning opportunities, heterogeneous linguistic resources and local language ideologies, creating emerging patterns of everyday language use with peers.

The seniors: Trajectories of Yup'ik language learning and use

Chapter 5 documented how small children in Piniq developed their everyday language use over time within multistranded relationships and overlapping social networks. Youth in Piniq who were arbitrarily grouped by age in elementary school, as well, developed shared group stances and patterns over time (e.g. Gutiérrez et al., 1995) as they took classes together for up to 12 years and socialized one another, negotiating individuals' language learning experiences.

The five seniors in 2000–2001, for instance, evidenced how the individual language socialization contingencies described in the previous chapter could align in favor of young people's continued use of Yup'ik as an unmarked language of peer culture. Two seniors were the oldest children in GB families. Three out of five seniors were younger siblings in older families with both RS and GB children and had been socialized by strong Yup'ik-speaking siblings and cousins, as well as parents. All five seniors had lived in Piniq their entire lives. Each of the students spoke Yup'ik comfortably, and were also proficient in English.

Considering the school trajectories of the original members of the senior class highlighted how knowing Yup'ik did not 'hold children back' from learning English or academic achievement in school. Studies have shown how American Indian and Alaska Native students in general, and Yup'ik students, in particular, often feel pushed out of schools that do not reflect their lives and communities, schools that do not appear to provide a pathway to future goals, and schools marked by disciplinary conflict, racism, uncaring teachers and/or low expectations (Deyhle & Swisher, 1997; Freed & Samson, 2004). In 2001, the district that served Piniq and surrounding Yup'ik villages struggled with a school-leaving rate of 52%. In other surrounding Yup'ik districts, the school-leaving rate was as high as 80%, with individual schools witnessing 100% loss of secondary students by their senior year (Freed & Samson, 2004).

Chapters 3 and 4 documented some of the challenging circumstances plaguing the local school and secondary program in Piniq. The senior class in Piniq, like many classes before and after them, experienced high attrition during high school, and the reasons students left reflected an array of conflicts and hopes. After reportedly becoming disgusted with the incompetent math teacher described in Chapter 3, two youth from the original senior class moved away from Piniq hoping to find better education elsewhere, one to a boarding school with a good reputation, and another to a nearby village. Two students moved with their families for economic opportunities elsewhere, and a seventh student had been retained a year.

Two 'outta here' students had dropped out of school to try life in Anchorage, only to come back when the economics of life in the city proved daunting. The four students who started with the senior class in ninth grade who never graduated from high school all had low productive skills in Yup'ik. In contrast, the students who made it to graduation under extremely challenging circumstances in Piniq were all strong Yup'ik-speaking youth, unlike their school-leaving counterparts.

The senior group also evidenced how young people's life contingencies, individualized language learning opportunities and accumulated linguistic resources shaped pockets of everyday Yup'ik use among subgroups of youth, even as young people's increasing use of English overall became a driving force of family and community-wide language shift. Strikingly, five years into the 'tip' into English in the youth culture of Piniq, the seniors used Yup'ik as an unmarked peer language with one another. Their daily language practices generally mirrored those of the RS group in the 1990s as the youth told stories and jokes, talked about daily events and accomplished goals such as planning a prom together predominantly in Yup'ik. Yet, after receiving minimal Yup'ik literacy instruction, the seniors also expressed insecurities about writing in their heritage language, as we have seen above.

The seventh grade: Negotiating divergent language trajectories

Compared to the senior class above, the seventh-grade class in 2000–2001 reflected a more typical mix of life contingencies and linguistic competences for GB youth. For instance, the group was much more impacted by migration than the seniors, and 4 of the 12 students who stayed in Piniq for the school year 2000–2001 had lived in English-speaking towns as child migrants with their parents. Three more students flowed back and forth to English-speaking hubs and villages over the course of the year.

Like child migrants in the RS group, youth from the GB group who flowed into Piniq generally did not speak extended Yup'ik beyond single words and simple phrases, if they used any Yup'ik at all. They also expressed linguistic insecurities about speaking Yup'ik, as we will see in the following chapter. Still, those who stayed in Piniq for years developed receptive competences over time, which they used to interact bilingually with Yup'ik-speaking youth.

Strong Yup'ik speakers comprised roughly a third of the seventh-grade class, and evidenced how both family circumstances and efforts shaped individualized affordances for learning to speak Yup'ik. One younger sibling from a transitional family with RS and GB children had spoken Yup'ik growing up with RS group siblings. The oldest child and a younger sibling from two young but strong Yup'ik-speaking families had grown up speaking Yup'ik together as cousins.

A fourth strong Yup'ik speaker in the seventh-grade group, Evan, had initially spoken English elsewhere, yet had been adopted into a strong Yup'ik-speaking family in Piniq as a young child. When Evan's adopted parents brought him to Piniq, they enlisted older siblings from the RS group in a family-wide Yup'ik immersion effort similar to that of Jenny's family described in Chapter 5. By the time Evan was in seventh grade, he spoke Yup'ik well for his age. He also achieved in school, received recognition for a district-wide writing assessment piece in English describing a day of seal hunting with relatives in 2001.

Strikingly, some of the strong Yup'ik speakers in the group described how individual children of mixed heritage had been saved from being *kass'aqs* through such family immersion efforts. In the following interview segment, John and Tom, two strong Yup'ik speakers in the seventh-grade group, described a young child who had been adopted into a local family:

LTW: Did your parents talk to you in Yup'ik, or=
Tom: =Most of the people talk to their kids in Yup'ik.
John: Like Lilly Tom, you know her? She's sharp in Yup'ik. She was going to be a *kass'aq* (*white person*) you know the hair? And the eyes? She, [Name], my auntie, she started speaking in Yup'ik to her, started eating Yup'ik food, and then while she got taller, she started speaking in Yup'ik.

Tom was an older sibling in a strong Yup'ik-speaking family; John was a young sibling in a large family, yet had grown up with Yup'ik-speaking cousins. Both spoke Yup'ik frequently with one another and around peers. Like most youth and individual class groups at the time, however, the seventh-grade students used much more English than Yup'ik with one another, and much less Yup'ik than the seniors and RS youth. Negotiating their wide-ranging linguistic repertoires with one another, the seventh graders and their GB peers also forged a distinctly local peer culture.

Yup'ik use in local youth culture during language shift

Among upper elementary to high-school-aged GB youth, some individuals spoke Yup'ik comfortably with peers, maintaining Yup'ik discourse patterns and morphology as their unmarked frame for local peer interactions, even as they borrowed English words and phrases in everyday talk. In the following interview, for instance, John, from above discussed a local basketball game with me and another Yup'ik-speaking student (underlined endings discussed below):

1. **John:**   Last week Kyle-*aq*   Last week Kyle
               akngirtellruuq.   *got hurt.*

2. **LTW:**   *Qaillun⸮ Ayaksaitua*   *How⸮ I never*
               Tallimeritmi. Qaill'   *went on Friday.*
               ayuqellrua⸮   *How did it go⸮*

3. **John:**   [*Village name*]-*armiut*   *When the people from*
               maantellratni, elbow-*arluku,*   [*Village name*]
               aug'um short referee-*m*   *were here, he got*
               [*Village name*]-*mium*   elbowed, *and that* short
               count-*arpek'naku*   referee *from* [*Village name*]
               tangvang'ermiu.   *didn't* count *it, even though*
                                                    he was watching.

4. **LTW:**   Hmm, I wonder why.   Hmm, I wonder why.

5. **John:**   Call-*aksaitaa.*   *He never* call-*ed it.*

6. **LTW:**   I heard one of   I heard one of
               the games they, it was   the games they, it was
               really close until   really close until
               right at the end.   right at the end.

7. **John:**   Yeh Bill-*aq. tuani,*   Yeh Bill, *right there,*
               kina⸮ First-*aamek* both   *who⸮ At* first he made
               shots make-*arlukek.*   *both* shots. *They had a*
               Time out-*arluteng,*   time out, Ben *coming in,*
               Ben-*aq iterluni* side   *shot a* side shot *and he*
               shot-*amek, nutegluku*   *sunk it. They were thankful*
               ekluku-llu. Quyaluteng   *because they* won.
               win-*allruami.*

As John told basketball stories, he studded his narratives with English words and phrases (e.g. 'last week' 'elbow', 'short referee', 'count', 'first', 'both shots make', 'time out', 'side shot', 'win'), incorporating the words into Yup'ik by adding Yup'ik postbases and endings. By considering the underlined endings in turn 7, we also see how John shaped the basketball stories in accordance with Yup'ik storytelling norms (Jacobson, 1995), using a set of tense-neutral subordinative endings encoding person and transitivity, including:

-luni (3rd person singular subject of an intransitive verb)
-luteng (3 or more subjects of an intransitive verb)

-luku (3rd person singular object of a transitive verb)
-lukek (3rd person dual objects of a transitive verb)

A direct translation of John's story in turn 7 would overtly mark tense via the post-base *-llru-* in the final phrase below, looking something more like this:

John:	Yeh Bill-*aq. tuani, kina?*	Yeh Bill, *right there, who?*
	First-*aamek* both shots	At first *making both* shots.
	make-*arlukek*. Time out-*arluteng,*	*They having a* time out,
	Ben-*aq iterluni* side shot-*amek,*	Ben *coming in, shooting*
	nutegluku ekluku-llu.	*a* side shot *and sinking it.*
	Quyaluteng win-a-	*They being thankful*
	llru-ami.	*because they* won.

John's pattern here of borrowing English words within a Yup'ik morphological frame was common among strong Yup'ik-speaking GB youth, as among strong Inuktitut speakers elsewhere (e.g. Allen, 2007). Chapter 5 documented how strong Yup'ik-speaking young children like Willie used the subordinative for telling simple stories, yet how increasing groups of young children with reduced Yup'ik language-learning opportunities most often demonstrated a very different pattern of translanguaging – that of inserting single Yup'ik words and/or simple phrases into utterances and stories framed by English word order (e.g. Allen, 2007).

GB youth who spoke mostly English used extensive Yup'ik tokenism with peers in 2001. Young people sprinkled their English speech with common Yup'ik discourse markers such as *kaca'a* (*oh no*), *aren* (*I mean*) and *icugg* (*like*), and used Yup'ik pronouns for emphasis, as in a student's assertion, '*Wiinga* (*me*), I would want to live in [village name].' Youth also borrowed Yup'ik nouns and used the ending –(a)*q* to create standalone English words out of Yup'ik verb bases. Regularly, youth borrowed words from Yup'ik for bodily functions (e.g. Zentella, 1997) as in the common statements 'I almost *miryaq* (*threw up*),' and 'who *leq*'d (*farted*)?' Youth combined Yup'ik body terms with English words to make hybrid insults, such as 'You're so *teq*-fat (*butt*-fat).' Much less frequently, youth also attached single Yup'ik word endings to English statements when talking with strong Yup'ik speakers, as in one girl's declaration in an argument over movies, 'You like the Matrix? Boring-*aartuq* (*it is*).'

Kinship terms can have a high degree of specificity and focus within Indigenous languages (Woodbury, 1993). However, Indigenous youth in shifting communities elsewhere have lost many of the kinship terms used by their grandparents and parents (Dauenhauer & Dauenhauer, 1998; Schmidt, 1985). Even relatively strong Yup'ik-speaking students in 2001 in Piniq did not use many of the specific kinship terms in Yup'ik, and replaced some commonplace kinship terms with English counterparts such as 'Grandma'. Still, youth underscored their affection and connections to relatives through use of other Yup'ik kinship terms such as *'apii'* for grandad, and *'iluq'* and *'ilung'* for male and female cousins.

Most GB youth also used specific Yup'ik subsistence-related terms. For instance, young people knew the Yup'ik nouns distinguishing smaller pieces of fast-melting ice from larger pieces used to keep drinking water cold in local steamhouses, and the three terms distinguishing a small, medium and large bearded seal. Youth also regularly borrowed Yup'ik words for animals and objects, specific land conditions, and verbs related to subsistence actions or occurrences into English statements and interactions, as in the following side of a phone conversation in which David asked another young man about his day:

David: You went hunting؟
David: Was it *qailiq*؟ (*wavy*؟)
David: Was it *ugtaq*؟ (*a seal on an ice-floe*؟)
David: How come you didn't *teguleq* (*take really fast*) it؟
David: I wouldn't if I were you; we need more *issuriq*s (*spotted seals*) in the ocean.

Young women, as well, borrowed terms for describing subsistence activities, as in the following example from Amy as she talked to a friend:

I *eritaq*'d (*pluck*ed) the bird, then I *allguq* (*took the skin off*) it.

Not surprisingly, youth were more familiar with Yup'ik terms related to contemporary activities than terms for items no longer encountered in village life, such as beams for traditional *qasgi* (sod houses). Individuals who lived with grandparents were generally more familiar with the specialized vocabulary of local elders than their peers. Youth who participated heavily in subsistence activities, as well, also tended to know the most Yup'ik vocabulary and were among the strongest Yup'ik speakers for their age.

Youth also used subsistence-related verbs, interspersing hunting verbs to heighten the effect of dramatic moments. Youth yelled *'Nutegluku!'* (*Shoot it!*)

at basketball games like adults around them. In another example of how hunting verbs in Yup'ik could spontaneously intensify group interactions, one student's voice shrieked *'Tuquskiu!'* (*'Kill it!'*) over 30 students cheering in English at the pitch of excitement as students burst open a homemade piñata in a class party.

The following chapter further details how GB youth used Yup'ik to learn subsistence practices and socialize one another as they took up local responsibilities and related gender roles. Below, however, we will see how GB youth employed a much wider range of linguistic resources to shape a highly localized bilingual peer culture during language shift.

Local style and bilingual resources

It was beyond the scope of the study to fully document young people's everyday language practices during rapid language shift. Nevertheless, the following section overviews some of the patterned ways young people in Piniq fashioned a specific group aesthetic out of wide-ranging linguistic resources.

In many contemporary contexts, Indigenous languages are being replaced by local dialects of English. In communities experiencing language shift and endangerment, specific discourse patterns, word choices or other shared norms in diverse 'village' or 'American Indian' Englishes may also mark Indigenous identities and continuities (Henze & Vanett, 1993; Kwachka, 1992; Leap, 1993). During language shift in Piniq, youth used multiple Yup'ik-influenced English features as one set of localized linguistic resources, such as Yup'ik-influenced phonological stress patterns, exclamations and bids for topic in conversation.

Yup'ik is known among linguists for its alternating stress pattern. GB youth commonly used similar patterns for emphasis in 'village English'. In the following examples of declarations from youth, for instance, underlining indicates a marked jump upwards in pitch:

Ex. 1:   [Shouted after someone took a picture of a girl with a camera]:
Oh <u>man</u>, He <u>fl</u>ashed to Sa<u>man</u>tha.

Ex. 2:   [Shouting over student noise while asking for the third time how to grade an assignment]:
How <u>many</u> <u>wrong</u>, how <u>many</u> per<u>cent</u>age?

Ex. 3:   [Protesting a substitute teacher's directions]:
Tom <u>gave</u> this as<u>sign</u>ment.

Echoing the Yup'ik exclamation, *'Angli-lli!'* (*'too much!'*), GB youth also commonly left dislocated the intensifier 'so' in local English use, as in the exclamations 'So lots it is!' and 'So puny it is!' They additionally used the rejoinder 'even me', echoing local uses of *'Wiinga-llu'* (*and me*) as a localized way of saying 'me, too'. Often, youth used 'even me' as a patterned bid for sharing a related story in conversational turn-taking, as we can see in the following example:

Student 1: My dad went hunting yesterday, caught lots.
Student 2: Even me, my dad went hunting yesterday.

Like adults and RS youth, GB youth regularly used onomatopeic sound words (Roth-Gordon, 2007) incorporating iconic Yup'ik sounds, such as the common sound words for gun shots in subsistence narratives, 'Trr', and 'Prr' with 'rr' representing the back velar voiceless fricative.

Slang terms and phrases are common markers of global and local peer cultures, and change rapidly (Mendoza-Denton, 2008; Roth-Gordon, 2007). In some instances, youth transformed existing English terms and phrases from RS youth as they tailored local youth culture to a particular time and place. For instance, RS youth periodically exclaimed 'Holy cow!' in the 1990s; by 2001 GB youth had phonologically reshaped the exclamation. Drawing out a low-pitched 'o' for the first syllable, youth emphasized the second syllable with a shortened, upswing in pitch and backed vowel: 'Ho:<u>leh</u>!' They also used the term much more frequently than their RS predecessors. In 2001, young children had begun to pick up the exclamation from older siblings, using 'Ho:<u>leh</u>!' with one another.

GB youth introduced new English slang in 2000–2001, such as the popular phrase for placing blame, 'Cause of <u>you/name</u>!' GB youth called 'cause of <u>you</u>!' or 'cause of [<u>name</u>]!' in wide-ranging situations, blaming individuals for lost points in sports games, or, in one instance, loudly faulting a peer for sharing a homework answer that turned out to be wrong. The phrase was also less frequently used as a humorous boast, as when a student got a point for his team in a game, and smilingly proclaimed, 'Ooh, cause of <u>me</u>!'

Patterned uses of token Yup'ik, Yup'ik-influenced English, and English slang flowed through peer culture. As youth responded collectively to specific situations, these linguistic features also appeared together in classroom discourse, as we can see in the following exchange when a math teacher gave seventh-grade students one minute to finish a problem before grading an assignment:

Teacher: 1 minute.
Student 1: 'Ho:<u>leh</u>!'
Student 2: *'Kaca!'* (*Oh no!*)
Student 3: So <u>hard</u> these are!

Youth in shifting communities often stop producing new words in endangered languages (Schmidt, 1985). GB youth in Piniq coined almost no new Yup'ik terms during rapid language shift, with the exception of one telling and derogatory hybrid term:

Ex.:	*kassa-*	*ssuun-*	-dy
Translation:	*white person-*	*device associated with N*	-dy
Gloss:	someone who acts like *a white person*		

As local adults increasingly accused youth of wanting to be like whites by speaking English, youth found new ways to stigmatize nonlocal stylistic practices, versus English use, as acting white. Youth did not use *kassassun*dy to call out or stigmatize one another's language choices. Instead, youth built upon historically rooted negative stereotypes of white people as tending too critically to cleanliness, and described peers as *kassassun*dy if they tried to be 'too perfect' and/or particular about dress, hair, and glossy, globalized youth style.

Not surprisingly, however, references to global media generally filled the banter of the GB group.

Connecting with one another through global media

In multiple ways during language shift, GB youth, like adults and their older RS counterparts in Piniq, consumed, creatively refashioned, and referenced TV, music and movies with one another, bringing multiple worlds into school spaces through everyday socializing. Contemporary youth also integrate their worlds, disrupting the tedium of school and shaping relationships with one another by mixing popular media and local references into classrooms (Rampton, 2006). During downtime in classes, GB youth compared their media use, sometimes teasingly calling back and forth claims about peers having bad taste in movies or music, as in one instance where boys insulted one another with accusations of 'Backstreet Boys!' and 'Country Music Orchestra!' Flipping through sports magazines, students also teased one another by comparing themselves to basketball stars in pictures making slam dunks or losing points, saying, 'See that? That's me (pointing to the dunker), that's you (pointing to the opponent). Me (dunker), you (opponent).'

Commonly, students hummed, sang and voiced lines from movies as prevalent forms of connecting socially through media use (Rampton, 2006). During one class observation, a group of three girls in the corner quietly tried out a cheer and accompanying arm movements from a cheerleading movie

Bringing It On. A little later two boys imitated the main character in the movie *The Sixth Sense*, throwing one another scared looks and claiming, 'I see dead people', then laughing at each other. Another boy crooned a line from a popular song, pretending to woo a girl as he tried to get her to help him with an assignment.

Like the RS group, GB group members also sometimes joked by consciously blurring the boundaries between Yup'ik and English. One student, for instance, spontaneously scrawled 'Wazz *Apii* (*grandad*)!' on the blackboard at the beginning of Yup'ik class, blending the media catch-phrase 'wazzup' from a famous commercial with the Yup'ik endearment for a grandfather.

Like youth elsewhere, young people in Piniq sometimes played with the authoritative voices and discourses around them such as those found in educational campaigns surrounding local issues. Two students taunted one another in a gym class, for instance, saying, 'What's wrong with you, you kill too many brain cells sniffing gas?' Youth, however, seemingly never mocked elders' *qanruyutait* or Christian teachings, showing how both sets of discourses carried particular force in Piniq.

Connecting to the world wide web

Between the RS and GB group, youth in Piniq became connected to the world wide web. Similar to many lower class minority and/or rural youth elsewhere in 2001, the GB group primarily had access to personal email accounts and the internet through computers located at the school. In many ways, internet connections allowed GB youth to increase their everyday participation in local and translocal forms of communication. Youth used email through a school district server to interact daily with Yup'ik youth in and out of Piniq. One high-school-aged youth noted that he had starting mostly using email for contacting youth in other villages, saying, 'I don't write to the people from here cause it's a waste of email time, you could just tell 'em later on'. In after-school study halls, youth surfed commercial websites, checking out sites devoted to selling global youth culture, such as cosmogirl. com, and downloading new music from popular culture sites like MTV.com. Youth also visited commercial websites related to local activities, such as sites advertising flashy new snowmobiles.

Observations and interview data suggested that some youth in 2001 were also using new internet connections to access and share Christian discourses within local and regional networks. Some GB youth found an internet story about a scientist who broke through the surface of the earth to hear the screams of Hell, which could be heard by following a link on the web. Others discussed and circulated second internet printout, a 'Letter from the Devil', encouraging readers to continue bad behavior and refuse Jesus.

Mary, a high school girl, also described how she had become a 'personal counseling service' over email, serving 'clients' including Yup'ik peers from other villages. The girl reported using Christian beliefs to discourage youth from committing suicide, warning peers, 'No matter what you are going through now it won't get better, just a hundred times worse in Hell if you do it.' Mary's words here underscore the importance of situating young people's acts of linguistic survivance in time and place. A recent youth participant action research project in Inuit communities in Canada compared villages with relatively high and low incidents of suicide, and found three common themes appearing across narratives of well-being from Inuit community members of all ages and sexes: (1) the central importance of family, (2) traditional values and practices, as well as (3) 'the importance of talking, whether to family, friends, or others in the community' (Kral & Idlout, 2006: 65). If we analyzed Mary's discussion of Hell over the internet with peers simply as 'non-traditional' or, worse, interpreted her acts as a straightforward evidence of 'internal colonization' following earlier missionizing efforts, we might miss the ways in which Mary's actions were rooted in lifelong experiences in a localized Christian church run by community members. We would also misinterpret the act of linguistic survivance on the part of a Yup'ik youth who recognized 'the importance of talking', and used new forms of communication to extend peer networks and keep youth alive in an Indigenous region wrestling with high suicide rates, and periodic youth suicide epidemics in particular villages (Fienup-Riordan, 2001).

In their downtime, GB youth commonly integrated their multiple local and translocal worlds in the daily flow of life. When visiting my home and helping me make cookies on a long summer afternoon, for instance, a group of 4th–6th-grade students made local shapes such as *piluguks* (*calf-high skin boots*) and Christian crosses, while eagerly telling me a ghost story from another village and the plotline of a favorite scary movie. They then spontaneously asked if they could tape themselves singing church songs from a global Christian media group.

Youth in Piniq further integrated symbolic resources and authoritative discourses to interpret powerful life experiences. One senior, for instance, shared a story in Yup'ik of how he crashed his snowmobile and almost died, then was discovered and saved by his cousin. When I asked the boy to retell the story on tape, he told it in English, using Yup'ik words for land features as well as Christian prayer. Backing up his assertion that he had been very close to death when he was saved, the boy referenced both local traditional beliefs about people's spiritual experiences before freezing and information about body temperatures and hypothermia learned from the Discovery Channel on satellite TV.

Thus, rather than simply 'walking in two worlds', like the RS group, members of the GB group participated in multiple local, regional and global spheres. Their local and global worlds ranged from the secular to the sacred, as they merged first-hand experiences in a unique subarctic environment with Yup'ik teachings, and mainstream and Christian media. Youth negotiated various authoritative voices in local and global settings, as they made sense of their personal experiences and connections to others. Within their local, bilingual peer culture, youth also used talk *in* Yup'ik and talk *about* Yup'ik to reinforce powerful local language ideologies and negotiate relationships in particular ways, as we will consider below.

The 'when' and 'how' of Yup'ik language allegiance

In the rich underlife of local classrooms and in everyday exchanges, the GB group used much more English than the RS group. Nevertheless, GB youth used Yup'ik for many of the same purposes as their older peers. Local and nonlocal young people's interactions continued to serve as a rich site for illuminating the discourse norms of local peer culture and the ways that youth used language strategically to spontaneously mark and/or erase boundaries along various lines of difference. In 2000, youth migrants with relatively developed Yup'ik competences generally found ways to fit into local life more easily than those without. However, in at least two instances, GB group members picked up on dialectal differences to exclude newcomers to the village. Such instances were particularly striking, since the newcomers involved spoke Yup'ik more fluently than many GB youth in Piniq at the time.

Students entering Piniq from urban areas with little knowledge of Yup'ik commonly faced challenges as they sought to establish a place within local peer culture. In the seventh-grade group, for instance, a boy named Harold was sent to live with cousins and, in his local guardian's words, 'try out village life for a while'. After an initial period of excitement, Harold had a difficult time adjusting to Piniq. A month after Harold arrived in Piniq, students were asked to write 10 sentences using state-of-being verbs in a class assignment. Some of Harold's classmates started their assignments by writing down sentences like 'I am full-blooded Eskimo,' and 'I am a Yup'ik.' Harold wrote the following:

I don't like Piniq.
It's boring.

Anchorage is way better.
In Anchorage you can play game station
I don't know Yup'ik.
Nobody will teach me Yup'ik.

During the above assignment, Nathan, another boy in the class, sat across from Harold. Above we saw how, in an interview, Nathan described his own insecurities speaking Yup'ik after living away from Piniq for years as a child. In this instance, however, Nathan played down the difficulty of learning Yup'ik and the need to speak Yup'ik other than in perfunctory tokens. After reading Harold's answers, Nathan asserted, 'Yup'ik people will teach you, say *"quyana"*, that's *"thank you"*.'

When Harold volunteered to play one of two roles in a Christmas skit developed by seventh-grade students, his classmates' responses further highlighted how GB youth used Yup'ik to distinguish themselves from urban peers. After a few rehearsals, students complained loudly, 'It's too cheap. We need to use someone who can speak Yup'ik, it would be better.' Harold was replaced with one of the strongest Yup'ik speakers in the class, and the other major role in the skit was given to another strong Yup'ik speaker. After a month Harold returned to Anchorage, and the skit was eventually performed completely in English.

In other instances local youth negotiated differences in their linguistic repertoires establishing a fleeting interactional equilibrium (Kramsch, 2002) through Yup'ik–English codeswitching. Multiple researchers have noted how bilingual speakers may translate statements when they do not receive responses to their initial statements or questions. In contrast, strong Yup'ik-speaking GB youth commonly fine-tuned codeswitched utterances after apparent misunderstandings. In one such instance, John from above teased a friend, 'Oh man, Cal, you burned a hole in this [indicating a fishnet] with your *tuqniq leq* (*powerful fart*).' When his friend Cal looked back at him without responding, John restated the punchline of his teasing insult with one less Yup'ik word: 'Your powerful *leq* (*fart*).'

GB youth did not put down peers for speaking Yup'ik, or vocally associate Yup'ik with poverty or backwardness like youth in some Indigenous communities experiencing language shift elsewhere (Lee, 2007; Pye, 1992). Youth sometimes teased one another, however, for mispronouncing Yup'ik in a pattern that further helped explain many students' seeming reluctance to use more than token Yup'ik with peers, and students' growing feeling that they 'spoke Yup'ik wrong'. Like youth in bilingual urban communities elsewhere (Jørgensen, 2005), GB youth also sometimes called explicit attention to societal norms as they sparred in verbal interactions, highlighting one another's lack of Yup'ik skills through spontaneous, racialized insults. One lengthy exchange of teasing insults between two youth ended, for instance, when one stated, 'You're a *kass'ayagaq* (*little white person*), you only speak *kass'aq* (*white/English*).'

In other instances, youth policed one another's increasing uses of English. Earlier in the interview below, Mary commented that she would like to hear young children speak Yupik to her in the future, and voiced concerns about language endangerment. The following segment starts with me repeating her earlier comment as a prompt:

LTW: But you'd rather see them speaking Yup'ik.
Mary: I'd love to see that, I'd love to hear them speak Yup'ik to me.
LTW: How come?
Mary: Cause it'd bring back memories, or know that our language is going to go on forever, not go away like other languages have.
LTW: Like, how would it be for you if your language goes away?
Mary: I'd be half dead, not knowing how to be able to speak Yup'ik to someone. And they wouldn't understand if I spoke to them. Like, I know this one, and then if I talk to them in that language, they're gonna look at me funny and wonder what I'm saying, it's like, '*Tua-ll'-am* (*not again*) English, do I have to speak to you in English again?' I've heard that before.
LTW: You've heard that from, or people say that.
Mary: I've heard it before, and kinda sounded funny to me, cause that person she was speaking to, he spoke Yup'ik, but he started using English more often and he started forgetting the language.
LTW: Then what did he say, or *callrua* (*what did he do*)?
Mary: Got mad and left. Didn't like that, so I had to sit there and think how the future would be if we spoke English only.

Mary's assertion that she'd be 'half dead' without speaking Yup'ik echoed many other young people's claims of strong emotional attachments to Yup'ik during language shift. Her description of the interaction between two high school students also highlighted how, for GB youth, calling attention to the fact that someone used English was generally interpreted as an insult with no easy response.

Summary

In 2000–2001, individual and subgroups of GB youth used Yup'ik extensively, though overall use of Yup'ik in youth culture had dramatically decreased from the mid-1990s. During language shift, GB youth used a broad set of symbolic resources, including token Yup'ik discourse markers and specialized terms, Yup'ik-influenced English phonological features and bids for topic, as well as slang terms to deeply situate local youth culture within particular relationships at a particular time and place. Along with peers, youth also found ways to localize mainstream, Yup'ik and Christian references and discourses, drawing upon new email internet connections to consume and circulate flows of information, and to participate in local, regional and national networks.

During rapid language shift, youth also used both Yup'ik itself and talk about Yup'ik as particularly powerful social resources. As the increase in young people's use of English became a driving force of local language shift, local adults critiqued young people's language choices and voiced concerns about language endangerment. Youth themselves, on the other hand, regularly expressed community language allegiance, even if such expressions of allegiance could sometimes mark social boundaries in ephemeral, situated ways, and/or reflect the complexities of historically rooted practices and generational disjunctures. As with the RS speakers, young people's allegiance to Yup'ik also generally broke down when it came to the area of Yup'ik literacy in the school-based writing system.

GB youth used Yup'ik as an in-group code to both strategically shut out nonlocal peers and teachers at times, and learn from local adults, even as youth wrestled with dwindling Yup'ik learning opportunities and increasing linguistic insecurities. Youth also used Yup'ik for creative purposes, even as they spoke mostly English. Taken together, the examples above show how youth demonstrated multiple forms of linguistic survivance in relation to individualized language socialization trajectories, as they used varying bilingual competences to navigate daily interactions and social relationships with adults and youth. In the following chapter, we will consider how youth like Amy, Mike, Nathan and their strong Yup'ik-speaking counterparts like Mary, Tom, John and Evan further demonstrated linguistic survivance as they learned *yuuyaraq* and related land-use practices, forging connections to community, place and peers while taking up local responsibilities and related gender roles in the contemporary, shifting subsistence society.

7 Subsistence, Gender and Storytelling in a Changing Linguistic Ecology

Men and women share the large bulk of linguistic practices and communicative resources in society. Nevertheless, societal conditions, expectations and socialization processes also produce gender differences and differential access to language learning opportunities (Eckert & McConnell-Ginet, 2003; Pavlenko & Piller, 2001). While the preceding chapters have noted such gender differences, the presentation of findings have, until this point, emphasized how wide-ranging long-term and short-term processes were setting up the conditions for local language shift, and how both girls and boys were participating in the linguistic transformation of Piniq through their increased use of English.

As previous chapters document, the degree to which individual GB youth used Yup'ik with peers largely depended on access to Yup'ik language learning resources and opportunities. When the GB group were growing up, starting from early childhood, a wide range of contingent circumstances shaped young people's affordances for learning and using Yup'ik, including, at the very least, (1) where individuals spent their childhoods, (2) how individuals were situated within the make-up of their particular family sibling orders, (3) who children played with in and out of school, (4) what type of language program they received as elementary youth and (5) how families negotiated ongoing language socialization practices at home, and within extended family networks over time. Individuals and chance groupings of youth were never free of these contingencies, and to a large degree, varying language learning opportunities shaped young people's everyday language 'choices'. When personal circumstances aligned to form subgroups of strong Yup'ik-speaking youth, such as the senior class in 2001, groups of GB youth used predominantly Yup'ik with one another like the RS group before them.

GB youth also integrated wide-ranging symbolic resources and shared many ways of communicating as they participated within local youth culture, and in shared local and global worlds. Youth who could speak Yup'ik comfortably generally held high status within their peer groups. Both boys and girls used talk *in* and talk *about* the Yup'ik language as a resource for strategically marking in-group membership along local, peer group and ethnic lines, and additionally acted as Yup'ik language advocates.

Youth in general oriented toward language ideologies and authoritative discourses in their local environment, overtly valuing Yup'ik as a connection to a unique identity. Almost all youth in the GB group, as well, commonly used Yup'ik terms related to subsistence. Yet, as we will see below, for a short moment in time, subsistence and related linguistic practices also produced salient gender differences between young men and young women's Yup'ik use during language shift. Young *nukalpiat* (*real hunter*) culture was highly visible among GB boys, as within the RS group. Within GB youth culture, extended Yup'ik discourse also became linked to a particular kind of storytelling that was largely, but not solely related to boys' hunting practices: the land-related adventure story.

Section I overviews the ways in which youth were socialized to take up local responsibilities and gender roles over time in Piniq. Section II situates and highlights GB young people's everyday language practices and subsistence narratives, documenting how young hunters used both Yup'ik and new forms of translanguaging as they (1) took up local roles and alignments, and (2) negotiated related notions of community, place and gender as young members of a shifting, contemporary Indigenous subsistence society.

Section I: Gender Roles and Local Responsibilities in Piniq

At the time of the study, boys and girls in Piniq had a wide variety of responsibilities related to local gender roles as seen in Table 7.1.

Maintaining households in rural Alaska five hundred miles off the road system without running water involved many daily activities related to local gender roles. In an interview below, Mary from the previous chapter humorously described her perceptions of young people's gendered responsibilities:

LTW: How does growing up as a boy and growing up as a girl compare in Piniq to you.

Mary: Boy? I don't know. I know about a girl, you have to do what you have to do, like go out berry-picking, egg-hunting, grass-picking, home chores, house chores.

Table 7.1 Young men's and women's responsibilities

Type of responsibility	Young men's/boys'	Young women's/girls'
Subsistence-related work	Hunting birds Hunting seals Fishing Berry-picking Working on mechanics	Cleaning birds Cleaning seals Cleaning fish Egg-hunting Berry-picking Collecting tundra plants for vegetables, medicine and tea Preparing food
Household chores	Cutting ice for water in winter Making a steambath with wood Getting mail from the post office Taking trash to the dump Pumping stove oil for household heating systems Dumping the qerrun (honeybucket) Dumping wash water Collecting/buying wood	Babysitting Cleaning the house Cooking Doing dishes Doing laundry
Wage work	Clerking at the local store Commercial salmon fishing	Clerking at the local store Babysitting

LTW: Like what are the girls' chores?

Mary: They do the dishes, sweep the floor, do the laundry, clean the table, clean the rooms, sweep the floor, cook, cut up something, pluck, wash the body parts. Mostly the guys, they prefer hunting and dumping something, and that's all they ever do.

LTW: Hmm ... hunt and dump.

Mary: [Smiling] Uh-huh, hunt, dump, sleep, eat.

As youth and adults noted in 2000–2001, and I myself observed, the most common place to hear extended Yup'ik among the GB group was also in boys' stories about their activities that involved venturing out onto the land. As Mary remarked earlier in the interview above:

The girls speak mostly English, and once in a while Yup'ik but the boys they prefer Yup'ik because it's easier to ... use, easier to understand, especially when they talk about hunting, snowmachine-riding. And girls, they talk about boys, homework, how boring it would be, boys and style, what's in, and they can't say anything about those unless they speak English.   (4/3/01)

Above, Mary painted a picture of male and female language choices as marked opposites among the GB group, linked to typically male and female topics for discussion. Yet, as we have seen previously, young people's cumulative resources for learning Yup'ik could outweigh any overriding gender effect making Yup'ik a particularly 'male' or 'female' language during language shift. Boys and girls also discussed the same range of topics, even as they differed in the amount of time and the degree to which they used extended Yup'ik to talk about subsistence (e.g. Aries & Johnson, in Eckert & McConnell-Ginet, 2003). Both boys and girls discussed stereotypically female topics such as fashion, haircuts and body types (Cameron, 1997), for instance, as in instances when groups of boys discussed who was the 'boniest' boy in the school, and approvingly noted how one boy changed his hat to match hip hop style. Both young men and young women also shared ghost stories, and recapped and reenacted exciting TV shows, movies and/or the exciting events from sporting events or local life.

At the same time, the separation in boys and girls' roles and responsibilities in Piniq meant the relative predominance of subsistence stories varied. In classes that were split with a mix of Yup'ik skills evenly distributed among boys and girls, boys would talk about going out on the land experiences more commonly than young women. In 2000–2001, especially during peak fall and spring hunting seasons, simply walking around Piniq, I regularly ran across small groups of boys speaking intently together on the boardwalk, the school steps, school hallways and classroom floors. From a distance, hunting stories were easy to recognize: typically one boy's hand would motion shooting a gun, another hand would go up in the air, then twist and flop down limply like a bird falling, quickly flip over to indicate a kill on land, or move downward to motion an animal in the water. As one drew closer, the stories were often, though not always, in Yup'ik.

To understand how gender influenced young people's everyday language use during language shift, here we will continue to conceptualize subsistence as a set of practices deeply embedded in specific sets of social relations and ideas about multiple types of human–human, male–female and human–animal relationships. Situating gender and young people's language choices within this system, we will also highlight how youth connected through discourse with local adults and peers, developing and transforming local practices as they learned to carry out adult roles in a specific community in a particular subarctic setting, at a particular moment in time.

Learning subsistence

In the 1990s and in 2001, boys and girls in Piniq took on local roles and responsibilities, developing shared and varying 'ways of engaging' in community activities (Gutiérrez & Rogoff, 2003: 22) in relation to specific relationships, personal circumstances and family networks, as well as assumptions about gender. Young children commonly started learning their local responsibilities as legitimate peripheral participants (Lave & Wenger, 1991), intently observing same-sex adults in the daily forms of household and subsistence work listed above (Rogoff et al., 2003). Adults also commonly involved young children in local work by giving them small, related tasks (Philips, 1983). Young boys might help on their first trip cutting ice for water, for instance, by putting pieces of ice in a sled. Girls age two might start helping older relatives skinning seals by putting strips of seal blubber into jars for rendering the fat into seal oil, a popular condiment for dried food.

Growing up in Piniq, both boys and girls also took on increasingly challenging responsibilities and developed competencies over time. Household chores and subsistence work were scaled in complexity. Babysitting took less skill than doing laundry; dumping the honeybucket took less skill than building a steam. Hunting and cleaning birds (young men's and young women's tasks, respectively) also took less skill than hunting and/or cleaning seals (young men's and young women's tasks, respectively).

As in many other Indigenous subsistence societies, boys and girls in Piniq acquired ecological knowledge through apprenticeship with local adults, as well as exposure to oral traditions. When and how young people developed specific competences in subsistence-related work, however, partially depended on the ways in which groups of related nuclear families distributed expertise and resources within extended family networks. In one family network, a grandmother was the primary seal-skinner, and a junior high girl learned to cut up food years later than her best friend who had no such grandmother nearby. The age at which boys took on hunting responsibilities also depended on the availability of their fathers and uncles as teachers, and to some extent, their sibling order. Among the seventh-grade group, for instance, almost all boys had caught their first seal. Like some of the young *nukalpiat* in the RS group, one boy had caught his first at age six. Many other boys, however, were catching their first seals at age 12.

As in other Yup'ik communities and subsistence societies in the Far North, girls' and boys' responsibilities in Piniq were somewhat flexible (Brumbach & Jarvenpa, 2002), contingent upon both the make-up of individual families as well as particular situations (Hensel, 1996). In one family of all boys, sons helped with dishes and laundry, but not with cooking or cleaning animals. In a family of all girls and a second family with young sons, older girls dumped the sink wastewater, but only rarely dumped honeybuckets, since they were seen as not strong enough. Likewise, older daughters helped cut ice, but only a few young women hunted. Boys participated in some women's activities, especially those that involved going out to the tundra such as berry-picking and egg-hunting. In some families, husbands regularly got up early, making coffee and cooking breakfast for their wives. Men's and women's roles were also more flexible when traveling out of Piniq. Men cooked for themselves, for instance, while out hunting with friends. For the most part, however, hunting and cleaning animals and spiritual tasks related to hunting (such as dumping the honeybucket for boys) were the most highly gendered local responsibilities.

Young people's socialization into subsistence also varied depending on families' connections to other villages, and whether families owned additional resources such as fish or berry camps. Most families traveled to and from Piniq regularly for subsistence in summer, using boats with outboard motors to participate in fishing and berry-picking. A few extended families, however, spent weeks at remote locations, fishing, cutting up and drying salmon, or picking berries.

Young people's expressed interest in learning, as well, helped determine when they took on new responsibilities. Describing how she taught her children and grandchildren to cut up seals, one grandmother noted that, 'It depends on how that child is, some are wanting to do things earlier than others.' One fourth-grade girl learned how to cut up a seal before her older sisters because she expressed an interest. Apprenticing boys into potentially life-threatening endeavors, however, such as hunting in spring ocean ice conditions, men also made regular judgment calls about how and when to involve youth in specific activities based on their knowledge of individual youth, weather conditions and the relative risks involved.

As boys and girls learned to participate in subsistence, they were socialized to specific ways of thinking about the connections between human–animal, as well as human–human relationships. Young children and older youth harvesting food from the tundra or ocean were generally taught to show respect for the animals who offered themselves by 'not playing with' or wasting food (for comparison with other subarctic hunting societies, see Nadasdy, 2003: 88–92) and to state their thanks for every meal by saying *'quyana'* (*thank you*). Many boys and girls in the mid-1990s and in 2001 followed traditional spiritual practices to insure the continuation of abundant harvesting and the return of animals, such as refraining from traveling on the ocean for berry-picking or hunting if a relative had recently died, or disposing of fish and animal bones in the river, versus the town dump, although church-going families, especially, varied in the extent to which they followed these teachings.

As Chapter 2 describes, youth were also socialized to share food and do chores for elders without pay to influence the outcomes of hunting and have a *piniq* (*strong, good*) life, as well as to listen carefully and respectfully to adults' teachings, avoiding the impulse to 'follow one's mind'.

Gender and going out on the land

As youth in Piniq learned subsistence, they also learned shared and gendered ways of navigating the local landscape, as they participated within 'a complex system of travel, preparation, and logistics preceding harvests or kills and the intricacies of butchering, processing, and distribution following kills' (Brumbach & Jarvenpa, 2002: 208). Unlike in places with paved roads, changing weather and land conditions made getting from point a to point b in Piniq vary from season to season and day to day. During two spring weeks in which ice was melting rapidly, for instance, nightly steam conversations commonly started with hosts asking guests for daily updates on how they crossed Piniq given changing areas of hard or soft snow, mud, pools of ice-water and/or stretches of traversible boardwalk. Traveling in and out of the village at particular times of year, as well, involved navigating and judging pathways over a dynamic landscape. In deep winter, even the most mundane tasks out on the land could prove life threatening for youth. In fall and springtime, elders also urgently shared specific *qanruyutait* with youth about remaining safe when traveling on changing ice conditions.

Going out on the land provided one of the most popular local activities – that of going snowmobile-riding on the tundra. During late fall, winter and early spring, students cruised at night in pairs, on dates, or in large groups, as in one instance when a caravan of youth on twelve snowmobiles tore out of Piniq in the setting sun. As an extension of boys' regular winter and spring activities, young men were the most likely to own or have use of family snowmobiles. As soon as the land froze over each year, the back of the school was lined with snowmobiles. Students' snowmobiles were status symbols; youth all knew who had which snowmobile, and boys often discussed which snowmobile models and makes were the flashiest and most powerful. Snowmobiling also had its own accompanying slang terms, such as one group of boys' use of the term 'hooker' for a girl trying to get a ride on a snowmobile.

Through accumulating experiences going out with adult relatives and friends, both boys and girls in Piniq learned local landmarks and spots for specific subsistence activities. Both girls and boys also learned to find and travel established snowmobile trails between villages in winter. Yet, through regular activities boys spent much more time out on the land, learning to read the markings and fluctuations in the local environment under the watchful eye of local adults, older peers and one another.

In many societies, female responsibilities are tied with household-bound responsibilities such as caregiving and cooking, while boys' and young men's roles take them farther from home (Rogoff, 2003). Younger, mixed groups of boys and girls went egg-hunting close to Piniq. By age 12, young women might spend long days farther away on the tundra together, egg-hunting or collecting plants. For much of the year, however, girls' responsibilities were relatively housebound.

As Mary noted, many girls helped with the everyday running of the household. Some girls processed and cooked birds alone, though most participated in food processing activities with older women, and were just learning how to process seals with their mothers, grandmothers or aunties. Some food-processing activities doubled as intergenerational women's social gatherings in local spaces. In a visit to one family, for instance, I joined a group of grown daughters, daughters-in-law and younger girls working together with a respected local grandmother, sitting on the floor of her house on cardboard, forming a circle around a large pile of birds. As church songs from a homemade tape played from a back room, together we plucked the birds, filling garbage bags with feathers while the women shared stories, jokes and comments in Yup'ik. Young cousins happily romped in and out of the room, staying out of the women's way. On nearby couches, a few young men also hovered around the circle's outskirts, enjoying the laughter and banter of the group.

Visiting the same household later that spring, I observed a different learning arrangement, as two adolescent cousins learned to cut up their first seal in their grandmother's foodhouse. Surrounded by the extended family's stacks of seals, the girls worked quietly and intently on skinning a large seal together. Their mothers checked on them periodically, offering lessons about specific tasks such as how to bend a seal's flipper in order to cut the joint properly, and videotaping the historic family moment for the future.

Boys' subsistence and daily household work, in contrast, involved going out on the land, and navigating changing land conditions. Individual boys and young children checked the mail at the local post office on foot, weather permitting. At other times, boys checked the mail by picking up and hauling boxes home in sleds or carts pulled behind snowmobiles or All Terrain Vehicles (ATVs), respectively, depending on the season. Individual boys also pulled sleds and carts using snowmobiles and ATVs to haul trash to the local dump beyond Piniq.

Boys described how they had practiced hunting together around the outskirts of the village as young children, using slingshots on small birds. As boys grew older, they also used vehicles to venture further out onto the land on their own or in groups. Preadolescent and adolescent boys took snowmobiles away from Piniq to locate clean frozen ponds and lakes, chop chunks of ice with a pick, load ice into a sled and pull the sleds back home, before hauling buckets of ice inside to melt for drinking and wash water. Some older boys also accompanied their fathers taking longer snowmobile trips in springtime to buy wood from dealers in Bethel, or to cut down and collect wood upriver for nightly steambaths.

By age 12, many boys went out to the ocean by boat with older cousins or brothers or adults, typically only hunting seals with adults. They also commonly walked on the tundra and took boats along local waterways with peers to hunt birds. As boys got older, one marker of competence was taking a boat or traveling by snowmobile on the tundra without adults. Many preadolescent boys took their initial solo trips by snowmobile to a nearby village, approximately 20 miles away. Boys also took boats out into the local river, starting by following well-traveled channels and later moving along nearby stretches of ocean. As young men reached their twenties, many learned to travel longer distances, graduating from collecting wood or seal-hunting with adults to doing these things alone.

Section II: Learning Place, Language and Gender in Everyday Subsistence Stories

Telling everyday stories, narrators 'evaluate specific events in terms of communal norms, expectations, and potentialities: communal ideas of what is rational and moral' and a 'communal sense of the appropriate and the esthetic', coming to 'understand, reaffirm and revise a philosophy of life' (Ochs & Capps, 1996: 30). Asserting that 'stories are our theories', Indigenous education scholars highlight how Indigenous narratives document the survivance of peoples who have passed on and adapted Indigenous knowledge systems under circumstances of rapid social transformation (Brayboy, 2005). For youth, as well, stories 'are theories, ways of testing what others feel and think and how they and their friends stand in contrast with others' (Heath, 1994: 216). Indigenous youth, like minority youth and peoples elsewhere, may tell stories about knowledge and experiences that directly counter broad societal discourses about their own subordinate place in society (Lee, 2009). Young people's everyday stories may also more indirectly articulate the 'tensions, fears, competitions, marginalized areas of knowledge from which they draw' (Heath, 1994: 210), in the face of both potential community disjunctures and shared community struggles.

'Native stories of survivance are prompted by natural reason, by a consciousness and sense of incontestable presence that arises from experiences in the natural world' (Vizenor, 2008: 11). As Basso states, 'Whenever the members of a community speak about their landscape – whenever they name it, or classify it, or tell stories about it – they unthinkingly represent it in ways that are compatible with shared understandings of how, in the fullest sense, they know themselves to occupy it' (Basso, 1996: 74). Even girls' and boys' seemingly mundane subsistence stories in Piniq evidenced a deep, consistent engagement with land-use practices within a specific linguistic ecology, as well as young people's linguistic survivance and active presence as Indigenous youth learning a 'highly emplaced' community knowledge system (e.g. Brayboy & McCarty, 2010). Commonly, within group interviews, when I asked young and older boys and girls about subsistence topics or themes, youth became animated, sharing local information in rapid-fire succession, laying out shared evaluative stances toward subsistence. In 2001, young people's storytelling about subsistence also served as a particularly productive site for considering how youth integrated language learning, language mainte-nance and language shift with the learning of community, place and gender during the sociolinguistic transformation of their community.

Girls and storytelling about gathering

During language shift, girls in Piniq shared positive associations with land-related adventures, including gathering eggs in the spring and berries in the summer from the tundra. One high school girl, for instance, talked about how her summer was ruined when she sprained her ankle and could not go to her family's camp to pick berries. Other girls, as well, shared stories about going out to gather tundra tea and a plant called *quagciq* in the spring.

Many older women in Piniq looked forward to spring egg-hunting as their favorite time of year, and adults and young people shared stories of how they used local knowledge of bird behavior to strategize where to find eggs on the tundra. Two young cousins asked me if it was true that cranes chased people, and excitedly described going to various spots by boat, finding nests with eggs, and the time one girl's mother threw her an *uqiquq* (*seal party*, described in Chapter 5) to celebrate her daughter's find of multiple swan eggs.

Girls' stories of egg-hunting often centered around humorous retellings of unexpected events, such as falling into the mud or ponds while walking on the marshy tundra, or surprising encounters with birds who left or defended their nests, as in the following story from Patty, a high school girl known for her good sense of humor (underlined word discussed below):

Patty: One time when Egg-hunt-*arualriakut* (*We were going* egg-hunting, *even though we weren't sure we were going to get anything. Literally: We were playing* egg-hunting), we went by walking. We found few of em, green-*aat augkut* (*those* green *ones*), those eggs, <u>*kangaqcaalriakut* (*We slowly plodded on*)</u>.
[...]

Patty: Since we got tired of looking for it, we left, went farther, that river? Towards the old village?

LTW: Um hmmm.

Patty: Then, around there ... *pekvallagilriakut* (*the bird suddenly flew out of its nest*), then, I looked there, *icuw'* (*like*), it was right there? And I was walking past it? As they were walking by the river bed? Then, *pekvallagilua, tatamllua* (*a bird flew from its nest in front of me, it startled me*), really scared? I was really scared then, all of a sudden ... *tengvallagluni! (suddenly took off into the air)* [laughs] And I went, 'Holy cow!' [laughs]. I was scared, my eyes were big. Then I checked, and the others came?
Nekanaqluni (it was irksome)! They went *pgg* on my head. *Nekanaqluni (it was irksome)!* And then took 'em and put 'em in the bucket. Then left? And there was *ciikaqs (loose diarrhea)* on it. [laughs].

Young women learned animal behavior through their experiences going out on the land. Relatively strong Yup'ik speakers in the GB group also creatively maintained aesthetic and affective dimensions of connections to place through codeswitching in subsistence stories told mostly in English. As we see above, Patty used specific Yup'ik verbs stems combined with postbases and subordinative endings (described in Chapters 5 and 6) to contrast the movements of birds alighting from their nests to birds lifting up into the air:

Ex. 1:   *pek-vallag-ilua*
Translation: *To fly from its egg – intensifier – 1st person singular subordina-*
                   tive subject
Gloss: *I had a bird suddenly fly out of its nest on me.*

Ex. 2:   *Teng-vallag-luni*
Translation: *To take off into the air – intensifier – 3rd person singular*
                   subordinative subject
Gloss: *It suddenly took off into the air.*

To heighten the interactional moment, Patty repeated Yup'ik verbs with intensifying postbases. She also peppered her story with specific Yup'ik utterances capturing emotional states (*tateme- llua, to be startled* – 1st person singular subordinative) and expressions of annoyance (*nekanaqluni!*), as well as commonplace English expressions for surprise ('Holy cow!'). Using a sound word, *'pgg'* made from an iconic Yup'ik velar voiceless fricative, Patty also reenacted the bird's response as she tried to take the eggs.

Years after this interview, a Yup'ik language consultant helped me correct my original transcription and translation of the segment above. As we huddled together over my laptop and a tape recorder, listening repeatedly to the segment, the consultant's comments underscored how stories like the one above evidenced young people's linguistic survivance. At one point, the consultant broke from our shared concentration on Patty's words and paused to laughingly comment how the narrator made her egg-hunting experience, 'sound really fun.' The consultant's comments brought home for me how, during language shift, youth were able to render engaging stories of shared community experiences by translanguaging.

At the same time, the consultant's comments also highlighted how youth simultaneously confused local adults with their rapid Yup'ik morphological changes, as well as their increasing use of English. A few minutes later, noting how Patty had said *kangaq-caa-lriakut*, instead of *kangaq-caara-lriakut* (*we slowly plodded on*), shortening the verbal postbase – *qcaar(ar)*, 'to keep on trying to V despite difficulties' (Jacobson, 1984: 538), the consultant also commented, 'If I or my peers spoke like this when we were young, we would have been teased for speaking babytalk.'

Boys learning to seal hunt

Through their everyday subsistence experiences, boys also integrated their learning of language, land-use practices and gender. Nathan and Mike from Chapter 6 described how they regularly listened as older men talked with one another in Yup'ik over marine radios as they determined when to go out, where to go and who to bring with them, judging weather conditions, and other men's reports of their experiences. In the following excerpt, Mike and Nathan also highlighted their engagement with the local subsistence practices as they described learning to seal hunt alongside adults:

1 **Nathan:** Sometimes, me, me and my *apii* (*granddad*) only go alone . . . It's fun when we go spring hunting.
2 **Mike:** For seals.
3 **Nathan:** Yup.
4 **LTW:** What's your favorite kind of hunting.
5 **Nathan:** Seal=
6 **Mike:** =Seal hunt, everybody.
7 **LTW:** What's it like?
8 **Mike:** It's cool, cold, really,
9 **Nathan:** /Fun/
10 **Mike:** /really/. . . close, real.
11 **Nathan:** Yup.
12 **Mike:** You'll catch *maklaar* (*bearded seal*), big=
13 **Nathan:** =Really big, really fat, blubber.
14 **Mike:** And sometime the adults say, they'll cut 'em up, '*tangvauriqluci*' (*watch carefully, be ever vigilant*, see discussion below)
15 **Nathan:** They cut, cut, cut their head?
16 **LTW:** Um hmm.
17 **Nathan:** If they cut their head, put it in the water, say '*Cali taikina*, come back again.' Throw it in the water.
18 **LTW:** Um hmm.
19 **Mike:** I did that at, uh, fall.
20 **Nathan:** I did that when we cut a *maklaar* (*bearded seal*).

Above, Mike and Nathan recounted and reenacted the ways they used Yup'ik with adult mentors, and how men used Yup'ik with youth while hunting to issue directives, direct boys' attention to the visual details of animals and the local environment, and to cultivate an appropriate state of mind for interacting with animals and the world around them. Nathan described how they used the simple Yup'ik prayer, '*Cali taikina*' ('*Come back again*'), and returned heads of hunted seals to the water (lines 17 and 18), enacting the belief that seals treated with respect will return to hunters. In their description, Nathan and Mike also used Yup'ik terminology to reference specific seals (line 12, 20 *maklaar*-bearded seal), as well as terms of endearment for older relatives (line 1 *apii*-grandad).

As Mike quotes an adult mentor (line 14), his utterance *'tangvaur-i-qluci'* also highlights the challenges and strengths of heritage language learners who may evidence linguistic errors, yet still be acquiring heritage language phrases and vocabulary, as well as powerful concepts about learning, through their participation in community activities (e.g. Valdés, 2005). *'Tangvaur-i-qluci'* echoes a common refrain used by adults when instructing youth to pay careful attention – *'Tangvaur-a-qluci'* or 'Be vigilant' (Walkie Charles, personal communication).

Mike and Nathan further overlapped their speech (lines 9, 10), latching onto one another's statements (lines 12, 13) as the excitement of recalling subsistence sped the interaction moment. Mike's offhand comment about seal-hunting being 'everybody's' favorite hunting in line 6, as well as the pacing of the boys' statements about seal-hunting above, stand in marked contrast to local worries that English-speaking youth 'wanted to be like whites'. Complicating their self-descriptions in Chapter 6 as language 'losers' and 'forgetters', Mike and Nathan additionally offered contrasting evidence above of the ways they used Yup'ik prayers, ecological terminology, endearment terms and teachings.

In 2001, youth with both relatively strong and weak productive competences in Yup'ik used Yup'ik to acquire knowledge embedded in the everyday life of Piniq. Through their bilingual storytelling about subsistence, youth in Piniq also found ways to reinforce connections to community and place during language shift. By looking closely at boys' interactions below, we will continue to explore how boys integrated their learning of gender, language and land-use practices in ways that produced, for a short time, the particularly visible links between Yup'ik and boys' stories of going out onto the land.

Bird-hunting and land-related adventure stories

The most popular RS and GB boys were generally hunters, as well as strong athletes. Local youth and adults also noted how some boys were particularly knowledgable about subsistence. In the following example, we can see how two seventh-grade boys challenged one another, exchanging claims about being 'dumb' for not seal-hunting:

Student 1:   Dumber, you never seal hunt.
Student 2:   Dumber, I never see <u>you</u> seal hunt.
Student 1:   Neh, I went out on Friday.

In 2001, the preadolescent boys quoted above were just beginning to navigate the local landscape on their own, though they were years away from the practical knowledge they needed to take a boat out by themselves in treacherous spring conditions. At the same time, the boys were old enough to have their first adventures going out alone with one another by boat for fall bird-hunting. Through their related stories, boys in Piniq commonly underscored their shared experiences and developing expertise as they began to travel and hunt in self-directed groups of peers. The following two excerpts were taken from an interview with John and Tom, two of the young *nukalpiat* and strong Yup'ik speakers in the GB group. John from Chapter 6 described below one of the experiences he shared with Tom during fall bird-hunting (underlined endings discussed below):

1   Uh, *imarpigcaaqellruukut,*   Uh, *we were going out to the ocean,*
2   Uh, Short cut-*arluta,*   Uh, *we took a* short cut,
3   *Tua-ll', uqsuqamek tangerrluta,*   *Then, we saw a mallard, the other was*
    nacaullget aipait.   *a Canadian goose.*
4   *Uqsuqat-llu, nutegluki wii.*   *And the mallards, I shot them.*
5   *Nutg-aar-luku,*   *After I shot it,*
    uitaqa-rraar-lua,   *after I waited,*
    Nerraar, nerqe-rraar-luni,   *Ate after, after it ate,*
    tuqu-luni. Aqvaluki.   *it died. I went to go get them.*
6   *Cukangnaqesqellua Tom, etganani.*   *Tom told me to try to go fast while it*
                                          was shallow.
7   *Ayagluta tegginani [River name],*   *We were going to go to [River name],*
    eqataryaaqluta time-aunata.   *but we didn't have time.*

By participating in hunting with adults, boys in Piniq learned to read the land, navigate the local spaces and local bodies of water, identify animals based on close observations of birds' markings and behavior, and to interpret conditions that might affect their survival in local subarctic conditions. In the description above, we also see how boys practiced careful observation and planful thinking (Heath, 1998, 2008) when hunting with their peers, reading animal behavior and local landmarks, while judging currents, local routes and navigating river channels in order to make it to good spots for subsistence, find and hunt animals, and get themselves home safely within the timelines determined by ebbs and flows of local waterways.

Comparing John's narrative above to his basketball narrative in Chapter 6, we further see how subsistence narratives could also call out extended Yup'ik use. John used strikingly little codeswitching above, and his use of Yup'ik postbases and endings evidenced strong Yup'ik speakers' use of relatively complex morphology. As in the basketball narrative, John employed the tense neutral subordinative mood (underlined above) to create a locally recognizable story frame. John first marked past tense at the beginning of the storyframe with the postbase -llru:

Ex.:   *Imarpig- caaqe- <u>llru-</u> ukut*
Translation: *Ocean-going out-<u>past tense</u>-3rd.pl.ending*
Gloss: *We were going out to the ocean*

In lines 4–5, John then embedded both human and animal actors within the Yup'ik frame using subordinative mood endings (-luki (3rd plural obj.), -luku (3rd sing obj.), -lua (1st sing subj.), -luni (3rd sing subj.), -luki (3rd plural obj.)), switching object referent from plural to singular to plural again, and indirectly marking changes in subjects (Jacobsen, 1995; see also Fienup-Riordan, 2005) as he described shooting a group of birds, watching and waiting for a single bird to eat and die, then going to collect multiple birds.

In line 6, John rendered the peer interactions involved with situated judgment calls by using a compound verbal postbase -sqe- 'to ask or tell the topic of the derived sentence to be the topic of embedded sentence' (Jacobson, 1995: 328), and the first person subordinative as the subject of the embedded verb in line 6 as follows:

Ex.:   *Cuka-   ngnaqe-   -sqe-   llua*
Translation: *Be fast-   try to-   tell (obj) to- 1st p. subordinative*
Gloss: *Told me to try to be fast*

As young men told hunting stories, they filled listeners in on where they went and what they caught. Yet, stories such as the ones above also evidenced how boys were learning to see themselves in adult roles, and to practice these roles as they interacted with a particular local environment. For strong Yup'ik speakers, shared subsistence experiences and stories also offered opportunities for extended Yup'ik discourse with adults and peers. Below, we will see how youth in general, and boys, in particular, negotiated connections between gender, language and place in their interactions with one another.

Enforcing gender roles through teasing

Children initially learn locally available gender roles through their interactions with adults; as youth grow older, they also socialize one another to take up gender norms through everyday peer interactions (Eckert &

McConnell-Ginet, 2003). GB youth, like their older RS counterparts, reinforced commonplace local assumptions about hunting as a male activity through teasing. Amy, for instance, recalled her peers' response when she tried hunting:

LTW: Did you ever try hunting?
Amy: No, just one time, long time ago we went boat riding, and my dad let me shoot, and the boys kept thinking I caught a bird. [laughs] It was so embarrassing.
LTW: Did you catch one?
Amy: Neah. Unh-unh. I just shot, tried to shoot that thing. That bird where the shell's staying? I tried to shoot that with my brother's or dad's gun.
LTW: And boys thought you caught a bird.
Amy: Yeh, my classmates, they just go 'Oh, Amy caught a bird, Amy caught a bird, she's a boy!' [laughs]

Amy went on to describe how boys teased her about the size of her feet and for being strong, and how she vehemently denied being 'like a boy'. Some younger girls, in contrast, proudly shared with peers how they had tried hunting. One girl, for instance, told a mixed group of boys and girls about her experiences of ptarmigan hunting, prompting one boy to tease another about being bested by a girl in hunting, 'Ho:leh, Betty *anagtaaten* (*beat you*) Joe!'

Through collaborative storytelling with one another, young people also opened up spaces for jointly interpreting and negotiating local gender expectations in interaction (e.g. Eder, 1998), as we will see in the following section.

Gender and local knowledge in collaborative storytelling

As youth tell stories together, they commonly repeat and embellish one another's descriptions, providing evaluative comments and remarks about one another's experiences and behavior, using the flexibility of discourse to engage in culture-building within peer culture (Eder, 1998). In 2001, the young hunters in the study were actively developing new competences as they learned to navigate the local landscape with one another, yet they still made many mistakes. Through collaborative, animated storytelling, GB boys reinforced the excitement of hunting by adding dramatic details, pointing out one another's errors, and sometimes rebutting one another's version of events (e.g. Heath, 1994). As the boys shared their mistakes with one another, they also negotiated their understandings of gender behavior and their positions in local peer culture. The following example starts with Tom from Chapter 6 asking John from above how many birds he caught on a recent hunting trip together.

1 **Tom:**	xxxx *Qavci uqsusqat* xxxx, What two꞉ /Three꞉/	Xxxx How many *xxxx mallards,* What two꞉ /Three꞉/
2 **John:**	/Maybe three/	/Maybe three/
3	*Nutgaluki tamaaguirraarluni,*	*Shooting them after it went that way,*
4	*Tua-ll'*	*Then*
5	*Waten piyaaqerraarlua, yaa- yaarraarluni*	*After I tried this, over- after going over there*
6	*'Rrrr' [Boat sound with a voiced back velar fricative] Caqirrluni.*	*'Rrrr' [Boat sound with a voiced back velar fricative] It turned.*
7	*'Nut'egki ampi!'*	*'Shoot them now!'*
8	*Trr trr trr [Gun sound with a voiceless back velar fricative]*	*Trr trr trr [Gun sound with a voiceless back velar fricative]*
9 **Tom:**	/One fell/	/One fell/
10 **John:**	/Ig-/ One fell,	/Fell-/ One fell,
11	*atauciq teguluku*	*I took one,*
12	*Alinglua.*	*I was scared.*
13 **Tom:**	[Laughing] Really scared of the birds.	[Laughing] Really scared of the birds.
14 **John:**	*Waten piqtaallruuq,*	*It was doing this,*
15	it was breathing scared꞉	it was breathing scared꞉
16 **LTW:**	Um hmm꞉	Um hmm꞉
17 **John:**	Like a human꞉	Like a human꞉
18 **LTW:**	Umm.	Umm.
19 **John:**	Like 'Huuh,' [Sucks in breath] like that, suffering꞉	Like 'Huuh,' [Sucks in breath] like that, suffering꞉
20 **LTW:**	Umm.	Umm.
21 **John:**	I was gonna take it꞉	I was gonna take it꞉

22 **LTW:**	Umm hmm?	Umm hmm?
23 **John:**	Bird I held, 'Wshhh'	Bird I held, 'Wshhh'
	[Flapping his hands]	[Flapping his hands]
24	I went,	I went,
25	'Ohhh! *Nutek*	'Ohhh! *Give me*
	taiteqerru!'	*the gun!'*
26	'No *kiingan teguluku.*	'No, *just take it.*
	Alingnaituq.'	*It's not scary.'*
27	*'Alingua!'*	*'I'm scared!'*
28 **Tom:**	[Smiling] And then I	[Smiling] And then I
	just went to took it off	just went to took it off
	the neck.	the neck.

Young men often compared their actions, sometimes humorously 'telling stories on themselves' about times that they broke with expected cultural norms (Eder, 1998), and/or highlighting times when they met local expectations in new situations. Above, we see how John and Tom, as young hunters, negotiated understandings of gender norms through shared storytelling of their land-related adventures. In lines 12–27, Tom and John laughingly remembered how John became afraid of a dying bird's movements, and thought he needed to use a gun to kill the bird. In line 28, Tom emphasized his own contrasting calm, more mature behavior as a hunter as he simply twisted the bird's neck.

Reenacting and performing previous hunting interactions in storytelling for others, the youth further underscored links between hunting and Yup'ik use. In interviews, Tom often chose to speak to me in English, while John generally used Yup'ik. In lines 15–24, John shifted into telling me the story in English, but he voiced his interactions with Tom in Yup'ik at the most exciting moments in the story, as when Tom told John to shoot the bird (line 7), the moment when John declared his fear as the bird flapped in his hand, and when Tom turned down John's request for a gun (lines 25–27).

The story above additionally evidences multiple commoplace features of young people's subsistence stories. John used locally recognizable sound words, for instance, to imitate gunfire and boat sounds, 'rrrr' and 'trr trr trr' in lines 6 and 8, bringing the listener into the moment. To demonstrate how and why the bird's movement had scared him, John also used paralinguistic features including hand gestures for the bird's flapping wings (line 23), and a breathy sound to imitate the dying bird as he compared it to a suffering human (line 19).

As strong Yup'ik-speaking boys conarrated subsistence stories like the ones above, they commonly reinforced the connection between Yup'ik and local land-use practices. They also brought the thrill of hunting and Yup'ik as the language of hunting into their interactions in other physical spaces. As we will see below, boys who described insecurities about speaking Yup'ik also used Yup'ik as they shared subsistence narratives, while they demonstrated another form of linguistic survivance.

'Getting by' in hunting stories

As youth like Mike and Nathan from above engaged in everyday subsistence storytelling with peers, they, too, increased their use of Yup'ik, yet their stories often evidenced how GB youth used patterned tokenism to 'get by' in local peer culture. In the following example, Mike tells a seal-hunting story in a group interview with strong Yup'ik-speaking peers, using the kinds of codeswitching that rapidly became prevalent among youth between the mid-1990s and 2000.

> Even James almost, first we killed the baby one, there were two when I was shooting. *Nayicuar* (*baby spotted seal*), it used to *pugeq* (*pop up*) really far. Then later on after it *anglluq* (*dove down*), *pugeq* (*pop up*) again, and then we killed the *pitaq* (*catch*). First we put it on ice, we went down '*rrrrr*' (boat sound with voiced back velar fricative), '*trrr*' (gun sound with voiceless back velar fricative). It was really fast, when it was gonna *anglluq* (*dive down*) we shot.

Like growing groups of young people in 2001, Mike did not use Yup'ik postbases or word endings, and kept the 'grammatical frame' (Myers-Scotton, 1998) of his story in English. Nevertheless, Mike integrated common Yup'ik hunting terms with many of the same locally recognizable storytelling features seen above. Mike got the floor by linking his story to the preceding story through the patterned bid for topic 'even (name)' described in Chapter 6. Using the word ending –*(a)q* to making hybrid standalone words from Yup'ik verb bases, Mike also expressed most of the story's action through Yup'ik nouns and verbs referencing common objects and actions related to hunting, including specific ecological terms for seals, and the movements of seals appearing on the surface of the water ('*pugeq*'), and diving down ('*anglluq*'), before rapidly disappearing. Like other youth, Mike included commonplace sound words for boat and gun sounds. He additionally used replays and direct statements to emphasize the fast action of key moments as he described working in moving boats on the ocean and making quick decisions while hunting seals.

Mike also used Yup'ik to share stories and gain the attention of stronger hunters and Yup'ik speakers such as Tom and Evan, as we see below (underlined terms are discussed below):

1	**Mike:**	*Kavialuq* caught *maklaar* (*bearded seal*) at Friday.
2	**Tom:**	Did they go out Friday?
3	**Mike:**	*Kavialuq* and Ned's dad.
4	**Evan:**	*Cikigaq?*
5	**Mike:**	Ned's dad.
6	**Evan:**	*Cikigaq.*
7	**Mike:**	Who's *Cikigaq?*
8	**Tom and Evan:**	Ned's dad.
9	**Mike:**	Yeh. *Cikigaq* caught *maklaar* (*bearded seal*). You know when we go down, we go that way? I mean, that- this way? And then, there was a *maklaar* (*bearded seal*) right there. *Issuriyagaq* (*one year old spotted seal*), Frank said took 'em, and then ... We were shooting that one, and then they went that way. And they xxx this way, and then they shot it. It went 'Qrr ch: ... vvuu tksh;' on the second one. Almost/ sink./
10	**Evan**	/Was it in/ the water? Under water? When they harpoon it?
11	**Tom:**	Evan-am *pugtangraan nutenqiggluku* (*shot it again even though it was floating*)
12	**Evan:**	Neh, it was gonna *kit'aq* (*sink*) it was like this, its back, very big, and it was going down. First it went like this 'ch:' /staying on the water/.
13	**Tom:**	/And then it was/ it was floating.
14	**LTW:**	Hmm.
15	**Mike:**	*Tegullruan?* (*Did you take it with your hands?*)
16	**Evan:**	Harpoon.

As in other Yup'ik villages at the time, Piniq community members received multiple Yup'ik and English names, comprising 'webs of many ... strands weav(ing) each person inextricably and uniquely into the community' (Fienup-Riordan, 2000: 194). As youth in Piniq were mentored in learning subsistence, they also entered into new relationships with older community members. In interviews, young hunters commonly worked together to identify adults' Yup'ik names, socializing one another to reference adults as adults. Over multiple turns above (lines 1–9), Tom and Evan influenced Mike to use the Yup'ik name of an adult hunter in lieu of the more childlike English description 'Ned's dad', before allowing Mike to describe a hunting event.

In the GB group, strong Yup'ik speakers like Tom and Evan also sometimes used Yup'ik to emphasize relative positions of power with peers as they negotiated the floor in everyday storytelling sessions (e.g. Jørgensen, 1998). After Evan asked Mike for a clarifying detail about a seal hunt he witnessed above in line 10, Tom gained the floor in line 11 by using a relatively complex statement in Yup'ik, *'pugtangraan nutenqiggluku'* (*'shot it again even though it was floating'*). In doing so, he shifted the conversation from strong Yup'ik speakers and hunters listening to a minimal Yup'ik speaker with less hunting experience, to strong Yup'ik speakers sharing an in-joke about a different story.

During language shift, youth who reported linguistic insecurities used simple phrases in Yup'ik to position themselves as knowledgeable participants in conversations about subsistence. In line 15 above, for example, Mike used a clarifying question in Yup'ik to regain the floor:

Ex: *Tegu-llru-an⸮*
Translation: *'Take'-past tense-2nd singular subject/3rd singular object*
Gloss: *Did you take it⸮*

In his question, Mike demonstrated his knowledge of how to make simple statements in Yup'ik, combining a single, common verbal postbase to mark tense, *-llru*, with a transitive word ending marking subject and object. Nevertheless, Mike stuck to the type of simple Yup'ik construction that became increasingly common among youth in 2000–2001.

As GB youth told subsistence stories during language shift, they emphasized local relationships, and developed collective understandings and aesthetic expressions of community and place. They also strategically negotiated their divergent positions as youth who were more and less confident using Yup'ik morphology as they jointly oriented toward Yup'ik as the language of subsistence. Examining the underlined words above, we can further see how youth were in the process of losing linguistic 'forms whose possibilities of use ha[d] been explored and learned for many generations' (Woodbury, 1998: 256), including the demonstrative system described in Chapter 5. At line 9, Mike briefly summarized for his listeners where he went in a single hunting trip, using six instances of the demonstratives 'this', 'that' and 'there' and three instances of the verb 'go' (underlined in the excerpt above). Above, Mike oriented his listeners by combining hand gestures with English approximations of Yup'ik demonstratives. Mike also called up shared experiences and knowledge of land, asking in line 14, 'You know when we <u>go down</u>, we <u>go that way</u>?'

In similar interactions, there was little evidence that young people could not follow one another when they substituted relatively nonspecific English counterparts for Yup'ik demonstrative terms. Nevertheless, it is easy to imagine how Yup'ik demonstratives and related verb stems might dramatically affect the level of detail in the story above, or any similar description of navigating on land. In 2000 and 2001, elders, parents, Yup'ik teachers and youth themselves noted that Yup'ik demonstratives and related verb stems were disappearing from young people's Yup'ik use. As one parent described,

> And everything to them is *tageq* (go up an incline), everywhere, like they don't have the meaning of direction. If they don't . . . like, toward the river? *Wani* (*Here*). Toward the airport? *Piani* (*Up, away from the river*). Toward the [building's name in Yup'ik] building? *Agaani, agaani.* (*Across there, across there*). *Man'a-ll' tuai, un'gaani* (*And this one, downriver, extended*). *Tua-i-ll', agaani* (*Then, across there extended*)? If you're talking about *agaani* (*across there extended*)? My generation: '*Qaqatartua* [building's name in Yup'ik] building-*amun'* (*I'm going to go to the* [building's name in Yup'ik] building). *Atraqatartua kuigem tungiinun* (*I'm going to go down in the direction of the river*). *Tagqatartua elitnaurvigmun* (*I'm going to go up to the school*). *Un'gaavet, waten, uterteqatartua* (*Downriver, like this, I'm going to go back home*) . . . *Ellait-llu tua-i* (*And then they*), if our kids talk? '*Tagqatartua*' (*I'm going up*). That's all they say, '*Tagqatartua*' (*I'm going up*). '*Tagqatartua, kiingan*' (*I'm going up, only*). That's the only word they started using from Wes's generation.

Young people's flattening of the Yup'ik demonstrative system raised local questions about the significance of losing a linguistic orientation to land. As we saw in Chapter 5, some adults also noted how young people's loss of demonstratives was contributing to intergenerational miscommunication, as adults increasingly doubted that young people could understand Yup'ik and accommodated by speaking English at home.

Learning through risk

All teaching and learning involves mutual risk and relies upon the development of trusting relationships over time (Erickson, 1987). In societies that are changing rapidly and communities where other upward paths of mobility are less evident, young people's performance in risky endeavors can serve as the ultimate measure of 'how youth are doing' (Heath, 2000). Survivance stories of land-use experiences further 'highlight the situational sentiments of chance' and 'the risk in nature' (Vizenor, 2008: 11).

Many youth in Piniq had stories of times they became lost or faced danger when traveling with adults by snowmobile, though boys more regularly faced the risks of navigating a heterogeneous natural world, with ever-changing weather, land and ocean conditions (Kawagley, 1995). Among villagers, it was commonly stated that, 'You risk your life every time you go to the ocean.' Boys had stories of dangerous ocean experiences when boats were almost crushed in ice flows. They also commonly referred to the potential danger of encountering aggressive mother walruses, and lessons about how to shoot a walrus from underneath, if a walrus hooked its tusks over the side of a boat, so the force of the bullet would lift the massive head and tusks up and off without tipping the boat into the Bering Sea.

When asked about his most powerful learning experience in or out of school, a high school senior with a strong academic record quickly mentioned his experiences on the tundra, saying: 'Like, when you go into trouble, you learn a lot from that. You learn not to do it again, like to watch out for the signs of this or that happening again.' Notable in the young *nukalpiat's* stories and reflections, as well, were young people's descriptions of regular apprenticeship experiences, and their respect for adult men as knowledgeable mentors with lessons for managing risky ventures in the subarctic environment.

As we see below, through their participation and discussion of controversial hunting practices, young hunters further used storytelling to make sense of disjunctures between local and scientific views of environmental practices, and potential threats to local land-use practices.

Subsistence regulation and local alignment

Like young *nukalpiat* in the RS group, GB youth negotiated conflicting ideologies of cultural and ecological preservation. Boys also witnessed and found themselves in risky situations as young hunters vis-à-vis government agents who were seen as threatening the very livelihood of the community through the policing of local subsistence practices. 'Youth use stories to suggest what taking risks might mean … (and) the restraints that outside authorities and the inevitable outcomes their own actions can have over them' (Heath, 1994: 219). Together through storytelling, GB boys shared the ways that community members and peers responded to the risks of continuing subsistence practices that had been declared illegal. In one group interview, for instance, four boys described how villagers were against the Fish and Game officials for 'trying to take over hunting' by checking freezers and boats for lead shot and/or Emperor Geese, an endangered bird, and threatening to fine villagers who broke related regulations. In their stories, boys sometimes weighed how they should act in relation to controversial issues such as whether to use lead shot, as local men had done for decades, or to accept scientific discourses about toxic contaminants (Kafarowski, 2009). Through discussion of their lived experiences and the situated responses of hunters, GB boys also expressed concerns that 'local control of their land and their lives' was in jeopardy (Fienup-Riordan, 2001: 555).

Youth sometimes coated their stories about how they and other villagers had responded to Fish and Game agents with humor, yet through storytelling they also simultaneously shared and worked out their interpretations of serious matters facing their community (e.g. Heath, 1994). As they replayed their own choices and the choices of other peers and adults through group conversation, at moments the boys challenged one another for not taking the risks involved with breaking hunting regulations seriously. At other times, the boys teased one another and indirectly critiqued individuals for taking risks too seriously.

In 2000 and 2001, the tensions above ran as an undercurrent in boys' talk, appearing periodically when everyday banter turned serious, or when I asked boys to share their overall experiences learning about hunting. In spring 2001, the conflicts with Fish and Game intensified as agents lived in Piniq for two weeks, going house to house to exchange steel for lead shot, and checking boats as villagers returned from hunting. During this time, young *nukalpiat* shared daily stories with one another of hunters' encounters with Fish and Game agents. Boys also spontaneously acted out imagined scenarios of standing up to the agents, drawing upon media-based forms of interpersonal aggression to imagine responses to situations that they perceived as threatening their communities' livelihood. Through their stories of the ways that they and others handled hunting-related confrontations, as well as enactments of hypothetical scenarios, GB boys took up shared stances toward the contested hunting practices of their community. In other instances, they voiced varying interpretations and disagreements over appropriate and effective local responses to increasing land-use regulations.

In 2000–2001, boys consistently described participation in local subsistence activities and snowmobile riding as the best parts of rural Alaskan living. Girls, as well, mentioned subsistence activities, especially the ones involving 'going out' to the tundra, as one of the best parts of growing up in Piniq. Both boys and girls regularly engaged with subsistence practices out of school, as individuals and small groups of youth, adults and family members 'traveled different paths, gain(ing) knowledge of dangers and opportunities' (Lemke, 2000: 282) along individualized and shared trajectories of subsistence. Hearing *qanruyutait* (*teachings*) and engaging in everyday subsistence practices alongside adults, young people developed trusting relationships and interacted with fluent Yup'ik-speaking mentors who, in turn, passed on specific knowledge of the local ecology.

In the process of participating in subsistence and sharing their experiences, youth maintained, and also helped generate community knowledge, as they 'integrat(ed) short-term processes of discovering, telling, and re-telling' (Lemke, 2000: 282) while circulating in the ecosocial networks of their community. Youth in Piniq further learned to synthesize 'specific experiences over geographical journeys and time', accessing and adding to a 'cumulative knowledge on a timescale and spatial scale that no individual could match' (Lemke, 2000: 282) as they took on adult roles alongside their peers. As in other places, this knowledge was unevenly acquired through individualized and gendered learning trajectories, creating inter- as well as intragroup differences in boys' and girls' knowledge of subsistence. Subsistence practices also brought boys face-to-face in particular ways with the power dynamics and dissonance of competing local, scientific and environmental discourses about land-use practices. Undoubtedly, groups of girls and boys together, and groups of girls on their own discussed the tensions around government regulation of subsistence. In the research, however, none of the girls raised these topics in interviews, nor did I hear these conversations.

Girls' subsistence experiences were more geographically restricted, and provided fewer daily risks than boys'. While girls and women had to be careful of weather conditions when traveling by boat, older boys and men often piloted the boats, and they rarely faced anything as dangerous as ocean ice or walrus mothers. Young women faced risky choices related to the regulation of subsistence, facing a $100 fine per egg, for instance, if they harvested Emperor Goose eggs. By the time women were egg-hunting, however, the Fish and Game agents had left Piniq. Girls' subsistence stories played a much smaller role in local peer culture than those of boys, and girls' connections to Yup'ik in subsistence stories were also much less visible during language shift.

Negotiating in- and out-of-school learning trajectories

As Chapters 3 and 4 document, some local adults and teachers including myself tried to make connections between young people's in- and out-of-school learning. In general, however, links between school learning and local life were tenuous, and youth had little opportunity to integrate the knowledge that they gained through subsistence with the content of school lessons. Youth also found little guidance in negotiating what could sometimes be profound disjunctures between local, state and scientific discourses, though individuals varied in the ways in which they responded to these disjunctures.

As youth took on local roles and responsibilities, they largely learned on their own how to balance the time and physical requirements of their learning trajectories in- and out-of-school. Throughout the study, the school year was structured around the competing demands of academic and subsistence timelines, with teachers' vacation days shortened as much as the teachers' union would allow in order to accommodate the intense work in spring seal-hunting season. In key subsistence seasons, sometimes girls had trouble making it to school on time after staying up late to help take care of birds and/or seals. Some girls were also called home to baby-sit younger siblings. In general, however, girls rarely ran into trouble with absences.

One teacher noted in 2000–2001 how the students who did best in school seemed to be the ones with major responsibilities at home, and how balancing in- and out-of-school responsibilities took ongoing negotiation for girls, as well as boys, during intense springtime subsistence:

> Every once and a while, [...] I'm like, 'Why didn't you do your homework last night?' And, I remember getting on Mary's case for that. And, she's like, 'Ms. [Name] I'm so tired!' And, I said, 'Well, why didn't you do your homework last night?' She goes, 'Well, I had two walruses, three seals, and I can't remember how many birds to clean last night. And, I was exhausted and didn't do my homework.' I'm like, 'Okay.' So, sometimes it does get to the best of the kids. But, in general, I'd say the kids who seem to follow responsibility at home also do it at school.

Some of the young *nukalpiat* were also among the highest-achieving youth in school in 2000–2001, having figured out how to balance community and school responsibilities. GB young *nukalpiat*, like their earlier RS counter-parts, counted school absences carefully, sometimes coming to school sick in winter so they could miss school for spring seal-hunting without being retained. Nevertheless, as seal-hunting season arrived, some boys inevitably went over their limit and were held back.

As even the brief description of young people's lives above demonstrates, boys and girls in Piniq shared many learning processes, situational contingencies, and challenges in the ways that they took on local roles and responsibilities. Yet they also experienced key differences in their varying learning curves, risks and social experiences learning the subsistence way of life of their community.

Discourses of survivance and visions of the local future

Recent studies of second language learning and language shift have underscored the importance of considering how communities and individuals imagine their futures as a means to understanding learners' everyday language choices and relative investment in language development (Kulick, 1992; Kanno & Norton, 2003). In interviews, youth provided varied answers to questions about the future of Piniq. Four boys and one girl in junior high in 2001 described how the village might 'go back to the old days', with everything modern disappearing and life returning to a traditional lifestyle:

LTW: What do you guys think Piniq will be like in the future?
John: No light.
Tom: Go back to the old days.
John: Like sod-houses? Not this kind of clothes [gesturing to his windbreaker and pants]
LTW: Go back to the old days?
John: Use seal oil for lamp.
Tom: Start using *qayaq*s.
John: Yep. I <u>hope</u>.

Amy, the self-declared 'English girl' from Chapter 6 also described in an interview how Piniq would 'go back to the old days', elaborating how the village would experience 'hauntings', and how she would not want to experience this. One longstanding non-Yup'ik educator in the district reported that she regularly heard young people's talk about 'going back to the old days', and how she would respond by asking students how they would handle having no electricity. Yet, through their expressions and portrayals of 'going back to the old days', the young *nukalpiat* asserted possibilities of using aspects of tradition and history to center a present day life (e.g. Fienup-Riordan, 1991), 'offer(ing) a competing form of historical consciousness' and claim for legitimacy (Cruikshank, 1998: 136–137). Multiple local elders in the 1990s and 2000–2001 expressed concerns that youth were losing the knowledge of how to sustain themselves in the local setting. As we have seen, the young *nukalpiat* above cited the dependence on electricity as a contemporary contingency that might drive Piniq to withdraw from the cash economy and depend on itself, versus outside bureaucracies and flows of resources. A number of the young *nukalpiat*, as well, spoke positively of how they might rely on local knowledge as they described possibilities of returning to the past.

At the time, some adults in Piniq emphasized Christian Judgment Day as a second millennial vision of the future, and discussed global conflicts such as the first Gulf War and the Y2K bug as evidence of the impending Rapture, or end of the world. Christian millennial visions have been described as an ideological force of language shift in Indigenous communities in Papua New Guinea (e.g. Kulick, 1992). Talk about returning to the past and Christian transformations of life on earth evidenced varying local responses to dramatic sociohistorical changes in Piniq. Still, youth alluded to competing millennial visions of the ways Piniq might be radically altered in the future in only a small number of instances. While GB youth echoed local concerns about language endangerment, they much more commonly imagined Piniq as remaining mostly the same, with possibly a larger population and more amenities, such as a larger airstrip and a laundromat, projects for which the traditional council had received planning grants.

When asked the general question of 'how is it growing up in Piniq?', almost all boys would start by answering 'good', mention something like 'you get to go out' and then describe hunting. Girls, as well, described subsistence in positive terms, although they were much more likely to answer the question about life in Piniq, 'good, but a little bit boring' or just 'boring'. When asked about the future, most boys would say they wanted to stay in Piniq, or to return to Piniq after college, while boys who were the most peripheral to local family networks and/or the young *nukalpiat* group sometimes talked about leaving Piniq for good. Girls had a wider range of answers, including staying in Piniq, or moving away to Anchorage to live with friends.

In 2000–2001, as some GB youth reached high school, their discussions of the future increasingly focused on the local economy. Youth could generally get minimum-wage jobs like clerking in a store or babysitting, although some stores in 2001 began to post requirements that workers be able to speak Yup'ik. A small subgroup of boys age 12 and older also found jobs harvesting commercial resources away from Piniq, depending on family connections. Tom, for instance, worked with family members in commercial salmon fishing along the Kuskokwim River, and his peers spoke admiringly of the thousand dollars he could make in a summer. By high school, during the summer some boys commercially fished for herring in Piniq, or for salmon on larger boats in Bristol Bay.

Secondary boys shared their concerns, however, about job opportunities in rural Alaska, while voicing desires to remain connected to local subsistence practices, as well as Yup'ik elders, family members and peers. Here, Jack described the push–pull incentives to stay and leave Piniq:

LTW: Do you think you'll wanna live here in the future?
Jack: Well yes and no, yes because this is home, and hunting, and the things the boys do, or it's yes, yes, all yes, but someday I'd like to find a place where I could work like big salary.

Girls, as well, voiced economic concerns and hopes about staying close to local social networks. As Mary described, 'I grew up here and everything I want and know is here: the friends, the family and everything, and we get homesick, that's why we say it's boring sometimes when we travel.' Yet, Mary also worried that, if the population in Piniq continued to increase, 'I'm not gonna like that, too many people, not enough jobs, not that many jobs. It will be hard to find a job, a decent job.' Language ideologies and subsistence practices shaped young people's overall allegiance to Yup'ik as a language of community and place, young people's continuing functional, aesthetic and emotional uses of Yup'ik with one another, and the young *nukalpiat*'s marked and regular use of Yup'ik in hunting stories during language shift. Yet these combined forces could not make up for the multilayered processes that were rapidly undercutting young people's opportunities to learn to speak Yup'ik.

Summary

Like adults and RS youth, GB youth strongly associated Yup'ik with subsistence endeavors carried out within specific social networks and geographical spaces. In many ways, young people's experiences with subsistence also profoundly shaped their connections to Yup'ik as a language of community and place. Even as youth culture became a driving force of a community-wide language shift to English, young people underscored connections between Yup'ik and subsistence through patterned word borrowing, and the use of Yup'ik for telling stories about land-related adventures. Whether and when these connections called forth extended Yup'ik discourse, however, depended jointly on (1) young people's varying Yup'ik competences, (2) young people's widely varying gendered and individualized experiences with local land-use practices, as well as (3) in-the-moment rhetorical and interactional dimensions of language use.

The GB group generally maintained receptive and some productive competences in Yup'ik. Like some groups of 'semi-speakers' elsewhere, youth in Piniq also maintained allegiance to Yup'ik as a language of solidarity and an in-group code during rapid language shift (Dorian, 1989). At the same time, the local term 'getting by' and the academic term 'linguistic survivance' more accurately portray young people's complex relationship to language ideologies and evolving community patterns, emphasizing the active process through which youth acted jointly, making use of their bilingualism to create a distinct peer culture within a particular time and place. While GB youth used much more English with one another than their earlier RS counterparts, all of the youth in the GB group, from the strong Yup'ik speakers to the minimal Yup'ik speakers, were coming up with their own ways of getting by with adults and with one another in what remained a clearly bilingual, but changing world. Chapters 5 and 6 document how the GB group 'got by' using Yup'ik to listen, follow instructions, and ask and answer basic questions around local adults. Chapters 6 and 7 evidence (1) how stronger Yup'ik-speaking GB youth 'got by' accommodating friends who spoke less Yup'ik, while maintaining the status of Yup'ik within local peer culture, and (2) how GB youth with diminished access to Yup'ik language learning opportunities 'got by' with their stronger Yup'ik-speaking peers by using some of the tokenism, receptive skills and survival Yup'ik that helped them function with parents and local adults.

Yet there were distinct differences in the ways young people linguistically got by with local adults and one other. In some ways, the GB peer group exhibited less purism in assessing learners' productive competences; unlike adults commenting on young people's Yup'ik, young people themselves hardly ever marked one another's speech as 'taking a short cut' or stigmatized linguistic change. To participate fully as Yup'ik speakers among peers, however, demanded certain types of extended discourse that young people were not generally expected to produce for adults.

As we have seen above, young people's sharing of peer-directed, subsistence narratives both called out boys' and girls' remaining uses of Yup'ik, and simultaneously highlighted young speakers' increasing productive shortcomings in Yup'ik. While Yup'ik had a distinct role in peer life, at the level of narrative performance, the nature of that role could be cause for linguistic insecurity. Strong Yup'ik speakers used relatively complex Yup'ik morphology, and commonly animated a Yup'ik storytelling frame through extensive use of the subordinative mood. Weaker Yup'ik speakers created many stand-alone Yup'ik terms for subsistence, using the hybrid loan marker $-(a)q$ to express key actions in stories. These youth sometimes used beginner Yup'ik postbases and endings to negotiate interactions with stronger Yup'ik-speaking youth, yet rarely used Yup'ik postbases and endings to frame their own subsistence stories in Yup'ik.

Nevertheless, in stories about going out onto the land, youth reenacted the known as a way of entertaining one another, using multiple symbolic resources to highlight shared and emplaced knowledge and experiences with subsistence. As youth learned how to carry out complex local work, they distributed their accumulating knowledge of land conditions, animal behavior and in-the-moment subsistence strategies. Sharing rich everyday narratives about commonplace and unexpected experiences with one another in Yup'ik, English and a hybrid mix of both languages, youth also shared knowledge about situated uses of Yup'ik.

Boys, in particular, grew increasingly conscious about the political challenges to community land-use practices as they participated in hunting, and used storytelling to make sense of the political and social, as well as physical, risks involved in local land-use practices. GB young *nukalpiat* vocally opposed outside encroachment into their ancestral homelands, like the RS young *nukalpiat* before them and many other Yup'ik community members elsewhere (Fienup-Riordan, 2001). Like many Far Northern Indigenous hunters, they also faced the challenge of negotiating contradictory discourses about ecological sustainability and self-determination. Through collaborative storytelling about subsistence experiences with one another, reenactments and imagined enactments of encounters with Fish and Game agents, and discussions of prophecies, the young *nukalpiat* worked out what it was to act like men in a specific community, place and historical moment.

Young people's Yup'ik language development and language ideologies were part and parcel of their situated experiences with subsistence. For a short window in time, as local peer culture tipped rapidly into English, the differences in the extent to which boys and girls engaged in land-related adventures fostered a highly visible gender difference in the extent to which boys and girls used Yup'ik. Nevertheless, boys as well as girls negotiated gendered expectations and experiences with their individualized positions as relatively strong and weak Yup'ik speakers during the rapid sociolinguistic transformation of their community. With one another, youth also found many ways to express connections to local community members, knowledge, practices and places across linguistic boundaries, demonstrating linguistic survivance in the face of ecological and political challenges, as well as the particular challenges of language shift and endangerment.

Conclusion

Hold fast to dreams,
for when dreams go,
life is a barren field,
covered with snow.
(Hughes, [1926])

During my first year teaching in Piniq, these lines from a Langston Hughes poem stared at me from a poetry book recommended as part of the ninth-grade English curriculum. Out the window of the classroom, beyond a few houses, seemed to lay the very vision Hughes describes: a 'field' of snow stretching as far as the eye could see in every direction. The background of this study is the story of how I learned to consider the ways Hughes' metaphor did, and more often did not, reflect the lives of the young people in Piniq, and how I moved from seeing 'barren fields' outside the school to recognizing the dreams of local community members and the rich linguistic ecologies around me.

The background of the book is also a longstanding personal and academic struggle to understand the complexities of young people's experiences and language use in communities undergoing rapid sociolinguistic transformation. In the early 1990s when I first came to Piniq as a secondary teacher, most community members spoke Yup'ik comfortably and Yup'ik served as the unmarked language of adults' interaction and local youth culture. Yup'ik was clearly embedded within *yuuyaraq*, a uniquely Yup'ik way of life. Through their words and actions, villagers emphasized the importance of orally accumulated *qanruyutait* (*teachings*) in Yup'ik as a resource for fostering *piniq* (*strong, good*) lives and community stability, and adapted related socialization practices accordingly. Youth themselves used Yup'ik as the framing language of local peer culture, and for making connections and marking social boundaries when they traveled within the region and tested Alaskan university spaces. Nevertheless, elementary Yup'ik educators noted that young children were beginning to speak mostly English with one another, and were beginning to voice concerns about the possibility of language shift and endangerment. Older youth, as well, worried that Yup'ik might someday disappear.

Noting adults' and secondary students' everyday language uses, and listening to ways they talked about Yup'ik, local elders and local knowledge, the wholescale linguistic transformation of the community seemed so implausible. How could a rapid language shift be happening in such a remote, seemingly homogenous place, where youth expressed powerful feelings about Yup'ik as the language of their community? How could the Yup'ik language be *endangered*, given its vibrant use in the lives of adults and youth around me? And what did it mean for young people's academic and social development to grow up feeling like speaking English 'was a crime' and school was 'brainwashing' them to speak English, in a setting where adults were increasingly voicing concerns about the loss of a unique Indigenous language?

Working in relation to community members' concerns, as a teacher and researcher I followed overlapping lines of inquiry for roughly two decades, trying to understand how different types of linguistic resources are distributed in society, and how various unpredictable groupings of resources shape social identification (Wortham, 2006) and sociolinguistic change. Examining the movement of ideas and people helped me trace how multiple processes were eroding uneven Yup'ik language-learning opportunities over time. Through conversations and work with local community members, educators and others, I further sought to understand how multiple actors were co-constructing the linguistic transformation of Piniq in translocal as well as local social fields, and how the Piniq case related to entrenched questions about the schooling of Alaska Native and language minority students more broadly.

Detailing, parsing and synthesizing language socialization trajectories, ideologies and instances of linguistic survivance offered insight into the ways young people might take up new positions as speakers of their ancestral languages, and how the actions of both authorizing agents and youth themselves might play a role in envisioning and creating 'preferred futures' (Pennycook, 2001) for endangered language communities (McCarty & Wyman, 2009; McCarty *et al.*, 2009). Engaging with complex understandings of youth, culture, knowledge and language further provided fresh 'ways of thinking about how human communities continue to hold together, and how divisions that at one time seem deep', may recede and become reworked 'in the process of building alliances at another time' (Cruikshank, 1998: 2) across time and space.

As we have seen, the interplay of language ideologies, linguistic resources and local language uses were far from straightforward in Piniq during rapid language shift. At the time of the study, a legislative proposal to adopt English as an official language of Alaska made major headlines and was heatedly debated and passed; soon thereafter, local members of traditional councils in small Yup'ik villages challenged the measure in court. Local council members in Piniq, however, largely dismissed the ability of such formal measures to change local methods of self-governance, although they worried how broader changes at the state level might impact financial support for heritage language programming in the local school. For the most part, parents, youth and children in Piniq remained unaware of and unconcerned with these broader debates.

Careful and longitudinal examination of young people's everyday language practices in Piniq unearthed little evidence that youth started speaking primarily in English because of its appeal as a language of State and economic power, or global youth culture and new forms of media. Missing, too, was evidence that youth were in the process of marking their heritage language as linked to a marginalized ethnic, rural or low-income identity. Data on young families' struggles with language shift further countered the notion that adults' conscious decisions or shared ideological orientations toward speaking English were primary forces in the linguistic transformation of Piniq.

Rather, the study demonstrated how educational policies and practices, concurrent changes in patterns of migration, educators' and community members' emerging explanations of language shift, the ways youth tacitly and explicitly positioned themselves as Yup'ik language 'forgetters' in interactions with peers and adults, and adults' responses to young people's changing linguistic practices together shaped the community's trajectory toward language shift and endangerment. The study also underscored how linguistic resources and accompanying language ideologies were transformed along overlapping, patterned, yet individualized trajectories of differentiated interactions and experiences.

To understand and situate youth language practices in linguistic ecologies takes methods of analysis that 'begin long before discourse emerges as a linguistically articulated object, and ... continue long after the act of production' (Blommaert, 2005: 234). Chapters 2 and 3 traced how historical as well as contemporary changes in schooling, missionization and governance helped to shape the specific linguistic resources, language ideologies and forms of linguistic survivance during language shift within Piniq.

The Piniq case also underscores the importance of taking into account the mobility of language learners in an increasingly global world (Blommaert, 2010; Roth-Gordon & Woronov, 2009; Warriner & Wyman, in progress). Many contemporary youth in North American Indigenous communities live in linguistic ecologies characterized by increasing rural–urban interdependence as community members move between ancestral homelands, regional hub towns and urban spaces (Fienup-Riordan, 2000; McCarty, 2004; Patrick, 2005; Wyman, in progress). Socioeconomic forces pushed community members and children out of Piniq's distressed economy, even as parents, children and individual youth flowed back to Piniq to relocate themselves within family networks, schools, peer groups and ancestral homelands. Notably, individual youth also used mobility as a survivance strategy, moving to Piniq to escape the very challenging circumstances of rural suicide and urban violence, or, in other cases, moving out of Piniq in search of better educational or economic opportunities elsewhere.

As we have seen, Indigenous migration served as a scaled and powerful force of language shift in Piniq. Chapters 4–6 provide many examples of how children and youth developed linguistic insecurities about speaking Yup'ik as they were positioned and repositioned across English- and Yup'ik-speaking communities, and how the effects of even relatively temporary dislocations from Piniq lingered with individual language learners. The chapters also document how the varying flows of children and youth had reverberating, accumulating impacts on the local linguistic ecology in Piniq, as peer groups and families tipped into using English with young migrants. Still, former child migrants could at least partially overcome related linguistic insecurities when they were offered subsequent opportunities to learn Yup'ik. We have also seen how schools, families and young people in strong Yup'ik-speaking villages elsewhere offered possibilities for maintaining and developing heritage language learners' Yup'ik use.

Because youth language practices and local linguistic ecologies are continually shaped, it is important to exercise caution in trying to extrapolate lessons from what was going on in one place over the course of one decade, seen through the eyes of one person. The Piniq case should *not* be read as a prediction of what will happen in the future in Piniq itself, let alone elsewhere, given the multidirectional, contingent and complex processes of language shift, maintenance and revitalization described within this book. At the same time, looking at the Piniq case, we can take away some general points that help us understand highly dynamic sociolinguistic settings.

The first point is just how quickly language shift can take hold in peer cultures, families and communities. In the remote community of Piniq, (1) all but a small minority of adults were Yup'ik; (2) adults continued to speak to one another predominantly in Yup'ik; and (3) almost all adults initially chose to speak Yup'ik to their children. However, within five to ten years, the sociolinguistic dimensions of adults' interactions with young people, and young people's interactions with one another, changed rapidly. As we saw in Chapter 5, the dynamics of family language maintenance and shift also quickly changed to mirror those found among immigrant families in urban, diverse communities elsewhere.

Comparing the RS group (Chapter 4) to the GB group (Chapters 6 and 7) further highlights how dramatic sociolinguistic transformations can take place quickly within and between consecutive groups of youth, in spite of considerable continuities in local peer cultures and shared intergenerational concerns for language maintenance. Youth in both the RS and GB groups in the study were generally motivated by the idea that Yup'ik use tied them to authentic, longstanding community practices and struggles (Smith, 1999), even as individuals understandably rejected notions of authenticity that posited them as 'lesser than Yup'ik' in relation to circumstances beyond their control. Boys and girls in both groups of youth also demonstrated their valuation of Yup'ik in many ways, even as they used wide-ranging symbolic practices generatively and creatively.

Nevertheless, as Piniq began to linguistically restructure from the bottom up, dramatic, age-graded discrepancies rapidly emerged among adults, older youth and children. Young people's beliefs about language, identity and the social world around them also changed quickly in Piniq, as language socialization processes 'enter(ed) into dialogue with the hegemony of English' (González & Arnot-Hopffer, 2006: 232) in the relatively homogenous, remote space. Most adults used Yup'ik and expressed strong language allegiance, although they increasingly accommodated children's English use, and needed to use new strategies for maintaining Yup'ik at home with multiple children. GB youth actively negotiated local language allegiance with their learning of local gender roles, their individualized, divergent linguistic repertoires and their increasing insecurities about speaking Yup'ik. Young *nukalpiat* (*great hunter*)'s everyday storytelling and orientations toward subsistence remained particularly visible in youth culture over time. Yet even boys who demonstrated strong interest in remaining connected to Yup'ik as a language of subsistence grappled with emerging linguistic insecurities. Very young children in Piniq, simultaneously, began to express emerging, conscious and seemingly agentive 'choices' not to speak Yup'ik to one another.

The Piniq study highlighted the importance of exercising caution in making claims about the ways in which societal changes impact young people's connections to families and communities. For instance, contrary to commonplace assumptions about youth and media, examples in Chapters 4–6 evidence how newly available cable TV, video games and internet sites did not simply act as a straightforward 'cultural nerve gas' (Krauss, 1980), paralyzing young people's interest in local knowledge, practices, discourses and forms of language use. In contrast, multiple examples highlighted how Piniq youth used media to negotiate their relationships with one another, and how, in some instances, youth used media to very actively (1) make sense of their collective history as Yup'ik people; (2) negotiate authoritative Yup'ik, Christian and scientific discourses in their local environment; and (3) interpret local–outside controversies and ideological conflicts over particular land-use practices.

Even as the Piniq study underscored the importance of youth culture as a site of linguistic and cultural change, findings within also underscored the importance of exercising caution in making claims about the ways in which young people's practices transform existing community practices and funds of knowledge. Commonly, ethnographic studies of youth culture take place over periods that feel long to researchers at the time, yet are a blink of an eye, so to speak, in the historical development of community life. As such, researchers face challenges when they try to empirically link interesting observations about youth practice to broader linguistic and cultural transformations taking place over longer timescales. The entrenched challenges of analyzing macrosocial and microlinguistic phenomenon are perhaps 'at their most extreme' when we consider global phenomenon like the worldwide spread of English (Pennycook, 2001) and the worldwide endangerment of languages, let alone the salience of relatively ephemeral youth cultures in relation to these trends.

Ethnographic studies of the ways youth negotiate interactions with adults, peers and younger children in different situational and interactional contexts are important for seeing how language learners use linguistic repertoires on the ground. They can also help combat the stereotypes and assumptions about youth, language and society that naturalize language shift and endangerment in particular families, peer cultures and communities. However, there is much work to be done to see (1) how long- and short-term changes in society combine to close and open spaces for language learning; (2) how language learners' typical and atypical language socialization trajectories shape young people's linguistic repertoires and emerging practices; and (3) how accumulating language practices, as well as young people's everyday linguistic performances, do and do not 'ramp up' (Blommaert, 2005; Eckert & McConnell-Ginet, 2003) into broader patterns of sociolinguistic transformation, and/or the widespread Indigenization of global linguistic flows.

The longitudinal study of youth culture in Piniq highlighted how some visible changes in local youth culture, such as young people's overall increasing use of English, quickly came to play a driving role in language shift within families and community life. Using interactional data, the study also highlighted how seemingly subtle changes in young people's everyday language practices, such as young people's change from using Yup'ik to English grammatical frames in local patterns of codeswitching, played an important role both forwarding and obscuring local language shift (e.g. Myers-Scotton, 1998). Yet other visible, creative youth practices such as the young *nukalpiats'* and Mark's appropriation of hip hop-related linguistic features had relatively very little connection to processes of language shift, or the transformation and expression of local knowledge and practice.

By comparing examples within and across chapters, we have seen how young people continuously positioned themselves as Yup'ik language 'speakers' or language 'overhearers' in relation to individual and family language socialization trajectories, as well as local socializing institutions, even as young people's language uses and ideologies were dynamic, malleable and sensitive to the specifics of particular face-to-face interactions within peer networks. We also wrestled with the challenges of disentangling simultaneous influences on young people's everyday language 'choices' and language ideologies. In Chapter 5, for instance, we saw how young James from family 1 used increasing amounts of English upon entering school and playing with his cousins in Piniq, and then activated Yup'ik competences upon staying in a neighboring village, attending a school Yup'ik program and playing with Yup'ik-speaking peers elsewhere. We also saw how James, within months of returning to Piniq, subsequently refused to speak Yup'ik, claiming that speaking Yup'ik hurt his throat.

In Chapter 4, we saw how youth could partially reverse language shift through agentive and shared choices, as Graham, a previous child migrant and a friend who had spoken mostly English throughout high school later decided together to speak Yup'ik upon entering local life as young adults (although we also heard Graham describe challenges speaking Yup'ik comfortably after years of positioning himself as a non-Yup'ik speaker). Chapter 5 further demonstrated how, in multiple instances, families were able to disrupt processes of language shift, especially when parents worked together to recognize rapid changes in the local linguistic ecology, and marshaled linguistic, human and ideological resources through sustained efforts to support heritage language learning within young people's social networks.

This brings us to another important point: processes of language shift are highly contingent, multidirectional and subject to community members' strategic actions and everyday linguistic negotiations within face-to-face social networks. As we have seen, communities can move rapidly along trajectories of language endangerment in spite of families', educators' and young people's own conscious efforts to value and maintain unique languages as part of local knowledge systems and identities. Yet, even as contemporary global forces influence local actors, individuals and groups talk and act back through their local economic, political and religious practices, mediating the interrelationships between discourses, flows and practices differently with respect to different social spheres (Levitt *et al.*, 2003).

Chapter 6 documents multiple ways that young people talked back to the pressures of language shift and the painful local claims that youth wanted to be white by speaking English. In 2000–2001, youth made public calls for language activism, while individuals continued to use Yup'ik around their peers. Many youth voiced concerns about language endangerment, and some critiqued the ways that the local school was undercutting family attempts to maintain Yup'ik at home. Youth also sometimes denigrated the English use of individual peers, though most often such instances reflected momentary interactional power plays.

Even as Piniq experienced rapid language shift, adults and youth also talked and acted back by attempting to stem the increasing pressures on Yup'ik, and to disrupt dominant discourses of monolingualism and urban populations as a societal goal. Yup'ik educators and some non-Yup'ik allies worked to connect youth to local knowledge and bilingualism and biliteracy, even as broader school policies and hierarchies often constrained their efforts. As families and individuals flowed back to Piniq from English-speaking spaces, and maintained connections to Yup'ik lands, communities and extended family networks, child migrants used Yup'ik to negotiate their positioning as language learners within local social networks. Youth also used Yup'ik as they took up local roles and learned to participate in subsistence.

Relatively short-term changes did not provide quick fixes or full reversals of individual, peer group and family language trajectories of language endangerment. Taken together, however, the cases dramatically underscored how young people in Piniq, during rapid language shift, were 'emergent bilinguals' (Reyes, 2006). Each chapter also highlighted the kinds of long- and short-term efforts that might help support young people's development of bilingualism and biliteracy. Broadening our conceptual lens, we can further see how adults and young people asserted a sense of 'presence over absence' (Vizenor, 2008) and a unique connection to an Indigenous homeland through their use of English and translanguaging, as well as their use of Yup'ik.

Indigenous Youth Practice and Linguistic Survivance

Building on complex understandings of languages, speech communities and cultures, I have sought to demonstrate how endangered languages can be deeply related to a community's sense of itself and a community's sense of place in the previous chapters. Yet, by identifying wide-ranging instances of linguistic survivance throughout this book, I have also consciously avoided analytical positions and rhetorics that would posit Indigenous community members, in general, and Indigenous youth, in particular, as passively caught in cultural contradictions, as mere victims or tragic heroes, or as authentic or inauthentic Indigenous people based on imposed criteria such as the ability to speak a heritage language, adherence to traditional spiritual beliefs or acting in particular ways in relation to local environments.

In the current moment of worldwide language endangerment, many academics are writing about endangered languages, the large bulk of which are Indigenous languages, as important windows into the ways human minds discern and encode the world around us, and as systems that can be used to identify Traditional Ecological Knowledge (Harrison, 2007). Links between language and land-use practices run as a theme throughout the study of Piniq. As we have seen, Yup'ik language use in Piniq remained closely tied with young peoples' participation in a unique subsistence society, and their sustained engagement, observations and experiences with the physical world around them. Through subsistence talk that was particularly marked for Yup'ik use, as we saw in Chapter 7, youth in Piniq helped *egmirte* – *pass on* – and distribute ecological knowledge. Examining the use and disappearance of specific ecological terms and form-dependent expressions, like the demonstrative system highlighted within Chapters 5, 6 and 7, further underscored how unique local ways of orienting to a particular ecosystem were rapidly becoming lost during rapid language shift.

Yet, a primary focus on Indigenous languages as mere vehicles for scientific or ecological content also obscures the complex, socially mediated relationship between distinct people's historical struggles, ideologies, norms of behavior, learning experiences and languages uses in particular environments (see also Duchêne & Heller, 2007). *Yuuyaraq* did not exist as some static body of knowledge encoded in language. Yup'ik also helped connect individuals to histories, places and relationships in ways that extended beyond obvious or expected functions, expressions and practices. Community members' expressions of linguistic survivance powerfully included Yup'ik use and harkened to existing ways with words and specific Yup'ik resources at the time of language shift. For many community members, including youth, young people's rapid Yup'ik linguistic changes and overall increase in English use also raised deep questions about whether youth were figuratively, as well as literally, losing their sense of direction as they became poised to lose access to local elders' *qanruyutait* and related socializing genres. Community members of all ages also described and negotiated tensions, stresses and powerful emotions as they worried about maintaining intergenerational communication during rapid language shift.

Nevertheless, as we have seen, individuals and groups within Piniq used wide-ranging linguistic resources and language practices to assert a 'continuing presence over absence' (Vizenor, 2008: 1), and to act with 'a belief in their inherent rights to be who they are' (Brayboy, 2008: 341) within particular times and places. Community members expressed linguistic survivance in the ways that they developed new hybrid practices, appropriated political, social and religious rhetorics, and used new forms of media in relation to longstanding and emerging challenges. Youth used multiple symbolic resources to mediate land–language connections, shaping continuities in community practices in spite of their uneven competences during language shift. Through their bilingual practices and uses of English, as well as their uses of Yup'ik, young people also maintained and fostered connections to local adults, one another and a specific place as they simultaneously negotiated their learning of gendered roles related to subsistence. Boys further used hybrid mixes of languages to make sense of local and scientific discourses about land-use practices.

The specific examples of *yuuyaraq* and linguistic survivance presented within are mere pieces of a much larger, complex picture. By documenting these mere pieces, I have run the risk of underrepresenting the affective side of belonging to a particular community and place (González, 2001; Nicholas, 2009), and the deeper role of language in shaping intergenerational relationships and local adaptations to historically accumulating pressures. Nevertheless, by tracing how language use, local knowledge and community members' lived practices were interrelated in Piniq, I have tried to share an appreciation for the varying levels of expression of belonging, and the richness that came 'with the range and diversity of symbolic associations' that swam within a community's reach and moved a community on its course (paraphrasing Basso, 1996), in a particular place at a particular point in time. The study also critically highlighted schooling's consequences for young people's connections to family, peers and place, and Piniq's particular course toward community-wide language shift and endangerment.

Placing Schools in Linguistic Ecologies

As we have seen within, schools are embroiled in peer, family and community dynamics in key ways, even when the complexities of contemporary life and linguistic ecologies may make it appear otherwise. No schools fully determine the linguistic and social realities of Indigenous communities or youth, and Indigenous communities and youth have historically mediated the effects of even very oppressive schooling practices within their social networks in diverse ways (e.g. Lomawaima, 1994). Nevertheless, it is crucial not to lose sight of schooling's influence within linguistic ecologies, given the ways in which multiple communities are now finding themselves 'at the crossroads' of ancestral language maintenance and revitalization, or language endangerment (Benally & Viri, 1995; Taylor & Wright, 2002; Wyman *et al.*, 2010a, 2010b).

The Piniq case extends the evidence that schools are important, if highly contested and problematic, spaces for supporting endangered languages (Hornberger, 2008; McCarty, 2004; Wyman *et al.*, 2010a, 2010b), as well as community knowledge systems and diverse peoples' linguistic survivance. Around the world, the historical fallout from oppressive school policies has helped to set up the current moment of language endangerment, and many communities continue to live with the damaging effects of these earlier policies, even if community members respond to shared historical experiences of linguistic oppression in varying ways. The most significant challenges for the development of language revitalization efforts in Alaska Native and American Indian communities involve 'transforming the long-term effects of policies and practices that continue to condition language attitudes and choices in favor of English at the expense of mother tongues' (Lomawaima & McCarty, 2006: 138). Andrew's historically rooted fear of transitioning into English class in Chapter 3, and Anna's description of speaking English to her children to protect them from the abuses she experienced under oppressive school policies in Chapter 4 evidence how educational practices can live intergenerationally in schools, families and communities. As we saw in Chapter 3, as well, lingering assumptions that speaking Yup'ik would 'hold children back' echoed across time in Piniq, sometimes creating a language smokescreen (Zentella, 1997) in discussions of language and achievement, obscuring the ways that individual teachers' actions were undermining children's opportunities to learn in school.

Chapter 3 documented how social and linguistic hierarchies were also remarkably persistent in the local school in Piniq (e.g. Jaffe, 2007), in spite of changing educational leaders, teachers, policies and curricular approaches from 1992 to 2001. Small numbers of Yup'ik certified teachers remained concentrated largely at the elementary level in Piniq. The rotating cast of temporary white administrators and certified, mostly white, educators in Piniq also had disproportionate influence over the overall goals and the everyday structures and interactions within the local school. Broader struggles over policy and educational equity, and dominant language ideologies strongly impacted the local school's focus, language programs and everyday interactions.

As a result, even when the school was ostensibly working toward bilingualism, too often fractured, underdeveloped and changing programs inadvertently devalued Yup'ik and raised doubts about the community's commitment to language maintenance. Too often when students did not achieve in school, the first assumption was that their home language was part of the problem. Too often, patterns and discourses in school distorted and erased community bilingualism, the mixed nature of the local economy, local funds of knowledge, and the unique social, historical, economic and political circumstances of local life. Just as language shift became broadly apparent to community members, new government-mandated high-stakes testing practices also commandeered much of local educators' time and attention.

In the Piniq case, we have seen how seemingly short-term or subtle changes in contemporary school programs can create long-term challenges for young people's access to unique ancestral languages and knowledge systems. In Chapter 3, we saw how, in the 1980s, villagers in Piniq switched from using Yup'ik to using English as the primary language of instruction within a local bilingual program at the urging of a temporary local administrator from outside the community. Combined chapters within document how that change rapidly reverberated within peer networks, family life and community institutions, transforming local linguistic practices as vicious cycles of reduced resources for and increasing doubts about bilingualism intensified over time.

From 1992 to 2001, community members and educators who were vocal Yup'ik language advocates were often confused about whether and to what degree the local school was shaping the emerging uneven linguistic practices of youth. Many were also increasingly discouraged about the possibility of intervening and reversing processes of language shift, given the ways that rapid sociolinguistic transformation manifested through changing microinteractional details of elementary and secondary young people's interactions with one another, and families' changing experiences socializing children at home. Some parents and educators noted how forces beyond their control were constraining local language maintenance efforts, as they began to feel like they were 'getting suckered into English' (Janet in Chapter 5), or that they would have to change too many levels of local interaction and society in order to stem language endangerment.

Talented local educators also faced tremendous challenges putting their finger on where to intervene in overlapping, emergent processes of language shift, especially given their awareness that sociolinguistic dynamics were shaped by uneven life circumstances and ongoing social mediation outside of school. Outsiders entering this small but complex and dynamic setting for short periods of time commonly struggled to interpret multilayered differences with the families and young people around them, as well as understanding the school's impact on the local linguistic ecology, given differences in the linguistic competences of local students and community divisions around questions of heritage language programming.

As language endangerment became evident, some educators, community members and youth recognized that the local school was undermining heritage language maintenance. Yet many also falsely assumed that the school was largely responding to, rather than coproducing, both the ideologies and historical particulars of uneven processes of language shift. Many individual youth, like Nathan and Mike in Chapter 6, further pointed to single root causes out of school to 'explain' their own linguistic insecurities about speaking Yup'ik.

Together, these emerging interpretations of language endangerment and responses to language shift obscured ongoing effects of schooling on local language practices. From 1992 to 2001, community members grew increasingly aware of language shift, yet few noted how a specific overall reduction of bilingual programming had occurred between the Real Speaker and Getting By group. Only later, when conducting follow-up member checks with longstanding educators and parents, did I myself realize how the reduction in Yup'ik programming mapped to the year of Yup'ik educators' descriptions of local peer culture 'tipping' into English, RS and GB parents' descriptions of struggles to maintain Yup'ik at home, and young people's descriptions of their own linguistic accommodation with peers.

Schools and schooling are but one key force of language shift and revitalization (Fishman, 1991, 2001; Hornberger, 1997, 2008). Young people's experiences of language maintenance and endangerment are also deeply rooted within local relationships, practices, knowledge systems and geographical places. Yet, on many levels, schools influence the availability of linguistic resources and the production and distribution of language ideologies. When home–school disjunctures shape changes in young people's everyday language 'choices' with siblings, parents and extended family members, such disjunctures rapidly impact individual, peer group, and family tips into English, moving communities toward language shift and endangerment.

Learning from Youth Survivance and Looking toward the Future

As leading Indigenous education scholars assert, education is necessarily broad, political and 'occurs in the everyday ways we live life' (Brayboy, 2008:

343), as opposed to simply the ways in which teachers and students do schooling. In rural Alaska, as we have seen, the dreams of young people, families and communities to maintain their status as a people and connection to ancestral homelands, and the very nature of the relationship of language and schooling to those dreams are in constant negotiation. Indigenous youth culture and multilayered processes of Indigenous language shift, endangerment and reclamation are deeply embedded within these broader negotiations.

In many cases, the topics discussed within this book are forays into subjects that deserve a more complete consideration. Recently, scholars have begun to pay increasing attention to the roles and knowledge of Yup'ik women as resource managers, producers and local artists (Frink, 2002; Lipka *et al.*, 1998), and how Northern Indigenous women, as well as men, negotiate new bureaucratic discourses, regulations and institutions (Cruikshank, 1998; Hensel, 1996; Nadasdy, 2003), and interpret controversial land-use practices (Kafarowski, 2009). More research is needed to understand how both Indigenous girls and boys learn about land-use practices and related issues within their local environments.

Research is also needed to see how Indigenous youth negotiate, or might be supported in negotiating congruent and complementary, as well as contested, areas of ecological science, management and land-use practices. One recent effort to document global warming involved Yup'ik youth in documenting elders' observations of changing marine life and weather patterns in the Far North. In 2008, young Yup'ik hunters in Piniq and elsewhere also collaborated with environmental researchers to track whether Avian flu had reached North American migratory birds. Such efforts highlight the potential for involving youth in Indigenous and non-Indigenous knowledge exchanges, and for building upper-level bilingual and biliteracy skills around such exchanges, even if such efforts are likely to spotlight the complexities that arise when aspects of local knowledge do and do not integrate easily with Western scientific discourse (Cruikshank, 1998; Hensel, 1996; Morrow & Hensel, 1992).

Further research is needed on the gendered and racialized dynamics of rural Indigenous young people's decisions to stay or leave rural Indigenous homelands (Hamilton & Seyfrit, 1994), and how Indigenous youth negotiate language in society as they grow up in urban areas, move in and out of particular rural and urban settings and/or foster connections across geographical spaces through use of new media. Notions of race and gender in society are also commonly embedded within educational materials, structures and the dynamics of everyday school interactions in ways beyond those I have touched upon here (Eckert & McConnell-Ginet, 2003; Pavlenko *et al.*, 2001; Pollock, 2004; Wortham, 2006). Currently, multiple Indigenous youth are seeking access to Indigenous language learning opportunities, and becoming interested in forms of Indigenous activism in post-secondary settings (e.g. Charles, 2011; Lee, 2009). Such settings are important places for investigating (1) the ways in which young people encounter heritage discourses, and related concepts of language, gender and race in society; and (2) the ways in which heritage language learning opportunities might be part of broader efforts to create pathways to higher education for underserved communities.

Heritage language learners' orientations, in general, and Indigenous young people's orientations toward Indigenous languages, in particular, can vary dramatically by continent and nation (e.g. Makoni *et al.*, 2007), as well as local context and interactional situation (Blackledge & Creese, 2008). Educational reform, as well, takes long-term efforts and continued monitoring of both intended and unintended effects in and out of local schools in diverse contexts. The complexities of language, society and schooling can be daunting. Nevertheless, the Piniq case extends the evidence that many youth in diverse communities see heritage language learning as holding 'powerful connotations in terms of their sense of belonging and selfhood', and as a means of 'engag(ing) with sets of values and meanings, including emotion, memory and shared knowledge', even if they may complicate discourses about language, heritage and authenticity (Blackledge & Creese, 2008: 535–536). The study further suggested that youth can build relationships of trust and access community funds of knowledge (González *et al.*, 2005; Moll, 1992) within language shift settings through emplaced forms of language learning, sustained engagement in local activities, purposeful risk-taking and situated 'planful thinking' (Heath, 1998, 2008) alongside peers as well as knowledgeable adults.

Recurring patterns within the Piniq study also point to some relatively simple guidelines that language researchers and educators might use in future work with heritage language learners, in general, and youth in endangered language communities, in particular:

Guideline 1: Maintain the 'voice of human concern' (Hill, 2002) and human possibility when discussing language shift and language endangerment, giving youth the benefit of the doubt that they are not simply rejecting connections to heritage languages, community members, local knowledge systems and/or ethnolinguistic identities.

Guideline 2: Work to cultivate 'both/and' perspectives (Fishman, 1991) on heritage language learners' complex positions, countering discourses that position youth as speakers of dominant *or* heritage languages, practitioners of contemporary *or* traditional practices, connected to adults *or* their peers.

Guideline 3:   Emphasize existing heritage language resources and instances of bilingualism in communities, spotlighting vibrant community practices, multigenerational role models and young people's local roles, responsibilities and relationships.

Guideline 4:   Open and keep open heritage language programs.

Guideline 5:   Develop critical language pedagogies related to historical, contemporary and potential future forms of linguistic survivance within heritage and nonheritage language programs.

Guideline 6:   Attend to *when and how* particular discourses engage individual youth in learning languages as part of ongoing struggles to foster connections to particular people, histories, practices and lands, and *when and how* youth may experience messages about languages and identities as disenfranchising.

On a final note of qualified optimism, we can remember that shift in Piniq was happening in spite of the ways that young people continued to use their bilingualism to mark valuation of local languages, communities and practices, and to creatively integrate multiple forms of knowledge, experience and community participation. That valuation and generative quality of young people's linguistic practices is reason enough to have hope in the potentials of enlisting youth themselves in the work of Hornberger's 'language planning from the bottom up' (1996), taking young people's creativity as a potential source of inspiration for bilingualism, biliteracy and linguistic survivance.

Epilogue: Educational Policies and Yup'ik Linguistic Ecologies a Decade Later

In the 1990s, international scholars asserted that strong bilingual programs were desperately needed to support Inuit and Yup'ik language maintenance within the linguistic ecology of the circumpolar world. However, they also noted that extending and strengthening the bilingual education models described in Chapter 3 was unlikely, given the logistical and ideological hurdles involved in educational change in the Far North (Graburn & Iutzi-Mitchell, 1993). From the mid-1990s to the time of this writing, some things have remained the same, while much has changed within educational policy contexts, Yup'ik linguistic ecologies and Piniq. Schools in rural Alaska, like schools in the rest of the United States, continue to function in dialogue with nationalist ideologies of English monolingualism as the ultimate goal of education for the ideal state of society. Schools in Alaska Native villages also continue to need more Indigenous leaders and teachers, and this remains arguably the primary stumbling block for sustained educational improvement. In 1992 when I started as a teacher in Piniq, there were two Yup'ik principals in a district serving 22 villages; as of 2010, there are still only two, with one located in the immersion school in Bethel. The percentage of Alaska Native teachers in the local school district remains relatively high for Alaska, yet continues to hover around 25%. The average teacher remains in a village school only slightly more than two years.

Although both schools and local linguistic ecologies in the Yup'ik region continue to be shaped within accumulating, face-to-face interactions, over the past decade, it has become increasingly evident how standardizing educational policies can have dramatic consequences for the maintenance of community bilingualism and endangered languages. In 2001, schools in the Yup'ik region and schools across the United States began to focus on meeting state and federal educational accountability demands through performance on high-stakes tests in English. Some educators in Piniq, like others around the country, hoped that such new accountability systems would help to change deeply fractured educational efforts such as those described within this book.

From that time until 2010, new federally and state-legislated high-stakes assessment practices, funding structures and definitions of 'highly qualified teachers', positioned culturally and linguistically responsive educational programs as relatively 'low stakes' options (McCarty, 2008, see also Beaulieu, 2008). As a result, American Indian and Alaska Native (AI/AN hereafter) communities across the United States saw programs supporting students' learning of endangered languages become sidelined (Beaulieu et al., 2005). From 2003 to 2007, schools serving AI/AN students increased remedial math and reading instruction in English, while average math and reading scores for AI/AN students on a separate longitudinal National Assessment of Educational Progress remained largely flat. Leading scholars in AI/AN educa-tion referred to this as the 'double whammy', whereby Indigenous youth in the United States were deprived of access to their home language and culture in schools without gains in school achievement (Brayboy & Castagno, 2009: 41, see also McCarty, 2008).

Collaborative action research conducted by myself and colleagues in LKSD, the school district serving 14 out of 17 villages where children spoke Yup'ik in 1995, evidenced how the new educational policies placed major stumbling blocks in the way of Yup'ik educators attempting to focus village communities on long-term language development goals from 2002 to 2007. In 2007 and 2008, as might be predicted from the research literature, most village schools that achieved government-mandated academic progress goals used Yup'ik as a primary language of elementary instruction for 10 or more years prior. Nevertheless, community members in multiple villages became divided over local language programs. A number of schools in previously strong Yup'ik-speaking village also reduced their overall amount of Yup'ik instruction, evidencing the ways that damaging language ideologies about bilingualism lead to the reduction of heritage language learning resources (Wyman et al., 2010a, 2010b). Our study also found that multiple villages where children spoke Yup'ik comfortably in 1995 were experiencing some of the early, complex and uneven dynamics of language shift described in this book. Veteran Yup'ik educators in the study notably echoed themes from the longitudinal Piniq case within. Educators voiced, for instance, strong feelings about the importance of elders' *inerquutet* and *alerquutet* as a social and academic resource for Yup'ik young people's development. Educators also observed how language shift could take hold rapidly among young children, as seemingly subtle increases in numbers of children who did not speak Yup'ik comfortably and child migrants to English-speaking places, and decreases of Yup'ik school instruction shaped children's feelings of linguistic insecurity, and as young people's local peer cultures mediated resulting sociolinguistic changes (Wyman *et al.*, 2010a, 2010b).

Between 2001 and 2007, some principals in LKSD responded to community divides over the 'language of instruction question' and pressures from high-stakes testing in English by creating two separate language strands so that parents could choose between schooling their children in English or in Yup'ik at the elementary level. Two of the three villages found to be progressing most rapidly toward English in the study mentioned above were villages that offered such programs. Many of the communities maintaining children's Yup'ik language use, in contrast, had maintained Yup'ik as a primary language of instruction (Wyman *et al.*, 2010a, 2010b). Given the evidence within and studies elsewhere that Indigenous youth are keenly aware of ideological and educational crosscurrents around them (McCarty & Wyman, 2009), there remains a great need to understand how youth are perceiving and responding to these developments and new pressures.

At the time of this writing, Yup'ik educators in multiple villages, Yup'ik scholars and their non-Yup'ik allies are working to reverse dynamics of language shift similar to those described in Piniq, and to revitalize Yup'ik for village communities that experienced language shift a generation ago. In recent intergenerational work with adults and elders, Yup'ik college-level teachers created a master–apprentice program and 'study abroad'-like experiences for Yup'ik adults within strong Yup'ik-speaking villages to create a new generation of Yup'ik language teachers for villages that already experienced a generational shift to English (Alexie *et al.*, 2009). In the spring of 2008, the first class from the immersion school in Bethel described in Chapter 3 graduated from high school, and included the valedictorian from the regional hub town high school. In spring 2010, a Second Language, Acquisition, Teaching and Education program at the University of Alaska additionally graduated a cohort of Yup'ik educators with masters' degrees and two PhDs in language planning, language assessment, curriculum development and literacy. These language advocates are sharing their insights into strategies for developing linguistically and culturally appropriate materials, curriculum and assessments, and are connecting to a global network of Indigenous scholars, educators and allies elsewhere (Battiste, 2008). As part of this movement, Inuit and Yup'ik youth from Greenland, Canada, Alaska and Russia have also started meeting annually across national language borders, and have developed a web presence, hoping to further 'ignite a language movement' in the Far North (Tulloch *et al.*, in progress).

As of 2010, there remains a critical mass of Yup'ik speakers in southwestern Alaska, and a growing capacity and interest in intervening in processes of language shift through immersion efforts similar to those of Maori and Native Hawaiians elsewhere. Such an effort would require another historic push in the training of certified Indigenous teachers, and the development of related educational programs, materials and school spaces. The federal Esther Martinez act passed in 2006 offered symbolic federal support for such Indigenous language immersion efforts, and the National Indian Education Association recently lobbied for AI/AN immersion programs across the United States. Should such an effort take place, AI/AN students, including Yup'ik students, would likely see beneficial side effects including a more locally responsive, stable teaching force. Schools would also increase their potential to build dynamics of trust, versus distrust, over time within AI/AN communities, and to inform heritage language education and bilingual education efforts elsewhere.

Lomawaima and McCarty describe how efforts to incorporate Indigenous ways of knowing into formal educational efforts have often served as 'remarkable harbingers of new possibilities, new visions for Indian education' for their time, and how, even in instances where such efforts have been severely constrained and controlled by federal and state policies and schooling practices, they have also laid 'a foundation that later generations built on, directly or indirectly, as Native people increasingly took hold' of the local processes and mechanisms of Indigenous education (Lomawaima & McCarty, 2006: 108). The educators, scholars and youth described above are developing multiple new forms of linguistic survivance, offering new insights to the fields of language planning and policy and Indigenous education. It is my hope that they will find this book useful in their endeavors.

Within Piniq itself from 2001 to 2010, many of the local educators portrayed in Chapters 3, 4 and 6 got up every day and taught their classes, working to build students' educational futures under the challenging conditions of a local school that continued to rotate through new administrators and nonlocal teachers. Many elders who participated in the documentation project with RS youth in the mid-1990s passed on. Individual community members, including RS youth, described how they continued to read the elders' teachings, using the locally produced books in classrooms and home settings with children.

As the school in Piniq reorganized instruction to deal with the new educational mandates described above, the seventh-grade class described in Chapters 6 and 7 experienced a rough transition to high school; some of the young *nukalpiat* had the hardest time in school, and only half of the class had graduated six years later. Under pressure from high-stakes testing, the school in Piniq largely abandoned its Yup'ik program at the secondary level and cut back the elementary Yup'ik program to one hour a week by 2008. Students' test scores remained low. Individuals in Piniq advocated for implementing a local immersion program, while some aides from Piniq moved to work in the immersion school in Bethel.

Community-wide language shift for the most part continued. Many young parents in Piniq tried to socialize their children to speak Yup'ik, yet continued to speak of challenges maintaining Yup'ik at home as their children reached school age. Veteran educators noted how decreasing numbers of youth seemed to understand adults' sharing of *qanruyutait* (*teachings*) in Yup'ik, or even hybrid talks like the one from the local NYO coach in Chapter 6. As young people in Piniq increasingly spoke a local dialect of English, like youth in many shifting Native American communities elsewhere (Romero-Little & McCarty, 2006), many questions remained about their academic language development.

In some cases, unusual children, youth and families used mostly Yup'ik with one another, demonstrating how individual and family heritage language learning can continue with consistent effort and support within face-to-face social networks, even during community-wide language shift. Adults and youth also used longstanding and new forms of linguistic survivance to negotiate diverse circumstances, ways of being Indigenous, and to foster personal connections in and out of Piniq. In 2006, seven RS youth were sent to Kuwait in the first military deployment from the Yup'ik region to a foreign war. The night before they left, an elder sang the familiar hymn 'God Will Take Care of You' in Yup'ik, offering support to the youth who sat with their families in the local church. In the Yup'ik sermon that night, the local pastor compared their upcoming journey to that of the first men to go to the moon. While the youth were away, they and their spouses used email to negotiate the new stress as they raised their children in Piniq.

In 2009, community members started using social networking websites, extending a number of the rich language practices documented within, while developing a virtual presence and communicating with local and far-flung relatives and friends. As youth and adults shared comments and pictures on Facebook, many used English, Yup'ik and varying mixes of both languages, breathing new life into the school-based, phonemic Yup'ik writing system described in Chapter 3.

Ricky, the youngest child from family 1 in Chapter 5, had her first traditional dance in her mother's home village recently; her grandfather wrote her a special song in Yup'ik for the event. Moving to the lyrics and the beat of sealskin drums in the local school gym, Ricky's parents and relatives danced to celebrate her arrival as a young woman.

References

Aguilera, D. and LeCompte, M. (2007) Resiliency in Native languages: The tale of three Indigenous communities' experiences with language immersion. *Journal of American Indian Studies* 46 (3), 11–36.

Alaska Advisory Committee to the U.S. Commission on Civil Rights (2002) Racism's frontier: The untold story of discrimination and division in Alaska – Online document, accessed 11 January 2011. http://www.usccr.gov/pubs/sac/ak0402/main.htm

Alexie, O., Alexie, S. and Marlow, P. (2009) Creating space and defining roles: Elders and adult Yup'ik immersion. *Journal of American Indian Education* 48 (3), 1–18.

Alim, H.S., Ibrahim, A. and Pennycook, A. (2009) *Global Linguistic Flows: Hip Hop Cultures, Youth Identities, and the Politics of Language.* New York: Routledge.

Allen, S. (2007) Bilingualism or language shift in Inuktitut. *Applied Psycholinguistics* 28 (3), 515–536.

Baker, C. (2006) *Foundations of Bilingual Education and Bilingualism* (4th edn). Clevedon: Multilingual Matters.

Barnhardt, C. (1994) Life on the other side: Native students' survival in a university world. *Peabody Journal of Education* 69 (2), 115–139.

Basso, K. (1996) *Wisdom Sits in Places: Landscape and Language among the Western Apache.* Albuquerque, NM: University of New Mexico Press.

Battiste, M. (2008) The struggle and renaissance of Indigenous knowledge in Eurocentric education. In M. Villegas, S. Neugebauer and K. Venegas (eds) *Indigenous Knowledge and Education: Sites of Struggle, Strength and Survivance* (pp. 85–92). Cambridge, MA: Harvard Educational Review.

Bayley, R. and Schechter, S. (2005) Family decisions about schooling and Spanish maintenance: Mexicanos in California and Texas. In A.C. Zentella (ed.) *Building on Strength: Language and Literacy in Latino Families and Communities* (pp. 31–45). New York: Teachers College Press.

Beaulieu, D. (2008) Native American education research and policy development in an era of no child left behind. *Journal of American Indian Education* 47 (1), 10–45.

Beaulieu, D., Sparks, L. and Alonzo, M. (2005) *Preliminary Report on No Child Left Behind in Indian Country.* Washington, DC: National Indian Education Association.

Beckner, C., Blythe, R., Bybee, J., Christiansen, M., Croft, W., Ellis, N., Holland, J., Ke, J., Larsen-Freeman, D. and Schoenemann, T. (2009) Language is a complex adaptive system: Position paper. *Language Learning* 59 (1), 1–26.

Benally, A. and Viri, D. (1995) Dine Bizaad [Navajo language] at a crossroads: Extinction or renewal? *Bilingual Research Journal* 29 (1), 85–108.

Berger, T. (1985) *Village Journey: The Report of the Alaska Native Review Commission.* New York: Hill and Wang.

Blackledge, A. and Creese, A. (2008) Contesting 'language' as 'heritage': Negotiation of identities in late modernity. *Applied Linguistics* 29 (4), 533–554.

Blommaert, J. (2005) *Discourse: A Critical Introduction.* Cambridge: Cambridge University Press.

Blommaert, J. (2010) *The Sociolinguistics of Globalization.* Cambridge: Cambridge University Press.

Blommaert, J., Collins, J. and Slembrouk, S. (2005) Spaces of multilingualism. *Language and Communication* 25 (3), 197–216.

Bodenhorn, B. (1990) 'I'm not the great hunter, my wife is': Iñupiat and anthropological models of gender. *Inuit Studies* 14 (1–5), 55–74.

Bodenhorn, B. (1994) Gendered spaces, public places: Public and private revisited on the North Slope of Alaska. In B. Bender (ed.) *Landscapes, Politics and Perspectives* (pp. 169–203). New York: Berg Publishers.

Bougie, E., Wright, E. and Taylor, D. (2003) Early heritage-language education and the abrupt shift to a dominant-language classroom: Impact on the personal and collective esteem of Inuit children in Arctic Québec. *International Journal of Bilingual Education and Bilingualism* 6 (5), 349–373.

Brayboy, B. (2005) Toward a tribal critical race theory in education. *The Urban Review* 37 (5), 425–446.

Brayboy, B. (2008) 'Yakkity yak and talking back': An examination of sites of survivance in Indigenous knowledge. In M. Villegas, S. Neugebauer and K. Venegas (eds) *Indigenous Knowledge and Education* (pp. 321–339). Cambridge, MA: Harvard Educational Review.

Brayboy, B. and Castagno, A. (2009) Self-determination through self-education: Culturally-responsive schooling for Indigenous students in the USA. *Teaching Education* 20 (1), 31–52.

Brayboy, B. and Deyhle, D. (2000) Insider-outsider: Researchers in American Indian communities. *Theory into Practice* 39 (3), 163–169.

Brayboy, B. and McCarty, T.L. (2010) Indigenous knowledges and social justice pedagogy. In T.K. Chapman and N. Hobbel (eds) *Social Justice Pedagogy across the Curriculum: The Practice of Freedom* (pp. 184–100). New York: Routledge.

Briggs, C. (1986) *Learning How to Ask: A Sociolinguistic Appraisal of the Role of the Interview in Social Science Research.* Cambridge: Cambridge University Press.

Brumbach, H.J. and Jarvenpa, R. (2002) Gender dynamics in native northwestern North America: Perspectives and prospects. In L. Frink, R. Shephard and G. Reinhardt (eds) *Many Faces of Gender: Roles and Relationships through Time in Indigenous Northern Communities* (pp. 195–210). Boulder, CO: University Press of Colorado.

Bucholtz, M. (1999) 'Why be normal?': Language and identity practices in a community of nerd girls. *Language in Society* 28 (2), 203–223.

Bucholtz, M. (2002) Youth and cultural practice. *Annual Review of Anthropology* 31, 525–552.

Bucholtz, M. and Hall, K. (2005) Identity and interaction: A sociolinguistic approach. *Discourse Studies* 7 (4–5), 585–614.

Cameron, D. (1997) Performing gender identity: Young men's talk and the construction of heterosexual masculinity. In S. Johnson and U. Meinhof (eds) *Language and Masculinity.* Oxford: Blackwell.

Canagarajah, S. (1997) Safe houses in the contact zone: Coping strategies of African-American students in the academy. *College Composition and Communication* 48 (2), 173–196.

Canagarajah, S. (2004) Subversive identities, pedagogical safe houses, and critical learning. In B. Norton and K. Toohey (eds) *Critical Pedagogies and Learning Learning* (pp. 116–132) Cambridge: Cambridge University Press.

Castagno, A. and Brayboy, B. (2008) Culturally responsive schooling for Indigenous youth: A review of the literature. *Review of Educational Research* 78 (4), 941–993.

Charles, W. (2009) Indigenous youth bilingualism from a Yup'ik perspective. *Journal of Language, Identity, and Education* 8 (5), 365–368.

Charles, W. (2011) Dynamic assessment in a Yugtun second language intermediate classroom. PhD Thesis, University of Alaska Fairbanks.

Clifford, J. and Marcus, G. (eds) (1986) *Writing Culture: The Poetics and Politics of Ethnography*. Berkeley, CA: University of California Press.

Cleary, L. and Peacock, T. (1998) *Collected Wisdom: American Indian Education*. Needham Heights, MA: Allyn & Bacon.

Condon, R.G. (1987) *Inuit Youth: Growth and Change in the Canadian Arctic*. New Brunswick: Rutgers University Press.

Corbett, M. (2009) Rural schooling in mobile modernity: Returning to the places I've been. *Journal of Research in Rural Education* 24. Accessed 18 January 2012, http://jrre.psu.edu/articles/24-7.pdf

Cotton, S. (1984) Alaska's 'Molly Hootch Case': High schools and the village voice. *Educational Research Quarterly* 8 (4), 30–43.

Crago, M. (1992) Communicative interaction and second language acquisition: An Inuit example. *TESOL Quarterly* 26 (3), 487–505.

Crago, M., Annahatak, B. and Ningiuruvik, L. (1993) Changing patterns of language socialization in Inuit homes. *Anthropology and Education Quarterly* 24 (3), 205–223.

Crawford, J. (1995) *Bilingual Education: History, Politics, Theory and Practice*. Los Angeles: Bilingual Educational Services, Inc.

Crawford, J. (2000) *At War with Diversity: US Language Policy in an Age of Anxiety*. Clevedon: Multilingual Matters.

Cruikshank, J. (1998) *The Social Life of Stories: Narrative and Knowledge in the Yukon Territory*. Lincoln, NE: University of Nebraska Press.

Cummins, J. (2000) *Language, Power, and Pedagogy: Bilingual Children in the Cross-Fire*. Clevedon: Multilingual Matters.

Dauenhauer, R. and Dauenhauer, N. (1998) Technical, emotional, and ideological issues in reversing language shift: Examples from southeastern Alaska. In L. Grenoble and L. Whaley (eds) *Endangered Languages: Language Loss and Community Response* (pp. 57–98). Cambridge: Cambridge University Press.

deMarrais, K., Nelson, P. and Baker, J. (1992) Meaning in mud: Yup'ik Eskimo girls at play. *Anthropology and Education Quarterly* 23 (2), 120–144.

Deyhle, D. (1998) From break dancing to heavy metal: Navajo youth, resistance and identity. *Youth and Society* 30 (3), 3–31.

Deyhle, D. and Swisher, K. (1997) Research in American Indian and Alaska Native education: From assimilation to self-determination. *AERA Review of Research in Education* 22, 113–194.

Dorais, J.L. (1997) *Quaqtaq: Modernity and Identity in an Inuit Community*. Toronto: University of Toronto Press.

Dorian, N. (1981) *Language Death: The Life Cycle of a Scottish Gaelic Dialect*. Philadelphia: University of Pennsylvania Press.

Dorian, N. (ed.) (1989) *Investigating Obsolescence: Studies in Language Contraction and Death*. Cambridge: Cambridge University Press.

Dorner, L., Orellana, M.F. and Jiménez, R. (2008) 'It's one of those things that you do to help the family': Language brokering and the development of immigrant adolescents. *Journal of Adolescent Research* 23 (5), 515–543.

Duchêne, A. and Heller, M. (eds) (2007) *Discourses of Endangerment: Ideology and Interest in the Defence of Languages*. London: Continuum.

Eckert, P. (1989) *Jocks and Burnouts: Social Identity in the High School*. New York: Teachers College Press.

Eckert, P. and McConnell-Ginet, S. (2003) *Language and Gender*. Cambridge: Cambridge University Press.

Eder, D. (1998) Developing adolescent peer culture through collaborative narration. In S. Hoyle and C.T. Adger (eds) *Kids Talk: Strategic Language Use in Later Childhood* (pp. 82–94). Oxford: Oxford University Press.

Erickson, F. (1984) School literacy, reasoning and civility: An anthropologist's perspective. *Review of Educational Research* 54 (4), 525–546.

Erickson, F. (1987) Transformation and school success: The politics and culture of educational achievement. *Anthropology and Education Quarterly* 18 (4), 335–356.

Field, L. and Fox, R. (eds) (2007) *Anthropology Put to Work*. New York, NY: Berg Publishers.

Fienup-Riordan, A. (1990) *Eskimo Essays: Yup'ik Lives and How We See Them*. London: Rutgers University Press.

Fienup-Riordan, A. (1991) *The Real People and the Children of Thunder: The Yup'ik Eskimo Encounter with Moravian Missionaries John and Edith Kilbuck*. Norman, OK: University of Oklahoma Press.

Fienup-Riordan, A. (2000) *Hunting Tradition in a Changing World: Yup'ik Lives Today*. New Brunswick, NJ: Rutgers University Press.

Fienup-Riordan, A. (2001) A guest on the table: Ecology from the Yup'ik Eskimo point of view. In A. Grim (ed.) *Indigenous Traditions and Ecology: The Interbeing of Cosmology and Community* (pp. 541–558). Cambridge, MA: Harvard University Press.

Fienup-Riordan, A., Meade, M. and Rearden, A. (2005) *Yup'ik Words of Wisdom: Yupiit Qanruyutait*. Lincoln, NE: University of Nebraska Press.

Fishman, J. (1991) *Reversing Language Shift: Theoretical and Empirical Foundations of Assistance to Threatened Languages*. Clevedon: Multilingual Matters.

Fishman, J. (ed.) (2001) *Can Threatened Languages Be Saved?* Clevedon: Multilingual Matters.

Fortuine, R. (1989) *Chills and Fever: Health and Disease in the Early History of Alaska*. Anchorage, AK: University of Alaska Press.

Freed, C. and Samson, M. (2004) Native Alaskan dropouts in western Alaska: Systemic failure in Native Alaskan schools. *Journal of American Indian Education* 43 (2), 33–45.

Frink, L. (2002) Fish tales: Women and decision making in western Alaska. In L. Frink, R. Shephard and G. Reinhardt (eds) *Many Faces of Gender: Roles and Relationships through Time in Indigenous Northern Communities* (pp. 93–110). Boulder, CO: University Press of Colorado.

Gal, S. (1979) *Language Shift: Social Determinants of Linguistic Change in Bilingual Austria*. New York: Academic Press.

Gal, S. (1989) Lexical innovation and loss: The use and value of restricted Hungarian. In N. Dorian (ed.) *Investigating Obsolescence: Studies in Language Contraction and Death* (pp. 313–331). Cambridge: Cambridge University Press.

García, O. (2009) *Bilingual Education in the 21st Century: A Global Perspective*. West Sussex: Wiley-Blackwell.

Garrett, P. and Baquedano-Lopez, P. (2002) Language socialization: Reproduction and continuity, transformation and change. *Annual Review of Anthropology* 31, 339–361.

Gee, J.P. (2003) *What Videogames Have to Teach Us about Learning and Literacy.* New York: Palgrave Macmillan.

Gilmore, P. (2010) Language ideologies, ethnography, and ethnology: New directions in anthropological approaches to language policy. In T.L. McCarty (ed.) *Ethnography and Language Policy* (pp. 121–127). London: Routledge.

González, N. (2001) *I Am My Language: Discourses of Women and Children in the Borderlands.* Tucson, AZ: The University of Arizona Press.

González, N. and Arnot-Hopffer, E. (2002) Voices of the children: Language and literacy ideologies in a dual language program. In S. Wortham and B. Rymes (eds) *Linguistic Anthropology of Education* (pp. 213–243). Westport, CT: Praeger Publishers.

González, N., Moll, L. and Amanti, C. (eds) (2005) *Funds of Knowledge: Theorizing Practices in Households and Classrooms.* Mahwah, NJ: Lawrence Erlbaum Associates.

González, N., Wyman, L. and O'Connor, B. (2011) The past, present and future of 'funds of knowledge': Toward an engaged anthropology of education. In M. Pollock and B. Levinson (eds) *Companion to the Anthropology of Education* (pp. 481–494). Malden, MA: Wiley- Blackwell Publishers.

Graburn, N.H. and Iutzi-Mitchell, R.D. (1993) Language and education in the North: Status and prospectus report on the Eskimo-Aleut language International Symposium. *International Journal of the Sociology of Language* 99, 123–132.

Gutiérrez, K. and Rogoff, B. (2003) Cultural ways of learning: Individual traits or repertoires of practice. *Educational Researcher* 32 (5), 19–25.

Gutiérrez, K., Rymes, B. and Larson, J. (1995) Script, counterscript, and underlife in the classroom: James Brown versus Brown v. Board of Education. *Harvard Educational Review* 65 (3), 445–471.

Hamilton, L. and Seyfrit, C. (1994) Coming out of the country: Community size and gender balance among Alaska Natives. *Arctic Anthropology* 31 (1), 16–25.

Harrison, B. (1981) Informal learning among Yup'ik Eskimos: An ethnographic study of one Alaskan village. PhD thesis, University of Oregon.

Harrison, K.D. (2007) *When Languages Die: The Extinction of the World's Languages and the Erosion of Human Knowledge.* Oxford: Oxford University Press.

Haviland, J. (2003) Ideologies of language: Some reflections on language and U.S. law. *American Anthropologist* 105 (4), 764–774.

Heath, S.B. (1983) *Ways with Words: Language, Life and Work in Communities and Classrooms.* Cambridge: Cambridge University Press.

Heath, S.B. (1994) Stories as ways of acting together. In A.H. Dyson and C. Genishi (eds) *The Need for Story: Cultural Diversity in Classroom and Community* (pp. 206–220). Urbana, IL: National Council of Teachers of English.

Heath, S.B. (1998) Working through language. In S. Hoyle and C.T. Adger (eds) *Kids Talk: Strategic Language Use in Later Childhood* (pp. 217–240). Oxford: Oxford University Press.

Heath, S.B. (2000) Risk, rules, and roles: Youth perspectives on the work of learning for community development. *Zeitschrift Fur Erziehungswissenschaft* 1, 67–80.

Heath, S.B. (2008) Forward. In J. Simpson and G. Wigglesworth (eds) *Children's Language and Multilingualism: Indigenous Language Use at Home and at School* (pp. ix–xiii). London: Continuum.

Hensel, C. (1996) *Telling Our Selves: Ethnicity and Discourse in Southwestern Alaska.* Oxford: Oxford University Press.

Henze, R. and Vanett, L. (1993) To walk in two worlds – or more? Challenging a common metaphor of Native education. *Anthropology and Education Quarterly* 24 (2), 116–134.

Henze, R. and Davis, K.A. (guest eds) (1999) Authenticity and identity: Lessons from Indigenous language education [Theme Issue]. *Anthropology and Education Quarterly* 24 (2), 3–21.

Hill, J. (1998) 'Today there is no respect': Nostalgia, 'respect,' and oppositional discourse in Mexicano (Nahuatl) Language ideology. In B. Schieffelin, K. Woolard and P. Kroskrity (eds) *Language Ideologies: Practice and Theory* (pp. 68–86). Oxford: Oxford University Press.

Hill, J. (2002) 'Expert rhetorics' in advocacy for endangered languages: Who is listening and what do they hear? *Journal of Linguistic Anthropology* 12 (2), 119–133.

Hill, J. (2006) The ethnography of language and language documentation. In J. Gippert, N. Himmelmann and U. Mosel (eds) *Essentials of Language Documentation* (pp. 113–128). Berlin: Mouton de Gruyter.

Hill, J. and Hill, K. (1986). *Speaking Mexicano: dynamics of syncretic language change in central Mexico.* Tucson, AZ: University of Arizona Press.

Hinton, L. (1994) *Flutes of Fire.* Berkeley, CA: Heyday Press.

Hinton, L. (2001) New writing systems. In L. Hinton and K. Hale (eds) *The Green Book of Language Revitalization in Practice* (pp. 239–251). Oxford: Elsevier.

Hirshberg, D. (2009) It was bad or it was good: Alaska Natives in past boarding schools. *Journal of American Indian Eduction* 47 (3), 5–30.

Holm, A. and Holm, W. (1995) Navajo language education: Retrospect and prospect. *Bilingual Research Journal* 19 (1), 141–167.

Holm, W., Silentman, I. and Wallace, L. (2003) Situational Navajo: A school-based, verb-centered way of teaching Navajo. In J. Reyhner, O. Trujillo, R.L. Carrasco and L. Lockard (eds) *Nurturing Native Languages* (pp. 25–52). Flagstaff, AZ: Northern Arizona University.

Hornberger, N.H. (1997) *Indigenous Literacies in the Americas: Language Planning from the Bottom Up.* Berlin: Mouton de Gruyter.

Hornberger, N.H. (2002) Multilingual language policies and the continua of biliteracy: An ecological approach. *Language Policy* 1 (1), 27–51.

Hornberger, N. H. (2005) Student voice and the media of biliteracy in bi(multi)lingual/multicultural classrooms. In T.L. McCarty (ed.) *Language, Literacy, and Power in Schooling* (pp. 151–168). Mahwah, NJ: Lawrence Erlbaum Associates.

Hornberger, N.H. (ed.) (2008) *Can Schools Save Indigenous Languages? Policy and Practice on Four Continents.* New York: Palgrave Macmillan.

Hornberger, N.H. and Coronel-Molina, S. (2004) Quechua language shift, maintenance, and revitalization in the Andes: The case for language planning. *International Journal of the Sociology of Language* 167, 9–67.

Huskey, L., Berman, M. and Hill, A. (2004) Leaving home, returning home: Migration as a labor market choice for Alaska Natives. *The Annals of Regional Science* 38, 75–92.

Irvine, J. (1992) Insult and responsibility: Verbal abuse in a Wolof village. In J. Hill and J. Irvine (eds) *Responsibility and Evidence in Oral Discourse* (pp. 105–135). Cambridge: Cambridge University Press.

Iutzi-Mitchell, R. (1992) Bilingualism and educational language policy in the North: Framing the issues. Paper presented at *Language and Educational Policy in the North Conference.* University of California, Berkeley, 13–15 March.

Jacobson, S. (1984) *Yup'ik Eskimo Dictionary.* Fairbanks: Alaska Native Language Center, University of Alaska.

Jacobson, S. (1995) *A Practical Grammar of the Central Alaskan Yup'ik Eskimo Language.* Fairbanks: Alaska Native Language Center, University of Alaska.

Jaffe, A. (2006) 'Imagined competence': Classroom evaluation, collective identity, and linguistic authenticity in a Corsican bilingual classroom. In S. Wortham and B. Rymes (eds) *Linguistic Anthropology of Education* (pp. 151–184) London: Praeger Publishers.

Jaffe, A. (2007) Contexts and consequences of essentializing discourses. In A. Duchêne and M. Heller (eds) *Discourses of Endangerment: Ideology and Interest in the Defence of Languages* (pp. 57–75). Westport, CT: Praeger Publishers.

Jolles, C.Z. (2002) *Faith, Food and Family in a Yup'ik Whaling Community*. Seattle and London: University of Washington Press.

Jones, K. and Ongtooguk, P. (2002) Equity for Alaska natives: Can high-stakes testing bridge the chasm between ideals and realities? *Phi Delta Kappan* 83 (7), 499–503, 550.

Jørgensen, J.N. (1998) Children's acquisition of code-switching for power-wielding. In P. Auer (ed.) *Code-Switching in Conversation: Language, Interaction and Identity* (pp. 237–258). London: Routledge.

Jørgensen, J.N. (2005) Plurilingual conversations among bilingual adolescents. *Journal of Pragmatics* 37 (3), 391–402.

Kafarowski, J. (2009) Gender, culture and contaminants in the North. *Signs: Journal of Women in Culture and Society* 34 (3), 494–499.

Kagan, O. (2005) In support of a proficiency-based definition of heritage language learners: The case of Russian. *International Journal of Bilingual Education and Bilingualism* 8 (2/3), 213–221.

Kanno, Y. and Norton, B. (2003) Imagined communities and educational possibilities: Introduction. *Journal of Language, Identity, and Education* 2 (4), 241–249.

Kardos, S. (2002) 'Not Bread Alone': Clandestine schooling and resistance in the Warsaw Ghetto during the Holocaust. *Harvard Education Review* 72 (1), 33–67.

Kawagley, O. (1995) *A Yupiaq World View: Pathway to Ecology and Spirit*. Prospect Heights, IL: Waveland Press.

Kawagley, O. and Barnhardt, R. (2005) Indigenous knowledge systems and Alaska Native ways of knowing. *Anthropology and Education Quarterly* 36 (1), 8–23.

Kenner, C., Mahera, R., Jessel, J., Gregory, E. and Arju, T. (2007) Intergenerational learning between children and grandparents in East London. *Journal of Early Childhood Research* 5 (3), 219–243.

King, K.A. and Haboud, M. (2010) International migration and Quichua language shift in the Ecuadorian Andes. In T.L. McCarty (ed.) *Ethnography and Language Policy*. Abingdon: Routledge/Taylor & Francis.

King, K.A., Fogle, L. and Logan-Terry, A. (2008) Family language policy. *Language and Linguistics Compass* 2, 1–16.

Kleinfeld, J. (1973) *A Long Way from Home: Effects of Public High Schools on Village Children away from Home*. Fairbanks, AK: Center for Northern Educational Research and Institute of Social, Economic and Government Research.

Kleinfeld, J. (1979) *Eskimo School on the Andreafsky*. New York: Praeger Publishers.

Kral, M. and Idlout, L. (2006) Participatory anthropology in Nunavut. In P. Stern and L. Stevenson (eds) *Critical Inuit Studies: An Anthology of Contemporary Arctic Anthropology* (pp. 54–70). Lincoln, NE: University of Nebraska Press.

Kramsch, C. (1997) Guest column: The privilege of the nonnative speaker. *Publications of the Modern Language Association of America (PMLA)* 112 (3), 359–369.

Kramsch, C. (ed.) (2002) *Language Acquisition and Language Socialization: Ecological Perspectives*. London: Continuum.

Krauss, M. (1980) *Alaska Native Languages, Past, Present and Future*. Fairbanks, AK: Alaska Native Language Center.

Krauss, M. (1997) The Indigenous languages of the North: A report on their present state. *Northern Minority Languages: Problems of Survival, Senri Ethnological Studies* 44, 1–34.

Kroskrity, P. (1998) Arizona Tewa Kiva Speech as a manifestation of a dominant language ideology. In B. Schieffelin, K. Woolard and P. Kroskrity (eds) *Language Ideologies: Practice and Theory* (pp. 103–122). Oxford: Oxford University Press.

Kulick, D. (1992) *Language Shift and Cultural Reproduction: Socialization, Self and Syncretism in a Papua New Guinean Village*. Cambridge: Cambridge University Press.

Kwachka, P. (1992) Discourse structures, cultural stability and language shift. *International Journal of the Sociology of Language* 93, 67–73.

Lakoff, G. and Mark, J. (1980) *Metaphors We Live by*. Chicago: University of Chicago Press.

Langdon, S. (1986) *Contemporary Alaskan Native Economies*. New York: University Press of America.

Langlois, A. (2004) *Alive and Kicking: Teenage Pitjantjatjara*. Canberra: Pacific Linguistics.

Lanza, E. (1997) *Language Mixing in Infant Bilingualism: A Sociolinguistic Perspective*. Oxford: Oxford University Press.

Lave, J. and Wenger, E. (1991) *Situated Learning: Legitimate Peripheral Participation*. Cambridge: Cambridge University Press.

Leap, W. (1993) *American Indian English*. Salt Lake, UT: University of Utah Press.

Lee, T.S. (2007) 'If they want Navajo to be learned, then they should require it in all schools': Navajo teenagers' experiences, choices, and demands regarding Navajo language. *Wicazo Sa Review* Spring, 7–33.

Lee, T.S. (2009) Language, identity, and power: Navajo and Pueblo young adults' perspectives and experiences with competing language ideologies. *Journal of Language, Identity and Education* 8 (5), 307–320.

Lee, T.S. and McGaughlin, D. (2001) Reversing Navajo language shift, revisited. In J. Fishman (ed.) *Can Threatened Languages Be Saved? Reversing Language Shift, Revisited: A 21st Century Perspective* (pp. 23–43). Clevedon: Multilingual Matters.

Lemke, J.L. (2000) Across the scales of time: Artifacts, activities, and meanings in eco-social systems. *Mind, Culture, and Activity* 7 (4), 273–290.

Levitt, P., DeWind, J. and Vertovec, S. (2003) International perspectives on transnational migration: An introduction. *International Migration Review* 37 (3), 565–575.

Lipka, J., Mohatt, G. and the Ciulestet Group. (1998) *Transforming the Culture of Schools: Yup'ik Eskimo Examples*. Mahwah, NJ: Lawrence Erlbaum Associates.

Lomawaima, K.T. (1994) *They Called It Prairie Light: The Story of Chilocco Indian School*. Lincoln, NE: University of Nebraska Press.

Lomawaima, K.T. and McCarty, T.L. (2006) *To Remain an Indian: Lessons in Democracy from a Century of Native American Education*. New York: Teachers College Press.

Luykx, A. (2003) Weaving languages together: Family language policy and gender socialization in bilingual Aymara households. In R. Bayley and S. Schecter (eds) *Language Socialization in Bilingual and Multilingual Societies* (pp. 25–43). Clevedon: Multilingual Matters.

Makihara, M. and Schieffelin, B. (eds) (2007) *Consequences of Contact: Language Ideologies and Sociocultural Transformations in Pacific Societies*. Oxford: Oxford University Press.

Makoni, S., Brutt-Griffler, J. and Mashiri, P. (2007) The use of 'Indigenous' and urban vernaculars in Zimbabwe. *Language in Society* 36, 25–49.

Maira, S. and Soep, E. (eds) (2005) *Youthscapes: The Popular, the National and the Global*. Philadelphia, PA: University of Pennsylvania Press.

Marlow, P. (2004) Bilingual education, legislative intent, and language maintenance in Alaska. In J.A. Argenter and R. McKenna Brown (eds) *On the Margins of Nations: Endangered Languages and Linguistic Rights* (pp. 25–30). Barcelona, Spain: Institut d'Estudis Catalans.

Mather, E. (1995) With a vision beyond our immediate needs: Oral traditions in an age of literacy. In P. Morrow and W. Schneider (eds) *When Our Words Return: Writing, Hearing and Remembering Oral Traditions of Alaska and the Yukon* (pp. 13–26). Logan: Utah State University Press.

May, S. (2005) Language rights: Moving the debate forward. *Journal of Sociolinguistics* 9 (3), 319–347.

May, S. and Hill, R. (2005) Maori-medium education: Current issues and challenges. *International Journal of Bilingual Education and Bilingualism* 8 (5), 377–403.

McCarty, T.L. (2002) *A Place to Be Navajo: Rough Rock and the Struggle for Self-Determination in Indigenous Schooling.* Mahwah, NJ: Lawrence Erlbaum Associates.

McCarty, T.L. (2008) American Indian, Alaska Native, and Native Hawaiian education in the era of standardization and NCLB: An introduction. *Journal of American Indian Education* 47 (1), 1–9.

McCarty, T.L. (forthcoming) *Language Planning and Policy in Native America: History, Theory, Praxis.* Bristol: Multilingual Matters.

McCarty, T.L. and Wyman, L. (2009) Indigenous youth and bilingualism – Theory, research, praxis. *Journal of Language, Identity and Education* 8 (5), 279–290.

McCarty, T.L., Romero-Little, M.E. and Zepeda, O. (2006) Native American youth discourses on language shift and retention: Ideological cross-currents and their implications for language planning. *The International Journal of Bilingual Education and Bilingualism* 9 (5), 659–677.

McCarty, T.L., Romero-Little, M.E., Warhol, L. and Zepeda, O. (2009) Indigenous youth as language policy makers. *Journal of Language, Identity and Education* 8 (5), 291–306.

McDermott, R. and Tylbor, H. (1995) On the necessity of collusion in conversation. In D. Tedlock and B. Mannheim (eds). *The Dialogic Emergence of Culture* (pp. 218–236). Urbana, IL: University of Illinois Press.

McKay, S.L. and Wong, S.C. (1996) Multiple discourses, multiple identities: Investment and agency in second-language learning among Chinese adolescent immigrant students. *Harvard Educational Review* 66 (3), 577–608.

Meek, B. (2007) Respecting the language of elders: Ideological shift and linguistic discontinuity in a Northern Athapascan community. *Journal of Linguistic Anthropology* 17 (1), 23–43.

Mendoza-Denton, N. (2008) *Homegirls: Language and Cultural Practice among Latina Youth.* Malden, MA: Blackwell Publishers.

Menken, K. (2008) *English Language Learners Left Behind: Standardized Testing as Language Policy.* Clevedon: Multilingual Matters.

Messing, J. (2009) Ambivalence and ideology among Mexicano youth in Tlaxcala, Mexico. *Journal of Language, Identity, and Education* 8 (5), 350–364.

Mitchell, T. (2004) Doin' damage in my native language: The use of "resistance vernaculars" in hip hop in Europe and Aotearoa/New Zealand. In S. Whiteley, A. Bennett, and S. Hawkins (eds) *Music, Space and Place: Popular Music and Cultural Identity* (pp. 108–123). Burlington, VT: Ashgate Publishing Company.

Mohatt, G. and Sharp, N. (1998) The evolution and development of a Yup'ik teacher. In J. Lipka, G. Mohatt and the Ciulestet Group (eds) *Transforming the Culture of Schools: Yup'ik Eskimo Examples* (pp. 41–70). Mahwah, NJ: Lawrence Erlbaum Associates.

Moll, L. (1992) Bilingual classroom studies and community analysis: Some recent trends. *Educational Researcher* 21 (2), 20–24.

Morrow, P. (1990) They just want everything: Results of a bilingual education needs assessment in southwestern Alaska. In *Proceedings of the Symposium Languages in Contact/12th Annual Congress of Anthropology of Ethnological Sciences.* Institute of Linguistics, University of Zagreb.

Morrow, P. (1993) A sociolinguistic mismatch: Central Alaskan Yup'iks and the legal system. *Alaska Justice Forum,* 10 (2), 4–8. Anchorage, AK: Justice Center, University of Alaska.

Morrow, P. (1996) Yup'ik Eskimo agents and American legal agencies: Perspectives on compliance and resistance. *Journal of the Royal Anthropological Institute* 2 , 405–424.

Morrow, P. and Hensel, C. (1992) Hidden dissension: Minority-majority relationships and the use of contested terminology. *Arctic Anthropology* 29 (1), 38–53.

Moses, K. and Wigglesworth, G. (2008) The silence of the frogs: Dysfunctional discourse in the English-only Aboriginal classroom. In J. Simpson and G. Wigglesworth (eds) *Children's Language and Multilingualism: Indigenous Language Use at Home and at School* (pp. 129–153). London and New York: Continuum International Publishing Group.

Mougeon, R. and Beniak, E. (1989) Language contraction and linguistic change: The case of Welland French. In N. Dorian (ed.) *Investigating Obsolescence: Studies in Language Contraction and Death* (pp. 287–312). Cambridge: Cambridge University Press.

Myers-Scotton, C. (1998) A way to dusy death: The matrix language turnover hypothesis. In L. Grenoble and L. Whaley (eds) *Endangered Languages: Current Issues and Future Prospects* (pp. 289–316). Cambridge: Cambridge University Press.

Nadasdy, P. (2003) *Hunters and Bureaucrats: Power, Knowledge and Aboriginal-State Relations in the Southwest Yukon.* Vancouver, CA: UBC Press.

Napoleon, H. (1991) *Yuuyaraq: The Way of the Human Being.* Fairbanks, AK: Center for Cross-Cultural Studies, University of Alaska.

Nicholas, S. (2009) 'I live Hopi, I just don't speak it' – The critical intersection of language, culture, and identity in the lives of contemporary Hopi youth. *Journal of Language, Identity, and Education* 8 (5), 321–334.

Noordhoff, K. and Kleinfeld, J. (1993) Preparing teachers for multicultural classrooms. *Teaching and Teacher Education* 9 (1), 27–39.

Nortier, J. (2008) Types and sources of bilingual data. In L. Wei and M. Moyer (eds) *The Blackwell Guide to Research Methods in Bilingualism and Multilingualism* (pp. 35–52). Malden, MA: Blackwell Publishing.

Ochs, E. and Capps, L. (1996) Narrating the self. *Annual Review of Anthropology* 25, 19–43.

Ongtooguk, P. (1986) The annotated ANCSA. In P. Ongtooguk (ed.) *The Alaska Native Claims Settlement Act: Selected Student Readings.* Kotzebue: Northwest Arctic Borough School District.

Ongtooguk, P. (2000) Aspects of traditional Inupiat education. *Sharing Our Pathways: A Newsletter of the Alaska Rural Systemic Initiative* 5 (4), 8–12.

Oswalt, W. (1990) *Bashful No Longer: An Alaskan Ethnohistory, 1778–1988.* Norman, OK: University of Oklahoma Press.

Patrick, D. (2005) Language rights in Indigenous communities: The case of the Inuit of Arctic Quebec. *Journal of Sociolinguistics* 9 (3), 369–389.

Patrick, D. (2007) Indigenous language endangerment and the unfinished business of nation states. In A. Duchêne and M. Heller (eds) *Discourses of Endangerment: Ideology and Interest in the Defence of Languages* (pp. 35–56). London: Continuum Press.

Paugh, A. (2005) Multilingual play: Children's code-switching, role play, and agency in Dominica, West Indies. *Language in Society* 34 (1), 63–86.

Pavlenko, A. and Piller, I. (2001) New directions in the study of multilingualism, second language learning, and gender. In A. Pavlenko, A. Blackledge, I. Piller and M. Teutsch-Dwyer (eds) *Multilingualism, Second Language Learning, and Gender* (pp. 17–52). New York: Mouton de Gruyter Publishers.

Pavlenko, A., Blackledge, A., Piller, I. and Teutsch-Dwyer, M. (eds) (2001) *Multilingualism, Second Language Learning, and Gender*. Berlin: Walter de Gruyter.

Pennycook, A. (2001) *Critical Applied Linguistics: A Critical Introduction*. Mahwah, NJ: Lawrence Erlbaum Associates.

Philips, S. (1983) *The Invisible Culture: Communication in Classroom and Community on the Warm Springs Indian Reservation*. Prospect Heights, IL: Waveland Press.

Pollock, M. (2004) *Colormute: Race Talk Dilemmas in an American School*. Princeton, NJ: Princeton University Press.

Pratt, M.L. (1991) Arts of the contact zone. *Profession* 91, 33–40.

Pye, C. (1992) Language loss among the Chilcotin. *International Journal of the Sociology of Language* 93, 75–86.

Rampton, B. (1995) *Crossing: Language and Ethnicity among Adolescents*. New York: Longman Publishing.

Rampton, B. (2006) *Language in Late Modernity: Interaction in an Urban School*. Cambridge: Cambridge University Press.

Reder, S. and Wikelund, K. (1993) Literacy development and ethnicity: An Alaskan example. In B. Street (ed.) *Cross-Cultural Approaches to Literacy* (pp. 176–197). Cambridge: Cambridge University Press.

Reed, I. (1974) The Eskimo language workshop. In J. Orvik and R. Barnhardt (eds) *Cultural Influences in Alaskan Native Education* (pp. 57–62). Fairbanks, AK: Center for Northern Educational Research.

Reyes, I. (2006) Exploring connections between emergent bilingualism and biliteracy. *Journal of Early Childhood Literacy* 6 (3), 267–292.

Reyes, I. and Azuara, P. (2008) Emergent biliteracy in young Mexican immigrant children. *Reading Research Quarterly* 43 (4), 374–398.

Reyes, I. and Ervin-Tripp, S. (2010) Language choice and competence: Code-switching and issues of social identity in young bilingual children. In M. Shatz and L. Wilkinson (eds) *The Education of English Language Learners: Research to Practice* (pp. 67–84). New York: Guilford.

Rogoff, B. (2003) *The Cultural Nature of Human Development*. Oxford: Oxford University Press.

Rogoff, B., Paradise, R., Arauz, R., Correa-Chavez, M. and Angellilo, C. (2003) Firsthand learning through intent participation. *Annual Review of Psychology* 54, 175–203.

Romero-Little, M.E. and McCarty, T. (2006) *Language Planning Challenges and Prospects in Native American Communities and Schools*. Language Policy Research Unit. Arizona State University.

Rosner, V. (2009) Gender and polar studies: Mapping the terrain. *Signs: Journal of Women in Culture and Society* 34 (3), 489–494.

Roth-Gordon, J. (2007) Racing and erasing the playboy: Slang, transnational youth subculture and racial discourse in Brazil. *Journal of Linguistic Anthropology* 17 (2), 246–265.

Roth-Gordon, J. and Woronov, T. (2009) Youthful concerns: Movement, belonging and modernity. *Pragmatics* 19 (1), 129–143.

Ruiz, R. (1993) Language policy and planning in the United States. *Annual Review of Applied Linguistics* 14 (1), 111–125.

Ruiz, R. (1995) Language planning considerations in Indigenous communities. *The Bilingual Research Journal* 19 (1), 71–81.

Ruiz, R. (2009) Reorienting language as a resource. In J. Petrovic (ed.) *International Perspectives on Bilingual Education: Policy, Practice, and Controversy* (pp. 155–172). Charlotte, NC: Information Age Publishing.

Schieffelin, B. and Ochs, E. (1986) Language socialization. *Annual Review of Anthropology* 15, 163–191.

Schieffelin, B., Woolard, K. and Kroskrity, P. (eds) (1998) *Language Ideologies: Practice and Theory.* Oxford: Oxford University Press.

Schmidt, A. (1985) *Young People's Dyirbal: An Example of Language Death from Australia.* Cambridge: Cambridge University Press.

Scollon, R. and Scollon, S. (1981) *Narrative, Literacy and Face in Interethnic Communication.* Norwood, NJ: Ablex Publishing Corporation.

Sefton-Green, J. (2009) Youth, technology, and media cultures. *Review of Research in Education* 30, 279–306.

Shin, S. (2002) Differentiating language contact phenomena: Evidence from Korean-English bilingual children. *Applied Psycholinguistics* 23 (3), 337–360.

Silverstein, M. (1981) The limits of awareness. *Working Papers in Sociolinguistics* 84. Austin, TX: Southwest Educational Development Laboratory.

Smith, L.T. (1999) *Decolonizing Methodologies: Research and Indigenous Peoples.* London and New York: Zed Books.

Soep, E. (2006) Beyond Literacy and Voice in Youth Media Production. *McGill Journal of Education* 41 (3), 197–213.

Sommer, G. (1997) Towards an ethnography of language shift: Goals and methods. In M. Putz (ed.) *Language Choices: Conditions, Constraints, and Consequences* (pp. 55–76). Amsterdam: John Benjamins.

St. Denis, V. (2003) Real Indians: Cultural revitalization and fundamentalism in Aboriginal education. In C. Schick, J. Jaffe and A. Watkinson (eds) *Contesting Fundamentalisms* (pp. 35–47). Halifax, Canada: Fernwood.

Stromberg, E. (2006) *American Indian Rhetorics of Survivance: Word Medicine, Word Magic.* Pittsburgh, PA: University of Pittsburgh Press.

Taylor, D.M. and Wright, S.C. (2002) Do Aboriginal students benefit from education in their heritage language? Results from a ten-year program of research in Nunavik. *The Canadian Journal of Native Studies* 22, 141–164.

Thomas, W. and Collier, V. (2002) *A National Study of School Effectiveness for Language Minority Students' Long-Term Academic Achievement.* Santa Cruz: Center for Research, Education, Diversity and Excellence.

Tuck, E. (2009) Suspending damage: A letter to communities. *Harvard Education Review* 79 (3), 409–428.

Tulloch, S. (2004) Inuktitut and Inuit youth: Language attitudes as a basis for language planning. PhD thesis, University of Laval.

Tulloch, S., Coley, M. and Schuerch, G. (in progress) Igniting a youth language movement: Inuit youth as agents of circumpolar language planning. In L. Wyman, T. McCarty and S. Nicholas (eds) *Indigenous Youth and Bi/Multilingualism: Language Identity, Ideology and Practice in Dynamic Worlds.* New York: Routledge.

UNESCO (2003) *Language Vitality and Endangerment.* Paris: UNESCO. Retrieved 31 March 2011, from: www.unesco.org/culture/ich/doc/src/00120-EN.pdf

Usborne, E., Caouette, J., Qiallak, Q. and Taylor, D. (2009) Bilingual education in an aboriginal context: Examining the transfer of language skills from Inuktitut to

English or French. *International Journal of Bilingual Education and Bilingualism* 12 (6), 667–684.

Valdés, G. (1996) *Con Respeto: Bridging the Distance between Culturally Diverse Families and Schools. An Ethnographic Portrait.* New York: Teachers College Press.

Valdés, G. (2005) Bilingualism, heritage language learners, and SLA research: Opportunities lost or seized? *The Modern Language Journal* 89 (iii), 410–426.

Villegas, M., Neugebauer, S. and Venegas, K. (eds) (2008) *Indigenous Knowledge and Education: Sites of Struggle, Strength, and Survivance.* Cambridge, MA: Harvard Educational Review.

Vizenor, G. (1994) *Manifest Manners: PostIndian Warriors of Survivance.* Hanover, NH: Wesleyan UP of New England.

Vizenor, G. (2008) Aesthetics of survivance: Literary theory and practice. In G. Vizenor (ed.) *Survivance: Narratives of Native Presence* (pp. 1–23). Lincoln, NE: University of Nebraska Press.

Watahomigie, L. and McCarty, T.L. (1997) Literacy for what? Hualapai literacy and language maintenance. In N. Hornberger (ed.) *Indigenous Literacies in the Americas: Language Planning from the Bottom Up* (pp. 95–115). Berlin: Mouton de Gruyter.

Warriner, D. and Wyman, L. (in progress) Experiences of movement and mobility in complex linguistic ecologies: Implications for theory, method and practice. *International Multilingual Research Journal.*

Wei, L. (2002) 'What do you want me to say?': On the conversation analysis approach to bilingual interaction. *Language in Society* 31, 159–180.

Williams, B. and Rearden, N. (2006) Yup'ik language programs at Lower Kuskokwim School District, Bethel, Alaska. *Journal of American Indian Education* 45 (2), 37–41.

Wong-Fillmore, L. (2000) Loss of family languages: Should educators be concerned? *Theory into Practice* 39 (4), 203–210.

Woodbury, A. (1993) A defense of the proposition, 'When a language dies, a culture dies'. *Proceedings of the First Annual Symposium about Language and Society – Austin (SALSA). Texas Linguistic Forum* 33, 101–129.

Woodbury, A. (1998) Documenting rhetorical, aesthetic, and expressive loss in language shift. In L. Grenoble and L. Whaley (eds) *Endangered Languages: Current Issues and Future Prospects* (pp. 234–258). Cambridge: Cambridge University Press.

Woolard, K. (1989) Language convergence and language death as social processes. In N. Dorian (ed.) *Investigating Obsolescence: Studies in Language Contraction and Death* (pp. 355–368). Cambridge: Cambridge University Press.

Woolard, K. (1998) Introduction: Language ideology as a field of inquiry. In B. Schieffelin, K. Woolard and P. Kroskrity (eds) *Language Ideologies: Practice and Theory* (pp. 3–47). Oxford: Oxford University Press.

Wortham, S. (2006) *Learning Identity: The Joint Emergence of Identification and Academic Learning.* Cambridge: Cambridge University Press.

Wright, S., Taylor, D. and Macarthur, J. (2000) Subtractive bilingualism and the survival of the Inuit language: Heritage- versus second-language education. *Journal of Educational Psychology* 92 (1), 63–84.

Wyman, L. (2009) Youth, linguistic ecology, and language endangerment: A Yup'ik example. *Journal of Language, Identity and Education* 8 (5), 335–349.

Wyman, L. (in progress) Indigenous migration, schooling and linguistic ecologies: A Yup'ik example. *International Multilingual Research Journal.*

Wyman, L. and Kashatok, G. (2008) Getting to know the communities of your students. In M. Pollock (ed.) *Everyday Antiracism: Getting Real about Race in School* (pp. 294–298). New York: New Press.

Wyman, L., Marlow, P., Andrew, C.F., Miller, G., Nicholai, C.R. and Rearden, Y.N. (2010a) Focusing on long-term language goals in challenging times: Yup'ik examples. *Journal of American Indian Education* 49 (1 & 2), 22–43.

Wyman, L., Marlow, P., Andrew, C.F., Miller, G., Nicholai, C.R. and Rearden, Y.N. (2010b) High stakes testing, bilingual education and language endangerment: A Yup'ik example. *International Journal of Bilingual Education and Bilingualism* 13 (6), 701–721.

Zentella, A.C. (1997) *Growing up Bilingual: Puerto Rican Children in New York*. Oxford: Blackwell Publishers.

Zentella, A.C. (2005) *Building on Strengths: Language and Literacy in Latino Families and Communities*. New York: Teachers College Press.

Author Index

Subject Index

Alaska Native education: 17, 67–69, 71, 75, 88, 95, 100, 104, 120, 121, 129–130, 213, 276–277. *See also* bilingual education programs; bilingual education movement

Alaska Native Claims Settlement Act (ANCSA): 4, 44

alerquutet (prescriptions): definition, 38–39 42–43, 51, 63, 90, 130, 278. See also *inerquutet (prohibitions)*; *qanruyutait (teachings)*

assessment: Yup'ik proficiency exam, 21–22, 212; writing assessment, 119, 131, 215. *See also* testing

basketball: 42, 50, 116, 117–118, 123–126, 206, 216–217, 219, 221

Bering sea: 3, 6, 21, 55, 60, 136, 233, 234, 236, 242, 247–248, 251, 253

Bethel: 5, 18, 21, 34–35, 48, 68, 85, 87, 92, 112, 116–118, 128, 134, 137, 141, 143, 158, 159, 178, 180, 182, 236, 276, 278, 280

bilingual education movement: 72–76, 91–92, 157, 278–279. *See also* bilingual education programs

bilingual education programs: bilingual/bicultural, 79; curriculum and materials development, 73; dual immersion, 90–91, 280; immersion, 34–35, 92, 159, 163, 276, 278–279; local choices, 73–74, 78–79, 91–92, 95–100, 271, 277–278; PEP and transitional, 72–73, 76–79; strong, 76–77, 91–92, 276

bird-hunting and processing: 4, 6, 61–62, 67, 106, 128, 135, 137, 179, 218, 230–232, 235–236, 241–246, 252, 254, 273

boarding schools/boarding school experiences: 5, 38, 65, 68–72, 75, 79, 100, 213

Christianity: conversion, 4, 6, 43, 50–51, 130; discourses of, 222–224, 227, 256, 265; early Yup'ik schools, 4, 67. *See also* church; media consumption/use/reference Christian; missionaries Yup'ik dancing; Yup'ik writing systems

church: community role, 44, 50, 99; as a site of language maintenance and linguistic accommodation, 51–53, 64; participant-observation, 18, 20–21, 23–24, 30; young peoples' participation, 108, 140, 188, 205, 211–212, 223–224, 234, 280

classroom observations: 23, 81, 83, 88, 130, 211, 221–222, 224–225

codeswitching: *See* translanguaging

college: *See* post-secondary education

community: complexities defining, 10, 15; communities-of-practice, 13, 21. *See also* curriculum: community-based

contact zones: definition, 44; 44–53, 118–120

counseling: 49, 51, 90, 141, 223. *See also qanruyutait (teachings)*

court system: 45, 48, 128. *See also* tribal court